Eleanor Bailie

The Pianist's Repertoire

HAYDN

A graded practical guide

with a foreword by H.C. Robbins Landon

NOVELLO

London and Sevenoaks

Cat. No. 10 0303

Portrait of Haydn by Thomas Hardy from the
Collection of the Royal College of Music, London. Reproduced by permission.

Novello and Company Limited gratefully acknowledge the permission of Henle Edition
in allowing use of thematic extracts from their published editions of Haydn's Sonatas.

Registered office, trade orders, mail orders and hire library:
Borough Green, Sevenoaks, Kent TN15 8DT Tel: 0732 883261

Showroom, editorial, performance promotion and retail sales:
8 Lower James Street, London W1R 4DN Tel: 01-734 8080

Printed in Great Britain by Whitstable Litho Ltd.   All Rights Reserved

CONTENTS

ACKNOWLEDGEMENTS

This project would never have seen the light of day without the help of my dear friends, the late Jimmie McKay Martin, and Marjorie Roberts. They listened to the first ideas with patience and interest. Then, having decided that it was a worthwhile venture, they threw themselves wholeheartedly and, as I often feel, quite unaccountably, behind it. With amazing generosity they gave countless hours to reading drafts, and saw me through what seemed interminable teething problems. They bullied, cajoled, and with equal incisiveness, ruthlessly shot down many bad ideas, and buttressed those they thought better. No words can convey my gratitude for their steadfast encouragement and the benefit of their immense musical knowledge and experience. It is my great sadness that Jimmie died before the publication of this first book. I am also most grateful to Dr Hilary Box, who gave generous and invaluable practical help.

This large undertaking, as it has now become, has passed through many stages. I warmly thank the many kind friends who have read drafts, given encouragement, and made helpful suggestions throughout the long incubation period, particularly George and Cynthia Isserlis, whose support has been especially valuable. I am grateful too, to my daughters, who have been so patient through long months when I have been in perpetual motion between desk and piano. Finally, special and admiring thanks to Betty Black and Anne Perks, who in turn have gamely and cheerfully fought their way through reams of shamefully defaced foolscap to produce a manuscript of astonishing neatness and accuracy.

ELEANOR BAILIE
London, 1988

FOREWORD

Haydn's piano sonatas have enjoyed a curiously mixed reception. In the eighteenth century they were immensely popular, but by the beginning of the nineteenth century they were being quickly overshadowed by the piano music of Mozart (just then being published, in many cases, for the first time) and Beethoven. Although Haydn's piano sonatas and single piano pieces soon dropped out of the average virtuoso's repertory, they became increasingly important as teaching vehicles. All during the nineteenth and twentieth centuries, edition after edition of Haydn's piano music appeared throughout most of Europe and in north America. At the end of World War I the first Urtext edition appeared (ed. K. Päsler, Breitkopf & Härtel, Leipzig) but had little or no effect on the world of practical music-making because it never appeared except as part of the Haydn Collected Edition (*Gesamtausgabe*).

In the 1980s the situation has remained more or less constant with one notable exception. While hardly more than half-a-dozen piano works by Haydn appear regularly on the concert platform, their use by teachers has, if anything, increased: the sale of the Wiener Urtext-Ausgabe's edition of the sonatas has been little short of phenomenal (some eight printings at present writing). The one exception is the fact that all the sonatas have now been recorded many times, and students who might also wish to hear them on old instruments now have ample opportunity to do so.[1]

Hence it is abundantly clear that Haydn's sonatas continue to have a vast public, even if not in the concert hall. It is this vast public of teachers and pupils to which Eleanor Bailie's admirable book is directed. When one has read it, one is astonished why no one wrote it hitherto: it is an urgent necessity for teachers, and indeed for players of all kinds. Haydn's piano music is often complicated and formally wayward: its beauties do not, on the whole, lie on the surface. It is music whose appeal is primarily intellectual, requiring both thought and explanation. Eleanor Bailie has provided both in generous measure. No intelligent piano teacher should be without this knowledgeable and sympathetic guide.

H. C. ROBBINS LANDON
Foncoussières, 1988

---

1 On a beautiful grand fortepiano by Johann Schantz of *c*.1790, played by Paul Badura-Skoda on Astrée AS 913/4 — fourteen sonatas and four smaller pieces; on an early fortepiano by Walter of *c*.1780 by Franz Eibner, Landesmuseum Eisenstadt — two sonatas; on a reconstructed fortepiano by Malcolm Bilson on Titanic Records (TI 51, 52) — eight sonatas.

PREFACE

The solo repertoire for the piano is vast, far outstripping that for any other single instrument, or indeed for most other instruments put together. Many of us, players and teachers alike, stupified by this embarrassment of riches, find ourselves cruising along the same tracks, sticking to what we know, or to what we think the public knows and likes. To the large and growing body of amateur players, the choice is particularly bewildering. How, confronted with the huge output of, say, Beethoven, is the 'average' pianist to know which works lie within his capabilities, and which are most likely to appeal to him? To the enthusiastic adult amateur, in many ways often the most rewarding and receptive of students, I hope this series will be of particular help. I also hope it will be helpful to teachers in selecting material for their pupils, to professional players in choosing programmes, and to students at schools of music, universities and teacher training colleges; also to the compilers of examination and competition syllabuses, and to those planning courses for study, public or personal.

The objective of the series is threefold:

a) To provide reference books-cum-guides to help players and teachers find their way around the repertoire of the major composers for the keyboard, and to help in the choice of music to suit their playing tastes and teaching requirements.

b) To give suggestions and guidelines for study and performance.

c) To draw attention to the most rewarding (and particularly to some neglected) areas of the repertoire.

Each book consists of three sections:

i) A short introduction to the keyboard music of the composer, giving an outline of the distinguishing features of his style.

ii) A graded list of the keyboard works of the composer. The list aims to contain all the works that are published in generally available editions.

iii) Detailed commentaries on the study and performance of every work, or part or movement of a work up to a post-Grade 8 standard (called Grade 8 +).

The Lists of Works

The music is listed in order of difficulty in the following categories:

Grade 3 and under
Grade 4
Grade 5
Grade 6
Grade 7
Grade 8
Grade 8 +
Very advanced

The grading is based on the standards set by the various examining bodies, and is intended only as a general indication, and not as a *definition* of technical or musical difficulty. In grading the pieces the criterion has not necessarily been the suitability of each piece for performance, but rather its potential for worthwhile and satisfying study at the stage in question. No one likes the idea of 'grading' music (and obviously some of my grading standards will be questioned, as indeed are frequently the selections in recognized examination syllabuses); there is, however, no other way of giving an indication of the degree of difficulty of each piece. I have grouped the simplest pieces together in 'Grade

3 and under', since standards at this stage are flexible, and most novice players are anyway likely to be under the wing of a teacher.

The Symbols * and O

The '*' means that a movement or piece is specially recommended. While this 'awards system' is, of course, entirely personal, and perhaps presumptuous, it does at least give players a starting-point. It includes not just my own favourites, but also those movements or pieces which I feel are most likely to attract relative newcomers to Haydn. It is not suggested that the starred works are 'better', the unstarred 'worse' – indeed as I have studied the works more closely I have gone on rearranging the stars, and I hope that other players will do likewise! The works have been chosen because they are interesting to *play*, and not because of their significance in any formal or historical sense. The first movement of Sonata No. 29 in E flat, for example, is highly spoken of by more scholarly minds than mine, but for the majority of pianists it must surely pale beside its astonishing neighbours, the first movement of Nos. 30 in D and 31 in A flat.

The 'O' indicates **either** that a piece contains a number of wide stretches (not so common with Haydn) or octave passages, and is therefore unsuitable for players with small hands; **or** that in a musical sense it seems more suited to the older player. This applies more often in the earlier Grades, when although a piece is relatively simple technically, its content and sentiments may be somewhat esoteric. But these are, of course, generalized indications, for a talented child can be wonderfully intuitive musically. From about Grade 6 it is assumed that an octave can be stretched. And, of course, octaves can often be omitted by those with small hands, except where the octaves are particularly important to the texture of the music as, for example, in the second movement, 'Andante', of Sonata No. 5 in G.

The figure in brackets following the title of each movement indicates the approximate suggested Grade.

The Introduction to the Music of Each Composer

This aims to give some general pointers towards an understanding of the individual qualities of the composer. Rather than giving a potted biography, I have tried instead to show how his personality, and the circumstances of his life and times, have helped to shape and characterize his style.

The Commentaries on the Music

In this series, music both for complete beginners and for players in the 'Very Advanced' category is not (with occasional exceptions) discussed in detail. The beginner is catered for by numerous primers and albums of attractive pieces. At the other end of the scale players capable of tackling the Beethoven *Hammerclavier* or the Liszt Sonata in B minor are out on their own! And in any event we have to stop somewhere, or the project would become unmanageable in every sense. These books are primarily intended for that vast majority of pianists in the 'middle' range.

I had intended to finish the commentaries at Grade 8, but found so many works lying tantalizingly just beyond a conventional Grade 8 standard that I decided to add a Grade 8 +, rather open-ended, but in general stopping short of music in the 'Very Advanced' or 'Virtuoso' categories. In the case of Haydn, however, as will be seen, there are only five items listed under Grade 8 +, and none at all in the 'Very Advanced' category; and while some of the early Sonata movements, particularly the minuets, are on the face of it quite simple, there are few if any which can be called complete beginners' pieces. There is nearly always more than may immediately meet the eye − some feature of rhythm, texture, or expressive sense which calls upon a certain degree of musical or technical know-how. And while, for example, the third and fourth movements of Sonata No. 1 can, of course, be adequately played by a Grade 2 or 3 player, an experienced artist will find charming expressive subtlety in the spare, quietly moving lines of the third movement, and will create a little virtuoso gem with the Finale.

It is stressed that the commentaries are intended to deal only with the *practical* (in the sense of strictly non-musicological) aspects of the performance of each work or movement. There is as little technical jargon as possible, though a knowledge of general musical terms and of the basic principles of form is assumed; but matters of form and structure arise only when directly applicable to the performance of the music. I have tried to give an impression of the fundamental character of each piece, and to discuss its technical and musical demands as they arise. *Except where I am simply drawing attention to the indications of the composer, the suggestions for dynamics, articulation, tempo and general interpretation are entirely personal, and players are begged to treat them as such.* I realize, and indeed welcome the thought, that these suggestions will often be disagreed with − again they will at least provide a starting-point for players' own ideas. And, for help in getting one's own ideas moving, there is nothing like being given a proposition with which we can have the pleasure of disagreeing!

I have tried to anticipate the kind of pitfalls into which, as every teacher knows, the inexperienced pianist will almost invariably fall. In discussing the music in the earlier Grades, details are pointed out which it is assumed can be taken as read by more advanced players. Inevitably, certain exhortations recur many times in the commentaries: 'be sure to make it clear that LH octaves are "leading" '; 'show the implied emphasis on the tied upbeat', and such-like. But, since no one is going to sit down in an armchair and read the book right through, this was felt to be less irksome than to be continually referred to Sonata No. −, bar −, page −.

My overriding objective, in every instance, is to try to help the player bring the music to life. This is the area, the most important of all, where so many students fail; anxious to have every note in place, to get the 'style' right, hamstrung by the fear of 'overdoing' things, they opt for safety, with the resultant painful dullness of timid dynamics and neutral tone-colour. The careful learning of notes, and all the conscientious groundwork are to no avail unless we can then transcend the dots on the page. In the last resort, a performance, either in private or on the concert platform, is never just good or bad. It either comes to life or it doesn't. If we play ever so well, with every detail thought out, every note correct, but Haydn remains a cardboard silhouette in neat wig and livery, we fail. If, on the other hand, despite the odd note flying off in the wrong direction, and the occasional passage sounding too loud, too soft, too slow or too fast, we bring him to life as the great human being and the extraordinary musical genius that he was, we have succeeded.

Dear God, I can tell crotchets from quavers
Right notes from wrong;
I can correct time-values and an aberrant pulse . . .
I'll measure a phrase length, even in Haydn,
But only You can take the truly long view . . .
Dear God, I can manage the Notes;
Will You help with 'the Expression'?

from *Visitations* by Alexander Kelly
(by permission of Elo Press Ltd)

INTRODUCTION

The Music of Haydn

In our earliest musical memories we associate the names of Haydn and Mozart as though they were one and the same person. We hear talk of the Haydn-Mozart era; later, we read chapters on 'Haydn and Mozart and Sonata Form', 'The Symphonies of Haydn and Mozart', and so on. When, eventually, they begin to assume separate musical personalities, Haydn inevitably emerges as the lesser luminary – as a kind of jolly country uncle to the meteoric and far more charismatic Mozart. In many senses though, Haydn's gifts were almost as remarkable. Without doubt the bolder innovator, he immeasurably expanded the horizons of the symphony, the string quartet and the piano sonata. His output was colossal. He was, above all, a constructor, his inexhaustible imagination exploring, experimenting, and ceaselessly moving on.

The greater part of his working life was spent in the service of the Esterházy family. By today's standards his duties were unbelievably arduous. Not only was he charged with a continuous flow of compositions for the princely entertainment – no sinecure, for the Prince was a discerning patron – but also with the weekly organization of operas, masses and concert performances, with the engagement of musicians, the care and supply of instruments and music, and even with the copying of parts. On the other hand, he benefited from a ready-made audience, and a constant supply of capable players and singers. As he was to say later: 'I could experiment and observe what heightened the effect and what weakened it, and so could improve, expand, cut, take risks. I was cut off from the world, there was no one near me to torment me or make me doubt myself, so I had to become original'.†

He was the most natural and lovable of men. He came of sturdy peasant stock and inherited a robust and resilient nature. His legendary humour was combined with the true countryman's sense of the realities of life. He was blessed with a temperament which enabled him to accept the constraints and frustrations of his life as a liveried servant without bitterness. Equally, in later life he accepted the honours which were heaped upon him with unaffected pleasure, and without a trace of vanity.

So entrenched is the popular view of Haydn as 'little more than an amiable funster' (to quote John McCabe),‡ that we tend to forget the darker sides of his life and music. When his voice broke, and he was thrown out of St Stephen's Choir School, literally onto the streets of Vienna, he came nearer than any other of the great composers to starving in the proverbial garret. Later, locked in a miserable marriage, overworked, and consumed by a deeply-felt love that eventually turned sour, he often knew profound turbulence or heaviness of spirit. We should not be surprised, though we often are and indeed we often fail to notice, that his music is shot through with passion, fierceness, anguish, and again at other times with tenderness and warmth. The great C minor Sonata No. 33, the slow movements of Nos. 31 and 62, and the F minor Variations are hardly the offerings of a deft-witted musical clown. That he remained so predominantly optimistic and positive was due, not to shallowness of nature or lack of feeling, but rather to the sterling qualities of character which carried him so triumphantly through these hardships and sorrows. If we fail to understand this we perceive only half, and that only the lesser half, of the greatness of both the man and his music.

† The Master Musicians: *Haydn* (Dent).

‡ John McCabe, *Haydn Piano Sonatas* (BBC Music Guides).

Haydn's piano works have been overshadowed by those of Mozart and Beethoven. Barely a handful of his Sonatas are in the repertoire, or are even known to the majority of professional pianists. It may be that many of them are not material for the concert platform. But to the domestic pianist, to the competent sight-reader, Haydn offers a musical experience which no other composer can parallel. From the early suites of tiny movements to the commanding, fantasia-like expanses of the final Sonata in E flat major (No. 62), he enables us to observe, to follow, and in a unique sense, to feel party to the workings of a truly prodigious musical imagination. From the point of view of the teacher and student, Haydn's Sonatas provide a far wider range of material than do Mozart's. They are more experimental, and their textures and rhythms are more rugged and more varied. None, apart from the above-named Sonata, and perhaps the first movement of No. 60 in C major, is technically above a Grade 8 standard, and as an additional bonus, many of the one hundred and fifty-odd movements have the virtue of extreme brevity.

The 'typical' Haydn first movement does not exist. In each he embarks on a new adventure in structure and style, encompassing every imaginable variety of mood, from the defiance of Nos. 40 in E flat major and 47 in B minor, to the refinement and expressive grace of No. 54 in G major. Often the moods switch wildly almost from bar to bar, between exuberance and pathos, merriment and grandeur, demanding correspondingly mercurial responses from the player (see, for example, the first movements of Nos. 31 in A flat, 51 in E flat, and 60 in C). He was a developer *par excellence*, a user of fragments rather than a melodist. His plunges into distant tonalities can still astonish us today. His recapitulations are seldom mere re-statements, but demonstrate his irresistible urge to continue to 'work' his material. Again, he used the formality of the minuet as a vehicle for all manner of textural experiment, and his minor trios are often finely expressive. Much has been written on the subject of Haydn's ancestry, on the possibility that he was of Croatian, rather than German extraction, and of the folk influences he naturally absorbed from the mixed races and cultures of his native region near the Austro-Hungarian border. These influences are perhaps most obvious in his finales, which are typically full of spark and mettle, and often of rumbustious 'country' humour, abounding in his characteristically irregular phrase lengths and stomping, whirling or 'churning' dance-like rhythms.

Today, it is all too easy to be intimidated by that daunting body of arbiters to whom Jorge Bolet tartly refers as 'the Urtext crowd'. We fail Haydn lamentably if we burden his adventurous, but cheerfully practical spirit with too deferential an approach. His reply to a query as to his methods of composition demonstrates not only his disarmingly unpretentious attitude to his craft, but also his simple and genuine piety: 'Well, you see, I get up early, and as soon as I have dressed, I go down on my knees and pray to God and the blessed Virgin that I may have another successful day. Then, when I have had breakfast, I sit down at the clavier and begin my search. If I hit upon an idea quickly, it goes ahead easily and without much trouble, but if I can't get on, I know that I must have forfeited God's grace by some fault of mine, and then I pray once more for grace until I am forgiven'.†

† The Master Musicians: *Haydn* (Dent).

Some Matters of Style

Instruments

Haydn's lifetime spanned the transition from the harpsichord to the piano. He clearly welcomed the new instruments, and his later works exploit the resources of the keyboard in an orchestral and often Beethovenian manner. The movement for the performance of Classical and Baroque music on contemporary instruments grows apace. Nevertheless, the vast majority of grass-roots players, amateur and professional, will continue to play Haydn and Mozart on the piano, whether from choice or necessity. And I believe that that is as it should be. To enclose this music within the limits of the fortepiano (and I am not thereby suggesting that it was, or is, an inferior instrument) is to move it into a museum reserved for specialists. How absurd would Haydn, of all composers, have found such an idea, and indeed how amazed and delighted he would be to hear his music, resounding differently perhaps, but as freshly as the day he wrote it, on our modern instruments. This said, we should never forego an opportunity of playing an early instrument. We can learn more about Haydn's style in an hour's private colloquy with a fortepiano than through reams of learned treatises! The textures and articulation are immediately defined in marvellous clarity without the conscious effort that we automatically make on a modern piano. And orchestral sounds emerge like magic, again without our help, because they are indigenous to certain registers of the keyboard.

Dynamics

In Haydn's early keyboard works, as was the norm in the era of the harpsichord, there are no dynamic signs. Although the fortepiano was emerging, it co-existed for some decades with the harpsichord and clavichord. But composers were not fussy in those days, and indeed were unlikely to be in a position to dictate their choice of instruments. In the 1770s however, along with the rise of the fortepiano, dynamic markings, sometimes considerably detailed, begin to show in the Sonatas, notably in the first movement of the great Sonata in C minor, No. 33. But performers then were accustomed to far greater freedom of interpretation than is usual today, and gradations of sound (crescendos and decrescendos) were not generally indicated until considerably later, when composers had grown used to the capacities of the new instruments. Thus, although the sudden *forte* or *piano* is indeed characteristic of Haydn, in many other instances a *crescendo* or *decrescendo* may well be implied by the shape of the phrase, though not specifically indicated. Even when there are no dynamics, or they are only sparsely indicated, I have purposely made only occasional suggestions. On the other hand, such exhortations as 'come in boldly', 'listen acutely to the subtle chromatic inflections', 'articulate with the utmost brilliance', obviously carry their own dynamic implications. But again I stress that in the absence of Haydn's own indications these are only *suggestions* (see also the Preface, under 'The Commentaries on the Music'). Haydn's musical processes are so marvellously diverse, and his styles so multiform, that widely differing dynamic interpretations are often possible. Indeed, in various instances I have suggested that it is possible to *decrescendo* to *pianissimo*, or to *crescendo* to *forte* with equally convincing effect – we should not be afraid to experiment and, within bounds, to vary our interpretations from day to day.

We do, however, need to be careful to avoid oversonorous *fortes*. While it is both fruitless and affected to try to ape the instruments of Haydn's day, we must always bear in mind their lighter tone (which at the same time has a sharper, clearer attack) to which his textural, dynamic and expressive effects are geared. This does not mean that we dare not play loud, or that the dynamics need be pale – on the contrary, they must be projected and contrasted with the utmost verve – but that we need to aim for a bright, clear rather than 'thicker', Brahmsian sonority.

Sforzatos

Haydn's frequent *sforzatos* must be treated according to context – in a brisk *forte* passage, a sharp, firm, or indeed biting accent may well be indicated. Syncopated *sforzatos* sometimes occur in the late Sonatas with Beethovenian persistence (see, for example, the Finale of No. 61 in D major, a *tour-de-force* of its kind, and the first movement of No. 60 in C, bb. 76 – 80). On the other hand, a *sforzato* in the course of a melodic line in a *piano* context is more likely to indicate a gentle emphasis – a 'leaning' upon, or slight 'holding' of certain notes, important to the shaping and the expressive sense of the phrase. There are good examples of this in the slow movement of Sonata No. 60 in C major: in bb.9 – 10 see the stressed offbeat semiquavers in the LH, in the RH, and again in the LH. Also, in bb. 29 and 30 of the same movement, see the stressed minim thirds in the LH, implying a warm resonance, and certainly not a hard bump. Again in the first movement of No. 54 in G major, there are numerous instances of such expressive 'leans', either on main beats, or on offbeats, giving gently syncopated effects. (In some editions these emphases are sometimes marked *forte* rather than *sforzato*.)

Rhythm

Haydn's rhythmical figuration is often complex. Breezy march rhythms and vigorous stomping figures abound. He delights in the deployment of dotted rhythms, in gaiety, in solemnity, or in passages of high dramatic tension. Equally, triplets are freely used, especially in some of the early Minuets. As early as in Sonata No. 1 in G we find dotted rhythm and triplet figures alternating throughout the first movement, and the first movements of Nos. 13 in G and 16 in D, with their continually changing note values, are little minefields for the rhythmically insecure. This zest for intricate patterns, part and parcel of Haydn's irrepressible vitality, reaches its apotheosis in that jubilant explosion of rhythmic exuberance, the first movement of Sonata No. 62 in E flat. In performance, therefore, rhythmic vitality and precision are of paramount importance. Often the openings of, in particular, the first movements give little inkling of what is to come. When setting a tempo, therefore, it is sensible to try out the patterns of the different sections and find a pulse which gives a unifying meaning to the whole. Otherwise it is easy to start too fast (usually this way round, rather than starting too slow!) and suddenly find that your intended salvo of brilliant demisemiquavers has collapsed in an ignominious heap.

It is of paramount importance that we find and *physically* feel the individual, fundamental rhythmic pulse of every piece or movement that we play. This is as true (if not more so) in the case of Haydn as of any other composer. In order to find the pulse that 'feels' right (and this will inevitably differ from person to person), walk, dance, wave your arms, conduct, do anything that has a *physical* rhythm. All the 'mental' counting in the world will not help unless at the same time the rhythm is *felt* (in the solar plexus), as Ralph Kirkpatrick has so rightly said.† If we do not feel the beat we find ourselves fighting the music, uphill, all the way. When we do feel the beat, we find that we are 'going with' the music, and that the majority of apparent stumbling blocks simply melt away. Furthermore, it is essential to feel the rhythm *before* we start. It is no good launching in blindly, and then fumbling for the beat in the middle of bar 1. It is particularly important in the numerous Haydn movements that begin on an upbeat, that the beat is already 'in the system', so that the upbeat is perfectly timed to give a clear lead in.

This is as good a place as any to reinforce the plea, frequently made in the commentaries on individual movements, not to try to play too fast. When they do play Haydn, many

† Ralph Kirkpatrick, *Domenico Scarlatti* (Princeton University Press).

professional performers, whether from lack of understanding, or because they cannot resist showing off their finger techniques, take most movements at ridiculous speeds. Haydn is not a streamlined composer. Player and listener alike need time to enjoy his marvellous quirks of mind, to take in the passing scene, and to look into the strange corners of his music before passing on — all the things that we cannot do if we insist on driving on the motorways!

As has been said above, Haydn used the minuet structure to marvellously expressive effect. Nevertheless, whether the minuet or trio be vigorous, even stomping in character (see, for example, the Trios of the incomplete Sonata No. 28 in D major, or of No. 47 in B minor), or poignantly expressive (as the Minuet and Trio of No. 49 in C sharp minor, or the Trio of No. 43 in E flat), we must never forget that a minuet is a *dance* rhythm. Although students often *think* that they remember this, they forget (at risk of labouring this point) actually to 'feel' the beat. If the rhythm is floundering, and it is pointed out how essential it is always to show the 'stepping' **3/4** pulse, things usually fall miraculously into place! In this connection it is so often the LH (both in minuets proper and in numerous *tempo di minuetto*, or unnamed but nevertheless minuet-type movements), with its 'plain' notes or chords in crotchets or minims, that gives the steady rhythmic foundation for the figuration of the RH. (See, among many examples, the second movements of Sonatas Nos. 3 in F and 13 in G, and the Finales of Nos. 34 in D and 37 in E.)

Rests, Pauses and Rallentandos

Following on from the above, it is equally vital, in some senses even more so, to *feel* the beat through rests. Most players, it has been said truly, are afraid of silence! But failure to give proper value to rests is just as damaging to rhythmic equilibrium as failure to time the written notes. For example, in the first movement of Sonata No. 2 in C it is essential to *feel* the quaver rest on the 2nd beat of b.2, or the upbeat demisemiquavers will not be properly timed, and you will 'fall into' b.3. Similarly, in the first movement of No. 50 in D you will 'fall into' bb.9 and 17 unless you *feel* the silent 4th beat of bb.8 and 16. In the first movement of No. 44 in F, failure to feel and time the quaver rest accurately on the 1st beat of b.15 would cause the subsequent complex rhythmic passage to collapse like a pack of cards. Fortunate are those who are taught from an early age to count rests *physically* (e.g. with a slight intake or exhalation of breath on the beats) rather than merely mentally.

Similarly the beat needs to be *felt* through tied and held notes. For example, in the slow movement of Sonata No. 50 in D the quaver pulse must be felt securely *through* the 2nd beat of b.1 and the 1st beat of b.2, so that the 'upbeat' to the subsequent main beat (the semiquaver and the demisemiquaver triplet respectively) is accurately timed. Then in b.16 the quaver pulse needs to be felt through the long tied chord so that the demisemiquaver triplet 'upbeat' is perfectly timed and you do not 'fall into' the 3rd beat.

Silences have particular significance in Haydn. He will sometimes build up to a climax followed by a positively violent dramatic silence. Or he will suddenly snap off in mid air leaving us cliffhanging, or tail away a wisp of sound into silence. See the dramatic cut-offs, or pauses in the Finale of No.47, bb.18, 37, 123, etc; or in the first movement of No. 59, bb.52 and 107; the hectic jerk as we hurtle to a violent 'stop' in the Finale of No. 60, bb.10–11, or the effect of the sound disappearing to a whisper at b.68; or in No. 62, the pregnant stillness at b.45 amidst all the clatter of the first movement. If we do not allow full value of such rests and pauses we forfeit most of the drama, or the joke, as the case may be.

Players often wonder anxiously how long they should wait on a pause. There can, of course, be no clear answer. In my experience students, 'afraid of silence', almost never wait long enough. On the other hand, too long a wait of course destroys suspense and leaves a vacuum. The solution which I find never fails because it is *natural*, not calculated (and which I have seen an eminent conductor try to inculcate into a batch of sceptical students) is to suspend the breathing as you pause. Then, when the urge to take a breath becomes irresistible, you are naturally impelled onwards.

Often at the end of a movement I have said 'end without any *rallentando*'. This may be a personal fad, but it often seems more effective and more in keeping with Haydn's manner to end an 'Allegro' at full tilt. Again, in some circumstances, where a *pianissimo* ending is specified or implied, to disappear into thin air in tempo tallies better with Haydn's love of the unexpected than the more contrived effect of announcing the ending by a gradual slowing down.

Phrasing

Attention to, and understanding of phrasing is particularly important in view of Haydn's frequently irregular phrase lengths. This is one of the senses in which he is so innovative and unconstrained. If you are not sure about the length of the phrases, the golden rule, as ever, is to sing them. You will soon see how and when they begin and end, and how they are shaped, subdivided and punctuated. It is also often important to feel the onward movement over the subdivision of phrases. Take the treble line of the opening of the first movement of Sonata No. 33 in C minor. Be sure that as you 'finish off' the first half of the first overall phrase, with the slurred C to B natural in bar 2, you do not 'stop', but rather give the feeling of 'going on' as the quaver upbeat to b. 3 (A flat) leads on into the second half of the phrase. Similarly, having 'gone up to' and given full value to the quaver E flat on the 3rd beat of bar 6, and to the subsequent quaver rest, do then give a definite onward and upward lead with the upbeat demisemiquaver scale, towards a definite dotted quaver B flat on the first beat of b. 7. Then again, having finished the trumpet-call motif boldly on the quaver C on the 1st beat of b. 10, clear the sound and come in, *piano*, and precisely in time, with the solo treble line, without losing the overall continuity of this *three*-bar phrase. Or, to take a simpler example at the beginning of the first movement of No. 2 in C: having played the three opening chords in a vigorous, rhythmic and 'ongoing' manner, do not feel that you have 'stopped' on the chord on the 1st beat of b.2. Phrase mentally *over* the rest, so that while coming *off* the chord and *feeling* the rest accurately, you at the same time communicate the sense of 'moving on' through the demisemiquaver upbeat group into b.3. Thus while the first phrase subdivides into two parts, there is at the same time the sense of a longer overall phrase from bb.1 – 5. In slow movements particularly, it is often important to phrase mentally *over* the rests, so that while each fragment or sub-phrase is perfectly shaped in itself, you do not lose the shape and the 'onward feeling' of the overall phrases. (See in this connection the commentaries on, for example, the slow movements of Nos. 44 in F and 51 in E flat.)

Texture

Attention to clarity of texture is vital, particularly in Haydn's many passages of contrapuntal writing. A number of his first movements (for example in Sonatas Nos. 13 in G, 39 in D, and 51 in E flat) open with passages in two single and distinct lines, the RH admittedly with the predominant melody line, but the LH supplying a clear counterpoint with a melodic shape of its own. Another simple example is the tiny 'Andante' movement of No. 1 in G, written almost entirely in two distinct parts. And the second movements of Nos. 31 in A flat, 46 in E, and a number of complex contrapuntal passages (e.g. bb. 35 – 40 of the first movement of No. 51 in E flat) have to be studied with a Bachian sense of the equality of the parts. It is here that fortepiano enthusiasts come into their own, and there is no doubt that, as has been implied above, we do have to articulate and listen more acutely on the modern piano to achieve the transparency of texture that came more naturally on the older instruments.

Articulation

Articulation in Classical music is too large a subject to be discussed in detail here (Howard Ferguson, in his *Keyboard Interpretation* (OUP) has an excellent section on 'Phrasing and Articulation'), but it is a safe generalization to say that articulation, in fast movements at any rate, was less *legato*, and more detached and defined (whether or not slurs or *staccatos* etc. are indicated) than it was to become from the time of Beethoven onwards. A good example of this is in the Finale of No. 42 in G where, if the RH quavers were played *legato*, the effect would be unthinkably flat and dreary. For the opening of this movement I have suggested various possibilities for RH articulation, and here, as in many other instances, players must try out different details of articulation and decide which they feel helps the passage in question to 'speak' to the best advantage.

The position regarding different signs for *staccato* is extremely confusing. Wedges or dashes and dots occur (further complicated by different permutations in different editions) wtih no relevance, as it seems to the innocent player, to the situation in hand The same wedges, for example, appear over the fierce RH quavers in bb. 1 and 2 of the first movement of Sonata No. 40; and over the 'speaking' repeated quavers in bb. 25 and 26 of the first movement of Sonata No. 54 in G. We have to decide, according to the context, how short or sharp or alternatively, how just-detached and 'speaking' they should be. On the other hand the ♪ ♪ ♪ ♪ definitely indicate a *mezzo-staccato* and again 'speaking' interpretation. In the commentaries I often make a plea to avoid 'spiky' *staccatos*. This applies even to sharp, short *staccatos*. If they are 'plucked' as in a *pizzicato* on a stringed instrument, rather than whacked from above, they will sound melodic and vital, though sharp or even fierce, according to context, rather than 'spiky' and spidery.

In slow movements longer *legato* lines are often implied. Play as expressively as you will, but be sure that melody lines remain clear and never become thick and overfed with too much of a romantic 'Steinway' sound.

Pedalling

This leads to the vexed question of pedalling. I often meet students who are stuck with the fixed idea that it is 'wrong' to use the sustaining pedal in Haydn or Mozart. Apart from the fact that this misguided notion is, at any rate in relation to Haydn's later works, anachronistic (knee pedals and, later, foot pedals came into general use during Haydn's lifetime) the pedal is an essential part of the piano's mechanism, and without it the instrument comes only half alive. The opening chords of Sonata No. 62 in E flat would lose much of their grandeur if deprived of the pedal. And in the second movement of No. 59 in E flat, for example, if the long notes and chords on the 1st beat of bb.1, 4, 17, 21, etc, were not lightly pedalled, or the turbulent middle section liberally so, the movement would sound dry as dust. But the use of the pedal must be governed by the most vigilant ear (that organ which students are so reluctant to use) in order that the clarity of harmonies, lines, phrases, and articulation is never obscured. This means in effect that the pedal must be changed with every inflection of melody, harmony and articulation in every outer or inner strand of sound, which may necessitate, in a slow passage for example, changing the pedal with every quaver or even semiquaver. (It goes without saying that music should always be learnt without the pedal. Yet this is a procedure which even advanced students, while they will admit the logic of it, seldom seem able to discipline themselves to carry out.) It is important to realize that the depth to which the pedal is depressed has a marked effect on the sound. Thus if it is depressed to three-quarters, a half, or a quarter of its full depth, or even just very lightly touched, it will have in proportion, a lighter, less full and thick sound than if it is fully depressed. This lighter sound is obviously, in general, more appropriate to music of the Classical period, and indeed the slightest touch on the pedal will often give the light warmth of sound that we are aiming for in, for example, fine-drawn lyrical passages.

One hundred and fifty years on from the days of Chopin, that master of pedal sound, it seems it still is not generally realized that the role of the sustaining pedal is not merely that of a 'joiner-up' – it is also a vital means of defining, colouring and characterizing different effects of sound. Similarly the left pedal is not only a 'softener', it is another aid to the subtle colouring, and also the 'distancing' of sound, particularly valuable in some of the delicate orchestral effects in the keyboard music of Haydn and Mozart. The pedals are to the piano as the paintbrush is to the drawing – only in Classical music the painting is in watercolour (and that does not mean weak and wishy-washy) as opposed to thicker oils in the late Romantics. There are, it seems, few treatises on pedalling, but again Howard Ferguson has wise words on the subject† and there is an important and marvellously informative new book by Joseph Banowetz called *The Pianist's Guide to Pedalling* (Indiana University Press) (although I cannot agree with his view that in Haydn and Mozart 'the left pedal should seldom be used').

Ornaments

Ornaments, as every teacher knows, cause disproportionate panic and confusion, and create a real barrier to the enjoyment of 'early' music. Editors are the first to admit that Haydn's intentions cannot always be reliably determined from the sources, and no hard and fast rules can be given. The position is further complicated in that different editions, even the Vienna Urtext and Henle, give different versions of ornaments in numerous instances.

For example, the sign ⊹ , much used by Haydn, may mean ♫♩. or again either

♫♫ or ♫♫

i.e. a 'normal' turn, and is therefore inevitably interpreted differently by different editors.

The appoggiatura sign in the context of a group of semiquavers or demisemiquavers frequently causes confusion, even amongst relatively experienced players:

♪♩♩ or ♪♩♩

The appoggiatura here will be given a semiquaver or demisemiquaver value as the case may be, with the sense of a little 'lean' upon it. Thus in the Finale of Sonata No. 33 in

C minor the 𝄞

on the 1st beat of bb.1 and 21 will be interpreted 𝄞

with a 'lean' on the first note. Similarly in the first movement of No. 32 the 𝄞

at the end of bb.7 and 8 will be 𝄞

† Howard Ferguson, *Keyboard Interpretation* (Oxford University Press).

But the correct length to be given to appoggiaturas in general is open to different interpretations in different circumstances (and by different authorities!). I have in many instances suggested the value that may be given to an appoggiatura but once more it is stressed that these are only suggestions. If you have a reliable edition, it is well to try the 'given' value of an appoggiatura, and then if you feel this is unsatisfactory, to experiment with a shorter or longer version. In general, grace notes and ornaments will begin *on* the beat. And while trills and shakes are more likely to begin on the upper, rather than the main note, players must use their discretion on this point according to the circumstances. Students are in any event begged to learn the music first *without* the ornaments; to consider the structure of the music, to *listen*, and to *feel* the melodic, rhythmic and harmonic emphases, and then to incorporate the ornaments without distorting the fundamental structure − to accept that the ornaments are there to serve and to embellish that fundamental structure, and *not* the other way about. To begin by fussing about the ornaments is like trying to furnish the rooms before the house is built. Then, do experiment with ornaments according to the context, taking courage from the thought that even in the case of Bach, where 'rules' are in general more defined, eminent performers differ widely in their interpretation of the signs. Remember also that Haydn, most unpretentious but also most adventurous of composers, was the last person to be trammelled by imposed rules of thumb in such matters. It would not be practical for me to give suggested interpretations of all the ornaments that occur, and it is only where ornaments seem particularly problematic or numerous that I have done so. The Vienna Urtext Edition, as mentioned below (see under 'Editions') gives helpful suggestions in footnotes for the realization of some of the more complex or ambiguous ornaments. It also suggests where, as is often the case, it is more appropriate and/or more expressive to shorten an appoggiatura so that its effect is nearer to that of an acciaccatura. There is also a helpful short discussion of ornaments in the Preface. The Henle Urtext, excellent as it is, regrettably supplies no information on this, or on any other matters of style or interpretation. While no one regrets the passing of the overblown and ill-informed editions of the nineteenth century, I wish that the producers of beautiful modern urtext editions would realize that the average pianist is not a scholar, and in this era of the quest for authenticity, is sorely in need of practical information of this kind from these learned minds! In the new Associated Board selection of twenty-three Sonatas in four volumes (again edited by Howard Ferguson), excellently clear interpretations are written out above each ornament, and a comprehensive table and analysis of all occurring ornaments is given in each volume. His realization of the ornaments seems, wisely, to take account not only of what is 'correct', but also of what is practicable for the average set of fingers. The terror induced by ornaments usually impels players to try to 'get them in' as fast as possible. Particularly in an expressive slow movement the ornaments must be given time to 'speak', rather than, as is so often the case, clamped onto the melodic line as if the player had gone into a momentary spasm. And it is always preferable to have a *less* rapid trill (i.e. with fewer notes) that is clear and controlled, than one which tries to go too fast, 'jams', and grinds to a halt. In the case of figures such as

(as in the opening of the Finale in Sonata No. 44 in F), when an experienced player will play

 it is far better to play four clear notes

than six garbled ones.

Some Explanations and Amplifications

'Going to'

In case the frequent exhortation 'let the quavers "go to" the minim on the 1st beat', or 'feel that the semiquavers are "going to" a singing dotted crotchet', etc. is not quite understood, it merely means: feel the onward-moving impulse from the 'weaker' (usually shorter) notes, towards the 'stronger' (usually longer) one. This feeling of onward (but not hurried) movement towards stronger stressed notes is vital to the shaping of the phrases, and to the overall onward impetus of the music.

The Left Hand

Why, it may be asked, do I constantly harp on the concerns of the Left Hand? Its importance and true role is, I believe, in general greatly underestimated. In the vast majority of instances (although the roles are, of course, sometimes reversed), the Left Hand (LH) gives the fundamental rhythmic and harmonic foundation to the music. (In contrapuntal music it is naturally taken for granted that the LH, Right Hand (RH), and all the parts, are of equal importance.) Various composers at various times have pointed this out, and perhaps Chopin said it best: 'the LH is the conductor, it must not waver or lose ground; do with the RH what you will and can'. This applies as much to the music of the Classical period as to that of Chopin's own day. And Ralph Kirkpatrick, the great harpsichordist and teacher, describing his method of studying, for example, a Bach Prelude, said that he would 'nearly always start with the bass line'.† When the rhythm is going awry, and the motion of the piece is faltering, it is amazing, when a student is asked to pay attention to the LH, how naturally things will often right themselves. (See also, in this connection, under 'Rhythm', and also 'Texture' in 'Some Matters of Style'.) Often indeed the LH has the predominant rhythmic and/or melodic line and must take an emphatic lead − in the Finale of Sonata No. 6 in C, bb.46 − 54 for example, or the first movement of No. 39 in D, bb.63 − 77. In such cases, an exhortation such as 'let the LH octaves lead off boldly, with the RH offbeat quavers following evenly and relatively lightly' will be self-explanatory, as also will 'keep the RH figuration in place with steady LH chords', or 'let the RH figuration fit in with the steady LH, and *not* the other way about'.

Upbeats

Explanations of this term, not always familiar to or entirely understood by players who have never had experience of ensemble playing, are not always easy to find in musical dictionaries. It means the beat before, or leading to, the main accent. To take a simple example from the opening of the Finale of Sonata No. 42 in G major (the quavers marked x are the upbeats to the 1st beats of each subsequent bar):

A large, perhaps exceptionally large, proportion of Haydn's movements begin on the upbeat. It is always, therefore, as has been said above (see under 'Rhythm'), extremely important that the pulse of the movement is 'in the system' before you start to play, so

† Ralph Kirkpatrick, *Interpreting Bach's Well-tempered Clavier* (Yale University Press).

that the upbeat is perfectly timed, and gives a clear sense of 'leading in'. Often upbeats are even marked with a *sforzato* (see the first movement of Sonata No. 52 in G, or the Finale of No. 61 in D). Again, when upbeats are slurred (see the Finale of No. 59 in E flat) or tied (see the Finale of No. 39 in D) a degree of emphasis, a feeling of 'leaning' is implied. In the cases of the Finales of Nos. 39 and 61, these syncopated emphases (in the former implied, in the latter specified) put the rhythmic security of the player under considerable strain!

In the large majority of instances, in order to convey the 'onward' feeling, I use the term 'upbeat' rather than 'last beat'. So I will refer to the 'upbeat' to b. 2, for example, rather than to the 'last beat of b. 1'. Similarly, although it may be a loose use of the term, I may, in a movement in **4/4** time for example, refer to the 'upbeat to the 3rd beat of the bar'. An upbeat can consist of more than one note − it may consist of two quavers, or even a group of notes, or a quick scale (in the first movement of Sonata No. 51 in E flat, for example, the upward scale at the end of b.48 forms the upbeat to b.49, a particularly significant instance, as it is giving the 'lead' into the recapitulation). Or in the first movement of No. 4 in G the four demisemiquavers form the upbeat to b.1, and the semiquaver triplet the upbeat to b.3, and so on.

Alberti Basses (practising in dotted rhythm)
To inexperienced players rapid Alberti basses

are often a major stumbling block (this term *is* usually well defined in musical dictionaries). In the first movement of Sonata No. 10 in C, or the development section of the first movement of No. 42 in G, or the Finale of No. 53 in E minor, for example, it is vital that the LH bowls along evenly and clearly, giving lively rhythmic support to the RH. What often happens is that the thumb gets too heavy, so the rhythm starts to lurch, until the LH jams completely and the proceedings grind to a halt. In rapid Alberti LHs, the fifth finger (or occasionally the fourth) must give a sharp, light finger accent on the bass note, and the other three notes of each group (particularly the upper, 'thumb' note) must be kept relatively light. In a **2/4** bar, for example, the thumb will probably play four times on the same offbeat note (see above). Therefore it is this note that we want to hear proportionally least of, and so it needs to be the lightest. To this end, practising in dotted rhythms is particularly helpful:

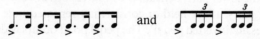

It is also useful to practise in triplets and all sorts of other rhythms (the French edition of those old friends, the Hanon exercises, gives a splendid selection of rhythms for this purpose). Whenever these passages occur, do practise the LH until it is perfectly secure before attempting to put the hands together.

Dotted Rhythms
Dotted rhythms, particularly when they persist through protracted passages, as they frequently do with Haydn, cause many an inexperienced (and sometimes not so inexperienced) player to bite the dust. Practise simple exercises at first, i.e. 'five finger exercises', scale figures, or simple broken-chord figures in a dotted rhythm

throwing the main weight onto the *dotted* notes, and keeping the semiquavers relatively light. Almost immediately, although the first few beats may be fairly well timed, the 'short' note, the semiquaver (or the demisemiquaver), tends to get gradually longer and heavier so that the overall beat is progressively undermined. The problem is that the player finds it difficult to *wait* for long enough on the *dotted* note, consequently the short note arrives too soon and it is therefore too long — it becomes 'tripletized', or in extreme cases even 'quaverized'! It is essential that the dotted note is felt as the *main* note, and it is often helpful, as is frequently suggested in the commentaries, to feel the short note as the *'upbeat'* to the dotted note.

If all else fails, walking around the room in dotted rhythm, pretending that the left leg is lame so that all the weight is thrown onto the right leg, can sometimes do the trick!

Chords
We usually think of a chord as a combination of three or more notes. In the commentaries, for the sake of simplicity, I refer to all combinations of notes (thirds, fifths, etc.) as well as to triads and larger combinations, as chords. In Haydn's time it would have been customary in many instances to 'spread' large or not so large chords. In various instances I have suggested this, but players should feel free to spread chords as or when they feel that it will improve their resonant or expressive quality.

Beat and Pulse
These terms are more or less interchangeable. The one may seem more appropriate than the other for reasons that can be sensed but not always defined! The connotations of 'beat' are more outward, defined, mathematical, than those of pulse, more inward, living, even metaphysical. On the other hand I might say, in a **4/4** bar for example: 'Come in clearly on the 6th *quaver pulse* of the bar', to differentiate between the quaver 'pulse' and the main crotchet 'beat'. Unless the term 'beat' is qualified ('quaver beat', 'crotchet beat', etc.), it always refers to the *main* beats of the bar, e.g. the *crotchet* beat in a **2/4**, **3/4** or **4/4** time and the *dotted crotchet* in a **6/8** time.

Pedal Points
This is a term not always clearly understood, and not to be confused with references to the sustaining, or soft pedal of the piano. It is particularly prone to cause confusion when it is referred to just as a 'pedal'. It derives from the foot pedal notes on the organ, which can be held beneath a series of progressions, often of considerable length, played on the manuals. On the piano it takes the form of a note (frequently the dominant) held, or consistently repeated, in the lower part, beneath the progressions or varying activities (often sequential) of the upper parts. If the held or consistently repeated note occurs in one of the upper parts it becomes an 'inverted pedal'. The pedal point occurs widely in folk music, when it is usually referred to as a drone or bourdon. And since Haydn enjoyed and used folk influences so freely, this effect is particularly prevalent in his music. Countless instances are to be found throughout the Sonatas, see for example, the first movement of No. 1, bb.17 – 19, and No. 36, bb.126 – 34; and frequently in the Finale of No. 62, bb.2 – 8, 10 – 16, 78 – 82, 85 – 90, and so on.

'Finish Off'
Failure to 'finish off' a phrase or figure properly is the cause of the frequent tendency to 'fall onwards' onto a subsequent beat or phrase, or over a rest. This applies particularly when the RH 'finishes' a phrase on a quaver, crotchet, or perhaps a dotted minim, and

the LH 'continues' to 'finish off' its own line, e.g.

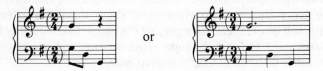 or

Hence my frequent exhortations to 'finish off' the LH clearly before leading on into the next bar. A good example of this occurs in the Finale of Sonata No. 4 in G. Here the LH must 'finish off' the two quavers neatly and in perfect time at the end of *each section* so that the RH can lead on with a clear quaver upbeat to b.9:

and so that the quaver rest at the beginning of each of the minor sections is perfectly timed, enabling the RH then the LH to lead off in a poised manner into b.25 and b.33

respectively.  Similarly, in the first movement of No.6

in C the RH figure must be 'finished off' neatly in b.8 over the LH crotchet fifth, so that the quaver rest will be accurately felt on the 2nd beat of the bar, ready for the RH to lead on with the quaver upbeat to b.9.

'Finishing off' in the LH is particularly important in numerous instances in minuets, when the RH may end a section on a crotchet, a minim, or a dotted minim, and the LH 'carries on' with the crotchets, which must continue in the precise 'stepping' pulse (see the Minuets of Sonatas Nos. 1, 2 and 3, and almost every early minuet movement).

'Rattle Out'
This is a personal term to suggest the kind of articulation in rapid semiquaver or demisemiquaver passages that is so brilliantly clear that the notes sound almost (but not quite) detached – an effect which occurs naturally with a fortepiano, or, of course, a harpsichord. On the modern piano we have to work consciously to counteract its more booming sonority, and produce a cleaner, more instant attack in our articulation.

Slurs and Tied or Syncopated Notes

Slurs are immensely important to the rhythmic and expressive character of the music. For some strange reason students who will happily 'show' them on a stringed instrument or in a vocal part, will ignore them when playing the piano. Consequently I frequently draw attention to them − I feel that the right effect is better conveyed by the suggestion of 'leaning on' rather than 'accenting' a slurred note.

Tied notes (or chords) always require a degree of emphasis, gentle and melodic, or strong even forceful according to context, in order that their sound shall carry over the subsequent beat or beats. Syncopated notes require a similar emphasis in order that they shall 'make their point' and that they shall also sound over the subsequent 'normal' beat. Hence, I frequently say: ' "feel" or "show" the implied emphasis on such-and-such a tied or syncopated note'.

Editions of the Sonatas

The numbering of the Haydn Sonatas is impossibly confusing to players. In the Peters Edition, and until recently in most other available editions, the numbering bears no relation to the order of composition. In the 1950s Hoboken issued his thematic catalogue of Haydn's works, and his numbering became more or less generally accepted. But since then the chronology of the keyboard works has been revised by Christa Landon for the Vienna Urtext Edition published by Universal, and to further complicate the issue, again by Georg Feder in the Henle Edition. The numberings here follow that of the Christa Landon/Vienna Urtext Edition, since this edition is now widely used, and since this is also the numbering used by H.C. Robbins Landon in his definitive work *Haydn: Chronicle and Works*. The Hoboken numbers are given in brackets. To further assist identification of the Sonatas by those possessing other editions, there is a reference table at the back of this volume. This shows the numberings of the Vienna Urtext Edition, the Hoboken Catalogue and the Henle Urtext Edition; the numbering of the Peters Edition (most representative of the earlier editions) is also given.

It is presumed that Haydn's earliest Sonatas (also called partitas or divertimentos) were composed for pupils. His early life is not sufficiently well documented for authorities to be able to date these compositions precisely, and it is assumed that many have been lost. The Vienna Urtext Edition groups the first eighteen Sonatas together as having been written before 1766, but in her preface Christa Landon states that a chronological order 'can only be suggested, not definitely established'.

The Henle Edition places the same eighteen Sonatas in two groups, at the beginning of Volume I, but in a different, and apparently less logical order. The first Sonata in Henle, in E flat major, is not published in the Vienna Urtext Edition, nor by Peters.

The preface to the Vienna Urtext Edition gives helpful information on interpretation, ornaments, etc. Suggestions for the execution of ornaments are, in many instances, also given in insets or footnotes to the music. The Henle Edition is equally authentic, but from the point of view of the player, less informative. In addition, Georg Feder's numbering is extremely complicated. The Peters Edition is, by today's standards, heavily 'edited'. But mercifully the editorial indications are given in light print, as opposed to those of Haydn himself, which are given in bold print. The same applies to the Breitkopf & Härtel Edition. Neither of these editions is as complete as the Vienna Urtext or Henle. Peters also publish a collection of '6 Easy Divertimenti' which correspond to Nos. 10, 14, 9, 1, 2 and 3 in the Vienna Urtext Edition. There are also numerous other collections and selections of various sizes, the longest published by Kalmus, and Schirmer. The Associated

Board has recently published a selection of twenty-three Sonatas, informatively edited by Howard Ferguson.

Bar Numberings

Bar numberings, tempo and dynamic indications, etc. are all taken from the Vienna Urtext Edition. For those with editions without bar numbers, there are two important points concerning the calculation of the numbers.

i) Bar 1 is always the first *whole* bar. Therefore, if a piece or movement is divided into 8-bar sections, and starts on an upbeat or half-bar, that upbeat or half-bar will be 'added up' with the part bar at the end of the section to make bar 8, and the first *whole* bar of the new section will be bar 9. In the Finale of Sonata No. 30 in D, for example, the opening upbeat is 'added on' to the end of the last bar of the first section to make a complete bar 8, and the first complete bar of the second section is bar 9.

ii) In cases where there are first- and second-time bars, only one of them is 'counted', in effect the second-time bar. See again the Finale of No. 30 in D, the seventh section, bb. 61 – 7: when this section is played for the first time, the first-time bar is bar 67, and when the section is repeated, the *second-time* bar becomes bar 67, and the first bar of the next section is bar 68. In both the Vienna Urtext Edition and Henle editions first- and second-time bars are calculated thus. However, in the new Associated Board selection of twenty-three Sonatas, the first- and second-time bars are *both* counted, so in the movements in which these occur there will be discrepancies in bar numberings.

Suggestions for Further Reading

Literature on Haydn's keyboard works is scanty. Many are discussed, of course, in H.C. Robbins Landon's monumental (but at the same time wonderfully companionable) work in five volumes, *Haydn: Chronicle and Works* (Thames & Hudson). In *Keyboard Music* edited by Denis Matthews (David & Charles) there is an informative section on Haydn by Eva Badura-Skoda. John McCabe's book *Haydn Piano Sonatas*, a new addition to the series of BBC Music Guides (which to my loss came out when this book was virtually finished) is warmly recommended. Both here and in his recordings of the Complete Piano Works, McCabe champions Haydn's keyboard works persuasively and incontrovertibly. Pianists who fall in love with Haydn's style – and who could not? – should investigate the Piano Trios. The complete edition, edited by H.C. Robbins Landon is published by Doblinger. Even if you cannot muster the other instrumentalists, the piano parts of these marvellous works (much undervalued like the Sonatas) offer a magnificent further field for exploration and study.

A GRADED LIST
OF HAYDN'S KEYBOARD WORKS

* = Specially recommended (see Preface).
O = More suitable for older players (see Preface).
The volume numbers refer to those of the Vienna Urtext Edition.

Grade 3 or under

VOLUME 1

Sonata No. 1 in G major (Hob. XVI/8)
   Second movement — Minuet
   * Third movement — Andante
   * Finale — Allegro

Sonata No. 3 in F major (Hob. XVI/9)
   * Finale — Scherzo (Allegro)

Sonata No. 4 in G major (Hob. XVI/G1)
   Second movement — Minuet and Trio

Sonata No. 7 in D major (Hob. XVII/D1)
   Second movement — Minuet

Sonata No. 8 in A major (Hob. XVI/5)
   Second movement — Minuet and Trio

Sonata No. 10 in C major (Hob. XVI/1)
   Third movement — Minuet and Trio

VOLUME 1B

Sonata No. 35 in A flat major (Hob. XVI/43)
   * Second movement — Minuet and Trio

MISCELLANEOUS PIECES

20 Variations in G major (Hob. XVII/2)
   Selected variations: see Commentary.

Arietta in A major with 12 Variations (Hob. XVII/2)
   Selected variations: see Commentary.

Grade 4

VOLUME 1

Sonata No. 2 in C major (Hob. XVI/7)
   First movement — Allegro moderato
   Second movement — Minuet and Trio

Sonata No. 3 in F major (Hob. XVI/9)
   Second movement — Minuet and Trio

Sonata No. 5 in G major (Hob. XVI/11)
O* Second movement – Andante

Sonata No. 6 in C major (Hob. XVI/10)
Second movement – Minuet and Trio

Sonata No. 9 in D major (Hob. XVI/4)
* Second movement – Minuet and Trio

Sonata No. 10 in C major (Hob. XVI/1)
Second movement – Adagio

Sonata No. 14 in C major (Hob. XVI/3)
Third movement – Minuet and Trio

Sonata No. 15 in E major (Hob. XVI/13)
O* Second movement – Minuet and Trio

VOLUME 2

Sonata No. 41 in A major (Hob. XVI/26)
Second movement – Minuet and Trio (Al Rovescio)

MISCELLANEOUS PIECES

20 Variations in G major (Hob. XVII/2)
Selected variations: see Commentary.

Arietta in A major with 12 Variations (Hob. XVII/2)
Selected variations: see Commentary.

Il Maestro e Lo Scolare (Hob. XVII/a/1) (duet)

Grade 5

VOLUME 1

Sonata No. 1 in G major (Hob. XVI/8)
* First movement – Allegro

Sonata No. 2 in C major (Hob. XVI/7)
O Finale – Allegro

Sonata No. 3 in F major (Hob. XVI/9)
O* First movement – Allegro

Sonata No. 4 in G major (Hob. XVI/G1)
First movement – Allegro
* Finale – Presto

Sonata No. 5 in G major (Hob. XVI/11)
* First movement – Presto (see Finale of No. 4)
* Third movement – Minuet and Trio

Sonata No. 41 in A major (Hob. XVI/26)
    Finale – Presto

Sonata No. 42 in G major (Hob. XVI/27)
    Second movement – Minuet and Trio
  * Finale – Presto

Sonata No. 43 in E flat major (Hob. XVI/28)
    * Second movement – Minuet and Trio

Sonata No. 47 in B minor (Hob. XVI/32)
    * Second movement – Minuet (Tempo di Menuet)

Sonata No. 48 in C major (Hob. XVI/35)
    Second movement – Adagio

Sonata No. 50 in D major (Hob. XVI/37)
O* Second movement – Largo e sostenuto

Sonata No. 51 in E flat major (Hob. XVI/38)
O Finale – Allegro

MISCELLANEOUS PIECES

20 Variations in G major (Hob. XVII/2)
    Selected variations: see Commentary.

Arietta in A major with 12 Variations (Hob. XVII/2)
    Selected variations: see Commentary.

Variations in D major (Hob. XVII/7)

Allegretto in G major (shortened arrangement of the Finale from the
String Quartet in G major Op. 33 No. 5)

Grade 6

VOLUME 1

Sonata No. 8 in A major (Hob. XVI/5)
    Finale – Presto

Sonata No. 11 in B flat major (Hob. XVI/2)
    * First movement – Moderato
O* Second movement – Largo

Sonata No. 12 in A major (Hob. XVI/12)
    First movement – Andante

Sonata No. 13 in G major (Hob. XVI/6)
 * Second movement – Minuet and Trio
 * Finale – Allegro molto

Sonata No. 16 in D major (Hob. XVI/14)
 * Finale – Allegro (sometimes marked Presto)

Sonata No. 17 in E flat major
  Second movement – Andante

VOLUME 1B

Sonata No. 19 in E minor (Hob. XVI/47)
 * First movement – Adagio
 * Finale – Tempo di Menuet

Sonata No. 28 in D major (Hob. XVI/5)
O* Second movement – Minuet and Trio

Sonata No. 30 in D major (Hob. XVI/19)
O* Second movement – Andante

Sonata No. 32 in G minor (Hob. XVI/44)
  Second movement – Allegretto

Sonata No. 34 in D major (Hob. XVI/33)
  Second movement – Adagio

VOLUME 2

Sonata No. 36 in C major (Hob. XVI/21)
O* Second movement – Adagio
 * Finale – Presto

Sonata No. 37 in E major (Hob. XVI/22)
  Second movement – Andante
  Finale – Tempo di Menuet

Sonata No. 38 in F major (Hob. XVI/23)
 * Third movement – Presto

Sonata No. 39 in D major (Hob. XVI/24)
 * Second movement – Adagio

Sonata No. 40 in E flat major (Hob. XVI/25)
  Second movement – Tempo di Menuet

Sonata No. 42 in G major (Hob. XVI/27)
 * First movement – Allegro con brio

Sonata No. 43 in E flat major (Hob. XVI/28)
  * Finale − Presto

Sonata No. 44 in F major (Hob. XVI/29)
    Second movement − Adagio
    Third movement − Tempo di Menuet

Sonata No. 46 in E major (Hob. XVI/31)
O* Second movement − Allegretto
    Finale − Presto

Sonata No. 48 in C major (Hob. XVI/35)
  * Finale − Allegro

Sonata No. 49 in C sharp minor (Hob. XVI/36)
    Second movement − Scherzando (Allegro con brio)
  * Third movement − Minuet and Trio (Moderato)

Sonata No. 50 in D major (Hob. XVI/37)
    Third movement − Presto ma non troppo − Innocentemente

Sonata No. 51 in E flat major (Hob. XVI/38)
  * Second movement − Adagio

Sonata No. 52 in G major (Hob. XVI/39)
O Second movement − Adagio

VOLUME 3

Sonata No. 53 in E minor (Hob. XVI/34)
O Second movement − Adagio
  * Third movement − Vivace molto (Innocentemente)

Sonata No. 57 in F major (Hob. XVI/47)
  * Second movement − Adagio (see No. 19)

Sonata No. 59 in E flat major (Hob. XVI/49)
  * Finale − Tempo di Menuet

MISCELLANEOUS PIECES

20 Variations in G major (Hob. XVII/2)

Arietta in A major with 12 Variations (Hob. XVII/2)

6 Easy Variations in C major (Hob. XVII/5)

Adagio in F major (Hob. XVII/9)

*Allegretto in G major (after a piece for Mechanical Clock
(Hob. XVII/10))

Grade 7

VOLUME 1

Sonata No. 8 in A major (Hob. XVI/5)
First movement – Allegro

Sonata No. 13 in G major (Hob. XVI/6)
* First movement – Allegro

Sonata No. 16 in D major (Hob. XVI/14)
* First movement – Allegro moderato

Sonata No. 17 in E flat major
First movement – Moderato

Sonata No. 18 in E flat major
First movement – Allegro

VOLUME 1B

Sonata No. 19 in E minor (Hob. XVI/47)
Second movement – Allegro

Sonata No. 20 in B flat major (Hob. XVI/18)
Second movement – Moderato

Sonata No. 29 in E flat major (Hob. XVI/45)
First movement – Moderato
Second movement – Andante

Sonata No. 30 in D major (Hob. XVI/19)
* Finale – Allegro assai

Sonata No. 31 in A flat major (Hob. XVI/46)
Finale – Presto

Sonata No. 33 in C minor (Hob. XVI/20)
O* Second movement – Andante con moto

Sonata No. 34 in D major (Hob. XVI/33)
First movement – Allegro

Sonata No. 35 in A flat major (Hob. XVI/43)
First movement – Moderato
Third movement – Rondo (Presto)

VOLUME 2

Sonata No. 36 in C major (Hob. XVI/21)
First movement – Allegro

Sonata No. 61 in D major (Hob. XVI/51)
  * First movement – Andante
  * Second movement – Presto

MISCELLANEOUS PIECES

*Arietta in E flat major with 12 Variations (Hob. XVII/3)

Variations on the Anthem 'Gott Erhalte'

O* Adagio in G major (from Piano Trio in E flat, see Hob. XV/22)

Grade 8

VOLUME 1B

Sonata No. 20 in B flat major (Hob. XVI/18)
  First movement – Allegro moderato

Sonata No. 29 in E flat major (Hob. XVI/45)
  * Finale – Allegro di molto

Sonata No. 30 in D major (Hob. XVI/19)
  * First movement – Moderato

Sonata No. 31 in A flat major (Hob. XVI/46)
  * First movement – Allegro moderato
  * Second movement – Adagio

Sonata No. 32 in G minor (Hob. XVI/44)
  First movement – Moderato

Sonata No. 33 in C minor (Hob. XVI/20)
  * First movement – Moderato (sometimes marked Allegro
    moderato)
  * Finale – Allegro

VOLUME 2

Sonata No. 40 in E flat major (Hob. XVI/25)
  * First movement – Moderato

Sonata No. 41 in A major (Hob. XVI/26)
  * First movement – Allegro moderato

Sonata No. 43 in E flat major (Hob. XVI/28)
  * First movement – Allegro moderato

Sonata No. 44 in F major (Hob. XVI/29)
  * First movement – Moderato

Sonata No. 47 in B minor (Hob. XVI/32)
  * Finale – Presto

Sonata No. 49 in C sharp minor (Hob. XVI/36)
  * First movement – Moderato

Sonata No. 50 in D major (Hob. XVI/37)
  * First movement – Allegro con brio

Sonata No. 51 in E flat major (Hob. XVI/38)
  * First movement – Allegro moderato

Sonata No. 52 in G major (Hob. XVI/39)
  * Finale – Prestissimo

VOLUME 3

Sonata No. 55 in B flat major (Hob. XVI/41)
  * First movement – Allegro

Sonata No. 56 in D major (Hob. XVI/42)
  First movement – Andante con espressione

Sonata No. 57 in F major (Hob. XVI/47)
  First movement – Moderato (see No. 19)

Sonata No. 58 in C major (Hob. XVI/48)
  * First movement – Andante con espressione
  * Second movement – Rondo presto

Sonata No. 59 in E flat major (Hob. XVI/49)
  * First movement – Allegro
  * Second movement – Adagio e cantabile

MISCELLANEOUS PIECES

Capriccio in G major (Hob. XVII/1)

*Andante con Variazione in F minor (Hob. XVII/6)

Grade 8+

VOLUME 3

Sonata No. 60 in C major (Hob. XVI/50)
  * First movement – Allegro

Sonata No. 62 in E flat major (Hob. XVI/52)
  * First movement – Allegro
  * Second movement – Adagio
  * Finale – Presto

MISCELLANEOUS PIECES

Fantasia (or Capriccio) in C major (Hob. XVII/4)

To My Teacher – Ruth D'Arcy Thompson

Author's Notes

1. The American equivalents for the British time-values used throughout this book are as follows:

semibreve	whole-note
minim	half-note
crotchet	quarter-note
quaver	eighth-note
semiquaver	sixteenth-note
demisemiquaver	thirty-second-note
hemidemisemiquaver	sixty-fourth-note

2. The following abbreviations have been used throughout:

LH	left hand
RH	right hand
b.	bar
bb.	bars

THE SONATAS

The order of the Sonatas, the bar numberings, and all dynamic indications etc. referred to below are taken from the Vienna Urtext Edition (unless otherwise stated) and may differ from those in other (particularly 'edited') editions. (See under 'Editions of the Sonatas' in the Introduction.)

* indicates movements that are specially recommended.

(O) indicates movements that are more suitable for older players.

The figure in brackets following the title of each movement indicates the approximate suggested Grade (see Preface).

No. 1 in G major
(Hob. XVI/8)

First movement – Allegro (5)*
This is a breezy, invigorating little movement, with a bright, clear texture.

bb.1 – 7   Set a smart march-like tempo, imagining a brisk step to each quaver pulse. Lead off from a perfectly timed RH upbeat, and then, placing the LH crotchet third firmly on the 1st beat of b.1, time the RH dotted rhythm figures with neat, military precision. Then be careful to place the LH quaver/crotchet thirds neatly in bb.2 – 4, to give a steady foundation for your immaculately timed RH semiquaver triplet figures. From bb.5 – 8 support the RH with a steady and firm LH line. The ornament on the 1st beat of b.6 can be played with an appoggiatura thus:

(see footnote in the Vienna Urtext Edition) or as an ordinary trill starting on the upper, or on the main note.

bb.8 – 16   Go to, and 'lean' well on the RH quaver appoggiatura on the 1st beat of b.8, making sure that the RH is perfectly co-ordinated with the two LH quavers, as you 'finish off' the LH line neatly down to the low quaver D. Then lead off clearly with firm LH quavers from the 2nd beat of the bar (playing these smoothly or slightly detached, as you choose – the essential is that they are steady), letting the repeated RH detached semiquavers follow evenly and relatively lightly. Through bb.10 – 11 keep the RH semiquaver/triplet figures in place with the help of continuingly steady LH quavers. 'Finish off' the figures of b.13 with clear unison quavers on the 1st beat of b.14. Then feel that you are 'leading on' from the high quaver D on the 2nd quaver pulse of b.14, and end the section in a bright *forte*, taking care to 'finish off' the LH neatly in b.16.

bb.17 – 44   Again lead in from a clear upbeat, and place the LH dominant pedal point resonantly on the 1st beat of b.17, holding it right through to b.19. Shape the curve of the inner LH quaver line smoothly, again feeling that the LH is 'leading', with the detached RH semiquavers following evenly in b.17 (as in bb.8 – 9). Through bb.18 – 19 feel that the RH offbeat semiquaver group, and the triplet semiquavers are fitting in with the steady LH quavers and *not* the other way about. 'Take over' with the RH again from the upbeat to b.20 and 'join in' clearly with cleanly articulated LH semiquavers on the second quaver pulse of b.20. Take care to poise yourself on the quavers on the 2nd beat of bb.21 and 23 so that you don't 'fall into' the upbeat to bb.22 and 24. Let your LH 'go on down' to a firm crotchet D on the 2nd beat of b.26, before you lead back into the recapitulation with a clear upbeat to b.27. Listen particularly to your perfectly placed bass octaves in b.28.

Second movement – Minuet (3 or under)

Though very simple in outline, the variety of RH note values within the steady crotchet pulse makes this an excellent little rhythmic study for novice players.

bb.1 – 16 Immediately establish your clear 'stepping' pulse as you lead in with confident RH crotchets (perhaps slurred), and 'join in' with a firm LH crotchet on the 2nd beat, playing the two LH crotchets in a clear, just detached style, giving equal weight to each. Carry on confidently, in perfect time, with the RH semiquavers going to a clear crotchet on the 2nd beat of b.2. This time feel that the 'equal' LH crotchets are 'going to' a firm crotchet on the 1st beat of b.3, as the RH quavers curve up through the bar. Take care to differentiate clearly between the 'plain' quavers through the 1st and 2nd beats, and the triplet on the *3rd* beat as you 'go towards' a firm 'lean' on the appoggiatura on the 1st beat of b.4. Give the appoggiatura a crotchet value and treat the ornament thus:

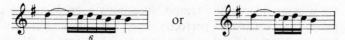

'Finish off' the phrase cleanly on the 3rd beat and lead on into the higher register in b.5 perhaps in a brighter tone, supporting the RH with steady and clear LH crotchet chords. Keep a steady crotchet pulse as the high 'solo' triplets curve through b.6, and support the RH again with a firm and steady LH through bb.7 – 8, listening to the three LH crotchets marching down through b.8 as you prepare to lead on in the second section. Play bb.9 and 10 perhaps in a quieter more expressive tone, and then 'open out' the tone through b.13 towards the 2nd beat of b.14. The LH crotchets through bb.7 – 8 and in the second section are best played in an even, just-detached 'stepping' style.

Third movement – Andante (3 or under)*

This is a particularly charming little movement. The poise and equilibrium of the RH melody line is dependent on the support of an even-moving and perfectly steady LH line, moving mainly in quavers. Study the lines carefully separately, therefore, giving as much attention to the shaping of the LH as to the RH.

bb.1 – 5 Lead off in a quiet, serene tone with a clear upbeat quaver 'going to' a firm dotted quaver on the 1st beat of b.1. Enter clearly with the LH on the 2nd quaver pulse of the bar so that the RH demisemiquavers can be perfectly timed. Let the RH repeated quavers 'speak' (rather than sounding spiky) with the feeling of 'going to' a clear singing and firmly slurred crotchet on the 3rd beat, and then curve the line smoothly down towards the 3rd beat of b.2, supported by the 'procession' of steady LH quavers. While the RH is shaped in a smooth but clear *cantabile,* the LH quaver can be *legato,* or, in my view, preferably slightly detached in an even 'stepping' style. Take care to 'finish off' the RH quavers neatly in b.2 as the LH 'goes on down' to a clear crotchet on the 4th beat, ready for the RH to lead on with the quaver upbeat to b.3. Make a little swell up to the high slurred crotchet B on the 3rd beat of b.3. Be sure to 'finish off' the three LH quavers cleanly in b.4 before leading off into the second section in a rather brighter and more open tone.

bb.5 – 9 Feel the 'lift' up to the D as you articulate the upbeat semiquavers to b.5 clearly. In bb.5 and 6 take care to carry the LH 'on down' to the bass note on the 4th beat, as in b.2. From the upbeat to b.7 and through b.7

support the RH clearly with the more resonant LH fragments, using these to help keep you steady as the RH moves momentarily into triplets. Then feel the implied onward leading emphasis on the RH crotchet upbeat to b.8 (placing the grace note figure confidently *on* the beat). 'Go up' resolutely to a firm-toned crotchet G on the sixth *quaver* pulse of b.8, balancing this syncopated note with firm LH crotchets on the 3rd and 4th beats, and then curve the line smoothly downwards towards a quiet, and carefully measured ending.

Finale − **Allegro** (3 or under)*

Play this deliciously racy little movement as merrily as can be.

bb.1-8   Set a rock-steady **3/8** pulse with an overall one-in-the-bar feeling. Practise the LH semiquavers carefully alone. It is helpful to practise at first

in a dotted rhythm [rhythm notation] and then [rhythm notation] (see

Introduction). Then when you practise the LH as written, make a light clear finger-accent on the first semiquaver of each bar. Play the RH quavers throughout in a sparky 'plucked' *staccato*. Go up to a ringing high crotchet D on the 1st beat of b.2, and then finish the first phrase off cleanly on the 1st beat of b.4, buoying the RH along with clear and mettlesome LH semiquavers through to the end of b.5. The 'changeover' at b.6 is an unsteadying moment for novice players. Feel that the LH quavers in b.6 are 'taking over' from the RH quavers in b.5, and let these LH quavers 'go to' a firm crotchet C on the 1st beat of b.7 beneath your busy RH semiquavers. Be sure to 'finish off' the detached LH quavers cleanly through b.8, making a tiny break before either returning to b.1, or leading on into the second section.

bb.9 − 24   Underpinning the RH with a resonant dominant pedal point and a clearly articulated inner LH line from the upbeat to b.10, let the 'keen' RH semiquavers curve up to the C on the 1st beat of b.11 and down again to a clear quaver D on the 3rd beat of b.12. Then *crescendo* vigorously as the LH octaves march down towards a resonant crotchet on the 1st beat of b.16 (octaves can, of course, be omitted by those with small hands). Then take care to collect yourself after the 3rd beat of b.16, allowing a tiny break again, ready to dash off into the reprise.

No. 2 in C major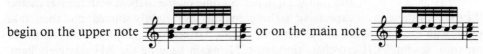
(Hob. XVI/7)

First movement − **Allegro moderato** (4)

This short movement has a bright fanfare-like character.

bb.1 − 10   Set a rock-steady *moderato* crotchet pulse (taking into account the coming demisemiquaver scale figures), and give the opening chords a ringing brassy quality, listening to the LH octaves marching firmly downwards, tonic, dominant, tonic. (Novice players had best not attempt the trill over the second chord.) The RH chords can be spread as indicated and this makes the trill easier. The trill could

begin on the upper note [music notation] or on the main note [music notation]

Be sure to give the crotchet chord on the 1st beat of b.2 its precise value so that you come *off* clearly, and *feel* the quaver rest on the 2nd beat, ready to shoot up, as if with a vigorous 'flick' with the RH upbeat demisemiquavers towards the 1st beat of b.3. Play the RH and inner LH quavers in a clear detached style through b.3, with the LH detached quavers carrying on through b.4 and into b.5 beneath firm RH crotchets. 'Finish off' the LH quavers cleanly in b.5, then make it clear that you are starting a new phrase with the RH on the 2nd beat of b.5, and support your cheerfully 'jogging' RH semiquavers with bright and rhythmic LH detached quavers from the upbeat to b.6. Feel that the LH is 'going to' a strong crotchet on the 1st beat of b.8 as the RH repeated-note figures *crescendo* 'keenly' upwards towards the 1st beat of b.9.

bb.10 – 23
'Finish off' the LH down to a resonant crotchet on the 2nd beat of b.10, and lead on with another ringing chord on the 1st beat of b.11. 'Lean' and linger fractionally upon the RH semiquaver on the 2nd beat of bb.11 and 13, then shoot to a clear quaver on the 1st beat of bb.12 and 14. These scales are less difficult than they look, providing that you keep steady, and make this definite 'lean-and-linger' effect on the first note without worrying too much about the precise differentiation between the semiquaver and demisemiquavers. The important thing is that you play the lower G precisely on the 2nd beat of bb.11 and 13, and arrive in one piece on the high G precisely on the 1st beat of bb.12 and 14. Support the RH through b.12 with a resonant lower dominant minim and steady inner LH quavers, and then take particular care to go up to a strong quaver on the 1st beat of b.14 where the high G is *not* supported by the LH. Give the RH appoggiatura on the 1st beat of b.16 a crotchet value, and feel the onward 'lead' of the LH semiquavers into the reprise at b.17.

Second movement – Minuet and Trio (4)
This minuet has a forthright air.

bb.1 – 16
Lead off in a vigorous tone. Feel the 'lift' in the RH up to the high crotchet C on the 2nd beat of b.1, and time the dotted rhythm upbeat figure to b.2 etc. with the utmost precision, supporting the RH with a resonant minim octave on the 1st beat of b.1, and with steady 'stepping' crotchets from the upbeat to b.2. The RH appoggiatura on the first note of b.4 could be treated either as a minim or as a crotchet – in either case 'go to' and lean well upon it, while also listening to the three LH crotchets marching steadily down through the bar. Then lead off into b.5 with a clear dominant chord, and shape the semiquaver figures in a more gracious tone up towards the high crotchet D on the 1st beat of bb.6 and 7. Take care to keep a steady crotchet pulse here when you only have the support of the LH on the 1st beat of these bars. Resume the more vigorous tone from b.9, and underpin the RH with strong crotchet chords on the 1st beat of bb.13 and 14. Be sure to 'come in' in perfect time with the RH semiquavers on the 2nd beat of b.13, and similarly in b.14 (making it quite clear in b.14 that the upward scale starts with a *quaver*).

Trio

bb.17 – 36
Having 'finished off' the LH crotchets cleanly through b.16, allow a tiny break, and then immediately establish a new character as you lead off into b.17 in the minor in a quieter, more thoughtful tone. Feel that the LH is 'leading' through b.17 with the detached repeated offbeat quavers following evenly and relatively lightly. Phrase the LH thirds smoothly down to a clear crotchet third on the 1st beat of b.18, and follow on in perfect time on the offbeat with the RH quaver thirds. Play these in an expressive 'sighing' manner as if lightly slurred; and then 'take over' with the LH, again in perfect time on the 1st beat of b.19. Concentrate firmly on your 'leading' LH crotchets through b.21, again keeping the RH relatively light, and taking care that the first and third semiquavers of each little RH figure (the C's) do not 'bump'. Feel that you are 'opening out' towards a resonant minim F sharp and

fuller toned RH in b.22. Listen to the onward movement of the LH quavers through b.24 leading downwards towards the 1st beat of b.25. Take care to keep a steady crotchet pulse as the treble scale opens out through bb.26 and 28. Be sure also to give the crotchet on the 3rd beat of these bars its full value, and a slight emphasis, as you prepare to 'take the LH down' again to a firm crotchet on the 1st beat of bb.27 and 29.

Finale – Allegro (5) (O)

This is a sturdy, bustling movement. The LH broken octave pattern is rather taxing for a small hand.

bb.1 – 12   Establish a brisk **3/8** pulse with an overall feeling of one-in-the-bar. Lead off with a clear ornamented crotchet in the RH (placing the turn *on* the beat) over 'keen' LH semiquavers. Do not labour the cross-rhythm on the upbeat to b.2 but, bearing in mind the one-in-the-bar pulse, play the triplet lightly, without disturbing the rhythm of the LH semiquavers, feeling that you are 'going up to' a strong crotchet G on the 1st beat of b.2. Be sure to give the crotchet on the 1st beat of b.3 its full value, so that you can lead on with a perfectly timed RH semiquaver, and LH quaver upbeat to b.4. Underpin the RH semiquavers from here with a firm and steady LH line – the LH quavers on the upbeat to b.4, and from the upbeat to, and through b.5 (and similarly from the upbeat to b.18, and through bb.28 – 30, etc.) could be either detached or *legato*. The essential is that they are clear and steady. Be sure once more to give the crotchets on the 1st beat of b.6 their full value so that you lead on into b.7 with a perfectly timed RH triplet upbeat. Carry the RH down through b.12 to a firm crotchet on the 1st beat of b.13 to give a good 'springboard' for the ascending LH broken octaves through bb.13 – 15.

bb.13 – 25   If the hand is big enough, practise the LH broken octaves (bb.13 – 15 etc.) at first in *plain* octaves. Then practise in dotted rhythms:

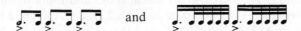

(see Introduction). Then, when you practise the passage 'straight', imagine that the broken octaves are slurred, so that the bass notes are stressed (this is hard work for the fifth finger), and the thumbs are kept relatively light. Finally, aim for your one-in-the-bar feeling and make an overall *crescendo* so that you are 'going to' a strong crotchet octave E on the 1st beat of b.16. Then 'bring in' your RH triplets confidently on the 2nd quaver pulse of b.16, and run down clearly, so that the RH semiquaver D coincides precisely with a firm LH crotchet F sharp on the 1st beat of b.17. Make sure that you 'finish' off the three LH quavers neatly in the last bar of the section, poising yourself for a clear subsequent 1st beat, as you either go back to b.1, or go on to the second section.

bb.26 – 55   Find a new, quieter and smoother tone colour for the minor moment, bb.34 – 7. Do not panic and lose your balance when you have to jump down a seventh in the LH (bb.45 – 6 and 51 – 2); keep a perfectly steady pulse through bb.45 and 51 (practising again in plain octaves at first) and poise yourself for the inevitable and natural slight break as you 'go down' confidently to a *firm* crotchet octave A on the 1st beat of bb.46 and 52.

No. 3 in F major
(Hob. XVI/9)

First movement − **Allegro** (5) (O)*

This short, but imposing movement has a declamatory, almost Handelian quality.

bb.1 − 15 Set a firm and very steady crotchet pulse, bearing in mind the hemidemi- semiquaver figures to come (bb.8 − 9 etc.). The opening bars have a bright woodwind, fanfare-like character. Lead off with a ringing crotchet chord (which can be slightly spread, as also at b.16), taking care to give this chord its full value. Then time the RH dotted rhythm figures with military precision over clear and steady LH octaves. 'Go to' a firm LH octave and clear RH quaver on the 1st beat of b.2. Then make a tiny break, and let the three repeated RH quavers 'speak' (rather than letting them 'run into' each other), feeling that they are 'going to' the ornamented quaver on the 1st beat of b.3. Support the RH from the upbeat to b.3 with neatly placed LH figures in quaver thirds, and feel the clear onward lead of the RH semiquavers on the 2nd beat of b.3 where the RH has a quaver rest. Be sure to *feel* the quaver rest on the 2nd beat of b.4, ready to lead on with a clear quaver upbeat to b.5 in both hands. Support the RH with firm LH crotchet chords through b.5, and with steady LH quavers through b.6. (The ornament on the 1st beat of b.6 can be treated as in the first movement of Sonata No. 1, b.6.) Take care to poise yourself on the 2nd beat of b.7 so that you don't 'fall into' the upbeat to b.8. 'Go to' a very firm LH crotchet octave on the 1st beat of b.8, and then 'snap' the RH hemidemisemiquaver figures smartly and jauntily, keeping steady with the help of firmly placed LH octaves. Make sure that the first note of each hemidemisemiquaver figure falls *on* each quaver pulse and does not anticipate it. Then, through bb.10 and 11 underpin the RH with perfectly steady LH quavers. Do indeed take care to place the LH clearly and accurately throughout the movement (see Introduction, 'The Left Hand') and also be careful not to hurry the *2nd* beat of those bars where the LH has a quaver rest (bb.2, 3, 8, 9, etc.) or a held dotted crotchet (bb.13, 14, etc.). At b.11 'finish off' the LH neatly down to the 3rd quaver C on the 2nd beat so that once again you do not 'fall into' the upbeat to b.12. Then 'come in' clearly with the RH upbeat semiquaver group on the offbeat, making sure that the lower RH semiquaver G is perfectly synchronized with the *LH* quaver upbeat to b.12. From here to the double bar, support your RH curving semiquavers with firm LH octaves. 'Finish off' the LH down to a firm low crotchet C on the 2nd beat of b.15, ready to lead off into the second section.

bb.15 − 42 Think of an even brighter, brassier sound here for the high quaver sixths (bb.17 and 19) and thirds (b.21). Again be careful not to hurry the 2nd beats of these bars, as you play the sixths and thirds clearly and deliberately. From the upbeat to b.25, again support the RH with a firm octave line in the LH, taking care to keep a steady pulse as you move briefly into triplets (bb.27 − 8). Then be sure to allow a full crotchet rest before setting off into the recapitulation.

Second movement − **Minuet and Trio** (4)

This is a rather strong 'masculine' Minuet. The Minuet and Trio are untypically similar in character.

bb.1 − 10 Lead off with a clear ornamented minim in the RH, placing the turn *on* the beat, and establish your secure Minuet rhythm with clear and steady rising crotchet octaves in the LH (small hands can omit the octaves). In the first four bars make sure that you define your note values properly, differentiating clearly between the RH triplet on the 3rd beat of b.1, and the two 'ordinary' quavers on the 1st beat of b.2, and similarly between the 'ordinary' quavers, then triplets, in b.3. Then take care to time the dotted crotchet and two semiquavers accurately in b.4 over steady LH crotchets. From the upbeat to b.7 underpin the RH triplet line with firm LH octaves. Then be sure to 'finish off' the section with perfectly timed LH crotchets in b.10.

bb.11 – 28 Through bb.11 – 12 shape the inner LH crotchet line evenly over the sustained lower tied C. Find a new, smoother tone colour for the minor moment (bb.15 – 18). Let the LH crotchets 'lead' steadily here with the syncopated RH line following evenly in smooth and expressive curves.

Trio

bb.29 – 44 Lead off with a resonant LH minim octave B flat on the 1st beat of b.29, and be sure to 'enter' with the RH third precisely on the 2nd beat. End the first phrase with a clear crotchet chord on the 2nd beat of b.32, and then be sure to give full value to the crotchet rest on the 3rd beat. Play the RH crotchet melody line buoyantly through bb.33 – 4 over even-running LH triplets. Then from b.37 let the RH triplet line curve easily over an even and steady LH crotchet line. Drop the tone to *piano* perhaps at b.37, and then *crescendo* towards b.40.

Finale – Scherzo (Allegro) (3 or under)*

The title here means simply a joke – not (since this is in a sturdy **2/4**) an antennal peek on Haydn's part towards his own, and of course, Beethoven's later 'scherzification' of the minuet.

bb.1 – 8 Set a lively but rock-steady **2/4**, and enter with a clear RH quaver upbeat, taking care to give this, and all similar quaver upbeats their full value, and a strong sense of 'leading in' or 'on'. These quaver upbeats could be either detached or slurred – or you could detach the upbeats to bb.1 and 5, and slur those to bb.9, 11 and 13. In any event, 'go to' a strong 1st beat of b.1, supporting the RH with a firm LH crotchet third, as if with a vigorous 'stamp', as the semiquavers ascend with 'rattling' clarity towards a ringing high crotchet C on the 1st beat of b.2. From b.2 underpin the RH with 'busy' but rock-steady LH detached repeated quaver chords. Let the RH 'go to' a strong slurred crotchet third on the 1st beat of b.4, and take care to 'finish off' the RH cleanly with the quaver third on the 2nd beat over a firm LH crotchet F, ready to lead on with a further clear upbeat to b.5.

bb.8 – 24 Come to a clear 'stop' on the unison crotchets on the 1st beat of b.8, being sure to come *off* cleanly, and *feel* the quaver rest on the 2nd beat ready to articulate the upbeat with perfect clarity as you either return to b.1, or lead on. Launch into the second section with renewed vigour, articulating the RH with pinpoint precision over 'rattling' LH semiquavers. (Deliver these with a short sharp accent with the fifth finger on the first note of each group – practising in this rhythm will help ♩ ♪♫ ♩ ♪♫ See Introduction.) Support the RH with a firm LH crotchet on the 1st beat of b.14, and a firm octave on the 1st beat of b.15. Then take care to co-ordinate the 'entry' of the LH quaver figure neatly on the upbeat to b.16, as the RH semiquavers 'go towards' a firm crotchet E; and *listen* to the three detached LH quavers marching down in precise time ready for the RH to hurtle off again from a perfectly timed upbeat to b.17.

No. 4 in G major
(Hob. XVI/G1)

First movement − Allegro (5)

Aim here to create as bright and transparent a texture as possible. Although there are no outstanding technical problems, this movement does present a considerable test of steadiness. Do feel a clear and steady crotchet pulse *before* you start. When setting your tempo, do not think so much of 'getting in' the demisemiquaver upbeats − rather think of a speed at which you can safely negotiate the little triplet passages in bb.22 − 4 etc.

bb.1 – 12   'Flick' the upbeat demisemiquavers clearly down to a definite, detached quaver on the 1st beat of b.1, and then, feeling the 'lift' up to the high RH third, detach the quaver thirds brightly, feeling that you are 'going to' a firm dotted crotchet third on the 1st beat of b.2. Then keep yourself steady through bb.2 – 3 with the help of immaculately placed LH quaver/crotchet figures (feeling that the quaver is the 'upbeat' to the lower crotchet on the 2nd beat) and be sure to differentiate clearly between the RH triplet upbeat to b.3 and the 'usual' demisemiquaver upbeats. Be sure also to 'finish off' the LH neatly down to the *quaver* on the 2nd beat of b.5 (beneath the smoothly slurred RH thirds), and to a firm *crotchet* on the 2nd beat of b.7, ready in both instances for the RH upbeat demisemiquaver figure to give a clear onward lead. Feel the implied 'lean' on the syncopated RH crotchet third in b.11, and do continue, here and throughout the movement, to keep yourself steady by playing all LH figures with the utmost precision.

bb.13 – 28   Slur the RH semiquaver couplets neatly in bb.13 – 16 over steady LH lines of descending quavers. (These LH quavers could either be *legato* or detached as you feel inclined − the essential is that they are steady.) Then from the upbeat to b.18 place the RH quaver fragments neatly over evenly pulsating LH semiquavers, being careful to 'feel' the 2nd beat of these bars securely in the LH, where the RH has a quaver rest. Similarly in bb.22 – 3, as you move into triplets, do 'feel' the 2nd beat in the *RH* when the *LH* has a rest, so that your crotchet pulse remains perfectly stable. Then in bb.24 and 26 support the RH with firm LH crotchets. Conversely, feel that the RH is 'taking over' with firm crotchets in bb.25 and 27, and end the section in perfect time.

bb.29 – 80   In the long sequential passage from bb.35 – 47, where Haydn develops the figures from bb.17 – 21, you may feel the urge to hurry for fear of being boring. Do exactly the opposite − maximize the rhythmic tension by playing as if you 'have the brakes on' (though of course without dragging), and make a gradual and deliberate *crescendo* from b.40 towards b.47. The greatest rhythmic danger area lies between bb.54 and 57. Be sure that the LH takes an emphatic 'lead', with the upbeat demisemiquavers running down deliberately to firm *crotchets* on the 1st beats of bb.54 – 7 (as opposed to 'flicking' down to detached quavers, as with the previous figures in the *RH*). Take particular care also to place the RH sixths here with immaculate precision, judging the tone carefully so that they balance, rather than swamp, the LH.

Second movement − Minuet and Trio (3 or under)

As John McCabe has said, this Minuet has rather a feeling of mock-solemnity.†

bb.1 – 22   Let the melody line sail through bb.1 − 4 over serenely moving, barely detached LH crotchet chords. Through b.1 feel that these LH chords are 'going to' the chord on the 1st beat of b.2, and then similarly b.4. Be sure

†John McCabe, *Haydn Piano Sonatas* (BBC Music Guides).

to come *off* on the 2nd beat of b.4, and to *feel* the crotchet rests. Then lead on with a quiet but firm LH crotchet chord on the 1st beat of b.5, taking care to 'follow on' in perfect time with the RH offbeat quavers, feeling the onward impulse towards a further firm LH chord on the 1st beat of b.6. Finish the section with neat formality, taking care to 'finish off' the LH crotchets cleanly through b.8. Then launch into the second section in quite a different, woodwind-like tone with resonant RH thirds over pompously strutting, bassoon-like LH detached broken octaves. Come to a clear 'stop' on the 1st beat of b.14 ready to resume the 'serene' opening figures from b.15.

Trio

bb.23 – 46 Lead off with a strong, almost stentorian bass octave on the 1st beat of b.23, answered in a lighter tone with the treble crotchets, 'going to' the ornamented minim of the 1st beat of b.24. 'Lean' a little on the ornamented crotchets on the 1st beat of bb.27 and 28 (playing the turns, here and in b.24, *on* the beat) and take care to place the LH crotchet chords with neat, dance-like precision on the 2nd and 3rd beats. Then show the more expressive quality of bb.31 – 4. Let the 'speaking', repeated RH crotchets 'go to' and lean well upon, the slurred minim on the 1st beat of bb.32 and 34, supported by even LH chords. Place the LH crotchets and then the minim clearly on the 1st beat of bb.35 – 7 so that the 'entry' of the RH triplets on each 2nd beat is perfectly timed. Take care not to hurry through b.38, allowing a tiny break after the 3rd beat as you prepare to go down to the strong LH octave on the 1st beat of b.39.

Finale – Presto (5)*

This mettlesome movement is identical to the first movement of No. 5. It has an amusing, rather 'cloak and dagger' minor, trio-like section.

bb.1 – 24 Set a smart and very secure **3/8** pulse with an overall one-in-the-bar feeling, and set off with the utmost rhythmic verve. Lead off from a clear quaver upbeat, and 'rattle out' your RH semiquavers over a firm LH octave line. Imagine that this LH line through bb.1 – 2 and 5 – 6, etc, is slurred

so that you 'lean' on the crotchet octave on each 1st beat. Then take care to articulate the quaver upbeat to b.4 neatly in both hands as you 'go to' the RH and LH quavers on the 1st beat of b.4. These quavers in b.4 could be slurred or detached, or the RH thirds could be slurred and the LH quavers detached. In any event make sure that you 'finish off' these two quavers cleanly in both hands, making a tiny break so that you don't 'fall into' the upbeat to b.5. Place the three quavers neatly in both hands in b.7 (these are best cleanly detached), and 'finish off' the two LH quavers neatly in b.8, so that once again you don't 'fall into' the upbeat as you either return to the beginning, or carry on. Take care not to clip short the value of the quaver on the 3rd beat of bb.10, 12, 13 and 14, or this time you will 'fall into' the *1st* beat of the subsequent bars. Think of the LH quaver octaves as clear upbeats to bb.11, 13, etc, rather than as 'tail ends' of bb.10, 12, etc.

bb.25 – 48 Allow the full quaver 'upbeat' rest to b.25, and poise yourself to find a completely new, very quiet and slightly mysterious tone colour as you lead off in the minor. If you play the RH turns (not given in Henle), place them neatly *on* the beat, and place the LH offbeat quaver couplets with neat precision, either detached or lightly slurred as you feel inclined. *Crescendo* a little as you ascend towards b.29, and then *diminuendo* again towards b.32. Lead off with clear though quiet, rather stealthy LH crotchet octaves at b.33, then 'take over' with the RH thirds on the 1st beat of b.35. You could make a little *rallentando*, and *diminuendo* to *pianissimo* through bb.39 – 40, as the previous little RH figure in thirds is repeated in the low register. Then you could either end the whole section in *piano,* ready to burst out again as you return to the *da capo,* or alternatively, *crescendo* dashingly from b.41 through to the *da capo.*

No. 5 in G major
(Hob.XVI/11)

The editor of the Vienna Urtext Edition considers this to be 'a combination of three unrelated movements', using the Finale of the previous Sonata, this time as a first movement. It is not published as a Sonata by Henle, but the second and third movements appear in the Appendix to their Volume 1.

(First movement – Presto (5). See Finale of No. 4.)

Second movement – Andante (4) (O)*
This is a pleasing and expressive movement, more likely to appeal to the older player. In any case, the particular warmth of the texture would be lost if a young player could not manage the LH octaves.

Set an easy-moving crotchet pulse with an overall two-in-the-bar feeling.
bb.1 – 6   (See footnote in Vienna Urtext Edition, and both Henle and Peters give an *alla breve* time signature.) Lead in from a smooth crotchet upbeat and shape the first little phrase neatly and smoothly over a quietly supportive LH. Start the trills here (and in b.4) on the upper notes, and do not attempt to scramble in too

many notes (six notes including the turn [♩♩♩] or even four notes

[♩♩♩]).   Take care to 'finish off' the first phrase clearly on the 2nd

beat of b.2 (imagining that the ornamented RH and the LH inner crotchets are slurred over the quietly resonant lower LH minim). Then be sure to *feel* the crotchet rest securely on the 3rd beat (or 2nd main beat) ready to lead on in a poised manner in both hands with the crotchet upbeat to b.3. From the upbeat to b.4 support the RH with steadily moving LH octaves. Do not attempt to fiddle around with fancy *'legato'* fingerings, but, keeping the LH very close to the keyboard, place the octaves quietly and deliberately so that they are barely detached and move like even 'steps'.

From the upbeat to b.7 feel the increasingly expressive quality of the RH.
bb.7 – 20   Feel that the repeated RH crotchets E flat in b.7 are 'going to' the ornamented crotchet on the 1st beat of b.8, supported by even LH thirds. Give the LH minim thirds in b.8 a warmly resonant tone, feel the 'onward lean' of the third on the 2nd main beat as you show the RH quaver rest, ready to lead on with the eloquent RH offbeat quaver figure. Feel the implied 'lean' on the RH dotted quaver on the 1st beat of bb.9 and 10, taking care to time the dotted rhythm figure neatly. Then feel the sense in which the RH quavers 'lead on' on the 2nd main beat of bb.9 – 12, where the LH has a crotchet rest. Balance the RH with quietly resonant LH fragments through bb.9 and 10. Then support the long span of curving RH quavers from the middle of b.10 with carefully placed LH octave fragments from the upbeat to bb. 11 and 12, and with the longer line of quietly 'stepping' octaves from the upbeat to b.13. Be careful

to place the LH upbeat to b.18 securely beneath the RH trill so that you do not 'fall into' b.18. Listen to the LH broken third figure 'entering' on the 2nd beat of b.18 beneath the even RH repeated crotchets. Do 'finish off' the three LH crotchets carefully in b.20, so that you are nicely poised to lead off again with the crotchet upbeat, as you either repeat or carry on.

bb.21 – 63   In bb.24 – 5 be careful to place the LH 'offbeat' crotchet chords precisely but quietly, so that you support, but do not disrupt the two-in-the-bar flow of the RH quavers. Take care to 'finish off' the previous phrase cleanly with the two RH crotchets in b.28, as you 'enter' clearly with the LH broken third figure on the 2nd crotchet beat of the bar. Then 'enter' equally clearly with the RH on the *4th* beat, and show the contrary motion contrapuntal movement of these LH and RH figures as they progress sequentially towards b.35. From bb.39 – 41 listen to the inner LH crotchet fragments over the sustained dominant pedal point, and then be careful to finish off the RH phrase down to the crotchet D on the 2nd crotchet beat of b.41 so that you don't 'fall into' the LH quaver 'upbeat' (E flat) to the 2nd main beat, as you prepare to lead back into the recapitulation.

Third movement – Minuet and Trio (5)*

This extraordinary movement has very much of a country air. It needs a brisker 'step' than the usual minuet, indeed the beat positively 'churns' as if the dancers are whirling and stamping, rather than moving with courtly grace.

bb.1 – 24   Lead off in sturdy unison through bb.1 – 4, 'going to' firm minims on the 1st beat of b.4. Then make a tiny break so that you lead off clearly with the upbeat to b.5 rather than 'falling into' b.6. Articulate the RH quavers with a vigorous 'churning' feeling as you 'go to' the 1st beat of bb.5 and 6 over firm LH chords. End the section cleanly with a bit of a 'plonk' on the LH detached crotchet on the 2nd beat of b.8. Then be sure to *feel* the crotchet rest, ready to set off into the second section with unabated vigour, underpinning the RH through bb.10 – 12 and 14 – 15 with lively LH quavers. The phrasing here is extremely disconcerting to the player as the first phrase 'carries on' with a 'link' through b.13 into a reiterated fragment through bb.14 and 15. Take care, therefore, not to lose your balance through bb.12 – 13, but let the LH quavers carry on steadily towards a firm crotchet B on the 1st beat of b.13, to support the ascending RH quavers which 'go on' in turn towards a firm crotchet A on the 1st beat of b.14. Come to a clear 'stop' on the 1st beat of b.16, and *feel* the two silent crotchet beats before launching back into the unison figure in b.17.

Trio

bb.25 – 55   Be sure to 'finish off' the three LH crotchets cleanly through b.24 before leading into the Trio, perhaps in a subdued, rather *sotto voce* tone, but without slackening the tempo, so that the recurring triplet figure has a 'twirling' character. Take care to keep perfect time as you place the octave on the 1st beat of b.25, and enter with the RH precisely on the 2nd beat. Feel that the RH is 'going up to' the crotchet on the 1st beat of b.26, with the LH thirds 'following on' on the 2nd beat, to 'go' in turn towards a firm 1st beat of b.27, and so on – so that the hands alternate through bb.25 – 32 with a continual 'ongoing' feeling. Take care once more not to lose your balance as the unexpected happens again: 'go to' a clear RH crotchet A on the 1st beat of b.32, and then 'join in' clearly with the LH on the 2nd beat of this bar as the section 'elongates' through to b.34. Similarly the first phrase of the next section is 'elongated' through bb.40 – 1. Support the 'churning' RH here with firm minim thirds. Come to a clear 'stop' in the RH on the minim on the 1st beat of b.43, as the LH leads on downwards with the octaves from the 2nd beat towards the 1st beat of

12

b.44 (perhaps making a little *decrescendo* here as you return towards the minor). Take care to keep steady from b.52, supporting the RH with firm LH octaves on the upbeat to, and the 1st beat of, bb.53 and 54.

No. 6 in C major
(Hob. XVI/10)

First movement – Moderato (5)

The predominating demisemiquaver 'turn' figures give a graceful, airy feeling to this bright, clear-textured movement.

bb.1 – 8   Set a sensible *moderato* crotchet beat, imagining a brisk step to each *quaver* pulse. Lead off from a clear quaver upbeat (a *legato* upbeat perhaps leads in better here), and then articulate the slurred demisemiquaver figures neatly (coming *off* on the quavers, but gently, not spikily), over precisely placed LH quaver thirds. Feel you are 'going up to' the RH 1st beat of b.2, 'leaning' well on this dotted quaver third as you articulate the LH semiquavers neatly, feeling that they in turn are 'going up to' the quaver C on the 2nd beat of the bar. Make it clear that the first subphrase ends on this 2nd beat of b.2 so that you lead on clearly with both hands into the second subphrase from the upbeat to b.3. Then shape the LH and RH lines with equal care through to b.4, being careful to 'finish off' the LH down to the crotchet on the 2nd beat, ready for the RH to take off again on the upbeat to b.5. The appoggiatura on the 1st beat of b.4 could have either a crotchet or a quaver value. In b.7 keep your inner LH quavers perfectly even above the sustained lower dominant, not allowing their steadiness to be disrupted by the RH trills. Give these RH trills just four notes starting on the upper note. Be sure to finish off the RH triplet/quaver figure neatly in b.8, and to 'feel' the quaver rest on the 2nd beat, before entering again with the RH upbeat to b.9.

bb.9 – 21   Support the RH figures through bb.9 – 12 with immaculately placed LH quaver chords. Play the unison figures boldly from the upbeat to b.15.

Then from the 2nd beat of b.16 let your RH melody line swing along buoyantly, over evenly pulsating LH semiquavers. Give the trills on the 2nd beat of bb.16 and 18 eight demisemiquaver notes, starting on the upper note.

Keep your RH triplets in place in b.20 with very steady LH quavers.

bb.22 – 59   At b.26 strike into the minor with a new, more urgent tone. Take care to keep steady at bb.31 – 3. 'Finish off' the quavers neatly in the first half of b.31, make a tiny break, and then lead off into the next series of fragments with a confident RH semiquaver E on the 2nd beat of the bar. Be particularly conscious that the RH needs to give a clear onward lead on the 2nd beat of each of these bars (bb.31 – 3) when the LH has a quaver rest. Again, be sure that you 'finish off' clearly on the unison G's on the 2nd quaver pulse of b.36, and, allowing the necessary slight break, 'leap up' deliberately with both hands, to the 2nd main beat of the bar, rather than lurching upwards in a panic and collapsing on the wrong notes!

Second movement – Minuet and Trio (4)

The Minuet is straightforward and open-textured with a predominant triplet rhythm.

Set off with a firm ornamented unison crotchet, placing the turn *on* the
beat, and keep your RH triplets perfectly steady to establish the precise
bb.1 – 26   Minuet rhythm. Feel that you are 'going to' a firm 1st beat of b.2, and
support the RH with even 'stepping' LH crotchets through the 2nd beat of b.4. Take
care to 'finish off' the RH and inner LH crotchets cleanly on the 2nd beat of b.4, over
the lower LH minim, and then to give the crotchet rest its full value. Lead on with
clear LH triplets on the 1st beat of b.5 and be careful to place the LH crotchet securely
on the 2nd beat of bb.5 and 6 so that the RH offbeat triplets can follow on evenly.
Be sure to 'finish off' the three LH crotchets in perfect time in b.8. At bb.9 and 11
be sure that you do not hurry the 'ordinary' quavers on the 1st beat and thereby 'fall
into' the 2nd beat of the bar. Similarly be careful not to hurry the 'ordinary' quavers
through b.10 as you listen to the onward lead of the LH quavers into b.11.

As is often the case, the minor Trio is more interesting than the Minuet.
bb.27 – 44   Realize throughout that the LH is 'leading' and feel that the RH is fitting
in with the LH lines, and *not* the other way about. Lead off with a singing
LH dotted minim C and let the curving RH quavers follow on evenly while you listen
acutely to the sustained and expressive LH lines. Take particular care to give both the
inner LH tied crotchet A flat on the 3rd beat of b.27, and the tied minim G on the
2nd beat of b.28, sufficient resonance to sing over into the subsequent bar. Release
the lower crotchet G on the 2nd beat of b.30, so that you can follow the upbeat quavers
smoothly down to the C on the 1st beat of b.31. In b.33 be sure to place the LH crotchet
G precisely on the 2nd beat as you show the RH quaver rest. Lead on evenly with the
LH quavers down towards a quietly resonant LH minim octave on the 1st beat of b.35,
and then shape the syncopated RH fragments smoothly and expressively over your steady
LH, feeling the implied gentle emphasis on the RH crotchets, C and B flat in bb.35
and 36 respectively. Then lead smoothly but purposefully into b.39 with the three upbeat
quavers, and feel the continuing onward impetus of these LH upbeat quaver figures
leading into bb.40 – 3, in perfect co-ordination with the three matching descending RH
quavers.

Finale – Presto (5)

This exuberant movement is much the most substantial of the Finales to
bb.1 – 10   these first few Sonatas. Set a lively but secure crotchet pulse, and give a
firm LH quaver chord on the 1st beat of bb.1, 3, etc. to give a good 'kick-
off' for the RH ascending figure. Then articulate the RH brightly as you ascend to
a clear dotted quaver on the 1st beat of bb.2, 4, etc. over rock-steady LH quaver chords.
The little trill on the 2nd beat of b.2 is awkward – think of it as a semiquaver triplet
with a little stress on the first note:

In bb.7 and 8 keep your inner LH quavers very steady over the sustained lower LH
dominant. It is best to slur the first pair of inner quavers in these bars, and to detach
the second pair (together with those in the RH). Give firm LH crotchet chords on the
1st and 2nd beats of b.9, letting the offbeat RH semiquaver figures follow relatively
lightly.

Feel that you are 'going to' a firm 1st beat of b.10, and 'finish off' the
bb.10 – 36   phrase with clear RH and inner LH quavers over a definite lower crotchet.
Then *feel* the quaver rest on the 2nd beat as you poise yourself to lead
on with a clear RH quaver upbeat to b.11. Keep a steady crotchet pulse as you articulate
the solo RH semiquavers through b.11, coming in firmly and neatly with the LH quavers

in b.12. Make a tiny break after the 2nd beat of bb.12 and 14 so that you lead on clearly with the upbeat to b.13, and similarly to b.15. From the upbeat to b.15, 'rattle out' your RH semiquavers over lively and very rhythmic LH detached quavers. 'Finish off' your LH neatly down to the crotchet G on the 2nd beat of b.20, as you poise yourself again to lead in smoothly with the RH slurred upbeat to b.21, in a new and more serious tone colour. Keep the LH offbeat quaver octaves as smooth as possible, imagining that they also are slurred, so that these 'rocking' RH – LH offbeat figures alternate very evenly. Be sure that neither hand 'hangs on' over the rests. Then finish off the RH slurred thirds neatly in b.26 over the LH crotchet octave, and 'feel' the RH quaver rest as you poise yourself yet again to lead in with the triplet upbeat to b.27. Feel that each of these triplet figures is 'going to' (as if in a tiny *crescendo*) a clear detached quaver on the 1st and 2nd beats of bb.27 and 28, steadying yourself with a firm LH crotchet third on the 1st beat of b.27 and similarly b.31. Then 'go to' a firm RH quaver on the 1st beat of b.32, and allow a tiny break so that you don't 'fall into' the LH octave and RH broken octave. *Crescendo* towards the end of the section with glittering RH semiquavers over rock-steady, but bright, not heavy LH quaver octaves.

bb.37 – 95   As you set off into the development, keep your vigorously articulated RH in place as before with steady LH quaver chords. Lead off boldly with the LH from the 1st beat of b.46, keeping the RH offbeat semiquaver figures relatively light though brilliantly clear. *Crescendo* with resonant LH octaves as you descend towards b.54. Then, it is effective to *diminuendo* to *pianissimo* towards b.58, keeping the LH *tremolo* very even and steady beneath your neatly slurred RH quaver figures. Do give full value to the crotchet rest in b.58 before launching back into the recapitulation.

No. 7 in D major
(Hob. XVII/D1)

First movement – Theme and Variations (5)

This is rather a dull movement. Nevertheless, short sets of variations such as this do provide useful teaching material. The LH of the theme is used as a 'ground' in each of the three variations. Do, therefore, learn it especially carefully on its own, absorbing its melodic and rhythmic shape, and ensuring that it always remains perfectly steady, and is never disrupted by the varying activities of the RH.

Theme

Set a steady and even crotchet pulse, lead off with a clear treble crotchet, and shape the lines of the RH and LH with equal care throughout bb.1 – 4. 'Lean' on the RH crotchet on the 1st beats of bb.5 and 6, and support the RH line here with evenly placed LH repeated quaver octaves (and similarly with the LH quaver chords in bb.13 and 14). Be sure to 'finish' off the LH neatly in b.8, and similarly at the end of each section in the variations. Set off into the second section with a rather fuller tone. Show the LH quaver rest on the 2nd beat of b.11, and then let the little LH fragment 'enter' neatly on the upbeat to b.12 beneath your smooth RH thirds. Feel the onward lead of the LH semiquavers into b.13 here, and in the similar bar in each of the variations. The LH quavers through bb.1 – 4, 9 – 10, etc, could be *legato* or detached, or perhaps varied in articulation through the variations – the essential is that they are carefully shaped and perfectly steady. The rather more vigorous character of the second half of the theme and each variation suggests a more detached LH articulation.

Variation 1

Lead off cleanly with the RH arpeggio in exactly the same tempo as the theme, and then let your RH semiquavers curve clearly and happily over *perfectly steady* LH quavers.

Variation 2

Here it is even more important that the LH gives a rock-steady foundation for the varied figures of the RH. Phrase your double RH lines boldly but smoothly through bb.33 – 4. Then 'lean' well on the dotted quaver octaves on the 1st beat of bb.37 and 38, and follow on with smooth and clear thirds over your steady LH octaves. Lean again on the RH 1st beat of b.39, then catch your balance by 'taking over' with the LH quaver line on the 2nd quaver pulse of the bar, with the RH detached semiquavers following relatively lightly. Then again, following a strong dominant chord on the 1st beat of b.41, lead on vigorously from the 2nd beat of the bar with firm and steady LH quavers. 'Lean' on the tied RH crotchet octaves on the 1st beat of bb.45 and 46 with a clear singing tone, ensuring that they sound over the 2nd beats of these bars.

Variation 3

Let your RH semiquaver triplets run happily over the LH ground, much as in Variation 1. Take care to keep a steady crotchet pulse through b.59, and ascend in a little *crescendo* towards a clear semiquaver D on the 2nd beat of the bar, where the LH has a quaver rest.

Second movement – Minuet (3 or under)

Like the first movement, this short Minuet (without a Trio) is rather plain. Shape the RH lines smoothly through to the 2nd beat of b.2, supported by clear and even LH crotchet chords. (Give the appoggiaturas in bb.1 and 9 a quaver value.) Be sure to bring the LH *off* cleanly after the 2nd beat of bb.2 and 3, also making a tiny break in the RH so that the RH triplet is clearly shown as the *upbeat* to bb.3 and 4. Then come *off* again on the 3rd beat of b.4 *feeling* the crotchet rest so that you enter again in perfect time on the 1st beat of b.5. Support the RH with firm crotchet chords on the 1st beat of bb.5 and 6, and be sure to give these 1st beats their full value so that you do not anticipate the little triplet run beginning on each 2nd beat. Be sure also to *listen* to the three LH crotchets descending through b.8 so that you do not 'fall into' the subsequent 1st beat as you either return to b.1 or carry on into the second section. Play bb.9 – 10 more expressively, 'leaning' well on the 1st beat of b.10 (giving the appoggiatura a crotchet value) and feel that the LH is 'opening out' towards a firm octave on the 1st beat of b.11 to support the RH triplet curve. Then in b.12 (again giving the RH appoggiatura a crotchet value) show the 'onward lead' of the LH quavers descending towards the 1st beat of b.13.

Finale – Allegro (5)*

This is one of Haydn's typically racy Finales. It is essential that the RH is controlled throughout by a clear and steady LH.

bb.1 – 22   At first, practise the first four bars without the ornaments, establishing a brisk but sensible crotchet pulse with boldly rising unisons through bb.1 – 2. Then add clear and lively RH mordents (or, as in some editions, turns) *on* the beat. In b.3 feel that your ascending scale is 'going to' a firm slurred crotchet third on the 1st beat of b.4 and then take care to 'finish off' the LH neatly down to the crotchet on the 2nd beat. From bb.7 – 10 keep your neatly articulated RH figures in place with lively and very rhythmic 'jogging' LH detached quavers. From bb.11 – 16 enjoy one of Haydn's favourite 'churning' effects, with vigorously articulated descending scales which 'return' to clear, strong quavers on the 1st beats of bb.12 and 14 (and to a firm crotchet F sharp on the 1st beat of b.16), over rock-steady but mettlesome LH quaver chords. 'Go to' strong unison crotchets on the 1st beat of b.18, being sure to give this beat its full value. Then lead off keenly with the LH quavers from the 2nd beat of b.18, with the RH offbeat semiquaver figures following relatively lightly but brilliantly as you *crescendo* recklessly (but keeping steady!) towards b.22.

bb.23 – 61   Lead off buoyantly again with the LH from b.23. Practise the LH alone at first from here to b.31, and then practise hands together in *chords* until you can negotiate the hand crossing confidently. If you really let the LH 'lead' you will find that the RH, which remains in virtually the same spot, will practically look after itself. Try to feel that the LH is sweeping up and down in continuous 'arcs' rather than in disjointed fragments. Go slightly quieter on the 2nd beat of b.31, and then feel an overall *crescendo*, with an increasingly resonant LH, towards b.39. Then take advantage of the full crotchet rest on the 2nd beat of b.31 to poise yourself for the reprise.

No. 8 in A major
(Hob. XVI/5)

We will pass over this Sonata. Some authorities are doubtful as to its authenticity, and in any event the first and third movements (Grades 7 and 6 respectively) are long and dull, with little harmonic or rhythmic variety, and a great deal of uncharacteristic padding. The middle movement is a very simple Minuet (Grades 2 – 3).

No. 9 in D major
(Hob. XVI/4)

First movement – Moderato (5)*
With its delightful variety of textures, and impressive, boldly modulating development, this is an outstanding piece for players of around Grade 5.

bb.1 – 7   Set a clear and steady crotchet pulse, bearing in mind the triplet and sextuplet figuration from b.14, and time the first phrase immaculately through to the 1st beat of b.3. Lead off with a confident RH dotted crotchet, articulating the turn here (and again those in b.5) clearly *on* the beat, and then go on to 'lean' with a singing tone on the dotted crotchets on the 3rd beat of b.1, the 1st beat of b.2, and on the appoggiatura on the 3rd beat of b.2 (giving this a crotchet value). Always feel the two semiquavers as 'upbeats' to these long notes, rather than as 'tail ends' to the previous beats. Keep your RH line in place with the help of perfectly timed LH quaver chords, not too *staccato* but neatly and evenly detached, ensuring that the second chord of each pair does not 'hang on' over the subsequent rests. Through bb.3 – 4 support your neatly shaped RH semiquaver figures with clearly placed LH crotchet thirds. From bb.5 – 7 articulate the RH figures cleanly over cheerfully 'jogging' LH quavers, being particularly careful that the RH turns on the 2nd and 3rd beats of b.5 (be sure to show the quaver rests) do not disrupt the LH rhythm. These LH quavers could be *legato*, or lightly detached, as you feel inclined – the essential is that they remain steady. Finish off the phrase with immaculately placed quavers on the 3rd beat of b.7, coming *off* cleanly to show the full crotchet rest on the 4th beat as you poise yourself to launch into the semiquaver passage-work from b.8.

Throughout bb.8 – 10 be sure that your crotchet pulse stays intact as the curving semiquaver figures alternate evenly between the hands. Help yourself to keep steady by placing the LH quaver octaves consciously and precisely on the 3rd beats of these two bars, and be sure that neither hand 'hangs on' when the other takes over. 'Jog' on cheerfully again through bb.11 and 12, and take care to place the two quavers at the end of b.12 accurately. Feel the last RH quaver A as an upbeat to a firm dotted crotchet B on the 1st beat of b.13. Arrive on firm unison A's on the 1st beat of b.14, and then swing easily into the triplet and sextuplet rhythm, keeping yourself steady from here to the double bar with the help of an immaculately placed LH. Feel the LH offbeat quaver chords or notes (bb.14 and 15 etc.) as 'upbeats', 'going to' the crotchets on the 3rd and 1st beats of these bars. Again, in bb.16 and 18 – 19 keep your RH demisemiquavers and trill in place with a neatly shaped LH fragment. Let the RH 'go down' to a firm LH octave on the 3rd beat of b.19, and be sure to allow a full crotchet rest to end the section.

bb.8 – 19

Set off confidently into the development, and then make a *diminuendo* through the second half of b.22, start *piano* at b.23, and then *crescendo* purposefully through to a resonant half-close on the dominant of B minor at b.28. Keep a steady crotchet pulse through this passage, ensuring again that the semiquavers flow evenly between the hands, and add resonance by 'leaning' a little on the lower LH semiquavers falling on the 1st and 3rd beats of bb.23 – 8. Strike off boldly in B minor at b.29, and drive on resolutely towards a further half-close on the dominant proper at b.35, leading back to the recapitulation. Through bb.33 – 5 feel the implied little 'surges' in both hands towards the uppermost notes of each curve (i.e. towards the 2nd and 6th *quaver* pulses of bb.33 and 34, and the 2nd quaver pulse again of b.35, with a final *crescendo* towards the unison A's on the 3rd beat). Feel the heightened intensity of the recapitulation as Haydn extends the semiquaver figures from the exposition, at bb.45 – 8. Do not lose your balance by 'snatching' at the high D in b.54, but rather 'go down' to a firm D on the 3rd beat of the bar and, without panicking, allow the slight natural break as you make the upward leap.

bb.20 – 57

Second movement – Minuet and Trio (4)*
This Minuet is pleasantly airy and gracious, with an almost waltz-like rhythmic swing.

Let the RH line sing in a bright clear tone through bb.1 – 4, showing the implied emphasis on the tied upbeat to b.3, over warm-toned, quietly resonant LH thirds. 'Point' the interrupted cadence into b.4, and be sure to 'finish off' cleanly in both hands after the 2nd beat of b.4, and to *feel* the silent 3rd beat. Then support the RH with a firm bass minim octave on the 1st beat of b.5, and 'go to' and 'lean' warmly upon the 1st beat of b.6, giving the appoggiatura a crotchet value. Take care to time the three LH crotchets precisely through b.8, and then 'go to' a clear LH crotchet third on the 1st beat of b.9, to support your immaculately timed RH triplet/crotchet figure. Place the crotchet thirds similarly very precisely on the 1st beat of bb.10 – 13, and then in b.13 'pick up' the opening phrase neatly again in the RH on the 2nd beat. Take care to 'finish off' b.18 cleanly, and then allow a tiny break to leap up calmly to the 1st beat of b.19, as the phrase unexpectedly opens out into the upper register.

bb.1 – 22

Trio

Here the RH is underpinned by an almost continuous LH crotchet line. Practise thoroughly 'hands separately', shaping the LH line just as carefully as the RH in a clear *legato* or perhaps just-detached light 'stepping' style. 'Point' the quaintly rustic character of the neat two-bar motif in bb.23 – 4 (and 35 – 6),

bb.23 – 44

articulating the dotted rhythm and the slurred couplets neatly, and then open out the tone a little through bb.27 – 8. Take care not to hurry the three LH crotchets ascending through b.30, and then lead off, perhaps in a fuller tone, into the second section, always supporting the RH with 'onward walking' LH crotchets. Then, as you 'finish off' the RH phrase on the 2nd beat of b.34, show the onward lead of the LH quavers down towards the 1st beat of b.35. 'Mount' confidently through bb.38 – 40 with firm RH quavers on the 'solo' 1st beat, 'joining in' clearly with the LH crotchets on the 2nd beats.

No. 10 in C major
(Hob. XVI/1)

First movement – Allegro (5)*
The patterns of this movement are untypically consistent, and some may find it dull. However, the character is forthright and vigorous, and it will, I feel, appeal to energetically-minded young students, provided that they can master the Alberti LH. Set a lively, but very steady crotchet pulse, and maintain an unflagging rhythmic impetus from first note to last.

bb.1 – 8   Begin by practising the Alberti bass (bb.1 – 5, 8 – 12, etc.) slowly and rhythmically.   Practise also in dotted rhythms: and

etc. (see also Introduction). 'Pluck' the RH detached crotchets in a vigorous and very rhythmic style, placing the turns clearly *on* the beat in bb.1 – 5 etc, with a little stress on the first note: When you put

the hands together, ensure that they are perfectly co-ordinated, and that the turns do not disrupt the rhythm of the LH. Make sure also that your RH comes *off* on the 2nd and 4th beats of bb.4 and 5. Let the LH 'go to' a firm tied minim on the 1st beat of b.6 to give resonant support to the RH scale figure ascending in a little *crescendo* towards a quaver A on the 3rd beat. Then listen to the LH rising chromatically to the 1st beat of b.7, as you prepare to come to a cheerful 'stop' on the dominant, with a bit of a 'plonk' on the 3rd beat of b.7.

bb.9 – 17   Articulate the RH quaver fragments neatly through bb.8 – 11, and be particularly careful to keep the LH steady when the RH has a quaver rest on the 2nd and 4th beats of these bars. You could detach all the RH quavers here, or slur those on the 1st and 3rd beats of bb.8 – 11. Let the LH 'go to' a clear crotchet on the 1st beat of b.12, and then support the RH with a firm crotchet sixth on the 3rd beat. Feel the implied emphasis on the tied RH crotchet on the 2nd beat of b.13, and keep steady here by letting the LH semiquavers 'go to' a firm crotchet C on the 3rd beat. Control your trill in b.14 with rock-steady LH quaver thirds, and go in both hands to firm crotchet G's on the 1st beat of b.15. Then let the LH crotchets take the lead through bb.15 – 16 with the RH offbeat semiquaver figures following evenly and relatively lightly, as you drive on to end the section with a clear dominant crotchet chord on the 3rd beat of b.17.

bb.18 – 50   Strike off boldly into the minor at b.18, and *crescendo* towards another 'stop' (here on the dominant of A minor) at b.23. Drop the tone to *piano* at b.24, but keep up the rhythmic impetus with quiet but rock-steady LH quaver chords beneath your neatly articulated RH figures. Then, as you 'lead' with the LH crotchets through bb.28 – 9, it can be equally effective either to make a *diminuendo* through b.29 (so that you move into the minor start of the reprise in *piano* and make a gradual *crescendo* towards b.35), or to *crescendo* through b.29 to launch into the reprise with renewed vigour. In either event, make your effect with conviction! If you adopt the first course, allow a little 'give' in the tempo through the second half of b.29, and start really quietly in b.30. Alternatively let your *crescendo* carry you through b.29 and into b.30 with a buoyant rhythmic drive.

Second movement – Adagio (4)
This is a pleasantly flowing movement, although young players particularly may find it rather dull.

bb.1 – 8　　Set a tempo at which the triplet melody line can flow in gracious curves over the even LH quavers. The motion must have an easy, on-going feeling that is never sticky, nor, on the other hand, hurried. Lead in from a clear *legato* quaver upbeat, being sure to give this its full value, and then show the curve of the RH through b.1 up to and down from the triplet on the 3rd beat of the bar, detaching the quavers on the 2nd and 6th quaver pulse of the bar gently, not spikily. Support the RH with perfectly even and steady LH quaver chords played as smoothly as possible; feel the gentle impulse towards the fourth on the 3rd main beat of the bar, and always feel that it is the *LH* and not the RH which is setting and maintaining the quiet, even pulse. 'Finish off' the phrase gracefully on the 3rd beat of b.2 as the LH quavers 'go on down' to the quaver on the 4th beat, and show the RH quaver rest as you prepare to lead on with the quaver upbeat to b.3. Show the different shape of the RH in b.3 as you curve up to the B after the 6th quaver pulse. Take care to 'finish off' the phrase cleanly with the two RH quavers in b.4 as the RH 'goes down' this time to a crotchet on the 4th beat. Let the LH 'go to' a quietly resonant crotchet on the 3rd beat of bb.5 and 6 as the RH expands on upwards through the second half of these bars. Then take care to 'join in' neatly and clearly with the LH on the upbeat to b.7 as the LH enters in more equal 'duet' with the RH. The LH quavers here (and from the upbeat to b.16) could be played smoothly, or in a very slightly detached 'stepping' style.

bb.9 – 17　　'Open out' the tone more expressively from b.11, listening to the descending LH line from the 3rd beat of this bar as you modulate to F major and then back to the dominant in b.13. Let the repeated notes 'speak' in an expressive 'ongoing' manner through the 1st beat of b.13, rather than sounding spiky or stuttering. Then expand the tone again as the RH curves around rather more freely through b.16, and then *diminuendo* down towards a gentle ending, finishing off with the three quietly 'measured' LH quavers.

Third movement – Minuet and Trio (3 or under)
The Minuet here is somewhat plain, but the minor Trio is more expressive, with useful lessons in offbeat 'entries' and syncopation for novice players.

bb.1 – 20　　Take care to set and maintain a perfectly steady minuet 'stepping' crotchet pulse, so that you avoid the tendency to 'clip' the RH crotchets on the 1st beat of bb.1 – 3, etc, and thus to 'fall into' the triplets on the 2nd beat. Shape the RH line in airy curves through bb.1 – 3, supported by resonant LH chords, feeling that you are 'going towards' the ornamented minim on the 1st beat of b.4, and similarly b.6. (Beginners can omit the trills.) Give the appoggiatura on the 1st beat of b.6 (and b.10) a crotchet value. From the upbeat to b.4 support the RH with clear 'stepping' LH crotchets, either *legato* or lightly detached. Be sure to 'finish off' the descending LH crotchets cleanly through b.8 before leading off into the second section in a more expressive tone. Listen particularly to the rising LH line through b.11 towards the G on the 1st beat of b.12.

Trio

bb.21 – 43

Strike a darker tone with the LH crotchet third on the 1st beat of b.21, and be sure to enter precisely on the offbeat with the *legato* RH quavers, feeling that this line is 'falling' towards a warm-toned slurred minim on the 1st beat of b.22. Underpin the RH here with even and steady LH crotchet thirds, with the feeling that they in turn are 'going to' the crotchet third on the 1st beat of b.23 (being sure to give this its full value), and so on. Expand the tone as you lead on into b.29 with a resonant LH crotchet sixth. *Listen* to the effect of the diminishing LH intervals as you place the chords clearly on the 1st beat of bb.29 – 31, with the RH offbeat quaver figures 'falling' expressively in perfect time. Then feel that the LH crotchets are 'leading' through bb.32 – 5, with the syncopated RH fragment (b.32) and the longer syncopated RH line through bb.33 – 4 following smoothly and expressively. Feel that you are 'going to' the 1st beat of b.35, again giving the RH appoggiatura a crotchet value, and then feel the onward lead of the three descending LH quavers into b.36.

No. 11 in B flat major
(Hob. XVI/2)

This is a splendid Sonata for players of about a Grade 6 standard. Apart from that of the uncharacteristic No. 8, it has the most substantial and complex first movement among the first twelve Sonatas. Both the first and second movements are considerable tests of rhythmic security.

First movement – Moderato (6)*

This movement is splendidly vital and full of rhythmic and expressive variety.

bb.1 – 10

Set a secure and sensible crotchet pulse, bearing in mind the coming triplet figuration, the snappy RH demisemiquavers figure (bb.12 – 13) and the sharp dotted rhythm figures in bb.36 and 37. Lead off from a clear detached RH quaver upbeat sixth, and play the opening RH figure like a little brass fanfare with bright, detached sixths and thirds over a resonant LH minim octave. Feel you are 'going to' a firm dotted crotchet third on the 1st beat of b.2, and time your triplet upbeats to bb.3 and 4 crisply, keeping steady in these two bars with the help of immaculately placed LH quaver/crotchet figures. Be careful to keep steady too in b.4. Place the two RH detached quavers (over a firm inner crotchet) and the LH detached quavers with absolute precision. Take particular care to place the LH quaver B flat cleanly on the 2nd beat of the bar beneath the RH rest so that you are poised to lead on clearly with the RH triplet and LH quaver upbeat to b.5. Support your clearly articulated RH with firm LH crotchet chords in b.5, and then, in b.6, similarly balance the LH figure with firm *RH* crotchets. Let the RH triplet figure 'go to' clear detached quavers on the 1st and 3rd beats of b.5 (and similarly in bb.7 and 8). In b.10 be sure to 'finish off' the LH neatly, down to a clear crotchet B flat on the 2nd beat. Having established a stable 2/4 pulse, be sure that you maintain it through thick and thin through all the varied figurations to come. Rhythmic insecurity in this movement is often the result of failure to 'place' the 2nd beat of the bar just as carefully as the 1st.

Place the RH grace note figure expressively *on* the 1st beat of b.11 and
bb.11 – 22   support this singing minim A flat with even LH quaver chords. Then also
be sure that each demisemiquaver figure is 'snapped' neatly *on* the beat
in bb.12 – 13, and balance yourself here with immaculately placed LH offbeat quaver
octaves. It is easy to degenerate into allowing these demisemiquavers to anticipate the
beat here, and thus to distort the rhythm. From b.17 slur the RH semiquaver couplets
neatly over steady LH detached quavers as you *crescendo* towards the 2nd beat of b.20.
Then from the upbeat to b.21 support the RH with a firm LH line. Take care to 'finish
off' the LH down to a clear crotchet on the 2nd beat of b.22 as you slur the RH crotchet
off to a neat quaver, then making a tiny break in the RH ready to lead on with the
RH triplet upbeat to b.23.

Let the RH upbeat triplets 'go down' to definite *staccato* quavers on the
bb.23 – 43   1st beat of bb.23 – 6, and note that the *second* RH quaver in these bars
is also *staccato* – students will almost invariably in such circumstances
allow the second quaver to 'hang on'. Keep yourself steady in these bars with the help
of perfectly placed detached LH quaver thirds. In bb.27 and 29 feel the 'lift' up to,
and implied 'lean' up on the syncopated high RH crotchet A flat, without disturbing
the rhythm of the LH quaver figures, and then steady yourself by letting the LH triplets
go neatly down to a clear crotchet on the 2nd beat of bb.28 and 30 beneath the slurred
RH crotchet and quaver. Phrase the RH slurred semiquavers expressively down towards
a warmly slurred dotted crotchet C sharp on the 1st beat of bb.32 and 34 over very
even LH quaver chords. Then change the r ood incisively on the 1st beat of b.36,
savouring the clash of the sevenths in either hand as you articulate the sharp RH dotted
rhythms over rock-steady LH quaver chords. Support the RH in bb.39 and 41 with
firm LH octaves, and in bb.40 and 42 feel the implied emphasis on the offbeat inner
LH crotchet F beneath your firm RH crotchets.

Go down from the perfectly timed RH semiquaver upbeat to a warmly
bb.44 – 61   singing dotted crotchet F on the 1st beat of b.44, and listen to the interesting
chromatic fragment in fourths (the RH and inner LH lines) rising smoothly
towards the 1st beat of b.45. Then *crescendo* perkily up to the high D in b.46, treating
the slurred grace notes like acciaccaturas, and bringing the hand *off* each quaver in
a *staccato*. 'Come in' clearly and confidently, but not too loudly, with the RH broken
octave semiquavers on the 2nd beat of b.48 (and 50 and 52). But then let the LH quaver
line 'lead' smoothly from the upbeat to bb.49, 51 and 53, realizing that the RH is
'accompanying' here. From the 2nd beat of b.56 articulate your RH semiquaver figures
neatly over very steady LH chords and *crescendo* through b.60 to end the section with
a ringing dominant chord.

Lead off boldly into the development in the dominant. Be careful not to
bb.62 – 148   lose your balance in b.68 – let the LH 'go down' to a clearly placed quaver
D on the 2nd beat of the bar, and poise yourself on this 2nd beat to avoid
'falling into' the upbeat to the subsequent bar. From bb.71 – 6 follow the ascending
sequential lines equally clearly in either hand. In typical Haydn manner, the mood
suddenly changes at b.77. Immediately catch the lamenting, sighing quality of the
descending slurred RH semiquaver couplets over evenly throbbing LH quaver thirds
and seconds. Then, just as typically, Haydn picks up the threads again from the 2nd
quaver pulse of b.84 in another ascending sequential passage. Let the LH quavers again
'lead' smoothly from the upbeat to bb.92 and 94 (as from the upbeat to b.49 etc.).
From the 2nd beat of b.95 Haydn 'borrows' the passage from the exposition (bb.16 – 22)
to lead us neatly back to the start of the recapitulation.

Second movement – Largo (6) (O)*

The emotional impact of this movement is new and striking. The music demands considerable musical maturity, and players at around Grade 6 may need help with some of the rhythmic patterns, particularly those from bb.12 – 14, which will need to be carefully worked out, even by experienced players. Feel the LH quaver chords like a melancholy (but not heavy) tread running through the movement. This is a good chance to learn the skill of playing repeated notes or chords as *legato* as possible: feel as if your hand is 'rooted' in the keyboard, and raise the hand as little, and as late as possible so that there is hardly any break in the sound. It is essential that these quaver chords remain perfectly steady within an easy moving, not too slow crotchet pulse, to give a secure foundation for the activities of the RH. Always feel that the RH is fitting in with the steady LH, and *not* the other way about.

bb.1 – 8
To set your tempo, try the first four bars, and then play bb.33 – 8, finding a speed at which these latter bars 'move' but at which, on the other hand, bb.1 – 4 do not sound rushed. Phrase the RH smoothly, giving a singing tone to the dotted quaver D's in b.1 over your even LH quaver thirds. Then feel the demisemiquaver triplet figures like light, smooth 'upbeats', 'going to' the slurred crotchet on the 1st beat of b.2, and then to the slurred quaver on the 3rd beat, and so on. Feel the overall continuity of the RH melody line right through from b.1 down to the crotchet G on the 2nd beat of b.4 (playing the turn *on* the beat here, in a leisurely, not 'clipped' manner). Spread the big chord generously on the 1st beat of b.7, and then let the syncopated RH melody line curve smoothly and expressively over rock-steady LH thirds. Do not collapse at the sight of the ornament in b.8. Feel the melody line continuing from b.7 right through to the low D on the 2nd beat of b.8, 'lean' on the C sharp on the 1st beat of the bar, and 'throw' the ornament and semiquaver lightly and smoothly down to the low D, making sure that the RH and LH unison crotchets coincide perfectly on the 2nd beat of the bar

bb.9 – 16
Articulate the turn *on* the 1st beat of bb.9 – 11 clearly and melodiously, and then give the little detached ascending scale a delicate (not spiky) woodwind colour. Through bb.12 – 14 keep your LH chords perfectly steady as you shape the syncopated fragments in the RH. Observe the demisemiquaver rests accurately, and feel each time that the two hemidemisemiquavers are 'going up to' an emphasized quaver (i.e. the high C's in b.12, and the high D's in b.13). Because the RH figures fall into two identical rhythmic groups in each bar you will find that you get a cross-rhythm effect, as if you have temporarily gone into a **6/8** pulse, with the *fourth* quaver chord feeling as if it falls on the 2nd main beat of each '**6/8**' bar. Just allow this effect to 'happen', and concentrate on keeping the quaver chords steady, and the 'normal' **3/4** will right itself in b.15.

bb.17 – 26
Let the RH demisemiquaver line follow on smoothly from a firm LH chord on the 1st beat of b.17, and curve expressively through to the dotted crotchet on the 1st beat of b.18. Shape the semiquavers smoothly in either hand through b.19 with the feeling that you are 'going to' a resonant LH chord on the 1st beat of b.20, and then be careful to keep your LH crotchet chords and RH ornamented quavers steady – it is easy to lose your pulse and go too fast here. In b.22 (and 23) let the RH demisemiquaver triplet 'go to' an emphasized tied crotchet F on the 2nd beat, and then follow the inner LH quaver line and the RH syncopated line smoothly over the lower sustained F. In b.25 define the RH dotted rhythm cleanly and

boldly, over strong ascending LH crotchet octaves, feeling the demisemiquavers as 'upbeats' to the subsequent beats, rather than as 'tail ends' to the previous beats. Then in b.26 do give the two crotchets and the rest their full value.

bb.27 – 54   In bb.31 – 2 feel the heightened intensity of the music as you shape the descending RH diminished 7th figures eloquently over your steady LH minor thirds. Then from b.33 listen acutely to the expressive interplay between the hands. Feel that the chromatic RH semiquavers are 'going to' a singing tied crotchet G on the 2nd beat of b.33, with the descending LH semiquaver fragment following on evenly and 'going to' the crotchet B natural on the 3rd beat, and so on. Make a gradual overall *crescendo* towards the eloquent half-close on the dominant at b.38. Let the demisemiquaver scales rise in an expressive *crescendo* through bb.39 and 41, towards singing tied crotchet C's on the 1st beats of bb.40 and 42, and then phrase the slurred RH demisemiquaver-quaver figures like little sighs over your steady LH chords. Let the syncopated RH line curve expressively, and with a resonant tone downwards then upwards through bb.43 – 4, and then 'open out' freely and even more expressively into the improvisatory solo semiquavers in b.45, as you curve down to 'meet' the steady LH quavers again in b.46.

Third movement – Minuet and Trio (5)*
This vigorous Minuet has an open texture and a lively mixture of dotted rhythms, triplets and semiquavers, etc.

bb.1 – 14   Time the first four bars meticulously, over a securely placed LH. In b.1 'feel' the held 2nd beat, thus ensuring that your firm RH dotted crotchet is given its full value. Show the 'lift' up to, and implied emphasis on, the RH dotted crotchet E flat on the 2nd beat of b.2, and time the dotted rhythms smartly through b.3. Keep a steady crotchet pulse through the curving triplets of bb.5 and 7 where the LH is silent. Feel that these triplets are 'going to' a warm dotted crotchet on the 1st beat of bb.6 and 8, and be particularly careful to place the LH crotchet thirds accurately in these bars. In b.9 let the LH semiquaver coincide with the last RH triplet note of the bar, and in b.10 (as also in b.14 etc.) do 'finish off' the three LH crotchets neatly beneath the RH appoggiatura, which could be given either a crotchet or a minim value. In bb.11 and 12 slur the RH semiquaver couplets neatly, but with a different, breezy, rather insouciant air, and again be sure to place the LH crotchet chords accurately on the 2nd and 3rd beats. Then take care to lead on into b.13 with a clear RH quaver upbeat, and time the dotted rhythm figure smartly on the 1st beat of b.13 above a resonant lower LH dotted minim.

bb.15 – 28   Lead into the second section in the high register in a clear bright tone, and do not allow the trills on the 1st beat of bb.15 and 16 to disrupt the crotchet pulse. Give the trills six notes including the turn

and yet again be sure to place the LH crotchets neatly on the 2nd and 3rd beats of these bars. Take care also to lead on with a clear RH quaver upbeat to bb.16 and 17. (In the Henle and Peters editions bb.25 – 8 are repeated, creating a four-bar discrepancy in the bar numberings of the Trio.)

Trio
bb.29 – 56   The LH plays a particularly important part in this beautiful and expressive minor Trio. Make it clear that the LH 'leads off' at the beginning of each phrase or fragment. Listen to the warm, horn-like quality of the LH thirds

(bb.29 – 30) and let the RH offbeat quaver fragments follow on smoothly. Place the detached RH quavers evenly over the smooth LH crotchets through b.31, and continue to 'lead' with the LH through bb.32 – 4, following evenly with the smoothly curving RH quavers (feeling the gentle implied emphasis on the tied RH quaver upbeats to bb.32 and 33). Be sure in bb.35 and 37 that you differentiate clearly between the RH triplet on the 2nd beat, and the 'ordinary' quavers on the 3rd beat (also observing that the offbeat quaver at the beginning of each of these fragments is an 'ordinary' quaver, and *not* a triplet). Phrase the LH thirds through bb.42 and 44 just as smoothly as the single crotchets through bb.41 and 43, and also differentiate clearly between the detached RH quaver thirds in bb.41 and 43, and the smoothly slurred syncopated descending fragments in bb.42 and 44. Ascend expressively in the LH towards a warm-toned minim third again on the 1st beat of b.45.

No. 12 in A major
(Hob. XVI/12)

First movement – Andante (6)
This movement opens promisingly, but although the undulating semiquaver triplets flow on pleasantly enough, it is unlikely that the player will find enough harmonic or rhythmic variety to maintain his interest. It will therefore not be discussed in detail.

Shape the opening RH phrase gracefully from a singing tied ornamented crotchet on the 1st beat, over even LH quaver chords. The charm of this opening phrase lies in its quiet, rhythmic flow, 'pointed' by the implied gentle emphasis on the tied B on the 2nd quaver pulse of b.3, and by the LH quaver rests on the 1st beats. From b.5, however, the rhythmic and harmonic progress becomes somewhat square. Maintain a steady quaver pulse to support the almost continuous flow of semiquaver triplets. It is particularly important that the RH ornamented quavers in b.21 remain perfectly steady, and that the LH flows on evenly through bb.22 – 4 beneath the easy-running long RH trill.

Second movement – Minuet and Trio (5)*
The simple Minuet has a clear, open texture.

bb.1 – 24   Set off with firm unison crotchets and time the RH neatly through bb.1 – 4 over an even, 'step-like' LH crotchet line. Do be careful to keep the RH triplets steady through the 1st two beats of bb.5 and 7 where the LH is silent, and then 'join in' clearly with the LH crotchets on the upbeats to bb.6 and 8. Be sure to give full value to the unison dotted minims in b.10. Then lead off into the second section perhaps in a fuller tone, supporting the RH with a resonant LH minim octave on the 1st beat of b.11. Be sure to differentiate plainly between the 'ordinary' quavers on the 1st beat of b.15, and the triplets through the 2nd and 3rd beats. Balance the RH with a warmly sustained LH third on the 1st beat of b.15, and then listen to the lower LH line ascending chromatically towards the 1st beat of b.16. Then 'finish off' the three descending LH crotchets clearly through b.16 before setting off into the reprise at b.17. The RH appoggiatura in b.16 could be given either a minim or crotchet value. Support the RH in bb.21 and 22 with a firm LH minim octave and third respectively.

Trio

bb.25 – 54

The minor Trio has a dark, and particularly expressive quality. Learn the LH carefully on its own. Change fingers (5 – 4) to ensure that the sustained chromatically descending bass dotted minim line remains perfectly *legato* while you also shape the inner LH crotchet fragments smoothly, ensuring that the tied upbeat crotchets sing over into bb.26 and 28. (Likewise change fingers (4 – 5) as the LH dotted minims ascend from bb.32 – 5.) Shape the syncopated RH fragments expressively over these even LH lines, from bb.25 – 30, showing all rests in either hand. Then follow the three long lines smoothly from b.31, always feeling that the LH is 'leading', and letting the syncopated RH line follow evenly, creating a close blending of the voices. Feel the 'lift' up to, and implied gentle stress upon the high RH syncopated crotchets falling on the 2nd quaver pulse of each bar. Lead off again with the LH after the double bar, and then from b.43 shape the fragments smoothly as before.

Finale – Allegro molto (5)*

This little Finale is cheerful and sturdy, with a positively driving rhythmic impetus. Set a brisk, very secure **3/8** pulse, with an overall feeling of one-in-the-bar.

bb.1 – 28

Practise bb.1 – 4 at first without the ornaments, giving *firm* RH quavers on the 1st beats over lively and rhythmic LH semiquavers. Be sure to observe the RH rests precisely – if the quavers are allowed to 'hang on' the rhythm loses its spring. Play the mordents (or, as in some editions, the turns) clearly *on* the beats. Let the LH 'go to' a firm crotchet on the 1st beat of b.5, and then support the RH with clear and steady LH quaver chords through b.6. Come to a clear 'stop' on the tonic at b.7, giving the crotchet, and the quaver rests their precise value. Articulate the RH fragments neatly through bb.8 – 11 over continuingly lively LH semiquavers. Support the tricky little RH semiquaver fragment through bb.12 – 14 with a firm and steady LH. At b.15 give a good 'kick-off' to the two-bar semiquaver figures with a brightly accented high B on the 1st beat. Then 'rattle out' the semiquavers vigorously as you 'return' towards accented B's on the 1st beat of bb.17, 19 and 21 over neatly dovetailed LH quaver fragments, creating one of Haydn's favourite 'churning' effects. Steady yourself with the three quaver chords in b.22, and then support the RH semiquavers with firm LH chords on the 1st beats of bb.23 and 24. Drive on to end the section with strong unison crotchets on the dominant at b.28.

bb.29 – 69

Lead off again with ringing unison E's on the 1st beat of b.29, and listen to the inner dotted crotchets descending resonantly over the lower 'drone'. Articulate your ascending RH figures vigorously, feeling that the RH is fitting in with the steady inner LH dotted crotchets, and *not* the other way about. Give a jaunty 'snap' to the slurred RH demisemiquaver figures in b.42, ensuring that the demisemiquavers are snapped *on* the quaver beats and do not anticipate them. Keep steady through bb.48 – 52, feeling that the RH semiquavers are 'going down to' a clear quaver on the 1st beat of b.49, and then that the LH thirds are 'going to' a firm crotchet third on the 1st beat of b.50, and so on. Support the RH scale figures with firm LH crotchets on the 1st beat of bb.52 – 5. Be careful to keep steady at bb.62 – 4: let the RH semiquaver scale descend to a *firm* quaver F sharp on the 1st beat of b.63. Then allow a tiny natural break as you leap up to place the two high F sharps neatly (rather than lurching upwards in panic), over steady LH quaver fifths.

No. 13 in G major
(Hob. XVI/6)

First movement – Allegro (7)*

This movement is full of rhythmic variety and harmonic interest. Be warned, in view of the intricacies to come, against starting too fast, and set a realistic and very steady crotchet pulse. The rhythmic patterns change almost from bar to bar, and the unifying influence of an absolutely secure crotchet pulse is essential.

bb.1 – 4   The first four bars have a clear and open texture. Lead off from a clear triplet upbeat 'going up to' a firm quaver G on the 1st beat of b.1. 'Enter' neatly with the LH on the 2nd quaver pulse of the bar, and shape the lines of either hand with equal care through to the 3rd beat of b.2. Let the three RH repeated quaver D's 'speak' in b.1 (rather than either just slurping into each other, or, alternatively, sounding spikily *staccato*), and then feel that you are 'going to' the tied syncopated quaver E on the 6th quaver pulse of the bar. 'Finish off' the first phrase with neat unison quaver G's in b.2. *Feel* the quaver rest on the 4th beat, and then think of a different, perhaps bassoon-like colour as you move into the lower register with the triplet upbeat to b.3. Time the LH fragment neatly in b.3 beneath your 'speaking' repeated RH quavers, feeling that this fragment is 'going to' the crotchet D on the 3rd beat. Then feel that the RH demisemiquavers are 'going to' a firm crotchet C natural on the 4th beat, and the LH upbeat dotted rhythm figure to a firm crotchet G on the 1st beat of b.4, so that you feel the effect of a steady crotchet pulse alternately between the hands. Then keep a steady crotchet pulse again as you swing into triplets from the 1st beat of b.4.

bb.5 – 10   From the upbeat to b.5 a little march-like figure enters. Time the dotted rhythms with military precision, with a sharp woodwind colour, and be sure that the 'entry' of the LH fragments is perfectly co-ordinated with the RH on the demisemiquaver 'upbeats' to the 2nd and 4th beats of b.5. In b.6 treat the grace note arpeggio like a spread chord, 'going up to' a singing tied crotchet G on the 3rd beat of the bar, and be sure to place the LH quaver A accurately on the 4th beat. Be careful to keep steady once more through b.7. Let the RH scale run up to a firm tied crotchet A precisely on the 2nd beat of the bar, with the LH quaver octave 'going to' a firm crotchet octave on the 3rd beat, and the RH 'going on up to' a clear dotted semiquaver on the 4th beat, so that you again feel the crotchet pulse alternating steadily between the hands. Then time the alternating RH and LH figures with equal precision through b.8 and the first half of b.9. From the 3rd beat of b.9 through to the 1st beat of b.10, let the syncopated RH line curve smoothly over even LH quavers, feeling the implied emphasis on each of the three syncopated RH quaver C sharps.

bb.11 – 18   From the upbeat to b.11 make a continuous chain of RH trills: start this upbeat trill with the upper note, then 'go to' and linger fractionally upon the *main* note of each of the remaining trills. Practise this passage at first, of course, *without* the trills, establishing the steadiness of the LH semiquaver chords, which must not be disturbed when the trills are added. Feel that the trills are fitting in with the LH chords, and not the other way about. Be careful to keep your steady crotchet pulse as you swing into triplets and sextuplets from the 4th beat of b.12. To this end take care to 'finish off' the previous phrase cleanly on the quaver chord on the 3rd beat of b.12. Then *feel* the dotted semiquaver rest so that the demisemiquaver 'upbeat' to the 4th beat of the bar is accurately timed. Support your RH with accurately placed LH quavers on the 3rd and 4th beats of b.13, and again with neat quaver octaves in the first half of b.14. Feel a new urgency as you turn towards the minor from the 4th beat of b.14. 'Lean' warmly on the RH dotted quaver on this 4th beat, and again on the 2nd and 4th beats of b.15, and articulate the demisemiquaver triplets clearly towards the subsequent quaver F naturals over even-running, but 'keen' LH semiquaver triplets. In b.16 let the RH demisemiquavers coincide with the third semiquaver of the second, third and fourth LH triplet groups.

bb.19 – 47 From b.21 Haydn sets off in a buoyant development of the opening theme, turning suddenly into A minor at b.22. Let the LH quavers 'lead' firmly through the 1st and 2nd beats of b.22 with the RH offbeat detached semi-quavers following relatively lightly. A peremptory interruption by a diminished 7th arpeggio on the 4th beat of b.25 leads to a dramatic interlude from b.27. (Again treat this grace note arpeggio like a spread chord, and be sure to give the crotchet C its full value, so that you don't 'fall into' the 1st beat of b.26.) 'Lean' urgently on the RH tied quavers on the 1st and 3rd beats of b.27, and let the demisemiquavers run down in a *decrescendo* to the quaver C's over evenly pulsating LH semiquaver thirds. Then from b.28 drive on, over your persistent LH semiquaver thirds and fourths towards the half-close in b.30. Then poise yourself on the quaver rest ready to enter with the march theme on the upbeat to b.31. Take care to keep a steady crotchet pulse through the sequential figures of bb.33 – 5, with the help of carefully placed LH quaver/crotchet octave figures.

Second movement – Minuet and Trio (6)*
This is a vigorous and rather 'masculine' Minuet.

bb.1 – 28 Place the first note of the grace note broken chord *on* the beat, 'going to' a singing upper tied D, and then time the dotted rhythms with the utmost precision. Think of the two demisemiquavers in b.1 as the 'upbeat' to the dotted quaver on the 3rd beat, and the semiquaver B as the upbeat to the 1st beat of b.2 (and so on), rather than as 'tail ends' to the previous beats. Place the LH crotchet precisely on the 2nd beat of b.1, and then feel the almost continuous LH crotchets like even 'steps'. Feel that the strong dotted rhythms in bb.1 – 6, and the triplets through bb.7 – 8, are fitting in with these LH 'steps', and *not* the other way about. Be sure to come *off* cleanly in the RH on the 3rd beat of bb.5 and 6, and then to time the semiquaver upbeat to bb.6 and 7 accurately over the clearly onward-leading LH crotchet octave. Listen to the resonant lower LH 'drones' through bb.11 – 14, and then articulate the RH fragments neatly in bb.15 and 16 over even LH crotchet chords. Feel that these even LH chords are leading on to support the RH offbeat quaver fragment through b.17, as you 'go to' and 'lean' well upon the double appoggiatura on the 1st beat of b.18 (giving these notes a crotchet value).

Trio
This minor Trio is outstandingly beautiful.

bb.29 – 58 Practise at first without the trills, keeping a perfectly steady crotchet pulse in your even LH chords while giving a spacious and expressive feeling to the rising RH triplets through bb.30, 32 and 34. Give the trills in bb.29 and 31, etc. four notes, starting on the upper note

From the upbeat to b.36 place the LH quaver/crotchet figures precisely as you shape the widely curving RH quaver line smoothly and eloquently. After the double bar sustain the lower, chromatically ascending dotted minim line resonantly as you listen to the 'close harmony' of the 'rocking' quaver figures in smooth thirds. From the upbeat to b.46 make sure that the LH 'leads' with a smooth inner crotchet line over the lower sustained pedal point D. Place the RH offbeat quavers neatly in a 'speaking' manner, making sure that they do not hang over the rests.

Third movement – Adagio (5) (O)*
This beautifully flowing 'Adagio' is ideal for older players at about Grade 5.

bb.1 – 6   Set an easy-moving crotchet pulse, in a tempo at which the semiquaver triplets will sound neither rushed nor sticky. Lead in from a clear quaver upbeat, taking care to give this note its full value, and shape the undulating RH lines smoothly and expressively over steadily moving LH quaver chords, bearing in mind Mozart's maxim (though without a sense of rigidity) 'in tempo rubato, in an 'Adagio' the LH should go on playing in strict time'. Show the gently syncopated melodic emphasis on the tied quaver D on the 6th *quaver* pulse of b.1, and also on the tied semiquaver 'upbeats' to the 3rd quaver pulse of b.1 and to the 2nd and 3rd quaver pulse of b.2. Feel the quaver rest on the 7th quaver pulse of b.2 like a 'breath', before starting the new phrase on the upbeat to b.3.

bb.6 – 25   Learn the LH alone from the 3rd beat of b.6, shaping the figures in thirds as smoothly as possible, and then when you add the RH trill, let it run easily and quietly, so that you do not (as inexperienced players invariably will) allow the trill to get hectic and loud, and to 'take over', leading to the faltering and the collapse of the LH! Keep steady as you approach this long trill, feeling the fourth quaver chord of b.6 as the 'upbeat' to the 3rd beat, and then do your best to concentrate on the LH, and to let the trill 'look after itself'. Let the LH 'go to' a firm crotchet third on the 1st beat of b.8, as you 'stop' the trill neatly on the first semi-quaver (of b.8). Then feel that the RH line is 'opening out' into resonant thirds and sixths. Support the RH with warm-toned LH chords from bb.8 – 10, taking care to keep steady through the second half of b.8. Make a little *rallentando* towards the six-four chord and pause in b.10. A short cadenza is intended to be inserted here, and similarly in the penultimate bar, for which suggestions are given in footnotes in the Vienna Urtext Edition. Do 'finish off' the LH down to the crotchet on the 2nd beat of b.11 before starting the new phrase with the RH quaver F. In bb.13 – 17 feel the punctuating effect of the quaver rests, like 'breathing' points as you shape the shorter melodic fragments eloquently, over your continuingly even LH quaver chords. Give a warm, resonant quali-ty to the 'harmonic' RH fragments in the first half of b.14 and the 2nd half of b.15.

Finale – Allegro molto (6)*
This movement is rumbustuously athletic and spirited. Set a smart **3/8** pulse, but not too fast, bearing in mind the triplet passages to come. Any problems that arise in this movement will almost invariably be due to rhythmic insecurity. Do therefore thoroughly absorb this secure pulse, and maintain it through thick and thin.

bb.1 – 10   Lead off with a boldly articulated ascending RH figure over a firm LH crot-chet third. Steady yourself in bb.2 – 3 with clear and meticulously placed LH quaver chords, and do take the RH *off* on the 3rd beat of these bars. Then lead off again clearly with the RH on the 1st beat of b.4, over a neatly shaped LH quaver fragment. Articulate the RH semiquavers vigorously through bb.6 – 9 over resonant dominant pedal point D's, and clear inner LH quavers. 'Finish off' cleanly in both hands in b.10, and do give full value to the quaver rest on the 3rd beat as you poise yourself to swing into triplets in b.11.

bb.11 – 34   Give yourself a good 'kick-off' with a clear ornamented quaver on the 1st beat of b.11 over a firm LH quaver chord, and continue to support your brilliant RH triplets with firm quaver chords on the 1st beat of bb.12 – 15.

Then lead off boldly with detached LH quavers from the 2nd beat of b.15, letting the RH offbeat triplets follow busily, but relatively lightly. Let the LH 'go to' a firm dotted crotchet octave on the 1st beat of b.19, and support the RH with a sustained LH through to b.22. Give a strong bass semiquaver A on the 1st beats of bb.23 – 6, and place the RH thirds or sixths clearly on the 2nd and 3rd beats over vigorously 'churning' LH semiquavers. Arrive on a firm 1st beat of b.27, and take care to keep steady through bb.27 – 8, feeling that the RH semiquaver triplets are 'going to' firm 1st beats of bb.28 and 29. Make a *diminuendo* from b.30 down to the double bar, supporting your neatly-spaced RH thirds with a steady LH tremolo.

bb.35 – 90   The greatest rhythmic danger area is between bb.39 and 45. Practise this passage very slowly and rhythmically. Feel that the RH in b.39 is 'going up to' a firm quaver C on the 1st beat of b.40, and that the LH in b.40 is 'going down to' a firm quaver F sharp on the 1st beat of b.41 and so on. It helps if you think of the LH broken octave on the 3rd beat of b.40, and b.42, as the *upbeat* to the subsequent bar. Do be sure also to differentiate absolutely clearly between the RH triplet, and the 'ordinary' semiquavers in b.39, and between the subsequent 'ordinary' semiquavers in the LH as they alternate with the triplets in the RH. It is effective to *diminuendo* through bb.50 – 3 and then to *crescendo* vigorously from b.54 as you lead back towards the reprise.

No. 14 in C major
(Hob. XVI/3)

The first movement (5) invites comparison with that of No. 10. In both there is a most untypical sameness of rhythmic pattern. But No. 10 is saved by its driving vigour and the emphatic sense of 'going somewhere'. Here we feel we are going gently nowhere, and most players will find the movement unrelievedly dull. Likewise the 'Andante' second movement (5): although the rhythmic patterns are more varied, it is long, and there is insufficient harmonic variety to maintain interest. As there is such a large field of splendid movements in the Grades 5 – 6 range, I therefore make no apology for passing over these two movements. The third movement, a Minuet and Trio, is more interesting.

Third movement − Minuet and Trio (4)
This is a bustling, cheerful Minuet, with a quietly flowing Trio in a subtly pointed two-part style.

bb.1 – 24   As John McCabe has pointed out, this is the first among Haydn's Minuets to start on an upbeat.† Take particular care therefore to set a brisk, clear, 'stepping' pulse *within yourself* before you start. Then articulate the upbeat semiquavers 'busily', but in perfect time, up to a bright crotchet G on the 1st beat of b.1. Support the carefully placed RH repeated C's with clearly placed LH rising crotchet thirds with the feeling of 'going up to' a strong minim on the 1st beat of b.2. Then, being sure to bring the LH *off* on the 3rd beat of bb.2 and 3, feel the implied emphasis and 'onward lean' on the high RH upbeat to bb.3 and 4, and support the RH through to b.6 with bright-toned and perfectly rhythmic LH chords. Give the trill on the 1st

†John McCabe, *Haydn Piano Sonatas* (BBC Music Guides).

beat of b.2 five notes (or three), starting on the upper note (with a slight emphasis on

the first note) 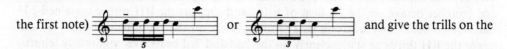 or and give the trills on the

1st beat of bb.3 and 4 four notes, again starting on the upper note. 'Go up to' a firm RH crotchet G on the 1st beat of b.6, and then 'come in' confidently with the triplets on the 2nd beat. Be sure to 'finish off' the two LH crotchets cleanly in b.8 before leading on with the upbeat to b.9 in a rather more gracious tone, perhaps slurring the crotchets on the first beat of bb.9 and 11. 'Go to' and 'lean well' upon the 1st beat of bb.10 and 12, giving the RH appoggiatura a crotchet value. Then articulate the semiquaver upbeat to bb.13 – 15 with whiplash clarity as you swoop upwards and down again to a resonant appoggiatura and chord on the 1st beat of each subsequent bar. 'Finish off' the phrase neatly on the 2nd beat of b.16, allowing a tiny break as you leap up to resume the opening motif on the upbeat to b.17.

Trio

bb.25 – 40

Lead into the Trio from the upbeat to b.25 with quiet clear quavers, and shape the curving line smoothly through to the double bar. Support the RH with carefully placed LH crotchet fragments from the upbeat to bb.26 and 28 (either *legato* or lightly detached) and 'lead on' clearly again with the high upbeat to bb.27 and 29. This Trio has something of the character of the musette, not only through the dominant pedal-point in the second section, but also in the subtle drone effect created by these high C's on the upbeats, and the inner RH C's through bb.25 – 6, etc. Support the RH with even 'stepping' crotchets from the upbeat to b.30, played either *legato*, or just detached. Listen carefully to the resonance of the long lower LH G, and the movement of the inner LH line through bb.35 – 8 and 39 – 42 beneath the curving line of your evenly moving RH quavers. Take care to give full value to the minim on the 1st beat of bb.38 and 42 before leading on with the subsequent upbeat quaver.

No. 15 in E major
(Hob. XVI/13)

This is an excellent choice as a complete Sonata at about Grade 5.

First movement – Moderato (5)*
This is a particularly rewarding piece for a comparatively inexperienced player. While conveniently short, it has at the same time the resonances and spacious contours of a much larger movement, as well as a radiant and expressive spirit.

bb.1 – 30

Set a steady and very *moderato* crotchet pulse. Lead off with a strong, warm-toned, spread E major chord, and then shape the quaver lines with equal care in either hand through to b.4. Take care to place the quaver chords precisely through b.3, and to 'finish off' the first phrase neatly on the 1st beat of b.4 with the RH triplet/quaver figure, over a clear LH crotchet octave. *Feel* the demisemiquaver rest on the 2nd beat, and then make a clean upward run towards a further strong E major chord timed precisely on the 1st beat of b.5. Lead off from the 1st beat of b.7 with even LH quavers, following on smoothly with the RH offbeat quaver fragments. Let the LH continue to 'lead' into b.11 to give a firm foundation to the RH semiquavers and triplets. Finish off the RH phrase neatly in b.12 (as in b.4), and then feel the LH semiquavers as an upbeat group 'going to' a resonant minim D sharp on the 1st beat of b.13. Then let the RH repeated semiquaver figure 'go' vigorously to a strong semiquaver on the 2nd beat of the bar, following on with the inner LH repeated semiquavers, 'going to' a strong tied minim on the 1st beat of b.14 (with the same effect again in b.16). Pursue the energetic onward movement of the RH semiquavers, supported by purposeful and steady LH quavers in a gradual *crescendo* towards b.20. Feel that your steady LH quavers are 'leading' as you descend through bb.20 – 1, and treat the RH semiquavers like slurred couplets. In b.23 'finish off' the two LH quavers cleanly, and then introduce a new, bright, clear tone for the fanfare-like figure starting from the RH high semiquaver 'upbeat' to the *2nd* beat of the bar. Define the RH dotted rhythm figures in thirds sharply and clearly over immaculately placed LH octaves in bb.24 and 25. 'Finish off' the RH phrase with clear detached quaver chords at the beginning of b.26, then 'take over' with a firm LH crotchet sixth on the 2nd beat of the bar, and feel that, in a rhythmic sense, the LH is 'leading' right through to the double bar.

Strike off boldly into the development. In b.32 show the inner LH line
bb.31 – 84 'following on' clearly from the RH in the previous bar, and pursue the
RH and inner LH lines energetically through to b.36 over a resonant lower dominant 'drone'. From bb.42 – 5 'lead' smoothly again with even LH quavers (as at bb.7 – 11) and through bb.45 – 7 support your determined RH semiquaver figures with a firm and clear LH. Keep your balance in b.47 by clearly marking the semiquaver G sharp on the 2nd beat of the bar, where the LH has a quaver rest. Then feel that your RH is 'going to' a firm quaver A on the 1st beat of b.48, and that the LH repeated semiquavers are 'going to' a firm crotchet D sharp on the *2nd* beat of b.48, so that you feel the hands 'taking over' from each other here on each beat. 'Take over' clearly with the RH on the 2nd beat of b.49, and stress these 2nd beats emphatically again in bb.50 and 51, when the LH has a quaver rest. Support this passage of high RH semiquavers with immaculately placed LH quaver figures through to b.53. In the recapitulation give increased buoyancy to bb.73 – 4 (compare them with bb.20 – 1), with firmly placed (though not heavy) LH octaves.

Second movement – Minuet and Trio (4) (O)*
In rhythmic and technical terms this is a simple Minuet and Trio, but as the Trio would lose much of its character if the LH octaves had to be omitted, it has been listed under Grade 4.

Minuet
This has a rather pensive quality. Play the RH repeated melody notes as
bb.1 – 24 smoothly and evenly as possible with the feeling of 'going to' the
ornamented minim on the 1st beat of b.2. Support the RH through to the 2nd beat of b.4 with even and steady yet 'on-going' LH crotchet chords. The trill on the 1st beat of b.2, starting on the upper note, could be 'long', so that it 'leads on into' the upbeat quavers to b.3, or it could 'stop' on the second crotchet beat. Be sure to give the RH dotted crotchet on the 2nd beat of b.4 its full value, *feeling* the held 3rd beat (while coming *off* in the LH), so that you don't 'fall into' the high quaver upbeat to b.5. Feel a slight 'lean' on the RH quaver on the 1st beat of bb.5 and 6, 11 and 12, as if these two quavers are slurred. Be sure to place the LH thirds clearly and steadily on the 2nd and 3rd beats of these bars beneath the sustained RH dotted crotchets, and

then listen to the LH fragment 'entering' on the 2nd beat of b.7. Take care to 'finish off' the LH crotchets cleanly through b.8 beneath the RH appoggiatura and minim thirds, ready to lead into the second section, perhaps in a more expressive tone. (The double appoggiatura here could be given either a crotchet or a minim value.) Take particular care to place the LH crotchet octaves clearly, like steady 'steps', in bb.21 – 2.

Trio

bb.25 – 52   Peters Edition gives this Trio some elaborate phrasing indications which belie the deliberate 'flatness' that Haydn seems to indicate here: the LH crotchet octaves are like stealthy 'steps' beneath the even RH quaver line. Keep the hand very close to the keys, and without fussing around with fancy fingering, place these octaves deliberately and quietly so that they are only slightly and lightly detached. Play the curving RH quaver line very smoothly over these 'stepping' *LH* crotchets listening acutely to the constantly varying intervals. The LH crotchets through bb.27 – 8, 31 – 2, and in the second section, could either be *legato* or slightly detached like the octaves. Take care to 'finish off' the two LH crotchets cleanly in b.8, and to *feel* the crotchet rest before leading off into the more sustained second section. After the double bar continue to place the inner LH crotchets evenly (observing the rests) over the sustained lower line. Keep this lower line smooth by changing fingers (5 – 4) on the tied dotted minims. Make this finger change neatly on the last beats of bb.34, 36 and 38, just after you have played the inner crotchet on each 3rd beat, making sure that you show the inner crotchet rests on the 1st beats of bb.35, 37 and 39.

Finale – Presto (5)*

This is another rumbustuous Finale, with a rollicking, strutting rhythm.

bb.1 – 18   Set a brisk and very secure crotchet pulse. Treat the opening like a little brass fanfare, lead off from a confident RH upbeat quaver sixth, and place the quaver/crotchet figures with the utmost precision in either hand, so that you feel a clear crotchet beat alternating between RH and LH. Support the RH thirds with firm LH octaves through bb.5 – 8, being particularly careful to place the LH octave clearly on the 2nd beat of b.6 when the RH has a quaver rest. Try going *piano* from the upbeat to b.9 when bb.1 – 4 are restated in the minor. From bb.13 – 18 feel that the LH is 'leading' rhythmically with clear but quiet detached repeated quaver octaves 'going to' firm crotchet octaves on the 1st beat of bb.14, 16 and 18, and letting the RH detached offbeat quaver thirds follow evenly and steadily.

bb.18 – 43   Give full value to the crotchet rest on the 2nd beat of b.18, then burst into *forte* at b.19, and let the LH line ascend vigorously towards b.22 as you 'rattle out' the RH semiquavers, savouring the E/D sharp clash in b.20. Mark the 2nd beat of bb.19 – 22 with a whiplash-clear accent on the high B's where the LH has a quaver rest. Then from b.23 reinforce your RH with resonant LH crotchet octaves as you drive on energetically towards b.27. Give full value to the unison crotchets on the 1st beat of b.27; and use the quaver rest to poise yourself to give the little treble figure in thirds, from the upbeat to b.28, a neat, woodwind quality, to be answered boldly with the unison figures from the upbeat to b.30. You could make a little *rallentando* through b.34, listening to the upward progression of the inner LH crotchets towards the dominant of B major. Then pick up the tempo smartly from the upbeat to b.36 and end the section in lively style. Give the RH quaver figure from the upbeat to b.36 a brassy, 'hunting-call' quality, and articulate the little fragments through bb.38 – 9 with pinpoint precision over 'keen' LH semiquavers. Support the RH trill in b.40 with firm LH crotchet chords, and articulate the LH semiquavers with brilliant clarity through b.42 as you go towards a ringing crotchet chord on the 1st beat of b.43.

You may like to drop the tone after the double bar, to *crescendo* gradually
bb.44 – 107   again towards b.59. Or you could set off in *forte* from b.44, *diminuendo*
from b.48 towards b.51, and then *crescendo* again towards b.59. In either
event do not allow your rhythmic impetus to slacken. Practise the LH Alberti
semiquavers slowly until your LH rhythm is quite secure. Practise also in dotted rhythms

and

(see also Introduction). Then be sure that the RH quaver fragments are neatly shaped,
and perfectly co-ordinated with your LH. You could either slur the two quavers on
the 1st beats of bb.44, 45, etc, or, alternatively, play all three quavers of each fragment
in a racy *staccato*. As in bb.19 – 22 in reverse, take care to *feel* the 2nd beat of bb.44 – 54
in the LH, where the RH has a quaver rest. Underpin the RH semiquavers with resonant
LH octaves from bb.56 – 9. 'Finish off' the two RH quavers exuberantly on the 1st
beat of b.59, and then seize the instant's break provided by the quaver rest to poise
yourself to lead back into the reprise with a clear upbeat sixth.

No. 16 in D major
(Hob. XVI/14)

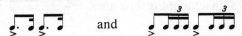

This is another splendid complete Sonata for players at a standard of about Grades 6 – 7.

First movement – Allegro moderato (7)*
This movement is rich in rhythmic detail and variety. Be cautioned therefore, by the
'moderato', remembering that 'Allegro' refers to style rather than merely to speed, and
establish a steady crotchet pulse at which the dotted rhythm figures of the first four
bars can be executed comfortably and clearly. Imagine a swinging 'step' to each *quaver*
pulse.

bb.1 – 8   Lead off from a neat semiquaver upbeat, and shape and time the RH dotted rhythm figures with immaculate precision through bb.1 – 4. Be sure
to differentiate clearly between the semiquaver 'upbeats' to the dotted
quavers in b.1 and the 1st beat of b.2, and the demisemiquaver 'upbeats' to the dotted
semiquavers in bb.2 – 3. Keep your RH in place with perfectly steady quavers in the
LH, feeling that the RH is fitting with this steady LH, and *not* the other way about.
Take particular care to keep a steady rhythm in the RH through b.2, when the LH
has a quaver rest on the 2nd beat. Feel that you are 'going to', and lean well upon,
the RH appoggiatura on the 1st beat of b.4, and 'finish off' the LH neatly down to
the crotchet D on the 2nd beat of the bar as you poise yourself to lead off again from
the RH upbeat to b.5. The logic of the suggestion in the footnote of the Vienna Urtext
Edition regarding the appoggiatura in b.4 is not clear. In my view a quaver appoggiatura
is better here and at b.40 etc, as at bb.8, 44, etc. (see also Howard Ferguson in the
Associated Board Edition). Define the RH dotted rhythms sharply from the middle
of b.6 and through b.7 supported by rock-steady LH quavers from the upbeat to b.7.
Be sure once more to 'finish off' the LH down to a clear crotchet on the 2nd beat of
b.8, and to give this beat its full value before leading on in perfect time into b.9.

bb.9 – 16   Keep yourself steady through bb.9, 11, 13 and 15 by 'leaning' well on the
LH crotchets on the 1st and 2nd beats, letting the offbeat semiquaver inner
LH, and RH fragments, follow relatively lightly; then go on to let the

LH quavers 'lead' evenly through the intervening bars (bb.10, 12, etc.), with the syncopated RH fragments following smoothly. In bb.11 and 15 when the RH triplets are in cross-rhythm with the LH, the 'lean' on the lower LH crotchets is particularly important; then concentrate on keeping your LH steady, imagining that you have four even LH semiquavers with a 'doubled' first note, and let the RH triplets fit in with your *even* LH, rather than (as inexperienced players invariably will) trying to fit in the LH with the *RH*.

bb.16 – 27   Let the RH 'go to' a singing tied crotchet on the 1st beat of b.17, and then follow the contrapuntal details meticulously in either hand. 'Go to' and 'lean' upon the slurred crotchets on the 1st beats of bb.18 – 20 over immaculately timed LH fragments. From bb.21 – 4 feel that the even LH quavers are 'leading' again, with the RH line following smoothly, showing the implied slight emphasis on the syncopated RH *quavers* (F sharp, D, B, etc.). Lean well on the RH quaver appoggiatura on the 1st beat of b.24, and collect yourself to 'flick' the RH demisemiquavers clearly and lightly down to the emphasized tied quaver spanning the bar line. Feel a light emphasis each time on the *first* demisemiquaver, placed precisely on the second beat of the bar, above the LH quaver rest, and support the RH with immaculately placed offbeat LH quaver figures.

bb.28 – 36   Feel the implied emphasis on the tied RH quaver E in b.28, and place a singing LH tied crotchet A beneath it on the 2nd beat of the bar. Then let the RH semiquavers 'go to' a singing tied crotchet D sharp on the 1st beat of b.29, and listen acutely as the LH and RH voices answer each other here in a close *legato*. A slight *rallentando* is suggested as you go towards the half-close at b.32. 'Lean' on the RH quaver appoggiatura on the 1st beat of b.32, and place the turn lightly over the second LH quaver. Then, allowing a tiny break, pick up the tempo at once, and feel that the reiterated RH triplet thirds are 'going to' firm slurred quavers on the 1st beats of bb.33 and 34 over neatly placed LH quavers. Time the demisemiquaver scale precisely from the 2nd beat of b.34, to 'go down' to a clear quaver B on the 1st beat of b.35. Be sure to 'finish off' the LH at the end of the section, giving a neat springboard for the RH semiquaver upbeat as you either go back to b.1, or on into the development.

bb.37 – 110   Take care to keep steady from bb.45 – 8; let the tied RH crotchets sing over the 2nd beats of the bars, and continue to feel your steady crotchet pulse as you time the little LH interjections neatly. Be sure that you differentiate clearly between the demisemiquavers in the second halves of bb.45 and 46, and the triplets in the second halves of bb.47 and 48. Then from b.49 shape your RH semiquaver and triplet fragments clearly, over resonant LH minims and even inner LH quavers (observing the rests precisely in either hand). From b.56 fit your offbeat RH triplet figures in neatly, over a smooth and clear lower LH crotchet line and even inner LH 'drone' as you *crescendo* towards b.59. Let the RH 'go on' here up to a strong high tied crotchet B on the 2nd beat of b.59. Feel the second LH quaver of b.65 as an 'upbeat' to the 2nd beat of the bar, starting a new phrase as you lead off with the LH into the long passage of even LH quavers with its equally smooth syncopated RH counterpoint. Create a very close, 'veiled' *legato* here, and then open out in a *crescendo* from b.71 as you lead back towards the recapitulation. In b.106, when the previous phrase is transferred to the lower register, give the reiterated triplet thirds figure a different, perhaps bassoon-like colour.

Second movement – Minuet and Trio (5)*

This Minuet has a firm, clear and open texture.

bb.1 – 22 Lead off with a clear RH crotchet, then show the implied emphasis on the tied crotchet on the 2nd beat of b.1, coinciding with the confident entry of the LH crotchets. Time the dotted rhythms precisely over steady 'step-like' LH crotchets. Let the LH lead into b.3 with a firm minim on the 1st beat, to give a springboard to the RH semiquaver scale entering on the offbeat. Then feel the implied syncopated emphasis on the tied second RH quaver in bb.5 and 6 over your perfectly steady LH crotchets. Be sure to 'finish off' the three LH crotchets precisely in b.8, and then take care to keep a steady crotchet pulse through bb.9 – 12. Practise at first without the trills. Give a strong RH A on the 1st beat of bb.9 and 11, and be sure to give full value to the LH crotchet rests. Then enter confidently with the LH on the 2nd beat, and make a light accent with the fifth finger on the first note of each group of semiquavers. Let these LH semiquavers 'go to' a firm crotchet C sharp on the 1st beats of bb.10 and 12, and then be sure to enter with the RH scales precisely on the 2nd beats of these bars. Take care to make it clear that the scale in b.10 begins with a *quaver* as opposed to two semiquavers in b.11.

Trio

Listen acutely to the fine minor resonances of this beautiful Trio, and follow all the part-writing smoothly and expressively.

bb.23 – 55 Lead off with a quiet but resonant lower LH tied dotted minim on the 1st beat of b.1, and let the two upper lines enter evenly on the offbeat. Then 'lead' with warm-toned RH dotted minim sixths on the 1st beats of bb.25 and 26, as you shape the LH quaver fragments expressively, letting the LH quavers 'go to' a clear crotchet G on the 1st beat of b.27. Feel that the LH is 'leading' through b.27 with the offbeat RH detached quaver chords following evenly. As the LH leads again through bb.30 and 32, note that the RH syncopated fragments are *legato* here. Let the RH 'go to' emphasized singing E flat minims on the 2nd beats of bb.33 and 35, and then phrase the LH thirds up towards the 1st beat of b.34 (and b.36), and the RH thirds down from the 2nd quaver pulse as if in a continuous smooth arc. After the double bar feel the gently heightened expressiveness of the music. In bb.39 and 41 you will have to get your RH thumb 'out of the way' so that the LH can repeat the middle C on the chord on the 2nd beat. The fraction of a second required to do this aids the implied slight emphasis on this diminished 5th. Listen to the inner LH line rising to a resonant high minim G sharp on the 2nd beat of b.44, and then allow a little 'give' as the LH leads smoothly down towards the sustained dotted minim D on the 1st. beat of b.46.

Finale – Allegro (6)*

This is a particularly sparky Finale – the wit is tinged with acerbity as Haydn jumps this way and that, and both player and listener need to have all their musical wits about them. Set a clear and very secure 2/4 pulse, and note the pattern of two-bar phrases (bb.1 – 2 and 6 – 7) and three-bar answering phrases (bb.3 – 5 and 8 – 10) which sets the bantering tone of the movement. The first phrase (bb.1 – 2) 'doubles back', astonishingly, into an immediate interrupted cadence.

Time the opening figure precisely with a rhythm as vital as a coiled spring,

bb.1 – 14 articulating the RH thus [music notation] and 'pointing' the

effect of the interrupted cadence. Be sure to *feel* and give full value to the crotchet rest on the 2nd beat of b.2 (and similarly in bb.5, 7, etc.). Then feel the smoother, more flowing character of the three-bar answering phrase, supporting the RH with a firm LH minim third on the 1st beat of b.3, and with a neatly shaped two-part fragment through bb.4 – 5. Underpin the RH semiquavers with rock-steady but lively LH detached quavers through b.9, and be sure to 'finish off' the LH clearly down to the crotchet A on the 2nd beat of b.10. Then set off from b.11 with sharply pointed RH figures supported by 'keen' LH semiquavers.

From bb.15 – 31 a firm and accurately placed LH is essential to steadiness.
bb.15 – 43   Place the LH quaver thirds neatly and firmly on the 1st beat of bb.15 and
16 to act as 'springboards' for your neat offbeat RH scale figures. Place the LH minim third even more firmly on the 1st beat of b.17; and let the RH scale descend to a firm crotchet appoggiatura on the 1st beat of b.18 over a neatly timed and articulated LH figure which in turn will 'go to' a firm LH fifth on the 1st beat of b.19. Feel that the LH is 'leading' through bb.19 – 22 with the RH offbeat semiquavers in bb.19 and 21 following relatively lightly. Then burst in with a *forte* LH minim octave F natural on the 1st beat of b.23, and support your 'rattling' RH semiquavers with resonant LH octaves all the way to b.31. Give full value to the crotchet rest on the 2nd beat of b.31, and collect yourself quickly to return neatly to the opening figure in b.32, now in the dominant. From the 2nd beat of b.39, let the cleanly articulated descending RH semiquaver figures 'go to' a firm slurred quaver (or appoggiatura, treating these just like the slurred quavers) on the 1st beats of bb.40 – 3 over neatly placed LH quaver figures.

After the double bar the music takes a more serious turn. 'Rattle out' your
bb.44 – 108   RH semiquavers from b.44 over a resonant dominant pedal point and
evenly placed inner LH quaver fragments, as you drive on towards a firm dominant chord at b.49. Then show, by a change of spirit, that you have switched to the minor at b.50. Give a firm chord on the 1st beat of b.54, and time this bar carefully, 'feeling' the held 2nd beat, before you 'flick' the upbeat triplet neatly towards the 1st beat of b.55. Collect yourself on the 1st beat of b.56 to 'lean' on the tied RH crotchet B flat on the 2nd beat (treating the second quaver (A) as the 'upbeat' to this B flat) and then follow the 'rocking' chromatic lines with close, creeping smoothness in either hand. From b.66 support the RH semiquavers with springy LH quaver chords as you lead to the half-close on the dominant at b.71, ready for Haydn's 'cut in' to the recapitulation in b.72.

No. 17 in E flat major

No. 18 in E flat major

Question marks hang over the authenticity of these two Sonatas. In Volume 1 of *Haydn, Chronicle and Works,* H.C. Robbins Landon says of No. 17, 'there is no evidence that Haydn had anything to do with this work'. And he states that No. 18 'has now been identified as a work by Kayser (Kaiser).' Since, in addition, pianists are unlikely to find much joy in ploughing through the somewhat lumpy first movements of either, I shall pass over both of these (both Grade 7). But the 'Andante' second movement of No. 17 (Grade 6) is pleasant, and the Minuets and Trios of both Sonatas are very worthwhile at about Grade 5. Brief notes are given below on these three movements.

No.17 – Second movement – Andante (6)

Find a comfortable speed for the triplet passage from b.8, and from this set the tempo for the movement as a whole. Otherwise it is easy to start too fast, and then, arriving at b.8, find that the triplets are too scurrying for a comfortable 'Andante'. Time bb.1 – 7 precisely, like neat little steps in a formal dance. Feel the implied 'lean' on the RH minor third on the 2nd beat of b.2, which 'bridges' the first and second halves of the first phrase. In b.6, 'go up to', and feel the syncopated emphasis on, the high dotted quaver C. Shape the 1st *LH* fragment (bb.1 – 2), the second fragment (from the upbeat to b.3), and the longer LH phrase (bb.5 – 8) with as much care as the RH line. Swing easily into triplets at b.8, and ensure that they flow evenly beneath your graciously phrased melodic line. Keep a steady crotchet pulse from bb.32 – 7, phrasing the RH semiquaver fragments and the LH thirds smoothly, and observing the rests meticulously in either hand. Let the LH crotchets 'lead' through bb.37 – 9 with the RH offbeat semiquaver fragments following relatively lightly. While it is probably 'correct' to allow the RH demisemiquaver and semiquavers in bb.9, 11, 13, etc. to coincide with the third semiquaver of the relevant LH triplet group (and to let the RH dotted quavers in bb.19 – 21 coincide with the second LH triplet), players may find a cross-rhythm effect more expressive.

Third movement – Minuet and Trio (5)

Practise bb.1 – 2 at first without the trills, timing the RH dotted rhythm precisely over evenly placed LH chords, and giving full value to the crotchet rest on the 3rd beats.

Then when you add the trills make sure that the precise

timing of these two bars is not disrupted. Keep a steady crotchet pulse through bb.3 and 5, differentiating meticulously between the dotted rhythm (b.3) and the triplets (b.5). After the double bar lead off clearly with the LH, *crescendo* up to a singing minim F on the 1st beat of b.10, and be sure to place the RH chords precisely. Place the LH chords firmly on the 1st beats of bb.13 – 15, letting the RH quaver fragments follow smoothly. Let the lower LH line 'lead' through bb.23 and 24 beneath the expressive RH offbeat quaver fragments, and carefully placed inner LH minims.

Trio

This expressive Trio presents a series of sequential modulations. Enter with quietly resonant unison crotchets, and then let the treble quaver line in b.27 'go to' a singing dotted minim on the 1st beat of b.28, with the inner quavers following on to 'go to' the inner B natural in b.29, and so on. Support your RH lines with clear LH crotchet octaves on the 1st beats, taking care to give these their precise value. Cultivate the skill of playing repeated notes as smoothly as possible, so that these quaver figures sound very even, rather than proceeding in a series of alternating hiccoughs and slurs; keep the hand very close to the keys, and raise the keys as little as possible, so that the sound of the repeated notes is as nearly continuous as you can make it. Continue this sustained effect with the RH sixths and thirds in bb.33 – 4. After the double bar *crescendo* gradually towards b.42.

No.18 – Second movement – Minuet and Trio (5)

Lead off clearly with the RH feeling the 'lift' up to the high crotchet on the 2nd beat of bb.1 and 2, coinciding with the clear 'entry' of each LH crotchet fragment. Observe the RH dotted quaver rests accurately in bb.1 and 2, 5 and 6, over a firm LH crotchet on each 3rd beat, so that the upbeats to the subsequent bars are perfectly timed. Keep a steady crotchet pulse as you descend through the scales (bb.9 and 11) towards singing dotted crotchet A naturals on the 1st beat of bb.10 and 12. 'Lean' well on the slurred crotchet B natural and C natural on the 1st beat of bb.16 and 18 respectively.

Trio

Lead off into the minor Trio with a *legato* LH crotchet line, letting the syncopated RH line follow smoothly and expressively. From b.33 let the lower LH G flat 'drones' give a sustained foundation for even inner LH crotchets and carefully shaped RH syncopated fragments. Then from b.38, and from bb.43 and 54 again shape the curves of the longer RH line expressively over the continuingly even and steady LH.

No. 19 in E minor
(Hob. XVI/47)

No. 57 in F major
(Hob. XVI/47)

The Vienna Urtext Edition gives two versions of this Sonata. No. 19, the earlier version, consists of an Adagio in E minor, with an Allegro and a Finale (Tempo di Menuet) both in E major. The later version (No. 57) has a new first movement in F major, the Adagio and Allegro are transposed, with slight variants, into F minor and F major, and the Finale is omitted. In the Henle Edition the Sonata appears in the earlier version, and in Peters in the later version, as No. 34.

First movement − Adagio (6)*

Though listed under Grade 6 this beautiful and finely expressive movement could perhaps be enjoyed by older players at an earlier stage. Feel the slow, siciliano-like **6/8** swing in an easy flowing *legato*, and find a tempo at which bb.9 − 10 'move' and do not feel sticky, but at which, on the other hand, the turns in b.11, and the demisemiquaver figuration (bb.16, 18, etc.) do not sound rushed.

bb.1 − 8   Lead off with a smoothly singing RH line supported by quietly resonant LH thirds. End this first phrase as if with a 'question' as you 'tail off' the grace note figure up to the quaver G on the 2nd beat of b.2 (placing the first grace note, E, *on* the beat). Then *feel* the quaver rest, and define the change of register and tone as you enter in a sonorous implied *forte* with the unison answering phrase from the upbeat to b.3. Be sure that you 'go on through' to the last of the repeated quaver E's in *forte* in b.4, so that in turn you define the contrast with the returning *piano* phrase from the upbeat to b.5. Take care here to *feel* the semiquaver rest so that this upbeat semiquaver group is perfectly timed. Feel the rests between all the phrases and fragments like 'breathing points' (e.g. the quaver rests on the 5th quaver pulse of bb.6 and 7, on the 5th and 6th quaver pulses of b.10, and the semiquaver rest on the 5th quaver pulse of b.15, and so on). Then while each rest is clearly defined, at the same time phrase mentally *over* the rests as a singer would, so that you create an overall sense of continuity, rather than proceeding in a series of stops and starts. From the upbeat to b.8 make a *diminuendo* as you draw out a little towards the pause, noting that the pause comes over the *rests* rather than on the dominant chord on the 2nd main beat.

bb.9 – 19 From b.9 introduce a fuller, more positive tone. Spread the big chords generously on the 1st beat of bb.9 and 11, and articulate the detached quavers strongly and melodically, not spikily, downwards through b.9 towards a warm-toned chord on the 1st beat of b.10. Then do not allow your pulse to be disrupted by the turns in b.11 (placing these *on* the beat). These powerfully impelled fragments are answered with a more yielding phrase from the upbeat to b.13. Feel the yearning quality as you 'lean' on the quaver appoggiaturas against carefully placed LH quaver chords on the main beats of b.13. Treat the grace notes in b.15 like very gentle, not clipped, acciaccaturas. From the upbeat to b.16, as you move into the ornamented version of bb.13 and 14, and indeed throughout all the similar melodic passages, do preserve your secure **6/8** pulse in the LH chords. Feel, as you shape the demisemiquaver figures gracefully, that the RH is fitting in with these steady LH chords and *not* the other way about. Take care to give the tied RH quaver A its full value on the 2nd main beat of b.17 so that the subsequent triplets are perfectly timed. Do not 'snatch' at the high D on the 1st beat of b.18, but rather feel a leisurely slurred effect up from the grace note B, as indicated in the Vienna Urtext Edition. Place this grace note (and the one in b.17) *on* the beat, again like a 'not clipped' acciaccatura.

bb.20 – 47 From the upbeat to b.24 let the demisemiquaver figuration flow easily over your very steady LH chords, always feeling that you are 'going to', and 'leaning' upon the slurred quavers on the main beats of bb.24 – 7 (as on the appoggiaturas in bb.13 and 16). Carry your full tone over from b.32 into b.33, listening to the 'horn-like' quality of the RH thirds. You could then either continue from here in a warm resonant tone, or alternatively make a gradual *diminuendo* towards b.37. In any event 'carry on' your melody line in thirds down to a clear quaver on the first beat of b.34, and then feel the upward leap to the high C as a wide melodic 'arc' (and similarly in b.35) rather than as a disjointed lurch. Feel the delicate hesitancy of the little demisemiquaver fragments from the upbeat to b.43, and take time to point the interrupted cadence (bb.45 – 6). Then show the horn-like sound again of the RH quaver augmented fourths, and listen to the beautiful inner RH descending melodic fragment from the 2nd beat of b.46 as you slow towards the pause. Then poise yourself on this dominant chord, ready for the *attacca.*

Second movement – Allegro (7)

Whether this stocky movement sounds bucolically comic, or boringly repetitive is entirely up to the player. Set a comfortable **2/4**, like a cheerful jog (not too fast, bearing in mind the sextuplet figuration from the upbeat to b.45), and keenly 'point' all the humorous touches.

bb.1 – 35 Lead off from a lively detached upbeat and play the opening RH figures in a jolly 'peasant' style over steady, detached LH quavers. Observe the RH quaver rests precisely (bb.1 and 2, etc). Let the LH 'go on down' to a firm crotchet E on the 2nd beat of b.8 with a bit of a 'plonk', and then lead off with a clear RH quaver upbeat to b.9. (Similarly 'finish off' with clear quavers in *both* hands on the 2nd beat of bb.11, 14, 21, etc. so that in each instance you are poised to lead on with the RH quaver upbeat to the subsequent bar.) Let the RH dotted crotchet B's sing out on the 1st beat of bb.9, 10, etc. – the offbeat LH quaver figures could well be *legato* here. In bb.15 – 17 (and 28 – 33) 'go to', and 'lean' on the slurred appoggiatura-like treble crotchets, over precisely placed LH offbeat quaver chords. Be sure to *feel* the quaver rest on the 2nd beat of b.18, before leading on with the RH upbeat. Note the slurred RH quaver couplets (bb.20 and 23) and support the RH semiquavers through bb.24 – 7 with steadily 'jogging' LH quavers. Treat the grace note G sharps like jaunty acciaccaturas (bb.34 – 5) and come cleanly *off* (jokily) on the 2nd beat of b.35.

Place the LH crotchet octave firmly on the 1st beat of b.36, then feel your
bb.36 – 138   steady crotchet pulse as the slurred RH semiquaver figures ascend towards
the 2nd beat of b.37. 'Finish off' the LH broken octave quavers neatly in
b.39, and make a tiny break as you leap up to enter with perfectly steady and clear high
RH semiquavers on the 2nd beat, supported by quiet, but clear and definite LH quaver
thirds from the upbeat to b.40. 'Go to', and feel the implied 'lean' on the tied treble F sharp
on the 2nd beat of b.42. From the 2nd beat of b.44 keep the LH quaver thirds perfectly
steady, and let the alternating RH offbeat sextuplet and 'ordinary' semiquavers fit in with
this *steady* LH, and not the other way about. Take particular care to place the LH thirds
securely on the 2nd beat of bb.44, 45 and 46, where the RH has a semiquaver rest. In
b.47 run neatly up the demisemiquaver scale, over a firm LH crotchet third, to arrive on
a clear upper quaver B precisely on the 2nd beat, and finish off the section in perfect time.
Listen to the neat piece of bi-play between the hands (bb.73 – 7), and through bb.78 – 82
be careful to preserve a steady crotchet pulse, making it clear that the second chord of
each LH quaver couplet falls on the 2nd beat of these bars beneath the RH semiquaver
or quaver rest. Do observe the rests accurately here in either hand, and again treat the
grace notes like acciaccaturas. Mark the switch to the minor at b.90 with an emphatic
change of tone colour. Then keep the LH quavers rock-steady through the sequential
'working-out' passage (bb.92 – 6), and come to a clear 'stop' on a firm dominant chord
on the 1st beat of b.97, ready to lead on with a strong upbeat to b.98.

Finale – Tempo di Menuet (6)*

Here Haydn toys delightfully with his material, continually changing tack, or changing
the expected pattern by the repetition of a short phrase: see, for example, how bb.3 and
4 are repeated in bb.5 and 6. Then in b.8, he throws in a 'skipping' variant of the RH
crotchets of b.2.

Spread the opening broken chord (placed *on* the beat) up to a singing minim
bb.1 – 29   B, and immediately establish your minuet movement with clear, 'stepping'
LH crotchets. Time the RH dotted rhythms smartly through bb.3 – 4 and
5 – 6 over immaculately placed LH chords. Be sure to come *off* on the 3rd beat of b.6,
and to give the crotchet rest its full value. 'Skip' the RH figures, through b.8, over a firm
LH minim and crotchet. Lead off clearly with the RH on the 1st beat of b.11, and then
let the LH crotchets 'take over' in b.12, with the two detached RH quavers following evenly
and relatively lightly. 'Lead' again with the RH tied C sharp on the 1st beat of b.13, and
be sure to place the two LH crotchet thirds neatly in this bar. Let the LH 'lead' through
bb.16 and 18, 'going to' a firm crotchet D sharp on the 1st beat of bb.17 and 19, with
the RH offbeat detached quavers and the longer quaver fragments following on evenly.
Then in bb.23 and 25 time the RH dotted rhythm figures precisely, over immaculately
placed LH chords. (Feel the demisemiquavers as light, snappy 'upbeats' to the subsequent
beats, rather than as 'tail-ends' to the previous beats. See also Introduction.) Then support
your curving RH scale figures with firm LH crotchet thirds on the 1st beats of bb.24,
26 and 27. Be sure to 'finish off' the LH neatly through b.29.

From b.32 Haydn launches into a passage of serious part-writing. Give a
bb.30 – 68   firm LH crotchet octave on the 1st beat of b.32, and let the RH quavers
enter clearly and smoothly on the offbeat, with the LH quavers 'following
on' clearly in b.33 beneath the steady RH crotchets. Listen to the LH quavers leading
on through b.35, and let the treble dotted crotchets on the 1st beat of bb.36 and 37 sing
out through their full value (also taking care to place the inner RH fragments precisely)
over the flowing LH quaver line. From bb.44 – 8 preserve a firm crotchet pulse as you

co-ordinate the two lines of dotted rhythms precisely over the sustained lower LH B's. Then show the lighter skipping effect of the detached RH 'dotted rhythm' through bb.50 – 1 (as in b.8). Keep steady here with the help of even, 'stepping' LH crotchet octaves. Through these passages of dotted rhythms, again feel the semiquaver as the 'upbeat' to the subsequent beat. Be sure to 'finish off' the LH clearly on the 2nd beat of b.53, ready for the RH scale to enter confidently on the offbeat.

No. 20 in B flat major
(Hob. XVI/18)

First movement – Allegro moderato (8)
This is the first of the Sonatas to show occasional dynamic marks. The first movement is light and airy in texture, and the melodic line is decorated with some complexity, incorporating turns, syncopations, flowing triplets, and all kinds of varied rhythmic figures. At first the music may seem dull, but it has an easy charm that grows upon the ear, and there is an interesting development section. The RH turns in bb.1, 5, etc. can be fitted in quite comfortably providing that you heed the 'moderato' and do not set off too fast. Establish and maintain, therefore, a leisurely moving **2/4** pulse at which all ornaments, demisemiquaver runs and figurations will sound flowing rather than brilliant. Feel an easy walking step to each quaver pulse.

Practise bb.1 – 2 at first without the turns, in immaculate time, and feeling *bb.1 – 13* the implied emphasis on the tied RH quaver on the 2nd quaver pulse of b.2.

Then when the turns are added, ensure that neither your crotchet pulse nor your neat dotted rhythms are disrupted. Various interpretations of these ornaments are possible. The one given in the Vienna Urtext seems the smoothest and most feasible, in practice simplified to with the turns incorporated with the upbeat semiquavers, and thus *anticipating* each quaver beat. Be sure to place your LH thirds precisely in bb.1 – 2, and then keep the RH dotted rhythms in place through b.3 with the help of steady LH quaver chords. Let the LH 'take over' in a poised manner from the RH, on the 'upbeat' to the 2nd main beat of b.4, and 'go on down' towards a firm crotchet B flat on the 1st beat of b.5. Be particularly careful to place the LH quaver third accurately on the 2nd beat of b.6, and the LH quavers accurately on the crotchet beats of b.7, to give a steady foundation for the RH triplets and demisemiquavers. Lead off with a singing ornamented RH tied crotchet D on the 1st beat of b.9, and then ensure that the triplet arabesques alternate evenly and gracefully between the hands. Let the LH triplets 'go to' a clear crotchet on the 2nd beat of b.9, and b.11, beneath the tied RH crotchet.

Count, and *feel* the rests patiently through b.13, and then, coming in precisely *bb.13 – 39* on the upbeat to b.14, let the reiterated syncopated treble figures move smoothly over evenly placed LH fragments. (Note that the LH *upper* single quaver B flat on the upbeat to bb.15, 16 and 17 is 'separate' from the lower LH fragment F and E natural.) Count carefully at b.17, 'feeling' the held 2nd main beat, and then from the second half of the bar articulate the sequential RH figures neatly through to b.20, again over a carefully placed LH. From bb.20 – 6 follow the lower LH line smoothly, while also sustaining the syncopated inner LH 'drones' on C. Fit in all the RH figuration neatly over this steady and sustained LH. Observe the RH detailing precisely in bb.21 and 23, showing the semiquaver rests, and 'leaning' lightly on the slurred semiquaver on the 2nd main beat of these bars. Continue to follow the LH lines evenly through bb.25 – 8 beneath a smoothly moving syncopated RH line. Be very sure to sustain the inner LH tied F from the 2nd quaver pulse of b.26. Throughout this whole passage (bb.20 – 8) do feel that the RH figures are fitting in with your steady and even LH, and *not* the other way about. 'Match' the LH and RH answering figures through bb.29 – 33, feeling that each is 'going to' the quaver appoggiatura on the 1st beat of the subsequent bar. Give a clear LH quaver B flat on the 1st beat of b.33, and then let the demisemiquavers flow evenly, supported by carefully placed LH quavers on the 1st and 2nd beats of b.34 and the 1st beat of b.35. Mark the LH octaves, taking time to 'point' the interrupted cadence boldly at bb.35 – 6, and being careful to dovetail the RH neatly with the LH on the demisemiquaver 'upbeat' to the 2nd main beat of b.35.

bb.40 – 69   'Lean' on the RH slurred semiquavers on the 1st and 2nd main beats of bb.45 – 6, and place the offbeat LH quavers carefully 'beneath' the RH semiquaver rests. From b.48 Haydn expands on the reiterated *legato* figures from bb.14 – 16. Descend steadily in both hands in a full tone from b.50 towards b.54. From the upbeat to b.60, let the syncopated RH line descend smoothly in contrary motion with the ascending LH quaver line, and be sure to place the LH thirds evenly beneath the partly syncopated RH line through bb.62 and 63. 'Go to', and 'lean' well on the treble D on the 1st beat of b.65, changing fingers so that this note can be smoothly slurred down to the C sharp on the 2nd beat.

bb.70 – 117   Give a bold LH octave E flat on the 1st beat of b.70, and proceed towards b.74 in cadenza-like fashion, playing the RH demisemiquaver figures in improvisatory style over resolute, declamatory LH octaves. 'Lean' warmly on the slurred minim chord in b.73, and poise yourself through the pause-effect on this chord to pick up the *a tempo* from the LH upbeat to the 2nd main beat of b.74, as you move into the recapitulation. Feel the sudden seriousness of the minor moment from the 2nd beat of b.80, and support the RH triplets with resonantly sustained LH lines through to b.83. Take care not to lose your balance at bb.108 – 10. Let the RH demisemiquaver line descend to a firm semiquaver F on the 1st beat of b.109; place the high semiquaver A neatly, and then 'take over' with steady LH quavers, 'going to' a firm quaver E flat on the 1st beat of b.110, with the RH detached semiquavers following relatively lightly.

Second movement – Moderato (7)

Like the first, this movement is more interesting than it appears initially. It has the tempo of a minuet, easing here and there through bars of contemplative part-writing towards a sustained pause (see bb.33 – 5, 56 – 8 and 97 – 9). The melodic line is again extensively ornamented, but as in the first movement, the ornamentation will be found to fit in quite comfortably at the *moderato* tempo. Establish a clear minuet rhythm, at first without the ornaments, and then when you add these, ensure that this 'step-like' pulse is not disrupted.

bb.1 – 14   Lead off with clear and smoothly phrased RH thirds, 'going to' a warmly emphasized crotchet appoggiatura on the 1st beat of b.2, over precisely placed LH crotchets, taking care to observe the rests on the third beat of b.1 and the 1st beat of b.2. Time the RH dotted rhythms immaculately through bb.3, 5, etc, and again feel the 'lean' on the crotchet appoggiatura on the 1st beat of bb.4 and 8, and also on the tied crotchets on the 1st beat of bb.6 and 7. In b.9 let the LH leap up buoyantly from the bass detached crotchet to the detached crotchet on the 2nd beat of the bar (avoiding any suggestion of slurring), beneath the tied RH third, and then be sure that the LH semiquaver upbeat to b.10 dovetails neatly with the last RH semiquaver. Let the LH 'go to' a warmly sustained dotted minim fifth on the 1st beat of b.11, to support the expressive RH phrase entering on the offbeat.

Give a firm bass crotchet F on the 1st beat of b.15, and then phrase the treble
bb.15 – 45   thirds and LH answering fragments smoothly and warmly, ensuring that the
tied RH dotted minim third sings over the 1st beat of b.17. From bb.20 – 5 let
the partly syncopated treble line and the inner LH line sing expressively over the sustained
lower dotted minims, ensuring that the tied lower LH upbeat to b.21 and the inner LH
upbeats to bb.22 – 5 sing over the bar lines. Then again from b.27, follow the lower and
inner lines as carefully as the treble. Listen particularly to the inner RH line from b.31,
between the sustained treble line, and the steady LH crotchet line. Let the LH line 'go
to' a resonant tied dotted minim G on the 1st beat of b.33, and the treble line to a singing
tied minim B flat, as the inner line continues its descent towards the sustained tied upbeat
to b.34 (E natural). At the beginning of b.34 'take over' the inner tied E with the LH
as you *rallentando*, listening to all the sustained notes, towards the dominant 7th pause
chord. Practise this whole passage (bb.27 – 35) not only '*hands* separately' but also '*parts*
separately' (as also at bb.51 – 8 and 91 – 9). Pick up the tempo brightly from the upbeat
to b.36, observing the details of articulation in either hand. Take care to come off cleanly
from the detached RH quaver C on the 2nd beat of b.40, so that you don't 'fall into'
the subsequent broken octave semiquavers. From the middle of b.42, 'lean' warmly both
on the offbeat RH slurred thirds, or sixths, and also on the slurred crotchets on the 1st
beats of bb.43 – 5 over evenly placed LH crotchets, and end the section with neat formality.

Do have courage to give a full bar's rest at b.50. Then follow the expressive
bb.46 – 110   part-writing again through to the pause at b.58, taking particular care to
sustain the long lower notes. Feel that the LH is 'leading' with steady quavers
from the 2nd quaver pulse of b.62. Keep a steady crotchet pulse through the broken octaves
of bb.65 – 6 (practise at first in plain octaves). 'Take over' clearly with the LH on the
1st beat of b.66, and then feel you are 'going down to' a *firm* detached crotchet B flat
on the 1st beat of b.67 as you lead back into the ornamented reprise. From bb.77 – 82
phrase the treble line expressively over warmly sustained LH chords.

Sonatas Nos. 21 – 7 and Sonata No. 28

The Vienna Urtext Edition publishes the opening fragments of seven lost 'Divertimentos',
and also the longer fragment of the first movement of a further Divertimento in D major
(Sonata No. 28). Along with this comes a splendid complete Minuet and Trio (6)(O). An
'attempted completion' of the first movement is also given in the Appendix. The Henle
Edition gives these fragments (Nos. 21 – 7) in the Appendix to Volume 1. No. 28 in D
major is also given in Volume 1 as 'Sieben Sonaten, um 1765 – 1772', No. 4.

No. 28 in D major
(Hob. XVI/5)

First movement – incomplete.

Second movement – **Minuet and Trio** (6)(O)*

The Minuet is notable for its dramatic changes of register. Phrase the low-
bb.1 – 38   pitched RH melody line resonantly and purposefully through bb.1 – 8.
Support the RH with a firm LH octave line (bb.1 – 3). Then from b.5 keep
the RH dotted rhythm and triplet figures steady with a firmly placed LH crotchet line.
Feel the lighter, clearer texture as you switch to the higher register at b.9. Let the LH crotchets
'lead' through bb.10, 12, etc. with the syncopated RH line following smoothly. Give full
value to the crotchets on the 3rd beat of bb.13 and 14 (placing the turns *on* the beat) so

that you don't 'fall into' the 1st beat of the subsequent bars. Support the RH triplets through bb.15 and 16 with firm LH crotchet octaves on the 1st beat, and be sure to 'finish off' this first section with clear descending LH crotchets through b.18. Listen to the strong 'drone' effect of the lower LH sustained A's on the 2nd and 1st beat, alternately, of bb.19 – 22. Underpin the RH triplets through bb.33 – 6 with resonant LH minim octaves.

Trio

bb.39 – 88   The extraordinary, long minor Trio is commanding and declamatory. Strike off boldly with the LH minim octave, and define the RH dotted rhythms sharply over decisive LH octaves as the hands move dramatically apart in contrary motion through bb.39 – 40, 43 – 4 and 49 – 51. Be sure that you come cleanly *off* on the 3rd beat of bb.40 and 44, and then in b.50 on the other hand, *crescendo* resolutely through to the 1st beat of b.51. Then phrase the slurred 'answering' fragments (bb.41 – 2, 45 – 8, etc.) more yieldingly over smooth LH octaves. Ensure that the LH 'leads' from b.52, right through to the double bar. 'Lean' on the minim seconds on the 1st beat of bb.52 and 53, and phrase the RH fragments graciously. Then place the LH crotchet octaves clearly on the 1st beat of bb.54 – 6, and phrase the slurred RH thirds carefully as you *crescendo* towards b.57. Take care to keep steady here. Give firm 1st beats to bb.57 and 58, both in the LH minim octaves and with the RH thumb. Then articulate the treble fragments clearly and be sure to place the LH crotchet octaves firmly on the 3rd beats, keeping the RH upbeat sixths to bb.58 and 59 relatively light. Then let the LH 'go to' a firm B flat octave on the 1st beat of b.59. Be particularly careful to keep steady through bb.61 – 3 and 65 – 7. Lead off forcefully with the LH minim octaves here, and keep the RH dotted rhythms in place with steady LH crotchet octaves as you lead on down to the 1st beat of bb.63 and 67. Do feel that the RH dotted rhythm figures are fitting in with your steady LH octaves, and *not* the other way about. Here, as at bb.39 – 40 etc, do also feel the RH demisemiquavers as 'upbeats' to the subsequent dotted crotchets rather than as 'tail-ends' to the previous beats (see also Introduction).

No. 29 in E flat major
(Hob. XVI/45)

First movement – Moderato (7)

This is the most elaborate first movement so far encountered, and Haydn varies the subject matter of the exposition freely and characteristically in the recapitulation. The texture is refined, and there is a continuous flow of changing rhythmic patterns, but the overall effect is rather bland, and the movement seems long.

bb.1 – 18   The opening dotted rhythm figures of bb.1 and 2, with their elaborated versions in bb.5 and 6, have the character of a little oboe duet, and are answered by more flowing phrases, still with a precise two-part texture. Set an easy-moving but steady, very *moderato* crotchet pulse. Lead off from a clear quaver upbeat and time the RH line and the LH fragments with equal care, defining the dotted rhythms crisply. Be sure to come *off* in both hands after the 3rd beat of b.2 and to *feel* the silent 4th beat. Then phrase both the RH line from the upbeat to b.3, and the LH from the upbeat group to b.4 smoothly through to the 4th beat of b.4. Finish the RH phrase down to the quaver G on this 4th beat, and then show the last quaver of the bar clearly as the upbeat to b.5. Co-ordinate the demisemiquaver figures immaculately in both hands in b.6, feeling in each instance that these figures are 'going to' the quaver on the subsequent main beat. Place the LH quaver-crotchet fragments neatly as you shape the RH line smoothly from the upbeat to b.7 through to b.11. Then feel that the LH quavers briefly take over the 'lead' on the first two beats of b.11 ('going to' a strong crotchet E flat on the 3rd beat), with the RH offbeat quavers following evenly. Then 'take over' clearly with the RH again, on the 3rd beat of b.11 as you articulate the ascending broken chord semiquavers cleanly, and lead on with the RH through b.12. Place the RH quavers G and E flat clearly through the 3rd beat of b.12, and then 'lean' on the tied crotchet upbeat to b.13 as the LH imitates the RH semiquaver broken chord figure from the previous bar, rising towards a firm crotchet G on the 1st beat of b.13. Preserve a steady crotchet pulse through to b.19, keeping the RH figures in place with a steady LH through bb.13 – 15, and ensure that the LH 'leads' in a rhythmic sense from b.16 with the syncopated RH line following smoothly.

bb.19 – 44   Be sure to maintain an even tempo through the much more straightforward passage from b.19 – it is easy to find yourself getting faster here. Let the treble melody line sing freely over a quietly flowing Alberti accompaniment. 'Lead' with smooth even LH crotchets in b.26, with the RH offbeat semiquaver figures following evenly. 'Finish off' the RH phrase with a clear quaver B flat on the 3rd beat of b.27, over a firm LH crotchet, and then allow a tiny break as you leap up in a poised manner to start the new phrase clearly on the high quaver D. Similarly, show this figure 'entering' clearly on the 6th quaver pulse of bb.28 and 29. The slightly syncopating effect of these 'entries', together with the implied emphasis on the tied RH semiquaver upbeat to bb.28 – 30, on the tied quaver on the 2nd quaver pulse, and on the slurred quaver on the 4th quaver pulse, all create a complex rhythmic effect through these three bars. It is, therefore, vital that the LH remains perfectly steady. Be sure to bring the LH *off* on the quaver rest on the 4th beat of bb.27, 28 and 29 so that it 'comes in' again clearly with the upbeat quaver third to the subsequent bar. From the upbeat to b.31 (and 37) do not allow the steadiness of the three firm LH crotchet chords to be disrupted by the syncopated

RH turns (played approximately ⟨music notation⟩). Feel that the LH is 'leading', and

that the RH fits in with the LH crotchet pulse, and *not* the other way about. From the 3rd beat of b.37 let the RH melody line sing out buoyantly over an evenly pulsating Alberti LH. From the upbeat to b.43, support your precisely timed offbeat RH fragments with firm and rock-steady LH crotchet chords.

bb.45 – 96   Launch out boldly, into the more dramatic minor opening to the development from bb.45 – 50. Feel that the ornamented RH figures are 'going to' singing tied crotchets on the 3rd beat of b.45 and the 1st beat of b.46, etc. over steady but buoyant LH semiquavers. From b.50 the impetus seems to peter out, and the passage-work through the remainder of the development becomes repetitive and rather dull. Keep a steady crotchet pulse in the LH on the 2nd beat of bb.50 and 56, and on the 2nd and 4th beats of b.55, where the RH has dotted demisemiquaver rests. At bb.70 – 1 keep the ascending LH offbeat semiquaver figures in place with a steady and clearly 'leading' RH, and then in bb.72 – 4 let the minim chords in the *LH* give resonant support to the improvisatory RH ascending offbeat semiquaver figures.

Second movement – Andante (7)
This movement may seem dull at first, but its appeal grows with familiarity. Establish and maintain a tempo which moves, yet sounds leisured, allowing space to listen to the inflections of the curving semiquaver lines and to follow the expressive interplay between the hands.

bb.1 – 13   Lead in with a firm LH crotchet on the 1st beat of b.1, and follow the curves of the RH phrase smoothly through to b.4 over neatly shaped LH quaver fragments. Then let the LH broken chord semiquavers 'take over' from the RH crotchet on the 2nd beat of b.4, and go on down to a further firm crotchet on the 1st beat of b.5, ready to 'bring in' the RH again. Similarly, let the LH ascend to a firm crotchet D flat on the 1st beat of b.9, and then be sure to sustain the tied semiquaver upbeat to b.11 as the lower crotchet line leads on, with the RH offbeat semiquaver fragments following evenly.

bb.14 – 28   Let the ascending LH crotchet line 'lead' through b.14, with the RH offbeat semiquaver fragments following relatively lightly, and with the descending RH crotchets 'taking over' through b.15. Then when the LH has 'taken over' again in b.16, feel also that the RH semiquaver line is 'going towards' the RH slurred crotchet on the 1st beat of b.17, and similarly that the rising semiquavers in b.17 are 'going to' the slurred LH crotchet on the 1st beat of b.18, and so on, so that a continual onward movement is maintained between the hands. Listen to the warmly sustained RH chords through bb.21 – 2 while also shaping the LH semiquaver curves graciously. (The bracketed ties are not given in Henle.) Then sustain the lower LH dotted minims smoothly through bb.23 – 4 beneath the even inner LH crotchets as you listen to the chromatic inflections of the curving RH semiquavers. Let the RH tied minims sing from the 1st beat of bb.26 and 27 as you phrase the lower semiquaver lines smoothly up towards the 3rd beat of these bars (then feeling the three descending RH thirds as an upbeat group to b.27 and b.28). Then 'go to' and lean well upon the appoggiatura third on the 1st beat of b.28.

bb.29 – 73   From b.33 follow the minor-tinged interplay between the hands expressively, listening particularly to the more concentrated resonances of the 'duet' from the upbeat to b.37 through to b.39. Lead into this passage with a warm-toned LH tied crotchet upbeat to b.37. Then feel that the RH offbeat semiquaver fragment is 'going to' a resonant tied crotchet E natural on the 1st beat of b.37, with the LH semiquaver 'going to' the A flat on the 2nd beat, and so on. Again at bb.41 – 3 shape the upper lines smoothly over the sustained lower LH notes. Then give resonant LH dotted minim chords on the 1st beats of bb.44 – 7 to support the improvisatory RH figuration. Keep a steady and sustained crotchet pulse in the RH at bb.63 – 4, keeping the LH offbeat ornamented semiquaver figures relatively light. (As at bb.21 – 2, Henle does not give the bracketed ties here.)

Finale – Allegro di molto (8)*

This brilliant movement needs to be taken at a spanking tempo. It can, however, easily degenerate into rhythmic chaos unless the player maintains a firm grasp of the crotchet pulse. Set a smart but realistic 3/4 therefore, bearing in mind the Scarlattian repeated note patterns (bb.20 – 7) and the awkward semiquaver passage-work (bb.38 – 46).

bb.1 – 19   Lead off confidently with a strong LH minim third on the 1st beat of b.1, and feel that the LH is 'leading' through to b.5. Articulate the slurred RH quavers busily through bb.1 and 3, and then place the LH quavers firmly in bb.2 and 4, observing the rests precisely, and keeping the RH offbeat quavers (in b.2), and the slurred semiquavers (in b.4) relatively light. Let the RH semiquavers in b.5 'go to' a firm minim B flat on the 1st beat of b.6, and then articulate the LH figure neatly to 'go' in turn to a firm crotchet E flat on the 1st beat of b.7. From bb.7 – 10 place the LH detached crotchets clearly as you 'rattle out' the RH semiquaver passage-work. Let the RH scale figure descend towards a clear quaver G on the 1st beat of b.11, with the *LH* scale then ascending to lead off again with a firm crotchet E flat on the 1st beat of b.12, and feel the slightly syncopating effect of the slurred RH quavers entering on the offbeat in bb.12 and 13. 'Pluck' the LH *staccato* crotchets in as lively and rhythmic a manner as possible from bb.14 – 18, feeling that the LH is crossing back and forth in a series of wide 'arcs' (rather than in isolated plonks) and keeping the RH offbeat semiquavers again relatively light.

bb.20 – 29   'Leading' emphatically again with the LH, let the LH crotchet octaves rise vigorously through bb.20 and 22 towards the 1st beats of bb.21 and 23 as you 'pick out' the repeated RH semiquavers as sharply as possible. Then be careful to keep a steady crotchet pulse through bb.21 and 23. Do not spoil the effect of the upward leap in b.24 by taking the C with the LH. 'Go down' from the previous bar to a *strong* RH semiquaver C on the 1st beat supported by a firm LH minim third, and leap up to the E flat, without panic, allowing the natural break. Then in bb.25 – 7, keep the difficult RH repeated note figures in control with firmly placed LH chords. Both here and in bb.20 and 22 you will probably find that the old convention of changing fingers on repeated notes serves best (see Haydn's fingering in b.20), although there is no need to feel bound by it. In bb.28 – 9, through the alternating LH/RH semiquavers (another brilliant Scarlattian effect), keep steady by lightly marking the crotchet pulse in the *LH* (i.e. on the B flat, G and E flat in b.28, and so on).

bb.30 – 49   It is easy to come unstuck in bb.30 – 3. Let the RH scale take off from a *firm* detached LH crotchet on the 1st beat of b.30, and run up in a little *crescendo* towards a *firm* quaver on the 3rd beat of the bar. Then let the LH offbeat broken octave figure 'go down to' a *firm* detached crotchet on the 1st beat of b.31, and so on. Run up the scale towards a ringing quaver D on the 1st beat of b.34, and then be sure to *wait* and come in again precisely on the 1st beat of b.35. Be sure that the LH upbeat quaver chord figures 'go to' firm crotchet thirds on the 1st beats of bb.36 and 38. From bb.39 – 47 steadiness depends upon an absolutely rhythmic LH. The RH is far from easy. Practise it carefully alone, then practise *slowly* 'hands together', always feeling that your lively but absolutely steady LH is 'leading' in a rhythmic sense, and *not* the other way about. Be particularly careful to show that the rising LH upbeat quavers 'go to' firm crotchets on the 1st beat of bb.40 and 45, and to feel the 2nd beat of bb.39 and 44 securely in the *RH*, where the LH has a quaver rest. Then steady yourself on the 1st beat of b.47 to execute the little figures in thirds and sixths with neat formality, and 'lean' warmly on the minim appoggiaturas on the 1st beat of b.49, as you end the section in perfect time.

bb.50 – 136   Lead off again vigorously with the LH from b.50. From b.62 Haydn typically, and without warning, veers off into a more serious *legato* passage in the minor.

Do not, however, allow the rhythmic impetus to slacken. 'Go to' and 'lean' upon a warm-toned tied crotchet B flat on the 1st beat of b.62, and then continue to feel that you are 'going to' the slurred RH crotchets on the 1st beats of bb.63 – 7, supported by even, not spiky, LH repeated quavers. Support the descending RH scales through bb.68 – 9 with a strong, sustained A flat major chord, and let the RH plunge down to a resonant low tied A flat on the 1st beat of b.70. Build up the tone resolutely through bb.70 – 5, ready to strike off again with maximum vitality with the LH octaves at b.76. Steady yourself again on the 1st beat of b.81 (as at b.47) and play the little figures in bb.81 and 82 with military precision, sustaining the treble tied A flat warmly through to the 1st beat of b.83. Then let the RH thirds 'open out' from b.84 over the sustained LH B flat octave, and *crescendo* resonantly downwards, ready to set off into the recapitulation at b.86. Take plenty of time to 'lean' on the appoggiatura chord on the 1st beat of the last bar (as shown in the Vienna Urtext Edition) before the final spread chord.

No. 30 in D major
(Hob. XVI/19)

First movement – Moderato (8)*

As has already been said, it is impossible to point to a 'typical' Sonata by Haydn, or even to typical features. But this first movement, with its rugged textures, its bold orchestral registration and its inexorable rhythmic drive, represents a real landmark – a point of departure for the extraordinary series of adventures that constitute Haydn's mature keyboard works. Note the 'Moderato' and set a very measured crotchet pulse; too fast a tempo will undermine the imposing character of the opening theme.

bb.1 – 18   Play the first three bars with military precision. Lead off from a precisely timed demisemiquaver upbeat and 'go to' a singing tied crotchet F sharp on the 1st beat of bb.1 and 2. 'Come in' equally precisely with the LH on the 2nd quaver pulse of bb.1 and 2 beneath the tied F sharp, and hold the sharp RH dotted rhythms in place with rock-steady LH quavers. 'Go up to', and come cleanly *off* the detached quavers in both hands on the 2nd and 4th beats of b.3. Let the RH melodic line 'swoop' down from the clear dotted crotchet F sharp on the 1st beat of b.4, and up again to the G on the 1st beat of b.5 in continuous 'arcs' (rather than in a series of 'plonks') over even LH offbeat repeated quavers (giving the effect of low drumbeats). Continue this melody line sonorously down into the low RH register in b.8, over a continuingly carefully placed LH. (Treat the RH grace notes in bb.6 and 7 like not too 'clipped' acciaccaturas.) Give the appoggiatura on the 3rd beat of b.8 a crotchet value and *feel* the rest on the 8th quaver pulse of the bar, ready to lead off vigorously again with a perfectly timed upbeat to b.9. Keep the RH triplets in place in bb.10 – 11 with the same steady LH quavers, and in bb.12 and 13 time your demisemiquaver scales clearly and accurately to fit in with the LH 'drumbeats'. Be very precise with the jolting demisemiquaver figures in bb.16 and 17, 'snapping' them smartly *against* (and *not* anticipating) the rock-steady detached LH quaver chords. Make an overall slurred effect with these RH figures, bringing the hand *off* each semiquaver in a biting *staccato* (see Haydn's *staccato* marks in b.24). 'Go to' and give full value to the strong spread dominant chords (and crotchet rest) in b.18.

bb.19 – 25   In bb.19 and 20 feel the strong, tightly controlled rhythmic drive of the slurred RH demisemiquavers on the 1st beats, and the 'stabbing' reiterated *staccato* semiquavers accompanying the fierce descending LH *staccato* quavers. 'Pluck' these LH quavers with the utmost vigour, with the feeling of 'going to' the crotchets on the 1st beat of bb.20 and 21. Then from the middle of b.21 show the slightly syncopating effect of the RH slurred semiquaver 'upbeats' over the strong LH octaves as the hands move outwards in contrary motion. The mood changes dramatically from bar to bar here; exploit the sudden tragic quality of the slurred semiquavers in b.23 (over steady LH quaver thirds), and then 'snap' the demisemiquaver figures vigorously again as you descend in *crescendo* towards the resonant, sustained bass octave F natural which supports the improvisatory RH broken octaves through b.25. 'Open out' these broken octaves in an expansive curve up to, and down from the C natural on the 3rd beat of the bar.

bb.26 – 42   Resume the fierce rhythmic drive in b.26, on towards b.30. This time keep the reiterated quavers going tautly in the LH as you 'pluck' the RH quaver figure. 'Finish off' the LH, to a strong quaver E on the 2nd beat of b.30, and then time the alternating RH demisemiquaver figures and LH quaver chords immaculately and with perfect clarity, feeling the high-pitched exuberance of this passage.

Control the RH as it descends through b.32, with precisely placed LH quaver chords and octaves. Then from the middle of b.33 Haydn 'retracts', typically, into lighter and more formal passage-work. Place the RH figures neatly as the LH swings into triplets, without altering your crotchet pulse. Through b.38, control the descending RH triplets with carefully placed LH quaver octaves (as at b.32). From b.41 it is effective to make a *diminuendo* to end this section in *piano*. Time the RH figures in immaculate cross-rhythm without disturbing your LH sextuplets, and place the low RH bass A's with neat finality.

bb.43 – 102   Haydn pursues the vigorous figures of the exposition with relentless and Beethovenian energy in his splendid development section. Exploit his skilfully calculated resonances here to the full, maintaining an iron control of the crotchet pulse, and keeping the sound sharp and clear, never degenerating into coarseness or thumping. Be particularly careful to keep a steady crotchet pulse as the broken octaves descend through the second half of b.48, and feel that you are 'going to' a strong 1st beat of b.49. Observe the RH quaver rest precisely on the 2nd beat of bb.49 – 52, and then feel the subsequent RH quaver third as the 'upbeat' to the 3rd beat of each of these bars. From the middle of b.53 (savouring the clash of the B and C natural), support the stabbing ascending RH figures with firm LH chords descending in a resonant *crescendo*. Be particularly careful to keep a steady crotchet pulse from the middle of b.56 as the RH triplets plunge down over a strong sustained bass tied F sharp towards the astonishing confrontation of the E sharp and G on the 3rd beat of b.57. 'Lean' well on these tied RH crotchets from the 3rd beat of b.57 over the continuing stabbing figuration in the LH. Feel that each of these LH semiquaver figures 'goes to' a *firm* quaver (on the 4th beat of b.57, the 2nd beat of b.58, etc.) beneath each tied RH crotchet, as Haydn drives relentlessly onwards. Be particularly sure that the LH 'goes to' this firm quaver on the 2nd beat of b.59, and on the 4th beat of b.60, to steady yourself for the upward leap in the RH. 'Take over' with clear RH sixths from the upbeat to b.62 and *crescendo* indomitably towards b.64, observing the slurred 'upbeat' effect in the LH semiquavers (as in the RH in bb.21 – 2). Articulate the RH thirds strongly over resolute bass octaves from the 3rd beat of b.64, and proceed from the middle of b.66 in an even more jolting, Beethovenian manner than at bb.16 – 17, as you move towards the start of the recapitulation. Haydn's energy continues to spill over. At bb.74 – 8 he extends the material of bb.6 – 7 to a further three bars, and adds further bite to bb.79 – 82 (compare with bb.19 – 22).

Second movement – Andante (6)(O)*

This is a fascinating movement, perhaps more suitable for older players. Its melody leaps between bass and treble, with an equally mobile LH, sometimes supplying pointed punctuating fragments (as from bb.1 – 8), sometimes accompanying in persistent repeated chords or single notes entering on the offbeat (as from bb.13 – 17 and 21 – 36, etc.) In its spare texture and in its very individual motion, this movement recalls Scarlatti in some of his slower 'processional' Sonatas. Set a steady 3/4 pulse that feels unhurried and yet 'moves', and maintain the utmost clarity of line in either hand throughout.

bb.1 – 20   Feel that the LH in b.1 (and 5) rises from bass to treble in a wide 'arc' rather than as widely separated single notes. Then place the LH crotchets like detached 'steps', observing the rests precisely. Shape the RH figures neatly, entering clearly on the offbeat in bb.1 – 3, and playing the repeated quavers in a 'speaking', semi-*staccato*, not spiky, style. Let the LH leap up to 'lean' on the slurred crotchet third on the 2nd beat of b.5 as the RH phrase 'starts again', and similarly 'lean' on the slurred thirds on the 2nd beat of bb.6 and 7. Let the unison figures enter clearly on the 2nd quaver pulse of b.9 in a new, more pompous tone, and *crescendo* downwards towards a resonant RH dotted minim A on the 1st beat of b.11. Let this A, and the spread chord in b.12, sing out over vigorously 'plucked' LH *staccato* quavers. Then keep the LH accompanying offbeat chords steady, though with an 'ongoing' feeling, and as *legato* as possible, beneath the RH melody line from b.13. This is a good chance to learn the skill of playing repeated chords or notes (as in the LH, bb.13 – 17, or 21 onwards) as smoothly and evenly as possible. Feel that your hand is 'rooted' in the keyboard, and raise the keys as little, and as late as possible, so that the sound is almost continuous, creating an even, pulsating, rather than 'spiky' effect. Keep the RH semiquavers steady through bb.18 – 19, observing the details of articulation scrupulously, over a carefully placed LH.

bb.21 – 49 Then shape the wide spanning and resonant low-slung RH melody smoothly from the upbeat to b.21 through to b.33 over continuingly steady and even LH quavers. Keep a steady crotchet pulse as you define the RH dotted rhythms sharply from the 2nd beat of b.33 over persistent LH repeated quavers through bb.33 and 35, 'going to' a firm LH crotchet on the 1st beat of bb.34 and 36. Feel that the RH is 'leading' clearly through bb.37 and 38, with the LH detached offbeat quavers following steadily, and 'going to' a firm bass crotchet on the 1st beat of b.39. From b.41 feel wide 'arcs' again, this time in both hands, preserving perfect rhythmic continuity as the lines of both hands swoop up and down between the treble and low registers. From b.47 give the low RH thirds and sixths a 'horn-like' quality over steady bass 'drumbeats' as you end the section in perfect time.

bb.50 – 115 From b.59 keep a steady crotchet pulse, and sustain the dotted minims warmly as the hands 'answer' each other evenly in alternating quaver and semiquaver lines. Feel that the RH thirds are 'going to' a warmly sustained tied dotted minim third on the 1st beat of b.60, and then that the LH semiquavers in b.60 are 'going to' the dotted minim on the 1st beat of b.61, and so on. In b.64 do not allow the steadiness of the LH crotchet chords to be disrupted by the RH syncopated turns. From b.67 create a smooth and resonant low RH line above the plucked LH quavers and listen carefully as the RH 'divides' into two lines from the 3rd beat of b.70, over even LH octaves. 'Draw out' through b.111 towards the pause on the dominant. A short cadenza is indicated here, for which a suggested example is given in the Vienna Urtext Edition. It is then effective to *diminuendo* without *rallentando* towards a *pianissimo* ending.

Finale – Allegro assai ((7)*

Here Haydn is at his most impish and racy. There are twelve sections, each repeated, and each taking over from the previous section on the upbeat in a breathless chase. Having created a 'norm' with three sections of eight bars each, Haydn adds to the fun by throwing in extra phrases in the fourth and eighth sections. Aim for maximum brightness and clarity, and set a lively but realistic crotchet pulse, bearing in mind the semiquaver passage-work from b.45.

bb.1 – 44 Let the LH 'take over' from the detached RH upbeat, to lead off boldly from the 1st beat of b.1 (as again at b.9), with lively, detached quavers, with the RH quavers, similarly articulated, following steadily and relatively lightly. Then articulate the RH fragments neatly (bb.4, 7 – 8, and 11 – 12) over firm, supporting LH crotchets. Be careful to 'finish off' the RH phrase neatly with the quaver A on the 2nd beat of bb.4 and 12, so that you show the last quaver of the bar clearly as the upbeat to the subsequent phrase. Show the change to the lower, minor register with stronger, more strutting *staccato* unison quavers from the upbeat to b.17. Place firm RH minim thirds on the 1st beat of bb.21 and 22 over vigorously 'plucked' LH quavers, and then 'take over' again with the LH octave on the 1st beat of b.23. Be sure to 'lead' with the detached RH thirds through bb.27 and 29 – 30, but let the LH 'take over' with a firm crotchet octave B flat on the 1st beat of b.31 (and treat bb.33 – 5 similarly).

From bb.45 – 60 'rattle out' the RH semiquavers over vigorous and steady
bb.45 – 125 LH detached crotchets, feeling that, in a rhythmic sense, the LH is
emphatically 'leading'. Conversely, from b.61, keep the LH tremolo semiquavers in place with a steady *RH*, and then from the upbeat to b.64 control the *RH*
semiquavers with lively but steady *LH* quavers (and so on through to b.84). Again from
b.85 underpin your RH scale figures with clear LH detached crotchets. From the upbeat
to b.101 do not 'plonk', but rather 'pluck' the detached octaves as vitally as possible,
'leading', of course, with the LH from the 1st beat of b.101. In the last section, practise
the Alberti LH until it is perfectly clear and steady. Then when you put 'hands together'
ensure that the crotchet pulse is not disrupted by the dashing syncopated effect of the
RH slurred upbeat octaves. Take care to feel the *2nd* beat of these bars accurately in the
LH, where the RH has a quaver rest. Steady yourself by 'going to' and 'leaning' well upon
the slurred RH octaves on the 1st beat of bb.112 and 120, and be sure that the LH comes
off on the 4th quaver pulse of these bars, ready for the slurred RH quaver upbeat to lead
onwards. End with vigorous clear *forte* chords.

No. 31 in A flat major
(Hob. XVI/46)

First movement – Allegro moderato (8)*
This is another fine Sonata. The expansive, almost fantasia-like first movement opens
with a broad and rather stately melody. Set a sensible crotchet pulse, bearing in mind the
extensive sextuplet figuration to come. The right tempo will be one at which the various
rhythmic figures of bb.9 – 11 sound spacious and unhurried, but at which the sextuplet
passage from b.18 etc. flows easily without sounding sticky.

bb.1 – 17 Lead off with a singing ornamented RH minim, and phrase the melody line
in a broad overall curve through bb.1 – 3, over evenly placed LH offbeat
quaver chords. 'Finish off' the first phrase neatly on the 3rd beat of b.3,
and be sure to *feel* the crotchet rest on the 4th beat. Then in b.4 follow the line of the
sextuplet scale smoothly as it plunges down boldly and characteristically towards a singing
tied crotchet F on the 3rd beat, and carry your phrase on resonantly through to the 2nd
beat of b.6. Start the new phrase clearly on the 3rd beat of b.6, and then be careful to
preserve the sense of your steady crotchet pulse through the curving sextuplets in b.7. Start
a new phrase clearly again on the 1st beat of b.9, keeping your ornamented line in place
with continuingly evenly placed LH chords. 'Take over' with the LH, with a firm chord
on the 1st beat of b.13, and support the RH offbeat sextuplet figures through bb.13 – 14
with clear and accurately placed LH crotchet chords. Then on the 1st beat of b.15, 'take
over' with the *RH* and place the RH quaver thirds perfectly evenly (but slightly detached),
keeping the bass triplet broken octaves relatively light as you move in a purposeful *crescendo*
towards the pauses at b.17. 'Feel' the crotchet pulse through the rests and pauses, as you
poise yourself to give a firm 'lead' with the treble third on the 1st beat of b.18.

bb.18 – 23 Guard against unsteadiness as you follow the curving arabesques through
bb.18 – 19 by 'feeling' the triplets within the sextuplet groups (though without
obvious accents). 'Lean' on the RH third and second on the 1st and 2nd beats
of bb.18 and 19, and let the rising LH sextuplets 'go to' a firm crotchet E flat on the 3rd
beat of these bars (and similarly let the treble sextuplets 'go to' the crotchet third on the
1st beat of b.19). Support the sextuplets through b.20 with firm LH crotchet chords, and
through b.21 with steady inner LH quavers over sustained lower minims. Feel that the

LH is 'going down to' a resonant semibreve chord on the 1st beat of b.22, as the RH semiquavers 'open out' towards the trill and pause over the dominant 7th chord at b.23. 'Lean' on the minim appoggiatura and start the trill just after the 3rd beat, ending, and

waiting on the 4th beat: Support your RH with a

resonant, sustained LH chord.

bb.24 – 38   Then feel the surprise of the minim E natural on the 1st beat of b.24, and later, of the brush with the minor in b.31. Between these two points (bb.24 – 31), the mood changes, typically, from bar to bar: suddenly serious in b.24, perky in the second half of b.25 (treat the grace notes like acciaccaturas here), urbane in b.26, and so on. Let the syncopated RH line move smoothly over even LH crotchets through b.28, and articulate the ornamented quavers springily through b.29 as you rise towards a singing tied crotchet on the 1st beat of b.30. From the middle of b.32 let the airy sextuplet figuration flow and curve easily within a steady crotchet pulse with the help of a neatly placed LH. End the section with immaculately placed quaver chord figures, from the upbeat to b.38. The inexperienced pianist can find this movement difficult to hold together. The unifying sense of a steady crotchet pulse is all important, and must be felt unfailingly throughout, particularly through the long improvisatory passage in the development (bb.46 – 64).

bb.39 – 112   Practise bb.46 – 8 carefully 'hands separately', and then, keeping a rock-steady crotchet pulse, make sure that the hands are perfectly co-ordinated. Always feel that , in a rhythmic sense, the *quaver* fragments (rather than the semiquavers) 'lead' in either hand, i.e. the RH quavers 'le: · ' on the 1st beat of b.46, and the LH quavers on the 3rd and 4th beats, and so on. From b.49 again ensure that whichever hand has the quaver line takes the lead, i.e. the RH in b.49 and the LH from b.50, always keeping the offbeat triplet semiquaver figures relatively light. Take particular care to remain steady through bb.55 – 6, leading firmly with the LH in the first half of each bar, and 'taking over' clearly with the RH on the 3rd beat. There are many ways of shaping the dynamics in this long Bachian passage (bb.49 – 64), and you should follow your natural inclinations. It can, for example, be equally effective either to *crescendo* or to *diminuendo* towards the pause in b.64, providing that either course is followed with conviction. The essential is that the maximum rhythmic tension is generated by the maintenance of a tautly controlled crotchet pulse. From b.65 Haydn leads back to the recapitulation through a long, ornamented, cadenza-like passage. Lead up resolutely to the dramatic pauses at bb.69 and 72, and take care to place the LH slurred quaver octaves clearly and steadily beneath the tied crotchet (F) on the 3rd beat of b.70, and the 1st beat of b.73, with the feeling of 'going to' a firm bass octave on the 1st beat of b.71 and the 3rd beat of b.73. Then from the 3rd beat of b.73, lead back purposefully and very rhythmically to the start of the recapitulation at b.78. Haydn has still more surprises up his sleeve, notably the striking minor expansion of the opening motif from the 3rd beat of b.83. Then at bb.98 – 9 there is the quirky version of bb.24 – 5 in the low bassoon-like register, with a sudden two-octave leap into the treble on the 2nd quaver pulse of b.100. From bb.89 – 91 be careful to keep your persistent LH repeated quavers perfectly steady beneath the active RH offbeat triplet semiquavers. Avoid collapse at the beginning of b.94 by 'going to' a *firm* RH semiquaver and LH crotchet chord on the 1st beat, and then allow the necessary natural break as you leap up without panic to the high B flat. This splendid movement, rich in harmonic adventure and tonal colour, will repay the closest study.

Second movement — Adagio (8)*

This magnificent movement is remarkable for its concentrated part-writing, and arresting chromatic progressions; and once again Haydn recalls Scarlatti in the freedom of his RH melodic line, with atmospheric effects of trills and arabesques 'in imitation of twittering birds', as Eva Badura-Skoda has remarked.† The slower the pulse that you can sustain while still giving the feeling of movement, the finer the movement will sound; the sextuplets in bb.13, 14, etc, and the scales in double thirds (bb.21 and 24 – 5) must flow easily and without hurry.

bb.1 – 12
The first twelve bars (and the passage following the double bar), Bachian in feeling, have a rapt and pervasive stillness. Enter with a sustained 'doubled' D flat on the 1st beat of b.1, and shape the curving quaver line, and the sustained lower line through to b.4 with gliding smoothness. 'Start again' with another resonant D flat on the 1st beat of b.5, and enter evenly with the treble line on the 4th quaver pulse of the bar. (Practise not only 'hands separately', but also *parts* separately.) Sustain the lower LH dotted minims warmly through bb.9 and 10 as the expressive treble and inner LH fragments move evenly inwards in contrary motion; and continue to listen to the lower LH line through b.11 as it ascends towards the dotted crotchet E flat on the 1st beat of b.12. 'Lean' a little on the treble D flat in b.11, and listen to the lines of this descending scale towards the crotchet E flat on the 2nd beat of b.12 against the inflections of the lower parts. Then let the three LH thirds give a clear 'upbeat' lead towards a resonant A flat crotchet third on the 1st beat of b.13.

bb.13 – 28
From b.13 when the 'bird' trills enter, do ensure that you maintain a steady crotchet pulse. In b.13 let your LH crotchet chords give a firm foundation for the RH trills and scale, and then from b.14, let your evenly sustained LH lines continue to give resonant and stable support to the RH. There are various possible

interpretations of the RH trills here. In my view the short shake

is more atmospheric than the tamer-sounding turn effect 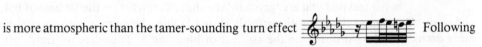 Following

the trills in b.13, let the soothing scale flow down easily from the 3rd beat towards clear crotchets (E flat and D flat) on the 1st and 2nd beats of b.14. Similarly let the next scale flow down to clear *inner* crotchets on the 1st and 2nd beats of b.15, and so on. Take care to keep these crotchets (on the the 1st and 2nd beats of bb.14, 15, etc.) steady above or beneath the offbeat trill (as the case may be) in perfect co-ordination with the LH. These bars are far from easy — listen acutely to the balance of the voices, and realize that absolute steadiness is vital. Practise again not only 'hands separately', but also *parts* separately, at first without the trills. When you put 'hands together' feel throughout the passage that the RH is fitting in with your imperturbably steady LH, and *not* the other way about. Rise in a *crescendo* with a singing treble line over a sustained LH through bb.18 and 19 towards a resonant spread chord on the 2nd beat of b.20, observing the pause and rest. Then let the RH scales in thirds descend easily from a singing tied crotchet third on the 1st beat of bb.21 and 25 over carefully placed LH octaves, and let the LH 'lead' smoothly through bb.22 – 4 and 26 – 7 with the syncopated RH thirds following smoothly. 'Go to' and 'lean' well on the appoggiatura chord on the 1st beat of b.28, and then spread the A flat chord freely on the 2nd beat.

†*Keyboard Music*, edited by Denis Matthews.

From b.29 follow the breath-catching inflections of the part-writing with
bb.29 – 80   an acute ear. Do ensure that all inner as well as outer tied notes are sustained
over the bar lines. Listen particularly carefully to the movement of the inner
RH line from bb.39 – 43, beneath the sustained treble line. In b.39 be sure to sustain the
treble minim F through the 1st and 2nd beats as the inner part 'crosses' up to the high
B flat. Change fingers (3 – 1) on this long F and take the inner quaver D flat on the 2nd
beat (and also perhaps the preceding quaver C) with the LH. At bb.46 and 48 'take over'
the dotted quavers on the 2nd beats (A flat and G flat respectively) silently from the RH
with the LH thumb, so that you can better poise the high triplet demisemiquaver figures,
with a clear yet distant effect. 'Draw out' a little through b.50 towards the pauses in b.51,
picking up the tempo on the upbeat to b.52. Time the upward arpeggio of b.60 (and 64)
to arrive on the upper F precisely on the 2nd beat of the bar (and similarly the arpeggio
in b.63, to arrive on the F on the *1st* beat of b.64). Phrase the LH lines smoothly and
warmly through bb.66 – 70 beneath the offbeat treble broken octave figures, ensuring that
the inner LH tied crotchets sing over the bar lines. Take time to 'point' the mysterious
interrupted cadence at bb.71 – 2, and then give full significance to the remarkable harmonic
progressions towards the pause at b.77, timing the reiterated three-quaver/crotchet figures,
so characteristic of Haydn, with quiet deliberation. Listen particularly to the rising inner
LH line from bb.75 – 7. A short cadenza is intended at b.77, and also, according to the
Henle Edition, at bb.20, 51 and 59. A suggested example is given for b.77 in the Vienna
Urtext Edition.

Finale – Presto (7)

This jolly, bustling movement is not altogether easy to control. Do not attempt to play
it faster than you can manage with safety and perfect clarity. It is essential to establish
and maintain a secure crotchet pulse from the first note to the last.

Lead off from a clear quaver upbeat and then feel that the semiquavers of
bb.1 – 37   b.1 are 'going to' a firm quaver appoggiatura on the 1st beat of b.2; then
in b.3 feel that you are 'going to' the slurred crotchet on the 1st beat of b.4,
and so on. Do support the RH with perfectly clear LH lines, being careful to sustain the
inner dotted crotchets properly on the 1st beat of bb.2 and 3. Take care to 'finish off'
the first subphrase cleanly in both hands with the quavers on the 2nd beat of b.2 so that
you start the next subphrase clearly on the quaver upbeat to b.3. Similarly, end the next
subphrase (or first overall four-bar phrase) clearly with the RH quaver C on the 2nd beat
of b.4, over the LH crotchet, so that you can leap up neatly to the high quaver upbeat
to b.5. Then give a firm RH lead with resonant minims on the 1st beat of bb.9 and 10,
letting the offbeat LH fragments follow neatly, and then similarly lead firmly with the
LH crotchets from bb.11 – 15. Let the RH scale descend through b.16 over firm LH crotchet
octaves, to end with a cheerful 'plonk' on the 1st beat of b.17. From the upbeat to b.18,
keep the RH semiquaver figures steady with neatly placed, detached LH quaver figures.
Take care to 'finish off' these LH quavers cleanly in b.19 (and particularly in b.21 so that
you *feel* the rest on the 2nd beat, poising yourself to lead on with the RH upbeat to b.22).
Give firm LH crotchet chords on the 1st beat of bb.22 and 24, and time the subsequent
LH quaver sixth and fifth chords precisely. Support the RH scales in bb.26 and 27 with
resonant LH minim chords. Then from the upbeat to b.30 'rattle out' the RH semiquavers
gaily over rock-steady but lively detached LH quavers.

From b.46 give a strong lead with the LH minim chords (showing the change
bb.38 – 143   from minims to crotchets at b.53), and conversely with the *RH* crotchets
from b.57, in both cases letting the offbeat semiquaver figures follow evenly
and brightly. From the upbeat to b.69, continuing through the long sequential passage

from the upbeat to b.73, 'rattle out' the RH semiquavers again over buoyant detached LH quavers. Then show the change of pattern clearly in the LH at b.82 to 'drone-like' lower crotchets (on the dominant) and offbeat inner quavers. 'Lean' on these lower LH crotchets, and keep the offbeat quavers short and relatively light, or you will collapse here! From b.120 articulate the curving lines of RH semiquavers cleanly but smoothly over firm and evenly sustained lower LH minims and even and steady, yet 'ongoing' LH inner repeated quavers. A *diminuendo* from b.138, towards a *pianissimo* ending is more stylish than a *crescendo* to a *forte.* Keep your LH tremolo very steady as you articulate each RH fragment more quietly, but with perfect clarity.

No. 32 in G minor
(Hob. XVI/44)

First movement – Moderato (8)

Set against the splendid adventures of the first movement of Nos. 30, 31 and 33, this movement may at first seem rather pedantic and finicky. The scale is smaller, the grain finer, and its expression is rather inward-looking, even secret. With its variety of textures and rhythmic figures it provides an exacting test of rhythmic poise.

bb.1 – 4   Set an easy-moving, but very measured crotchet pulse, taking into account the demisemiquaver scales and flourishes (bb.6 – 8, 13 – 14, etc.). Do take time to study the details of the first four bars carefully 'hands separately'. Lead in from a clear RH triplet semiquaver upbeat, and let your four quavers descend in immaculate time towards a 'lean' on the slurred crotchet on the 3rd beat of b.1. (These four quavers should be played in a detached, semi-staccato style, here and at bb.31, 46, 47 and 52. At bb.33 and 35, however, note that they are slurred. At b.3, and at b.48, both in the RH and then in the lower LH line, they could be either detached, *legato* or slurred, since Haydn's intention is not clear.) Slur the quaver couplet neatly on the 1st beat of b.2, and then 'lean' again on the slurred crotchet on the 3rd beat. Practise the LH with equal care. Note particularly the implied emphasis on the inner crotchet A on the 6th quaver pulse of b.1. When you put 'hands together' be sure to place the LH quaver thirds precisely on the 1st and 2nd beats of b.1 beneath the descending RH quavers, and then to place the LH detached crotchets securely on the 1st and 2nd beats of b.2. 'Finish off' neatly in both hands on the quavers on the 4th beat of b.2 so that the RH can lead off clearly with the triplet upbeat to b.3. Feel the implied emphasis on the treble, and LH tied crotchets on the 2nd beat of b.3, as the RH quavers descend into the inner line. Then detach the quaver chords neatly in b.4, 'going to' clear unison crotchets on the 3rd beat. Be sure to *feel* the quaver rest on the 4th beat, as you poise yourself to lead on with the triplet upbeat to b.5.

bb.5 – 14   The little section from the upbeat to b.5 acts as a linking passage, leading to the new melody starting on the 3rd beat of b.6. 'Lean' upon this ornamented dotted crotchet (C) then feel that the upbeat demisemiquavers are 'going to' a singing tied crotchet on the 1st beat of b.7, and so on. Keep this curving ornamented line in place with immaculately placed LH offbeat chords. Go very *legato* from the 3rd beat of b.10, listening carefully to the sustained LH lines, and with the feeling of 'drawing out' a little through the second half of b.11 towards b.12. Then pick up the tempo from the upbeat to b.13, and 'flick' each rapid descending arpeggio figure lightly and clearly down to the LH quaver B flat on the subsequent 1st or 3rd beats. Keep the LH quavers perfectly steady, feeling the implied syncopating 'lean' in *both* hands on the *2nd* and *6th quaver* pulses of bb.13 and 14. Take time to absorb this rhythmic effect in *slow* practice.

From the upbeat to b.15 follow the two sustained LH lines smoothly and
bb.15 – 30   evenly. Let the RH line, curving and flowing easily above, fit in with the
LH, and not the other way about. Then let the RH line 'take over' from the 3rd
beat of b.17, and sing freely above the LH offbeat rising semiquaver figures. In b.19 feel
the implied 'lean' on the tied RH second quaver B flat, and then come *off* cleanly in both
hands on the 4th beat so that you *feel* the quaver rest. Then play the little phrase from
the upbeat to b.20 in a rather 'throwaway' fashion, and 'finish off' the LH neatly on
the 4th beat of b.20 ready to lead off again with the RH quaver upbeat to b.21. 'Lean'
on the slurred RH sixths or thirds on the 1st and 2nd beats of bb.21 and 22 feeling that
you are 'going to' the dotted quaver on the 3rd beats. Then be sure to 'lead' with the
detached LH quavers from the 3rd beat of b.24, and with the slurred LH quaver thirds
in b.25, placing the detached reiterated RH semiquavers relatively lightly. Take particular
care to play the LH semiquavers clearly and steadily through the first half of b.27 – it
is easy here for the RH offbeat semiquavers to get too loud, and to 'take over', with a
consequent collapse of rhythm and balance. 'Lean' on the syncopated RH tied sixth on
the upbeat to b.29 and on the slurred crotchet sixth on the 4th quaver pulse of b.29 over
precisely placed detached LH crotchet B flats. Then lead into b.30 from the upbeat with
smooth LH thirds, with the syncopated RH fragment following evenly.

Exploit the improvisatory character of the development section to the full.
bb.31 – 77   'Lean' on the LH tied crotchet on the 2nd beat of bb.33 and 35 beneath
the sustained RH lines, and then let the semiquavers curve freely upwards,
towards the 1st beat of bb.34 and 36. Meanwhile, feeling that the treble line is 'carrying
on' from the LH, 'lean' similarly on the RH tied quaver upbeat to bb.34 and 36, and
listen to the RH semiquavers curving up to the high crotchet on the 3rd beat of these two
bars. Make a dramatic *crescendo* up to the high E flat on the 3rd beat of b.38, supported
by firmly placed LH offbeat quaver chords. Let the reiterated treble figures flow smoothly
and expressively through bb.39 – 42 over neatly shaped LH offbeat semiquaver figures.
Make the most of the demisemiquaver flourishes in b.45, going up to a dramatic pause
on the 4th beat. Bb.48 – 51 are not easy to manage, and careful *slow* and rhythmic practice
will be needed to achieve clarity and steadiness in the part-writing. Be particularly careful
to keep the triplet/quaver fragment going on in perfect time from the upbeat to b.49 in
the treble, then similarly in the LH from the upbeat to b.50. Support the RH through
b.49 with *steady* LH quaver chords. Following this extraordinary passage it is possible
either to make a slight *rallentando* towards the 3rd beat of b.51 with a short pause, or
to assume that Haydn intended to catapult us straight into the low-registered start of the
recapitulation. Whichever course you favour, carry it out with conviction. Shape the
semiquaver line from b.66 in free and improvisatory style, gradually slowing towards the
minim E flat on the 3rd beat of b.69. Support the RH with a resonant LH tied chord
from the 3rd beat of b.67, and then *listen* to the notes of the broken diminished 7th chord
from the end of b.69 as you hold them through until the 4th beat of b.70. Resume the
tempo with the upbeat to b.71, and then let the detached LH quavers lead clearly from
the second half of this bar (as in the corresponding passage from b.24).

Second movement – Allegretto (6)

This movement has a minuet character, of rather an acerbic cast. Establish a decisive,
'stepping' **3/4** pulse. Do not let this crotchet pulse be disrupted by the somewhat over-
ornamented treble line. It is vital that the frequently occurring ornamented upbeats (to
bb.1, 2, 3, etc.) are accurately timed and clearly played. They must give an emphatic, though
not too heavy, onward lead towards the slurred crotchets on the subsequent 1st beat.

57

bb.1 – 24   Keep the semiquaver before the turn on the opening upbeat light and short, and 'go to' a firm slurred 1st beat of b.1 (similarly with the upbeat to b.2 etc.). The turn can either *anticipate* the beat or be placed *on* it:

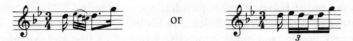

Maintain steadiness with accurately and firmly placed chords in the LH. 'Lean' particularly on the RH tied crotchets on the 1st beat of bb.4 and 5, where the LH has rests, and then be sure to place the LH precisely on the 2nd beat. After the first double bar continue to 'lean' on the RH slurred crotchets on the 1st beat of bb.7 – 10, and place the LH crotchet chords precisely on the 2nd beat of these bars. Time the dotted rhythms meticulously from the 2nd beat of b.10, being sure to 'enter' neatly with the LH on the upbeat to b.11. As always in such instances, feel the semiquavers as 'upbeats' to the subsequent beats rather than as 'tail-ends' to the previous beats (see Introduction). Let the LH 'go on' towards a clear detached crotchet on the 1st beat of b.13. Be careful to time the LH 'upbeat' semiquavers neatly in bb.16 and 18 so that the hands are precisely co-ordinated on the 2nd beats. Rise to a singing high slurred crotchet on the 1st beat of b.22, and observe the rests precisely so that the semiquaver upbeat to b.23 is perfectly timed.

bb.25 – 109   Adopt a more gracious tone as you move into the major from the upbeat to b.25. Maintain a steady crotchet pulse through the solo semiquaver curves (bb.26 – 7 and 31 – 2). Slur the RH quavers neatly from b.35, again being careful to place the LH chords precisely. From b.41 let the syncopated RH line curve smoothly over a very even LH lower crotchet line (feeling that the LH is 'leading'), sustaining the inner LH D through to b.43, and then ensuring that both LH lines move smoothly, through to the end of b.44. Conversely lead off from b.45 with the *RH* crotchets, letting the LH syncopated line follow smoothly. From b.53, in the linking passage leading back to the minor at b.56, 'lean' well on the RH 1st beats, slurring these crotchets smoothly down to the dotted quavers on the second beats, over clear and very neat LH semiquaver/crotchet figures. Make sure that these LH figures rise to a clear crotchet that is precisely co-ordinated with the RH dotted quaver. Through bb.64 – 7 phrase the syncopated treble line smoothly over the steady and warmly sustained LH lines. Keep a steady crotchet pulse from bb.68 – 80, 'leaning' again on the slurred crotchet on the 1st beat of bb.69, 70, etc. and let the RH semiquavers 'take over' smoothly from accurately timed LH figures in bb.69, 71, etc. Time bb.86 – 9 carefully – it is easy to lose the crotchet pulse here. Make it clear that the 3rd beat of bb.86 and 87 falls on the LH semiquaver G. Be sure to 'feel' the held 3rd beat of b.90, so that you don't 'fall into' the upbeat to b.91. From b.102 let the hands take over fluently from each other in the improvisatory build-up towards the dominant 7th flourish and pause at bb.106 – 7 (timing this flourish so that you arrive on the top quaver C on the 3rd beat of b.106), and then finish neatly in tempo.

No. 33 in C minor
(Hob. XVI/20)

First movement – Moderato (8)*

This Sonata, one of Haydn's most splendid, was written in 1771, coinciding, it appears, with a period of considerable turbulence in his life. The first movement, in its dramatic and expressive power, and in the impressive scope of its fine and extended development section, is outstanding by any standards, the more so in view of its relatively early date of composition. This is not music for children, however talented, nor for the faint-hearted, whatever their age! For the first time Haydn gives detailed dynamic instructions. Set a resolute, very steady, *moderato* crotchet pulse. At too fast a tempo you will reduce the stature of the music to mere jauntiness, and sound scrambled into the bargain. (You will know if you are too fast after only a few bars.)

bb.1 – 8   Lead off decisively in the RH in b.1, giving the thirds (and the sixths in b.2) a firm but expressive resonance, buoyed along by vigorously slurred offbeat LH quaver figures. Feel that you are 'going to' the ornamented slurred crotchet on the 3rd beat of b.2, while at the same time feeling the overall continuity of the RH melodic line right through the first four bars, underpinned by the complementary LH lines from the upbeat to b.3. Then from b.5 note the more fragmentary 'development' of the material of the opening bars. Be sure to 'feel' the quaver rest on the 6th quaver pulse of b.6, and then run up an immaculately clear demisemiquaver upbeat scale to lead off into a clearly defined ornamented treble melodic fragment in b.7, supported by evenly placed LH offbeat quaver chords. Then 'lead' into b.8 from a definite LH quaver upbeat 'going to' a firm minor crotchet third on the 1st beat (of b.8), and 'go to' firm detached unison C's on the 3rd beat of b.8, making sure that you come clean *off* on the 4th beat to give the crotchet rest its full value.

bb.9 – 26   This movement is alive with orchestral colour. Poise yourself on the previous crotchet rest, to arrest attention with the bold 'trumpet calls' in b.9, supported by smooth, but firm, LH crotchet chords. The quick turns, or shakes, are

not easy to manage. Start on the main note if you can

but if this is too difficult, start on the upper note    or

 The essential is not to disrupt the basic rhythm. Feel that the

RH is fitting in with the steady *LH* chords, and *not* the other way about. Then feel the gracious quality of the quiet answering solo melodic phrases. Show the emphases on the offbeat quavers in b.14 as melodic 'leans' not 'bumps'. Then feel the warm 'horn-like' tone of the RH melody in thirds from b.15, supported by smooth LH offbeat quaver figures. Let these LH figures rise to a clear crotchet on the 3rd beat of bb.15 – 17, and then feel the little emphasis on the *appoggiatura* third on the RH upbeat group to bb.16, 17, and 18. Listen to the dramatically widening intervals of the *tenuto* treble crotchet chords as you *crescendo* through b.18 supported by clear LH offbeat semiquaver broken octave figures. Treat these LH semiquavers as if they are slurred, and let the LH upbeat C flat broken octave 'go to' a firm B flat on the 1st beat of b.19. Then let the semiquaver figures flow in improvisatory style towards b.22. From here build up the rhythmic tension in either hand towards the 1st beat of b.24, going suddenly *piano* here in the LH as you move in *rallentando* towards the *adagio* 'cadenza'. Allow plenty of time here as you phrase the treble line expressively over the sustained LH chord, and 'draw out' the *pianissimo* sound effects towards the pause on the sustained dominant 9th in b.26.

Then resume the tempo smartly with a strong LH chord on the 3rd beat of
bb.26 – 37   b.26 and a vigorous 'snapped' dotted rhythm figure in the RH. (Be sure that
the demisemiquavers are snapped *on* the beat, rather than anticipating it.)
Keep a steady crotchet pulse through b.28 with the help of firm LH chords on the 1st and 3rd beats, placing the RH turns *on* the quaver beats. From b.29 support the RH with firm and steady LH quaver chords as you rise to a fierce 'stop' on the dominant 7th (of E flat major), on the 3rd beat of b.31. Then set off in b.32 with *even* LH triplets to underpin the neatly articulated RH descending demisemiquaver figures. Phrase the chromatic scale very smoothly from the upbeat to b.36, and finish the section with a quiet and immaculately timed figure in thirds in b.37.

Exploit the full strength of the Beethovenian treatment of the opening figure
bb.38 – 69   at the beginning of the development (bb.38 – 46). Listen to the resonance
of the powerful syncopated slurred *sforzato* bass quaver and held C in b.39.
Let the LH thirds 'take over' resolutely through bb.40 – 2, and treat the descending RH broken octaves (bb.41 – 2), as if they are slurred, 'leaning' on the thumbs. Let the RH 'take over' again in b.43, and drive on through the resonant descending passage leading towards the strong pause chord (on the dominant 7th of B flat minor) on the 3rd beat of b.46. Then set off again at b.47 with immaculately clear, rhythmic and evenly pulsating LH triplets. Let each RH demisemiquaver interjection run cleanly down towards a clear, almost fierce, detached quaver on each 3rd and 1st beat of these bars. Always maintain the forward impulse as you build the tension inexorably in tautly controlled rhythm towards the unison *fortissimo* figures of bb.61 – 2. Keep a steady crotchet pulse through bb.51 – 3, articulating the triplet flourishes with maximum vitality, and giving full value to the sonorous unison crotchets on the 1st and 2nd beats of b.52. Let the impassioned treble melody line ring out powerfully from the 3rd beat of b.55, through to b.59. Then notice how the accurate observance of the RH semiquaver rests serves to intensify the rhythmic tension through bb.59 – 60. Feel that each RH fragment is 'going to' an emphasized quaver on the 3rd beat of b.59 (G) and on the 1st and 3rd beats of b.60 (G and C respectively). *Crescendo* steeply through b.61 and then articulate the unison sextuplets through b.62 with lashing clarity. Do not then allow the tension to drop, but 'go on' over resolute LH octaves towards a violent 'stop' on the LH bass octave on the 1st beat of b.65. Poise yourself immediately to enter on the 2nd beat with a varied fragment of the 'gracious' phrase from b.10, which is then immediately interrupted by the 'trumpet' motif, which in turn throws us abruptly back into the recapitulation at b.69.

Show the heightened expressiveness of the recapitulation – the horn-like
bb.69 – 100   quality of the LH version of the opening figure from b.73, this time buoyed
along by the slurred quavers in the *RH;* and the abrupt silence in b.76,
followed by the plaintive *pianissimo* phrase, leading back into the 'normal' course of the recapitulation from the upbeat to b.78. End in strict tempo, timing the RH horn-like *piano* fragments with military precision from the upbeat to b.99, over the reiterated LH octaves. Feel these LH octaves like receding drumbeats leading, in *diminuendo*, to the quietest possible (but immaculately clear) *pianissimo* ending.

Second movement – Andante con moto (7)(O)*

This movement is equally remarkable. In complete contrast to the outer movements, it has a quality of coolness, even austerity, tinged here and there with warmth. The smooth lines of either hand are in constant, mainly contrary motion, sometimes moving closely together, and sometimes far apart, with curious and lightly mesmeric effect. Shape these lines with equal care, appreciating their differing character: the LH moves in almost unbroken lines of quavers, while the RH is more florid, more 'vocal'.

bb.1 – 25 Set an even crotchet pulse that feels leisured, yet 'moves'. Play the three crotchet E flats through b.1 in an even, 'speaking' manner, while 'bringing in' the LH quavers quietly and evenly, but definitely, on the 2nd quaver pulse. Then incorporate the ornaments and rhythmic figures smoothly into the RH line without ever disrupting the continuous procession of LH quavers. Feel the RH rest on the 3rd beat of bb.4, 8, 12, etc. as 'breathing points' before you start each new phrase, while at the same time showing the onward lead of the LH quavers towards the subsequent bar. Ensure that the LH thirds 'entering' on the 2nd quaver pulse of b.9 flow just as evenly as the previous single quavers. Treat the grace notes in b.9 (and in b.26) like gentle and 'speaking', not too clipped, acciaccaturas. Then let the RH line expand into a smooth chain of trills through b.10 up towards a singing tied crotchet C on the 2nd beat of b.11, above the calmly descending LH thirds. From b.14 feel that the quietly resonant LH thirds are 'leading' as you fit in the eloquent RH fragments neatly through b.14 and the first half of b.15, showing the 'punctuating' effects of the semiquaver rests. Then from the middle of b.15 let the syncopated RH quaver line 'follow' the even LH thirds in a close *legato*. Let the RH scale run down to a clear quaver on the 1st beat of b.21 (and b.24), and then (while showing the upward 'lift' in the RH towards the high quaver third) feel that the LH crotchets are 'leading' through these bars as you place the offbeat treble quaver chords precisely and relatively lightly. 'Go to' a clear quaver chord on the 1st beat of b.22, and then allow a natural break as you leap up in both hands to start the next phrase on the 2nd quaver pulse of the bar.

bb.26 – 67 Feel that the LH quaver thirds are 'taking over' on the 1st beat of b.31 from the three even RH crotchets in b.30 (having given a little extra emphasis to the tied upbeat crotchet), and from here feel the gently heightening intensity of the music, listening acutely to the chromatic inflections as the lines move more closely together. Then from the upbeat to b.36 shape the sustained lower LH line and inner line with equal care, beneath the expressive curving treble semiquavers. From b.47 listen to the resonance of the lower LH dotted minims as you shape the beautiful ascending inner LH quaver lines in contrary motion to the descending RH offbeat lines. Listen particularly here to the inner LH tied upbeat quavers singing over into bb.48, 49 and 50.

Finale – Allegro (8)*

The opening bars suggest the motion of a fast minuet, but this is soon overborn by the increasing feeling of turbulence. There is some kinship between the rhythmic impetus of the vigorous LH thirds in the opening of this movement (bb.1, 2, etc.) and in the opening of the first movement of the Sonata No. 59 in E flat major (Hob. XVI/49), written nearly twenty years later. Several other features also anticipate the later movement, notably the use of the broken thirds figure, and the sustained passage from b.41 to the double bar, closely akin to the passage in a similar place in the E flat Sonata.

bb.1 – 12 Set a resolute **3/4** pulse, give the crotchet upbeat its full value, and 'lean' on the RH slurred figures on the 1st beat of bb.1 and 2, coming *off* on the detached crotchet on the 2nd beat, over clear, detached LH crotchet thirds. Do place these LH thirds with vitality, accurately and *equally*, so that in the LH, in contrast to the RH, there is no suggestion of a slurred effect. Then 'lean' well on the RH dotted quaver on each beat of b.3, timing the dotted rhythm precisely, over smoothly phrased LH thirds. Then in bb.7 and 8, while articulating the RH exactly as in bb.1 and 2, though if anything leaning *more* on the 1st beat, place the LH third emphatically, almost with a jolt on the 2nd beats. Let the RH quavers descend determinedly through bb.9 and 10, and let the detached LH crotchets in b.10 'go to' a firm crotchet F on the 1st beat of b.11. 'Finish off' the phrase down to the LH crotchet on the 2nd beat of b.12.

bb.13 – 46
Lead on from a clear LH semiquaver upbeat towards a firm crotchet on the 1st beat of b.13. 'Come in' smoothly with the descending RH quaver line to 'go to' a singing tied minim on the 1st beat of b.14, with the LH quaver line 'carrying on' smoothly in b.14. Let the RH 'go down' to a firm quaver B flat on the 1st beat of bar 16 and, avoiding any sense of snatching, leap up calmly to start the new phrase on the high E flat. Then follow the interplay between the upper and inner lines evenly, over sustained LH dotted minims. Feel that the treble quavers in b.16 are 'going to' the crotchet and minim on the 1st and 2nd beats of b.17, as the inner quavers enter clearly, to 'go to' the inner crotchet and minim in b.18, and so on. Feel the agitated 'busyness' of the lines in both hands from b.21 while maintaining a resolute 3/4 pulse. Give firm LH octaves on the 1st beats of bb.21 and 22, and 'pluck' the LH quavers vigorously beneath energetically articulated RH semiquaver broken thirds, counting the quaver rests accurately at the end of bb.21 and 22. Then let the LH quaver line in bb.23 and 25 'go on to' strong crotchets on the 1st beat of bb.24 and 26. Give a strong melodic lead in the LH from b.27, crossing to the treble and back as in continuous 'arcs', accompanied by vigorous RH semiquavers. Note that the crotchets in the bass clef (bb.27 – 8) are detached, and the crotchets in the treble (bb.29 – 30) are *legato*. Then feel the defiance of the LH *staccato* crotchets on the 1st and 2nd beats of bb.31 and 32. In contrast, phrase b.34 smoothly, 'leading' with firm LH crotchets, while the offbeat RH thirds descend evenly from the emphasized tied upbeat. Then in bb.35 – 6 'rattle out' the RH semiquavers over vigorous and rhythmic detached LH quavers 'going to' a firm LH crotchet on the 1st beat of b.37. Let the solo RH line 'go to' a warm tied minim third on the 1st beat of b.39, with the slurred LH quavers likewise 'going to' the dotted minim B flat on the 1st beat of b.40. Sustain the long tied E flats in the outer parts (bb.41 – 4) as you follow the subdued inflections of the inner slurred thirds, and end the section peacefully, 'leaning' well on the slurred dotted minim chord (b.45).

bb.47 – 120
Set off forcefully again into the development. In the contrapuntal passage from bb.56 – 64 observe the detailing of either hand meticulously, always 'leaning' on the slurred RH crotchets on the 1st beats of bb.57 – 63. Feel the fierceness of the LH *staccato* figures in bb.67 – 71 (and 92 – 5) – be particularly careful to keep steady here. It is helpful to feel the 3rd beats of bb.67 – 71, where the LH has a rest, as *upbeats* to the subsequent bars. Make a *diminuendo* as you descend from the treble at b.74 towards a *pianissimo* at b.78, 'finishing off' as quietly as possible with the low bass LH slurred quavers. Then lead off again with *forte,* legato RH upbeat quavers, and note the slurred LH thirds in this varied re-statement of the opening theme. Give a bold melodic lead with the LH *legato* crotchet fragments at bb.97, 99, etc, and ensure that the semiquaver fragments divided between the hands in the intervening bars remain steady and even. Build up the tone through this passage, as you prepare to give full vent to Haydn's impassioned outburst from b.107. Sweep powerfully from bass to treble with the LH, giving firm bass crotchets on the 1st beats of bb.107 – 117, and 'leaning' also on the slurred treble 2nd beats, buoyed along by lashing RH semiquavers. Do not, in mistaken deference to notions of eighteenth-century 'style', underplay the 'nearly hysterical force' of this passage.† On the other hand, do not let the texture grow too heavy or 'Beethovenian'. Keep up the furious impetus, right down to the bass crotchet G on the

†H.C. Robbins Landon, *Chronicle and Works,* vol. 2.

3rd beat of b.119. Then collect yourself through the rests and pause of b.120 to return to normality with the upbeat to b.121.

Shape the chromatic semiquaver upbeats to bb.123 and 124 with 'sliding' *bb.121 – 52* smoothness. Then from the upbeat to b.125 let the LH thirds lead in a sonorous downward *crescendo* towards b.128, with the syncopated RH line following evenly. Let the solo detached RH quavers 'take over' from the LH crotchet F on the 1st beat of b.139 in an energetic *crescendo* up towards the high quaver F on the 4th quaver pulse of b.140 and then subside towards the extended version of the quiet sustained passage at the close of the exposition. 'Finish off' the slurred quaver figures quietly on the 1st beat of b.150 before 'coming in' sonorously with the *forte* quaver sixths on the 2nd quaver pulse of the bar, to lead down towards the resonant final chords.

No. 34 in D major
(Hob. XVI/33)

First movement – Allegro (7)

This movement is too long to sustain interest in its rather conventional material – a far cry indeed from the first movement of the previous Sonata in C minor – and it is discussed below in less than usual detail. Set a sensible crotchet pulse, not so fast as to endanger the clarity of the demisemiquaver figures, and set off in a bright and lively spirit.

Articulate the demisemiquaver upbeats lightly and cleanly, as they 'go to' *bb.1 – 24* clear slurred quavers on the 1st beat of bb.1 and 3, supported by firm LH crotchet octaves. Then finish off the phrases neatly in bb.2 and 4 with precise detached quavers in either hand and *feel* the RH quaver rest on the 2nd beat of these bars before leading on with the subsequent upbeat demisemiquavers. (Be particularly careful to *feel* the silent 2nd beats in similar instances, e.g. in bb.12, 24, 60, etc, so that you always lead on with a perfectly timed upbeat.) 'Go to' and 'lean' on the dotted crotchets on the 1st beat of bb.5 and 6 over precisely placed LH offbeat chords. Support the RH descending scale through b.11 with neatly placed LH quavers on the 1st and 2nd beats, and 'go to' firm crotchet unison D's on the 1st beat of b.12. Feel that the neatly slurred RH semiquaver figures in bb.13 and 15 are 'going to' the slurred crotchet thirds on the 1st beat of bb.14 and 16. Articulate the RH fragments neatly (bb.18 – 21) over even LH semiquavers, placing the RH turns *on* the 1st beats of bb.19 – 21. Give the slurred minim chord in b.23 and the rests in b.24 their full value.

Support the RH figures with firm detached quaver chords in bb.25 – 6. From *bb.25 – 68* b.27 listen to the continuity of the low RH line; a singing G natural in b.27 carrying into the semiquaver patterns of b.28, leading to a singing A natural in b.29, and so on. From bb.31 – 9 support the immaculately articulated RH with even but 'keenly' pulsating LH semiquavers. From bb.39 – 45 keep the scale patterns steady with firmly placed LH crotchets on the 1st beat of the bars. At b.52 take plenty of time for the pause, the *adagio* semiquaver figure and the two subsequent pauses. Then, at *tempo primo* treat the perky grace notes like acciaccaturas. *Crescendo* towards the spread dominant 7th chords on the 1st beats of bb.60 and 64, and finish the section in precise tempo, letting the LH quaver chords 'lead' through bb.66 – 7, with the RH offbeat semiquavers following relatively lightly.

Be sure to sustain the long bass F from b.69 through to the end of b.71, *bb.69 – 117* and to *wait* for the full three beats before entering with the RH on the 2nd beat of b.70. Then be sure, also, to sustain the tied and held notes in either hand from b.79. Enliven the semiquaver figuration from bb.92 – 7 with brightly detached ascending LH quavers, which 'go to' firm LH crotchets on the 1st beats of bb.93, 95 and 97. 'Feel' the silent beats once more so that you do not lose the pulse at bb.103 – 6, and then be careful to co-ordinate the scale in sixths immaculately through bb.107 – 8. Sustain the lower tied dominant pedal point from b.111 through to b.115 beneath the 'rocking' upper figures, and allow a generous pause after the dominant 7th flourish in b.116, before starting back into the recapitulation with all brightness, from the upbeat to b.117.

Second movement – Adagio (6)

This is a mellifluous and expressive movement. Find a tempo at which the sextuplets from b.9 flow easily, and at which the sustained b.10 sounds neither hurried nor sticky, and establish a measured, and very secure **3/4** pulse.

bb.1 – 8   'Lean' on the slurred RH dotted quaver and LH crotchet third on the 1st beat of b.1, letting the RH demisemiquavers 'fall' lightly towards the quaver C sharp, placed precisely on the 2nd beat. Then 'feel' the full crotchet rest on the 3rd beat and 'go to' and 'lean' again on the 1st beat of b.2, supported by a firm LH diminished 7th chord. Be careful to keep steady as you lead on with the 3rd beat of b.2, and through b.3, giving the slurred RH semiquaver 'upbeats' to each beat their exact value, and coming off gently, not abruptly, on the detached quavers. Support the RH with carefully placed LH quavers on the crotchet beats of bb.3 and 4. Despite the fragmentary nature of the melody line over bb.1 – 4, try to create an overall melodic curve rather than a series of isolated spiky fragments. Likewise think of the second phrase (bb.5 – 8) in a wide 'arc', up to the high F on the 3rd beat of b.7, and down to the G sharp appoggiatura and A in the bass clef on the 1st beat of b.8. Be sure, throughout these first eight bars, that the RH is supported by carefully balanced, and accurately placed, LH chords or single notes.

bb.9 – 17   Feel the full crotchet rest on the 3rd beat of b.8. Then give the RH sextuplets a good start with a warm but firm LH bass octave on the 1st beat of b.9, and let the RH line flow freely, but still rhythmically downwards towards a singing minim C on the 1st beat of b.10. Support the sonorous melodic fragment through b.10 (and through bb.12 – 13) with even and steady, yet 'ongoing' LH quaver chords. 'Finish off' this RH fragment clearly on the semiquaver C on the 1st beat of b.11 over a clear LH crotchet third, and then leap up calmly, as if in a graceful curve (rather than 'snatching'), to the high semiquaver C. Let the *staccato* triplets ascend towards the 1st beat of b.14 in a gently detached, not spiky style and then phrase the RH melody line warmly through to the end of b.16 over evenly-flowing LH sextuplet semiquavers. From b.16 let the LH sextuplets 'go on' to a firm quaver third on the 1st beat of b.17.

bb.18 – 32   Practise b.18 (and 21) carefully, 'hands separately', maintaining an even pulse, and then, when you put 'hands together', ensure that your smoothly co-ordinated sextuplets in tenths curve gracefully and without bumps to move smoothly into the melodic fragment at b.19. From b.28 let the LH sextuplets go smoothly to a warm-toned fourth on the 1st beat of b.29, to give a sustained foundation to the RH sextuplet curve. In bb.30 and 31, in accordance with the old tradition, let each RH semiquaver coincide with the last sextuplet of the LH group.

bb.33 – 52   Bear in mind your careful timing and phrasing of bb.1 – 4 as you play the ornamented version of these opening bars at bb.33 – 6. At bb.37 and 38 give sufficient definition to the first RH semiquaver of the bar to ensure that the LH can enter on the offbeat without causing a hiccough. Give a buoyant tone to the RH melodic line from b.39, and 'lean' warmly on the tied crotchets on the 2nd beat of bb.42 and 43. Let the RH semiquavers descend in improvisatory style through b.45, with the diminished 7th flourish then rising freely up to the high quaver on the 3rd beat of b.46, and then let the LH lead on clearly from the quaver upbeat, to a firm octave G on the 1st beat of b.47. Draw out a little towards the interrupted cadence (bb.47 – 8) and then let the high treble reiterated quaver figures 'speak' mysteriously, keeping a perfectly steady crotchet pulse as these RH quavers alternate with the LH sextuplet figures. Ensure that neither hand 'hangs on' over the subsequent rests here. Let the A major arpeggio curve easily and evenly through b.51, then 'lean' expectantly on the crotchet A on the 2nd beat of b.52, ready for the *attacca*.

Third movement – Tempo di Menuet (5)

This lively Tempo di Menuet is, in effect, a little set of variations on two themes, one major, one minor. Inexperienced players often find extended passages of dotted rhythms (which, as will be seen, prevail throughout the first 32 bars) difficult to manage. Do concentrate on keeping the *main* pulse clear and steady, so that you 'lean' on the dotted crotchets and keep the semiquavers short and relatively light. Always think of the semiquavers as upbeats to the subsequent dotted quavers rather than as 'tail-ends' to the previous beats (see Introduction).

Let the minuet tempo be fairly brisk, with precisely 'stepping' LH crotchets.

bb.1 – 16   Lead off from a clear and perfectly timed upbeat, and immediately establish your secure crotchet pulse. Feel that the RH is 'going to' the double dotted crotchet on the 2nd beat of b.2 while the LH 'steps' onward. Then in b.3 feel that the RH dotted rhythms are fitting in with the LH 'steps' and *not* the other way about, as you 'go to' the slurred crotchet on the 1st beat of b.4. Through bb.9 – 10 phrase the RH dotted rhythms more smoothly (but equally sharply timed) over smoothly phrased and very even LH crotchets. Be careful throughout the movement to 'finish off' the LH clearly on the 2nd crotchet of the bar, at the end of each four-bar phrase (e.g. in bb.4, 8, 12, and so on) so that you lead on with a clear and perfectly poised RH upbeat to the subsequent phrase.

bb.17 – 48   Give a new and sturdier feeling to the minor section from the upbeat to b.17, and support the RH with firm LH chords through bb.21 – 3 (and 29 – 30).

Leap up confidently to a firm dotted crotchet on the 1st beat of b.29, and steady yourself with a clear LH chord on the 2nd beat. From b.33 articulate the RH figures neatly over continuingly steady LH crotchets. Be particularly careful to place the LH crotchets clearly on the 2nd beat of bb.33, 34, 37, 41, 42 and 45, where the RH has quaver rests. Note the 'skip' of the RH in b.47 over the *legato* LH.

bb.49 – 88   Feel that the even LH crotchets are 'leading', in a rhythmic sense, from the 2nd beat of b.49 with the RH syncopated line following smoothly. From the upbeat to b.53 *crescendo* purposefully as the hands move apart in contrary motion towards the 1st beat of b.55. 'Lean' on the tied crotchets on the 1st beat of bb.57 and 61, and be particularly careful to place the LH chords precisely on the 2nd beats beneath these tied notes. Let the semiquaver upbeats rise to clear semiquaver D's on the 1st beat of bb.73 and 77 where the LH is silent, and then articulate the RH semiquaver curves brightly over your firm LH crotchet line. Then let the upbeats rise again to clear high D's on the 1st beat of bb.81 and 85 to give a good 'kick-off' to the passages of descending semiquavers. Listen carefully to ensure that these semiquavers alternate clearly and evenly between the hands, marking the crotchet pulse with a light accent in the LH.

No. 35 in A flat major
(Hob. XVI/43)

This is another lightweight Sonata. Although the outer movements contain no outstanding technical difficulties, they are long, and really need the understanding and imagination of an experienced artist to bring them to life.

First movement — Moderato (7)

Like that of No. 34, this first movement is rather conventional, and the rhythmic figuration is, for Haydn, unadventurous. So although there are pleasant and humorous touches, the movement feels rather monotonous.

bb.1 – 11   Set a brisk crotchet pulse. The 'Moderato' refers to the overall two-in-the-bar feeling indicated by the *alla breve* time signature. Lead off from a clear and neatly timed upbeat and be sure that the dotted rhythms in b.1 are also very precisely timed, over firmly placed LH crotchet octaves on the main beats. Give the trill on the 2nd crotchet beat (and similar trills in the movement, from b.21 etc.) six notes,

starting on the upper note: Feel that the upbeats to bb.2, 3 and

4 are 'going to' emphasized slurred minims on the 1st beat of the subsequent bars, and also feel the onward impetus of the LH slurred crotchets on the 2nd crotchet beats *beneath* these slurred minims. Be sure to come *off* the detached quavers on the 2nd main beat of bb.2, 3 and 4, ready to lead on with a perfectly timed upbeat to the subsequent bar. Let the LH dotted rhythm interjection in b.6 'follow on' in perfect time from the RH dotted rhythm in the previous bar. 'Lean' well on the RH slurred crotchets on the main beats of bb.9 and 10, keeping the LH detached crotchets on the 2nd and 4th crotchet beats relatively light.

bb.12 – 34   Swing into b.12 with even, 'speaking' RH crotchets, treating the grace notes like not too clipped acciaccaturas, over even and easy running LH triplets.
    Feel that you are 'going to' the appoggiatura and slurred minim on the 1st beat of b.13, and similarly in b.14 that you are 'going towards' the first beat of b.15. Be careful to *feel* the crotchet rest on the 2nd main beat of b.20. From bb.21 – 4 keep the ornamented RH in place (practising at first without the ornaments) with rock-steady detached crotchets in the LH as you *crescendo* upwards towards b.24. Then let the treble line flow on easily over the LH triplets through to b.34 being careful to keep the solo triplets steady through bb.25 and 27. Allow a fraction of extra time at b.34 for the unexpected interrupted cadence to register.

bb.35 – 40   Find a new, horn-like sound for the low RH tied minim A flat on the 1st beat of bb.35 and 36, over even LH crotchet chords, and articulate the RH broken chord and repeated quaver figure through bb.37 – 8 in a lively, and again horn-like style over accurately placed LH crotchet chords. Today, most pianists have discarded the convention of the 'compulsory' changing of fingers on repeated notes, although some teachers still drum in the old rule. In practice, in some instances, it works best to change fingers (see bb.83 – 4), in others to use a single finger, usually the third. I suggest that here through bb.37 and 38, this fingering will work best for most hands: 124, 333, 124, 333, etc.

bb.41 – 55   Lead off clearly with the RH dotted minim on the 1st beat of b.41, and keep your lively LH triplet scales steady in bb.41 and 42 by lightly marking the 2nd main beats of the bars (B flat in b.41 and G in b.42), beneath a firm and accurately timed RH. Do feel that the steady RH is controlling the LH scales, and *not* the other way about. Avoid snatching at the high LH E in bb.42 and 45, but, having 'gone down' to a firm C on the 1st beat of the bar, allow the natural fractional 'break' as you leap up, without losing your rhythmic balance. 'Go down' again to a firm LH minim A flat on the 1st beat of b.43, and help the clarity of the RH triplet figure in thirds by feeling a tiny *crescendo* up to and down from the 2nd crotchet beat, i.e. up to the C/A flat. It is effective to go suddenly *piano* at b.47, and to carry on to the end of the exposition with a tinkly, musical box sound, ending with perfectly placed *pianissimo* thirds in treble and bass. Treat the grace note on the upbeat to b.48 similarly to the upbeat figures to bb.49 and 50, 'snapping' each demisemiquaver neatly *on* the beat.

bb.56 – 92   Lead off purposefully into the development, and be careful to keep a steady crotchet pulse as the dotted rhythms alternate between the hands from bb.60 – 3. Feel each semiquaver as an upbeat to the next dotted quaver, rather than as the tail end of the previous beat (see Introduction). *Crescendo* vigorously up towards a ringing high minim D flat on the 1st beat of b.63, and feel through this bar that your firm and very steady *RH* is controlling the descending LH dotted rhythm figure. At the end of b.63 let the RH quaver B flat coincide with the LH semiquaver E natural. Then set off buoyantly on the long melodic passage from b.64 over evenly pulsating LH triplets. Rise to a *forte* towards b.78, and then let the scales run boldly down towards a new colour in the low register from b.80. (At bb.83 – 4 the repeated note situation is different from bb.37 – 8: try the fingering 432, 121, etc.). *Crescendo* through to b.87, letting the LH 'take over' with a firm C on the 1st beat of b.87 and then go *subito piano* again at b.88.

bb.93 – 148   From b.93 let the RH triplets 'open out' in improvisatory style, and then progress expressively through the quavers, then crotchets, in this 'written out' *rallentando* towards the 'Adagio'. Note the pause effect, allowing plenty of time for the trill at b.100, and feel that the 'turned' demisemiquaver ending 'goes on down' to 'finish' on the low E flat in the LH on the 2nd beat. At bb.129 – 130 (as in bb.41 – 2 in reverse) let the firm LH thirds control the RH triplets. From b.135 articulate the unison scales boldly and rhythmically, feeling the natural rise and fall to and from the upmost notes of each curve (i.e. to the C's on the 2nd triplet quaver of bb.135, 136 and 137, and then to the A flats on the last crotchet beat of b.137 and the 2nd crotchet beat of b.138). Make a *subito piano* at b.140 (or if you prefer, a little *diminuendo* effect from the previous upbeat) and play the last section in an even more tinkling and musical box style than the close of the exposition, disappearing to a tiniest *pianissimo* for the final thirds.

Second movement – Menuetto and Trio (3 or under)*

This is a brisk, breezy Minuet with rather a military air, and with an expressively flowing Trio.

bb.1 – 22   Lead off with an immaculately 'pointed' dotted rhythm upbeat 'going to' a clear detached crotchet on the 1st beat of b.1, in a bright, brassy tone.

Balance this figure with a carefully placed LH crotchet third on the 2nd beat, ready to lead on again with the next upbeat figure. 'Join in' confidently with the LH on the upbeat to b.3, and listen to the contrary-motion direction of the hands through b.3, 'going to' firm minims on the 1st beat of b.4. Take care to give this minim chord its full value before leading on with the upbeat to b.5. Support the RH from b.5 with clear downward marching LH detached thirds, and then with clear detached crotchets as you go towards a firm dominant chord on the 1st beat of b.8. *Feel* the silent 2nd beat before leading into b.9 in a more gracious tone. From the upbeat to bb.10 and 11 let the RH 'go to' and 'lean well' upon the slurred crotchet on the 1st beat of bb.10 and 11, while at the same time showing the implied emphasis on the LH *tied* inner upbeat to these bars.

Listen acutely to the resonance of these tied crotchets and to their resolution on the 2nd beat of bb.10 and 11, over the sustained lower minims. Shape the RH line very smoothly through b.12 over a sustained LH third, and then feel the implied 'lean' in both hands on the upbeat to bb.14 – 16, slurring the LH sevenths smoothly as indicated . 'Draw out' a little towards the pause, and *feel* the pause, on the *rest* and not on the 1st beat of b.16, before picking up the tempo smartly on the upbeat to b.17. End the section with emphatic ringing chords.

Trio

bb.23 – 40 Lead into b.23 with clear upbeat quavers in a quiet, smooth tone, and shape the curving RH melody line in lightly expressive style over steady and even, yet 'ongoing' LH quavers. Feel an overall dynamic curve up to bb.27 – 8, and down again towards a neat close on the unison crotchets on the 1st beat of b.30. Lead on with neatly slurred RH quaver couplets from the upbeat to b.31 over a carefully shaped LH crotchet fragment. Then draw out a little through b.33 towards an implied little pause through the 1st and 2nd beats of b.34. *Listen* to the descending lower LH sustained F to E flat through bb.33 – 4, and to the resonances of the tied inner LH *and* RH upbeats to b.34, and then pick up the tempo again from the upbeat to b.35.

Third movement – Rondo (Presto) (7)

As the opening theme (bb.1 – 8) appears no less than ten times (fifteen counting all repeats) with various small changes of detail, this movement needs to be made as snappy and witty as possible. Set a brisk, but not too fast, and absolutely stable crotchet pulse, bearing in mind the passages of semiquavers to come.

bb.1 – 45 Lead off from clear upbeat semiquavers, and articulate the RH quavers through b.1 in a bright detached style, immediately establishing your clear 2/4 pulse, with the feeling of 'going to' a firm dotted crotchet on the 1st beat of b.2. 'Follow on' smartly with the LH quavers in b.2 (these can all be neatly detached; or, at some of the varied appearances of the opening RH motif, the first three LH quavers could perhaps be *legato*, e.g. at b.66, or in the low register at b.184). In any event, shape both hands with equal care and precision, and feel that the overall four-bar phrase is 'going to' the ornamented slurred crotchet on the 1st beat of b.4. 'Finish off' the phrase neatly in both hands on the 2nd beat of b.4, ready to lead on clearly with the RH upbeat semiquavers. It is particularly important in this movement that all ends of phrases and ends of sections are likewise properly 'finished off' (as at bb.8, 26, etc.), so that the subsequent upbeat is perfectly poised. To this end, similarly take care to *feel* the quaver rest on the 2nd beat of bb.32, 38, etc. Show the more *legato* character of the curving RH quavers from the upbeat to b.9, and take care to place the supporting LH quaver/crotchet chord figure accurately and neatly. (This passage appears in varied form at bb.73, 133, and 199.) At b.18 exaggerate the pauses jokily, both on the slurred RH quaver on the 1st beat, and on the quaver rest on the 2nd beat; then snap back into tempo on the upbeat to b.19. Be careful to keep a steady crotchet pulse between bb.33 and 36. Feel that your steady LH quavers are 'leading', in a rhythmic sense, from the upbeat to b.33, and then 'take over' with the *RH* quavers from the upbeat to b.34, taking care once more to poise yourself each time on the 2nd beat of the bar. *Crescendo* towards the 1st beat of b.38, showing the slightly syncopating slur-*staccato* effect in your perfectly co-ordinated figures in tenths from the upbeat to b.37. Then make an echo effect from the upbeat to b.39, resuming the *forte* from the upbeat to b.41. 'Rattle out' the RH semiquaver scales (bb.42 – 5) over a securely placed LH, with the quaver upbeats 'going to' firm crotchets on the 1st beat of bb.43 – 5.

Let the RH scale figure descend towards a singing tied minim on the 1st beat
bb.46 – 98   of b.46 as you suddenly go very *legato* from this point. Then feel that the
LH quavers in b.46 are 'going to' the tied minim on the 1st beat of b.47,
and similarly that the RH quavers in b.47 are 'going to' the minim in b.48, and so on.
Ease the tempo in an implied *rallentando* from b.53 or so, making either a *crescendo* or
a *diminuendo* (either can be equally effective) towards the pause on the sustained dominant
7th chord at b.56. From bb.57, 65, and at all subsequent appearances of the opening theme,
make the most of all the changes of detail. Keep a steady crotchet pulse from bb.73 – 8
with the help of the LH slurred quaver figures placed accurately on the upbeat to, and
the 1st beat of, bb.74, 76 and 78, while also 'pointing' the high RH quaver at the end
of bb.73, 75, and 77. From b.91 control your exuberant RH semiquavers with lively and
rhythmic LH quaver figures. Make a little swell towards the high C on the 2nd beat of
b.92 where the LH is silent, and poise yourself *on* the 2nd beat of b.94, so that you don't
'fall into' the broken octave upbeat to b.95. Practise this RH broken octave passage in
plain octaves at first, over firm supporting LH chords or octaves (in bb.96 – 8).

Lead off clearly with lively RH quavers from the upbeat to b.99, feeling here
bb.99 – 123   that the RH quavers are controlling the LH semiquavers. Be particularly
careful here to poise yourself for a fraction of a second on the 2nd beat of
bb.100, 102 and 104 so that you don't 'fall into' the upbeat to each subsequent bar. Go
suddenly *legato* and *piano* from the upbeat to b.107, and then lead off clearly with the
LH detached semiquavers from the upbeat to b.109, letting the *RH* detached semiquavers
follow relatively lightly, and feeling you are 'going to' a firm LH crotchet third on the
1st beat of b.110. Then support the RH offbeat semiquaver figures with continuingly firm
LH chords on the 1st beat of each of the subsequent bars through to b.115. Then articulate
the diminished 7th flourish from b.115 in brilliant and improvisational style up to a ringing
crotchet D on the 1st beat of b.117. Allow full value to the rests before entering with a
piano LH octave at b.119, to *crescendo* in momentary seriousness towards a further full-
toned 'stop' at b.123.

Keep your balance at bb.127 and 131 – 2 by letting the LH quavers 'lead',
bb.125 – 227   with the offbeat RH detached quavers following relatively lightly. Lead off
boldly with the LH from b.165, again letting the RH offbeat figures (immaculately articulated) follow relatively lightly. Drive on from b.168 with tautly rhythmic LH
detached quavers, building the dynamics towards a grand *forte* half-close on the dominant
at b.182 (though perhaps making a *diminuendo* through from b.171 towards bb.174 – 5,
and then a re-*crescendo* towards b.182). Do not snatch (and thus overbalance) at the high
offbeat quavers in bb.193 and 197. Ensure that the *LH* quavers remain rock-steady, *feel*
your crotchet pulse, and fit the RH in with the LH rather than the other way about, and
you will find that there is more time than you think. Feel the implied emphasis on the
tied RH upbeat quavers to bb.200 and 202, and 204 – 8 above neatly placed LH
quaver/crotchet figures, or (from bb.205 – 7) crotchet chords. Sustain the last of these
tied upbeats through b.208 with a warm tone above jokily plucked *adagio* descending LH
quavers, and then phrase the little RH *cadenza* with mock expressiveness down to the pause
on the dominant on the 2nd beat of b.210. *Feel* the silent 2nd beat of b.221, and enter
in perfect time on the offbeat with the *pianissimo* triplets, supported by equally *pianissimo*
but clear LH octaves on the 1st beat of bb.222 – 5, and end with a sudden *forte* crotchet
chord on the 2nd beat of the final bar, in perfect time. (In the new Associated Board selection
of 23 Sonatas, in which this Sonata appears in Book 2, both 'first time' *and* 'second time'
bars are counted in this movement (see Introduction). This creates a discrepancy in bar
numberings from b.90 onwards.)

The next six Sonatas, Nos. 36 – 41, were published as a group in 1773, and were dedicated to Haydn's employer, Prince Nikolaus Esterházy. The first movements of the first four are less adventurous than some of those already encountered (notably those of Nos. 30, 31 and 33), though none is without charm. With Nos. 40 and 41 though, Haydn again breaks new ground with characteristic vigour and spirit of adventure.

No. 36 in C major
(Hob. XVI/21)

First movement – Allegro (7)

The texture here is light and airy. Long sequences of bright dotted rhythms (too long, most players will feel), are interspersed with passages of sextuplet and triplet arabesques. Establish a neat, march-like **2/4** tempo, not so fast as to endanger the clear definition of the dotted rhythms. Imagine a brisk 'step' to each quaver pulse. Aim for the utmost clarity of texture throughout, avoiding heaviness at all costs, particularly where the dotted rhythm figures are 'doubled' (as at bb.13, 17, 28, etc.). Think of a clear 'woodwind' sound in the opening bars, and a bright 'brass' effect at b.13. As always in passages of dotted rhythms, feel the short notes (here the demisemiquavers) as 'upbeats' to the longer notes (the dotted semiquavers or quavers or crotchets as the case may be) rather than as 'tail-ends' to the previous beats, so that you keep the demisemiquavers relatively light, with the feeling of 'going to' the subsequent stronger beat (see Introduction).

bb.1 – 35   Lead off with a perfectly timed RH upbeat, and feel that you are 'going up towards' the tied quaver C on the 2nd quaver pulse of b.1. Then feel the implied 'lean' on the slurred crotchets on the 1st beat of bb.2, 3 and 4. Give the ornamented dotted quavers in b.2 just three quick notes, i.e. F G F and D E D. It is essential to the rhythmic stability of this movement that the LH figures are immaculately timed throughout; let the RH dotted rhythms in the opening bars fit in with the perfectly steady LH quavers, and *not* the other way about. Make sure also that the occasional LH dotted rhythm figures, e.g. bb.6 and 10, etc, 'follow on' in perfect time, and are just as crisp as those of the RH. Let the LH in b.6 rise to a clear detached quaver on the 2nd beat ready for the RH upbeat to lead on clearly into b.7. Feel that the LH in b.10 is 'going on up to' a firm minim B flat on the 1st beat of b.11, and that the RH in b.11 is 'going on to' a firm slurred crotchet third on the 1st beat of b.12, and so on. Note the 'skipping' effect of the slur-*staccato* unison figures in b.17, taking particular care to co-ordinate the hands neatly as the LH 'enters' on the demisemiquaver upbeat to b.17. 'Finish off' clearly in both hands on the 2nd beat of b.18 ready for the RH to lead on in a poised manner from the upbeat to b.19. Be careful to keep a steady crotchet pulse from b.19; feel the implied emphasis on the treble tied quavers on the 2nd quaver pulse of bb.19 and 21, and be sure to place both the LH quaver thirds accurately in these bars (particularly the second, upper one which falls on the *2nd* main beat of each bar) as the RH prepares to swing into the sextuplets. Continue to time the LH meticulously from b.23, and follow the two *separate* LH lines clearly from the 2nd beat of b.24 through bb.25 and 26, *listening* to the inner tied crotchet on the 2nd beat of bb.24 and 25 singing over the subsequent bar line. Keep the crotchet pulse firmly in place again through bb.27 – 36. Make sure that the persistent dotted rhythms are perfectly co-ordinated, and equally sharply articulated in either hand, particularly when they are 'doubled', from the upbeat to bb.28 and 30.

bb.36 – 57   Sound a more serious note as you turn into the minor at b.36, and listen carefully to ensure that the triplet passage-work flows evenly between the hands. Feel that the LH triplets in b.36 'go to' a clear detached, but not spiky, quaver on the 2nd beat of the bar, and let the RH triplets 'take over' confidently to lead on to the quaver on the 1st beat of b.37, and so on. Lead off purposefully with the LH from the 1st beat of b.39, letting the offbeat RH triplets follow evenly and relatively lightly. Continue to 'lead' with a clear LH inner line from the 2nd beat of b.40, over the sustained lower pedal point. Build up the tone purposefully towards the 2nd beat of b.43, and descend with a resounding flourish towards a ringing quaver D on the 1st beat of b.45. Be sure to *feel* the 2nd beat of this bar as you prepare to lead off from the upbeat to b.46 with the ticklish, perky little figure in triplet semiquavers. Feel the implied syncopated emphasis on the tied RH quaver A in bb.46, 48, etc, and time these RH figures neatly over your evenly ascending LH quavers. This idea evidently amused Haydn, for here he states it four times, and then uses it again in the development and the recapitulation.

bb.58 – 149   No new material is introduced in the development section. Bring back the bright 'brassy' sound at b.64 ensuring that the RH-LH figures 'take over' from each other exuberantly, but with military precision. Sustain the tied inner LH A clearly from the upbeat to b.75 over a steady lower LH quaver line, and then continue to articulate the RH dotted rhythms incisively over resonant descending LH thirds through bb.76 – 7. Lead off boldly again with the LH from b.80, and build up the dynamics towards the B flat flourish (bb.85 – 6) and the big diminished 7th chords leading to the low A minor close at b.88. On the upbeat to the next bar, back comes the 'perky' figure. In the recapitulation it returns again after the concentrated build-up from b.126 over the long dominant pedal point. In each case the delightful absurdity of this figure is heightened by the 'seriousness' of the foregoing passage-work. From b.122 articulate the jagged RH dotted rhythms sharply again in both hands, continuing in the RH from b.126 over a resolute LH inner quaver line entering clearly on the 2nd quaver pulse of the bar. 'Retake' the dominant pedal point resonantly in bb.129, 130 and 131, and show the 'entry' of the inner RH line, coinciding with the syncopated re-taking of the pedal point in b.129.

Second movement – Adagio (6) (O)*

For players of about a Grade 6 standard this expansive and expressive movement contains especially valuable material for learning to shape a phrase while holding a slow beat. (The movement is perhaps more likely to appeal to older players.) Try bb.5 – 6, and then play from b.13, and find a tempo at which the turns, triplets, and demisemiquavers of bb.5 – 6 do not feel scrambled, and at which the semiquavers from b.13 flow easily and calmly, and do not feel sticky. Then establish a secure and measured 3/4 through bb.1 – 2. It is a good plan to count in quavers at first, until you have fully absorbed the feeling of the slow pulse.

bb.1 – 12   Give a full tone to the opening chord, spreading at least the LH, and ensuring that the notes of the tied upper RH third have sufficient tone to sing over the 2nd beat of the bar. Also ensure that you 'feel', and give full value to, this held 2nd beat. Then 'lean' on the upper, 1st note of the trill (A) on the 1st beat of b.2 (like an appoggiatura: see b.4), giving the trill an overall slurred effect, matching that of the LH slurred thirds. Do not panic at the sight of the ascending scale in b.2. There is plenty of time to fit it into the 3rd beat of the bar at this slow tempo. Divide the demisemiquavers mentally into one group of six notes and one group of seven to fit the quaver pulses. Feel the scale as an *upbeat* to b.3 as you crescendo through it, up towards the 1st beat of b.3. Then, while observing the slur-*staccato* effect through b.3 (detaching the quavers gently, though, and not spikily), do at the same time feel the continuity of the scale line, from the high A right down to the lower A on the 2nd beat of b.4. Then in b.5 incorporate the turns smoothly into the melodic line and curve the triplets gracefully as you 'go towards' the 1st beat of b.6. Observe the rests scrupulously over the first six bars, but at the same time do mentally phrase *over* the rests so that you feel an overall melodic line, rather than a series of stops and starts. Do also always support the melody line with warm-toned and accurately placed LH chords. Give a singing tone to the high minim A on the 1st beat of b.7, and be sure to place the LH crotchet thirds accurately on the 2nd and 3rd beats. Give full value to the minims through the 2nd and 3rd beats of b.8, and then let the RH semiquaver line follow on smoothly from a singing LH minim on the 1st beat of b.9, to move evenly into triplets on the 4th *quaver* pulse of the bar. Then phrase the ornamented melody line smoothly on through to the 2nd beat of b.12, while also listening to the inner LH line (showing the implied emphasis on the inner tied crotchet upbeats to bb.11 and 12), over the sustained pedal point G.

bb.13 – 28   Do give full value to the crotchet rest on the 3rd beat of b.12, and then lead off on the 1st beat of b.13 with a warm-toned RH G major chord, letting the LH semiquavers follow on evenly. Listen to the LH tied semiquaver upbeat (F) to b.14, resolving to the minim E on the 2nd beat of the bar, over the lower dotted minim C, as the RH semiquavers curve upwards. Then listen to the tied treble crotchet G singing over from the 3rd beat of b.16 into b.17, beneath the treble minim A, and continue to listen to the two sustained RH lines here as the LH semiquavers curve up towards the minim C on the 1st beat of b.18. Go resolutely into the interrupted cadence in b.20, and then take care to place the LH crotchet third accurately on the 3rd beat of b.21 beneath a singing tied RH D. Rise to a singing tied octave on the 2nd beat of b.22 (again placing the LH third carefully on the 3rd beat) and then let the sextuplet octaves descend smoothly and without panic to the quaver octave on the 1st beat of b.23. Then, keeping the LH crotchets steady through b.23, go up from the RH upbeat quaver fourth, as if in a wide 'arc', to a clear and firm treble tied crotchet third on the 1st beat of b.24. Place the LH spread chord resonantly on the 2nd beat, and let the detached, but not too spiky RH thirds descend within a steady pulse towards b.25. From b.26 listen to the 'horn-like' quality of the low RH line over very even LH semiquavers, and 'go towards' a warm 'lean' on the slurred chord on the 1st beat of b.28.

bb.29 – 64   Follow the curve of the LH semiquavers smoothly through b.29, showing the expressive 'lift' up to the E flat on the 2nd beat, and then, from the upbeat to b.30, phrase the RH melody line eloquently, at the same time listening to the inflections of the even LH semiquavers. In b.30 treat the grace notes like gentle and not too clipped acciaccaturas, and feel the implied 'lean' on the tied crotchet A on the 2nd beat of b.31. Let the offbeat slurred semiquaver couplets 'speak' through b.34 (again detaching the *staccato* notes gently, not spikily), and phrase the RH syncopated melodic line smoothly and expressively through bb.36 and 37 over a steady Alberti LH. Ease the tempo through the descending triplet scale of b.39 in preparation for the return to the opening melody in b.40. At bb.46 – 8 listen to the smooth movement of the three voices. In the LH at b.46 listen particularly to the inner line moving between the dotted minim sixths, and then to the inner semiquaver line as it moves on through b.47 from the F, tied from the previous bar. Through bb.51 – 2 take care to keep a steady pulse as you move back and forth between 'ordinary' and triplet semiquavers. As your LH detached crotchets 'lead' resonantly through b.61, feel that you are shaping the offbeat RH quavers in a wide 'arc', rather than in isolated plonks.

Finale – Presto (6)*
This racy little Finale is notable for its 'Scarlattian' special effects – the recurring twittering

72

bird figures in the RH on the upbeats to bb.15 – 16, 73 – 4, etc; the cuckoo calls in alternating hands, from the upbeats to bb.31 – 2 and 36 – 7; and the sudden spurt of 'Spanish' rhythm, bb.52 – 5. Set a smart, but very secure **3/8** pulse, feeling an overall one-in-the-bar.

bb.1 – 18   Time the first eight bars carefully, feeling the implied slightly syncopating 'lean' on the slurred upbeat quavers to bb.1 and 2, and 5 and 6, and placing the LH thirds neatly on the 2nd quaver pulse of these bars. Then show the 'normal' pulse clearly in bb.3 and 4. Articulate the RH semiquavers keenly through b.3, over a neatly shaped LH quaver fragment, and be sure to 'finish off' the quavers neatly on the 2nd beat of b.4, ready to lead on clearly with the upbeat to b.5. Similarly 'finish off' neatly on the 2nd beat of b.8, so that you show the quaver C as a clean upbeat to b.9. 'Rattle out' the RH semiquavers (bb.9 – 12) over lively and rhythmic detached LH quavers, and *crescendo* up to a clear quaver D on the 1st beat of b.13. Finish off this six-bar phrase with a neat chord on the 1st beat of b.14, and *feel* the quaver rest, then 'flick' the triplet upbeats jauntily down towards the *staccato* quavers on the 1st beat of bb.15 and 16, placing the LH offbeat quaver thirds neatly as in bb.1 and 2.

bb.19 – 48   Show the syncopating downward slurred RH upbeats to bb.20 and 21, while keeping the LH quavers perfectly steady. Feel that the LH quaver line is 'leading' from the upbeat to b.22 beneath your 'rattling' RH semiquavers, and on, over the sustained dominant pedal point (of G major) held from b.25 through to the 1st beat of b.30. (The tie here applies of course to the *lower* line, so the quaver D is played on this 1st beat.) Then do not allow the steadiness of your quaver pulse to be undermined by the further syncopating effect of the 'cuckoo' thirds 'rocking' between the hands. 'Lean' on the slurred LH upbeats to bb.31 and 32, and again on the slurred 1st beats in the RH, observing the rests accurately. Then 'lean' again on the pairs of LH slurred quavers from the upbeats to bb.33 and 38, creating a momentary cross-rhythm effect, and spurt on from b.40 towards the double bar with a lively RH line over immaculately clear and keenly rhythmic LH semiquavers.

bb.49 – 124   Let the LH lead decisively from the double bar through to the pause at b.67. 'Pluck' the LH quavers vigorously through bb.52 – 5, keeping the offbeat repeated detached semiquavers relatively light. Then from b.56 underpin your RH semiquavers with firm and resonant LH dotted crotchets. Drive on resolutely to b.66, drawing out a little through this bar towards the pause at b.67 over a strong LH tied octave on the dominant of A minor. Then, passing briskly from A minor, through F major and D minor, Haydn returns to the reprise from the upbeat to b.81. Feel the three quaver rests at bb.71 – 2 not as a vague vacuum, but as a breathless 'check' as Haydn decides in which direction to dash off next.

No. 37 in E major
(Hob. XVI/22)

First movement – Allegro moderato (7)

bb.1 – 8   This is a pleasing, warm-natured and relatively straightforward movement. Take heed of the direction, Allegro *moderato*, and establish a very steady crotchet pulse, starting off with a firm, warm-toned chord (perhaps semi-spread, as indicated on the 1st beat of b.3). Then shape the curving RH melody line smoothly through b.1 and into b.2, 'following on' with an even, and equally carefully shaped LH quaver line. In b.2 place the detached RH sixths, and the triplet and detached quaver third, neatly, like steps in a formal dance. Shape the two subsequent phrases with equal care, always taking particular care to listen to the LH quaver lines. Come to a clear 'stop' on the tonic chord on the 3rd beat of b.4, and *feel* the crotchet rest on the 4th beat before leading off decisively again with the tonic chord on the 1st beat of b.5. 'Go to' and 'lean' on the RH slurred crotchet sixth on the 3rd beat of b.6. Then come neatly *off* the quaver chord on the 4th beat, ready to lead on with a neat triplet upbeat to b.7, as you 'go to' the slurred crotchet third on the 1st beat of b.7. Feel the upward 'lift', as you go on to lean again on the dotted crotchet on the 3rd beat of b.7, and on the tied crotchet on the 1st beat of b.8, and time the note values neatly in b.8, allowing a full crotchet rest at the end of the bar. Support this RH line from the middle of b.6 through to b.8, with meticulously placed LH offbeat quaver broken octaves, or chords.

bb.9 – 24   Lead off with a smooth, expressive RH melody line from b.9, again over perfectly placed LH offbeat quaver thirds, feeling a gradual *crescendo* towards b.12. Slur the RH semiquaver couplets neatly through b.12, and observe the RH detailing precisely in b.13, over evenly pulsating LH semiquavers. Phrase the descending LH crotchets smoothly and resonantly through b.15 beneath even RH semiquavers. Then 'lean' on the tied quavers in both hands on the 1st beat of bb.16 and 18, being sure to give these notes their full value – then 'flick' the demisemiquaver figures lightly, returning to the F sharp quavers precisely on the *2nd* main beat, and then going on to 'lean' again on the slurred crotchets on the 3rd beats. 'Lead' off clearly with the *LH* semiquaver from the upbeat to b.17 (D sharp). Keep the detached semiquavers steady through b.17 by 'feeling' the crotchet pulse in the LH (though without over-obvious accents) on the E, C sharp, E and F sharp, letting the RH offbeat semiquavers follow relatively lightly, as you descend towards, and again 'lean' upon, the tied unison quavers on the 1st beat of b.18. Shape the slurred RH semiquaver couplets neatly from the middle of b.20 over a steady LH line, and time b.22 meticulously, 'going to' a definite detached crotchet on the 1st beat of b.23. Then articulate the perky RH dotted rhythms sharply, 'snapping' the demisemiquavers *on* the quaver beats, and *not* anticipating them, as you end the section in perfect time.

bb.25 – 42   Launch into the development with another resonant chord, and then slur the RH semiquavers neatly again through to b.29, over even LH semiquavers (bb.25 – 6) and then over neatly shaped LH quaver fragments (bb.27 – 9). Then phrase the RH melodic fragment warmly from the 3rd beat of b.29, rising to a singing tied crotchet D on the 2nd beat of b.30. From b.33 (as Haydn develops the material from b.7) keep a steady crotchet pulse with the help of neatly placed LH offbeat chords, 'leaning' as before on the RH dotted crotchets as you rise towards the dramatic pause at b.36. 'Lead' with the LH detached quavers through the second half of b.39, and then sustain the lower LH minims warmly through bb.40 and 41 (shaping the inner LH quaver fragments evenly, and keeping the RH offbeat semiquavers relatively light) as you move back towards the recapitulation.

bb.42 – 75   Here, as is so often the case, Haydn's recapitulation is extraordinarily free. From b.50 allow the cadenza-like RH semiquavers to flow in improvisatory style over the long tied dominant 7th chord, slowing through b.53 towards the *Adagio* and pauses at b.54. From bb.61 – 6, deal boldly with the 'development' of the material of b.15. Phrase the descending crotchet fragments smoothly and resonantly (and the *ascending* octaves, bb.64 – 5, perhaps in a more detached style) while listening acutely to the harmonic resonances of your even RH semiquavers.

Second movement – Andante (6)
This gently expressive 'Andante' moves pleasantly in curving and flowing triplet lines.

bb.1 – 28   Establish a leisured and easy-moving **3/8** pulse. Let the opening tied quaver B sing over the 2nd quaver pulse, and then 'go to', and feel the 'lift' up to, and implied emphasis on the RH tied B on the 2nd quaver pulse of b.2.

Support the RH with a smooth and carefully placed LH, and end the phrase with a neatly-timed dotted rhythm figure in both hands in b.4. Then give full value to the quaver rest at the end of b.4 as you prepare to enter in the lower register on the 1st beat of b.5. Be particularly careful to place the LH quavers precisely on the 2nd beat of b.1 and the 3rd beat of b.2 beneath the tied RH quaver. Let the RH line curve smoothly on through bb.7 – 10 over an even and singing LH line. In bb.11, 13 and 15 ensure that the RH tied crotchet D's sing clearly through their full duration, so that their sound 'carries on' to merge smoothly into the subsequent treble triplet line. Be sure also that the LH and inner RH triplet semiquavers 'follow on' evenly after these tied D's, and note the tied inner LH upbeats to bb.12 and 14. Take care to keep steady through bb.17 – 18. Lead off with a firm LH quaver on the 1st beat of b.17, and then let the RH 'go up to' clear detached quavers on the 2nd and 3rd beats. Keep the LH offbeat broken octaves relatively light, but feel that the *upbeat* broken octave is 'going to' a further firm quaver on the 1st beat of b.18. Support the RH offbeat figures with a firm LH, through bb.19 – 20, and then 'take over' with the RH on the 1st beat at b.21, showing the implied melodic emphasis on the tied upper RH quavers (A) on the 2nd quaver beats of bb.21 and 23. Go on to 'lean' on the slurred RH crotchet on the 1st beat of b.22, and then note the detailing of the upper RH and LH lines, showing the inner rests, through bb.24 and 25, as you make a gentle *crescendo* towards the slurred crotchets on the 1st beat of b.26. End the section gracefully, supporting the curving RH line with quietly resonant bass quavers on the 1st and 3rd beats of b.27 as you 'go to' and lean well upon the slurred crotchet fourth on the 1st beat of b.28.

bb.29 – 69   In bb.30, 34 and 35, again feel the implied 'lean' on the RH tied quavers on the 2nd beat, as in b.2. Take care to maintain a steady quaver pulse through bb.37 – 40. Feel the two semiquavers at the end of b.37 etc, as a clear *upbeat* figure, 'going to' a resonantly singing tied crotchet on the 1st beat of the subsequent bar. At bb.41 – 5 lead off firmly with the LH detached quavers, following evenly with relatively light RH offbeat triplet semiquaver figures. Lean warmly on the LH slurred crotchet thirds on the 1st beat of bb.58 and 59, and listen acutely to the modulating inflections of the RH quaver chords over evenly curving LH triplets through bb.62 – 5.

Finale – Tempo di Menuet (6)
Here the first two sections and their varied restatements are separated by two minor episodes. The second minor episode is in turn a 'developed' version of the first. Be sure to maintain the precise minuet movement throughout.

bb.1 – 16   Lead off with a singing RH minim G sharp and be careful to 'come in' with an accurately placed LH crotchet fifth on the 2nd beat of the bar. Place the RH crotchets evenly in b.2, but feeling the 'lift' up to the upbeat to b.3, as you go on to 'lean' on the crotchet appoggiatura on the 1st beat of b.3, and similarly on the tied crotchet B on the 1st beat of b.4. Finish off the first phrase cleanly on the 3rd beat of b.4, and then lead off clearly again with the tied crotchet on the 1st beat of b.5, being sure to continue to place all LH chords accurately. Tied and held notes are particularly important to the texture of the major sections and must always be given their implied slight emphasis, and sustained through their full duration; note, as well as the tied treble notes, the tied inner LH upbeat E spanning the bar line (bb.3 – 4) and the inner LH tied upbeat to b.6 etc. Time the RH dotted rhythm figures neatly in b.10 over a perfectly steady LH. Then be sure to place the 1st note of the RH demisemiquaver figure *on* the 2nd beat of b.11 (and not anticipating it) and listen to the subtle passing clash of the RH A natural and the LH A sharp near the end of the bar. Show the RH *and* lower LH tied upbeat B's to b.13, and then let the treble dotted minim C sharp sing out through b.13, while also listening to the ascending inner LH line. Then go on to 'lean' on the treble tied crotchet A on the 1st beat of b.14, making a slurred effect as the semiquavers descend to the detached G sharp on the third beat, and supporting the RH with a firm LH minim and crotchet chord, 'pointing' the effect of the interrupted cadence.

Show the sparer texture of the minor section. Lead off clearly with the LH
bb.17 – 62 detached crotchet on the 1st beat of bb.17, 19 and 21, following with immaculately timed RH figures, supported through bb.17 – 22 with a firm and rock-steady LH. Then let the unison scale figure rise boldly through b.23 towards the firm crotchets on the 1st and 2nd beats of b.24. Give firm LH crotchet octaves on the 1st beat of bb.25 – 8, as the RH figures rise in a cadenza-like but very rhythmic implied *crescendo* towards a strong detached treble third on the 1st beat of b.29. Feel the detached chord on the 3rd beat of each of these bars as a strong (and steadying) *upbeat* to the subsequent LH crotchet octave. Play the detached RH crotchet thirds on the upbeat to, and on the 1st beat of, b.30 in a neat echo effect, and then be sure to give full value to the two crotchet rests before leading off in the major again on the 1st beat of b.31. Preserve your steady minuet rhythm as the material of the first eight bars is varied, from bb.39 – 46, and again as the next eight bars are varied, from bb.55 – 62, with the help of a continuingly steady LH.

In the second minor episode lead off with warmly sustained lines in the RH,
bb.63 – 108 providing a firm upper foundation for the immaculately timed sequential figures in the LH. Feel in bb.63 and 65 that the LH is 'going to' the crotchet appoggiaturas on the 1st beat of bb.64 and 66. Keep steady from bb.71 – 6 by giving firm RH chords on the 1st beats, and letting the LH 'go to' firm detached crotchets on the 3rd beats. From bb.85 – 92 sustain the two LH lines warmly, giving a secure and resonant foundation for the curving RH quaver line. Let the syncopated RH line follow smoothly through bb.88 and 90 over the even LH lines. Then again from b.101 let the RH quaver line curve smoothly over warmly sustained LH thirds. 'Lean' on the RH slurred quavers through bb.104 – 6 over a sustained dominant pedal point and a warmly resonant inner LH line. Then divide the demisemiquaver arpeggio neatly between the hands (starting from a firm semiquaver A on the first beat of b.107, and arriving on the top C sharp precisely on the 2nd beat) and end neatly in tempo with clear crotchet chords.

No. 38 in F major
(Hob. XVI/23)

First movement – Moderato (7)*
This is an active and adventurous movement. It is an excellent choice for a nimble-fingered young player at about Grade 7. Set a tempo at which the long demisemiquaver passages from b.21 etc. can run easily and without a sense of hurry, and allow the movement to settle at a comfortable *Moderato* – think of a briskly swinging walking pace, one step to the quaver pulse.

Lead off with a clear and accurately timed upbeat, and time the RH dotted
bb.1 – 12 rhythm figures in b.1 with military precision over neatly placed LH chords.
Then feel the implied slightly syncopating 'lean' on the slurred quaver third on the 2nd quaver pulse of b.2, and go on to support the RH through b.3 and the first half of b.4 with carefully shaped and perfectly steady LH quavers. Be sure to 'finish' off the first phrase cleanly on the 2nd beat of b.4 before leading on with clear upbeat demisemiquavers to b.5. From bb.5 – 8 keep the varying note values and patterns of the RH in place with an immaculately placed LH. Let the demisemiquaver upbeats descend

cleanly and lightly to singing slurred crotchets on the 1st beat of bb.7 and 8, and to a yet stronger tied minim on the 1st beat of b.9. Place the LH offbeat slurred figures neatly in bb.7 and 8 and phrase the LH thirds in b.9 smoothly up towards the crotchet B flat on the 1st beat of b.10 beneath the RH tied minim. Also phrase the RH descending semiquaver thirds as smoothly as possible in b.11 ('leaning' a little on the first third of each quadruplet) with the feeling of 'going to' the slurred crotchet chord on the 1st beat of b.12.

bb.13 – 46   From the upbeat to b.13, let the treble melody undulate expressively over evenly pulsating LH accompanying semiquavers. Play the *staccato* RH semiquavers in bb.13, 15, etc. in a gently detached and 'speaking', not spiky, style and feel the semiquaver rests like 'breathing points' in a vocal line. Take care to keep steady in b.20 by letting your two light LH demisemiquavers 'go to' a firm LH semiquaver G, placed accurately on the 2nd beat. Then leap up neatly to let the detached LH semiquaver thirds descend neatly towards a *firm* LH crotchet third on the 1st beat of b.21, to give a good 'kick-off' to the RH demisemiquavers. From here through to b.44, keep your brightly articulated RH demisemiquaver passage-work in place with an immaculately placed LH, always thinking of the LH 'leading' the RH, and not the other way about. Show the detailing of LH slurs and detached notes very clearly from the upbeat to b.22. 'Go to' firm LH 1st beats of bb.26, 27 and 28. Find a new and more urgent tone colour at the interrupted cadence at b.29. Go from a a clear LH quaver octave upbeat to an implied *sforzato* or *forte-piano* on the LH octave A flat on the 1st beat of b.29. Then articulate your RH offbeat fragments urgently over rock-steady LH quaver chords, and go on to 'rattle out' the demisemiquavers from b.33 over vigorously 'plucked' LH quavers. Show a sudden change of colour again with the *tenuto* LH crotchets at bb.38 – 40, articulating the RH demisemiquavers more smoothly and 'harmonically' here. Keep your RH steady through bb.40 – 3 supported by smoothly phrased LH fragments from the upbeats to bb.41 and 43, and then drive on towards a firm dominant close at the double bar with clear and incisive RH detached quaver chords over 'whirring' brightly articulated LH demisemiquavers.

bb.47 – 60   Keep firm control of the crotchet pulse through the contrapuntal fragments of bb.51 – 3, taking particular care to place the LH quaver accurately on the 2nd beat of each of these bars (E, F and A respectively). Practise this passage carefully and slowly, counting in quavers at first. Feel that the LH is 'leading' through bb.54 – 7, taking care again to place the LH quavers firmly on the 2nd beats of these bars, and then feeling the last LH quaver of each bar as an emphatic upbeat to the subsequent 1st beat. Then 'take over' with the detached RH quaver thirds from the upbeat to b.58, and lead purposefully in both hands towards the half-close on the dominant of D minor at b.60.

bb.61 – 127   Achieving evenness of the divided demisemiquaver passage-work between bb.68 and 76 may prove difficult. Practise slowly and absolutely rhythmically

(and also in dotted rhythms: ♩. ♪ ♩. ♪   and   ♩ ♬ ♩ ♬   etc. See

Introduction), at first marking the *quaver* as well as the crotchet pulse. (In b.68, for example, be clear that the quaver pulse falls on the RH F, the LH D, the RH G and the LH E.) Cascade ebulliently downwards through bb.73 and 75, and steady yourself with emphatic LH quaver chords in the second half of bb.74 and 76. Aim for maximum clarity and brilliance in this whole passage. (H.C. Robbins Landon refers to its 'Scarlattian brilliance').†

†*Haydn: Chronicle and Works*, vol. 2 (Thames & Hudson).

Then drive on powerfully through bb.77 – 85, 'leaning' strongly on the slurred RH crotchet chords on the 2nd beat of bb.77 and 80 – 2, and articulate the detached quavers in the first half of bb.78, 81 and 82 with biting incisiveness, over the whirring LH demisemiquavers. Prepare for the recapitulation with exuberant flourishes on the dominant 7th (bb.83 – 5). Practise the RH alone perfectly rhythmically, from the upbeat to b.106 to the beginning of b.111. Then let the LH trill run easily, and do not let it get 'loud and hectic', and thus 'take over' and wreck the rhythm of the RH. Try to concentrate all your attention on the *RH* and to let the trill 'look after itself'.

Second movement – Adagio (5)*
This is a beautifully flowing and expressive movement.

bb.1 – 20
Establish an easy LH sextuplet and triplet motion with a leisured **6/8** swing. You will find that providing you maintain this easy rhythmic motion throughout, this movement will 'play itself'. Give the RH a warm and gracious tone, placing the turns unhurriedly on the 1st beat of bb.1 – 3, etc, and 'tail off' the demisemiquaver figure on the 2nd beat of each bar towards a gently detached quaver, rather than ending with a bump. While most pianists will conform to the old tradition, and co-ordinate the RH semiquaver with the sixth LH sextuplet in bb.1 – 3 etc, there is no doubt that a freer, slightly cross-rhythm effect is more expressive. Let the triplets ascend through the second half of b.3 towards a singing slurred RH quaver F on the 1st beat of b.4, and then curve gracefully downwards, feeling that the line is 'going on down' to the bass quaver C on the 2nd main beat. Give full value to the rests at the end of b.4, and then do observe the semiquaver rests in bb.5 and 6, like little breaths, as you shape the RH fragments eloquently over the evenly flowing LH. Let the trills in bb.7 and 8 sound leisurely and not hectic (starting them on the upper note) and ensuring that they do not

disrupt the evenness of the LH.      'Stop' the last RH trill

on the D flat (to coincide with the last LH note of b.8, also D flat), and then let the RH rise to a singing tied quaver D flat on the 3rd quaver pulse of b.9, taking care to place the LH dotted crotchets clearly on the 1st and 2nd main beats of this bar. Shape the RH smoothly down through b.10, listening to the intervals of the broken chord, and 'joining in' confidently with the LH after the 2nd main beat. Sweep up again towards a singing tied quaver on the 2nd main beat of b.11 over precisely placed, not spiky, detached LH quavers. Articulate the RH *staccato* semiquavers through the first half of b.14 in a gently detached, 'speaking' (again, not spiky) style. Listen acutely to the expressive inflections of the RH through the second half of b.17, and the first half of b.18, over resonant LH crotchets. In b.19 incorporate the turn and trills as smoothly as possible into the overall melodic curves, supported by carefully placed LH chords. 'Finish off' the first RH trill onto a clear semiquaver C on the 2nd main beat, and then leap up calmly without snatching (as if in a wide arc) to the high E flat. 'Finish off' the LH line smoothly down to the low A flat on the 2nd main beat of b.20.

bb.21 – 39
Let the LH 'go to' a firm crotchet third on the 1st beat of b.22, to support the descending RH broken chord figure entering on the offbeat. Then ascend through a resonant unison diminished 7th arpeggio towards singing crotchet A flats on the 2nd main beat of b.23 (placing the RH grace-notes *on* the beat) being sure to give these their full value. Listen to the curve of the LH through the second half of b.27 as it 'goes to' a resonant seventh on the 1st beat of b.28. From the middle of b.33 let the RH expand in improvisatory style, supported by a resonant LH. Listen to the full-throated inflections of the RH over the dominant pedal point from the 2nd beat of b.34,

and take time to 'point' the interrupted cadence as the RH 'goes to' a clear quaver A flat on the 1st beat of b.36. Let the volume of sound gradually subside from the first half of b.37, tailing the sound away towards the final bass quaver F.

Finale – Presto (6)*

bb.1 – 52
Let this delightfully busy movement be as bright and lively as possible, but set a realistic crotchet pulse, bearing in mind the occasional semiquaver passages to come. Lead in from a clear detached quaver upbeat, and 'point' the effect of the RH slurs on the 1st beats of bb.1, 5, 7, etc, by detaching the 3rd and 4th quavers clearly. Feel that the RH quavers and LH chords in b.1 are 'going to' the slurred and partly tied chord on the 1st beat of b.2, and similarly that b.3 is 'going to' b.4, and so on, 'leaning' well on the slurred crotchets on these 1st beats of bb.2, 4, etc. Make sure that all LH chords and figures are neatly placed and that rests are observed. It is important that the upbeat to each phrase or sub-phrase is clearly articulated. Be sure therefore to 'finish off' the first two-bar phrase on the 2nd beat of b.2, and then to articulate the RH upbeat to b.3 clearly, and similarly in bb.4, 6, etc. Take particular care again to 'finish off' the two LH quavers neatly in bb.8, 27, etc, and to observe the quaver rest, *feeling* the 2nd beat, so that you are poised to lead on clearly with the subsequent quaver upbeat. Note the slurs over the first *three* RH quavers in bb.10 and 12, and also shape the LH quaver fragments in thirds smoothly and neatly from the upbeats to bb.10 and 12. Feel the implied emphasis on the RH tied E flat upbeat to b.14, and keep steady here by letting the LH 'go to' a clearly placed B flat on the 1st beat of b.14, beneath the tied RH. Likewise keep steady at the beginning of b.22 by letting the LH 'go to' a firm dotted crotchet F beneath the RH tied quaver B flat, and 'go on' here with a clear LH line beneath your spanking RH semiquavers. Point the momentary minor inflections at bb.19 – 20. Support the RH semiquavers with vigorous LH dominant 7th chords on the 1st beat of bb.28, 29 and 30, and continue this *forte* dominant 7th flourish exuberantly down towards the detached quaver on the 1st beat of b.32. 'Point' the different detailings of bb.33, 35, 41 and 43 clearly and jokily, and listen to the inflections of the slurred LH crotchet chords in bb.37 – 8 and 45 – 6. Let the quaver figures alternate very evenly between the hands from b.48, from where it is effective to *decrescendo* to a *pianissimo* towards the double bar. You could either slur the LH broken quaver octaves like the RH quaver figures, or play them in contrast in a witty *staccato*.

bb.53 – 147
Support the RH diminished 7th flourish with a resonant LH chord on the 1st beat of b.53. Then place the alternating offbeat RH figures and LH quaver chords in meticulous time through bb.55 – 8. Let the LH 'take over' boldly from the upbeat to b.63, with the support of firm RH chords on the 2nd beats of bb.63 and 65, and the 1st beats of bb.64 and 66. Proceed through the sequential passage from b.68 either with lively and very rhythmic detached quavers in both hands, or, alternatively, in a smoothly 'gliding' *legato*. From bb.77 – 81 again support the RH semiquavers with firm LH crotchet chords. In b.83 let the LH 'go to' a clear quaver B flat on the 2nd beat, and let the LH 'lead' on through b.84, but with the RH then 'going to' a firm crotchet on the 1st beat of b.85. Practise bb.86 – 9 slowly and rhythmically to achieve perfect co-ordination between the hands, detaching all the quavers smartly. Listen to the lower dominant pedal point C from bb.90 – 3, and also place the inner LH fragments neatly here (while continuing to articulate the RH as brightly as before). From bb.104 – 11 follow the sustained inner LH and RH lines as carefully as the treble, over the longer dominant pedal point. Take time to practise this passage not only 'hands separately', but also *parts* separately.

No. 39 in D major
(Hob. XVI/24)

First movement – Allegro (7)

I have to own that I thought this movement long and dull, until I heard John McCabe's stunning recording of this Sonata, backed up by his eloquent advocacy of its special charms in his book.† Nevertheless I stick to the view that its appeal is somewhat esoteric, and can perhaps only be revealed by an experienced and imaginative artist.

bb.1 – 20 Set a lively but steady crotchet pulse and lead in from a clearly articulated ornamented upbeat with the feeling of 'going to' a singing tied crotchet A on the 1st beat of b.1. Enter evenly with the LH on the offbeat, and then ensure that the LH and RH lines are perfectly co-ordinated, and that you listen as carefully to the LH as to the RH. Feel the overall span of the RH line from the high upbeat right down to the F sharp on the 1st beat of b.4, and of the LH right down to the D on the 2nd beat. In b.8 take care to end your little triplet flourish with precisely co-ordinated detached crotchets on the 2nd beat of the bar, and then allow a full crotchet rest. 'Lean' on the RH diminished 5th on the 1st beat of b.9, and then feel the three RH quavers as an upbeat group 'going towards' a further 'lean' on the augmented 4th on the 1st beat of b.10, and so on. *Listen* to the resonances of these diminished or augmented chords on the 1st beat of bb. 9 – 12, supporting the RH through these bars with carefully shaped rising figures in the LH. Let the LH 'go to' a clear crotchet G on the 1st beat of b.13 to support the easy-curving RH semiquavers. At the end of this bar ensure that the LH semiquaver upbeat is neatly dovetailed in with the RH as you 'go towards' the slurred 1st beat of b.14. Then follow the yet longer span of the RH line in a broad sweep down from the upbeat to b.15 to the low appoggiatura and F sharp in b.18.

bb.21 – 51 Strike off in a bold *forte* with tautly rhythmic LH detached crotchets from b.21, letting the offbeat RH semiquavers follow keenly, but relatively lightly.

Reinforce the dynamics with resolute LH octaves from the 2nd beat of b.30, and 'go to' an emphatic crotchet octave D on the 1st beat of b.32. Then let the RH semiquavers 'go up to' a clear RH dotted crotchet E on the 1st beat of b.33, and steady yourself with firmly placed LH chords on the 2nd and 3rd beats of this bar. Following the firm unison crotchet A's on the 1st beat of b.34, observe the quaver rest, and poise yourself to enter neatly on the offbeat with once again perfectly co-ordinated quavers. Listen to the varying intervals as you climb towards the 2nd beat of b.38, and then keep a steady crotchet pulse as the RH semiquavers plunge down to strong unison crotchet D sharps on the 1st beat of b.40. Strike off boldly in the LH again from the 2nd beat, and then 'take over' with the RH crotchets from b.46, supported by lively and rhythmic LH semiquavers. Do not let your clear RH turns, placed *on* the beats, disrupt your rhythm through b.47. Steady yourself on the 1st and 2nd beats of b.49 and then play the three detached quavers here and in b.50 with immaculate precision.

bb.52 – 77 From b.52 shape the treble and inner LH curving lines smoothly, over the sustained pedal point A (and then, from b.56, D). 'Re-take' these long notes firmly on the 2nd *quaver* pulse of both b.54 and b.58. Feel that the inner LH line is 'going to' the tied G on the 1st beat of bb.53 and 55, and similarly that the treble is 'going to' the tied G on the 1st beat of b.54, and so on. Let the LH 'go to' a resonant fifth on the 1st beat of b.61, and then phrase the RH quaver thirds smoothly through bb.61 – 2. Feel that the LH line is going right on from the tied dotted minim E in b.61 through the quavers in b.62 to lead off yet again with a strong detached crotchet

†John McCabe, *Haydn Piano Sonatas* (BBC Music Guides).

B on the 1st beat of b.63. Maximize the dramatic tension of this passage by maintaining a taut crotchet pulse (as at bb.21 – 33, 40 – 5, etc.) as you make an overall *crescendo* towards b.76. Then plunge down to a resonant bass octave on the 1st beat of b.77.

bb.78 – 98 From the upbeat to b.81 follow the two RH lines resonantly and smoothly, over carefully shaped LH rising quaver figures, as Haydn expands on the material from bb.9 – 12. Place the RH crotchet thirds purposefully on the 1st and 2nd beats of bb.84 and 85 (avoiding a slurred effect) and take care to keep the LH broken octave figures steady. Support the descending RH semiquavers with resonant LH octaves on the 1st beat of bb.86 and 87. Place the LH crotchet octave and single notes defiantly on the 1st and 2nd beats of bb.88 – 91, again avoiding any tendency to a slurred effect, as you *crescendo* forcefully down towards the bass F sharp crotchet octave on the 1st beat of b.91. Steady yourself with firmly placed RH crotchet chords on the 2nd and 3rd beats, and end the passage with two more defiant LH crotchet octaves on the 1st and 2nd beats of b.92 before you poise your RH to enter smoothly on the offbeat with the treble figures in thirds. Then do not lose the sense of your crotchet pulse despite the cross-rhythm effect as these figures in thirds alternate evenly between the hands. Then, keeping the thirds as smooth as possible from b.95, 'draw out' in a little *ritenuto* through b.97 towards the pause on the dominant 7th chord at b.98, before leading to the recapitulation with a clear upbeat to b.99.

bb.99 – 155 From b.139 lead resolutely towards the interrupted cadence at b.142. Practise the LH carefully from b.143, leaning warmly again on the chords on the 1st beats. This reversed version of bb.9 – 12 is much more difficult. When you put 'hands together', avoid the tendency to let the RH offbeat quaver figures get too loud and then to throw you off balance and swamp the LH. Keep steady as you 'go down' firmly to lead into b.146 with a clear and definite upbeat sixth. End the movement with maximum vitality.

Second movement – Adagio (6)*

John McCabe also has a particular affection for this movement: 'The Adagio's opening theme, in D minor, is extraordinarily delicate, with its halting, pathetic tune, above a simple Baroque accompaniment – its restatement, in F, as a more continuous line' (from b.9) 'with flowing accompaniment, is like a ray of sunshine.'†

It is a good plan to try bb.9 – 12 and to find a tempo at which the RH figuration, particularly in b.11, flows easily and unhurriedly over the even LH quavers, and from this to settle on an overall tempo for the whole movement.

bb.1 – 8 Set a steady crotchet pulse from b.1 with evenly detached, not spiky, LH thirds. Follow the detailed articulation of the RH carefully and expressively, while feeling the overall melodic shape of bb.1 – 8. Lean on the dotted quavers on the 1st beats of bb.1 – 4 etc, timing the demisemiquavers accurately and lightly and letting the repeated detached quavers 'speak' in a melodic, and again not spiky style. Then, observing the quaver rests, place the detached offbeat RH quavers and the slurred quaver upbeats to bb.2, 3 and 4 accurately. Ensure throughout the first eight bars that all these RH melodic figures are kept in place by perfectly steady LH crotchets. 'Finish off' the slurred crotchets clearly on the 2nd beat of b.8, and be sure to give full value to the two crotchet rests.

bb.9 – 37 Moving into F major at b.9, continue to follow all RH detailing expressively over an even LH accompaniment, carefully implementing the effect of the *tenuto* lower crotchets and slurred inner quavers. In b.13, phrase the ascending

†John McCabe, *Haydn Piano Sonatas* (BBC Music Guides).

semiquavers in a gently detached, 'speaking' style. Do not panic at the demisemiquaver and hemidemisemiquaver scale in b.15, nor at the 'free' scale in b.21. Both will fit in quite easily to the slow pulse providing that the *LH* quavers continue to move evenly. In b.15 *crescendo* up the scale to arrive on the top A to coincide exactly with the LH slurred crotchet chord on the 4th beat of the bar. Be sure to give this 4th beat its full value, and then 'lean' on the tied RH third on the 1st beat of b.16, place the low C exactly on the 2nd beat, and 'tail away' the RH demisemiquaver thirds down to the detached quaver third on the 3rd beat. Rise to a singing tied minim F on the 1st beat of b.21, and start the 'free' scale almost immediately after the second LH quaver of the bar (A). It is easier at first when you are practising, to *play* the tied RH quaver (D) *with* the second LH quaver, and to divide the run into groups of five, six and five notes to fit with the second, third and fourth LH quavers of the bar. Then when you grow more confident you can let the groups merge more freely over your perfectly steady LH. Take time to 'point' the coming interrupted cadence as you move through the second half of b.21, letting the RH trill run easily over your steady LH. Then give full value to the crotchet rest on the 2nd beat of b.22, and 'come in' again with a resonant RH sixth and LH third on the 3rd beat of the bar. Place the RH fragments eloquently through b.23 over steady LH crotchets, and then let the detached RH thirds 'go on down' into the LH, to finish neatly on the 3rd beat of b.24, as if in a continuous line. Moving back to D minor at b.25, the music strikes a more profound note. 'Point' the inflection to the major on the 1st beat of b.26, and then phrase the syncopated RH line smoothly and beautifully through b.26 (and bb.29 and 34) over a continuingly even and steady LH. Make a gradual *diminuendo* from b.35 as the music hovers over the dominant pedal point, and 'carry on' the line of the detached semiquavers down to a quietly resonant bass A in b.37, and poise yourself on the pause to lead straight into the Finale.

Finale – Presto (7)

From a rhythmic point of view this movement is delightfully provocative and capricious.

bb.1 – 24   As will immediately be seen, the problem lies in maintaining control of the pulse, despite the persistent syncopating effects of the tied upbeats (to bb.1, 5, 7, 9 and 25 – 30, etc.). Establish a brisk, but not hectic 3/4, with an overall feeling of one-in-the-bar. Mark the implied emphasis with a 'lean' on the opening RH upbeat, likewise on the upbeat to b.5 etc, supporting these tied thirds with clear LH minims on the 1st beats of bb.1 and 5, etc. Be sure to come *off* cleanly on the 2nd beat of bb.2, 4, etc, so that the subsequent upbeat is always perfectly placed and timed. From the upbeat to b.3, phrase the RH sixths smoothly, feeling the 'normal' 1st beat of b.3. Show the 'drone' effect of the D's in the lower LH (bb.9 – 13) and in the inner RH (bb.10 – 13) as you support the RH with resonant LH chords. From the upbeat to b.14 control the RH quavers with a firm LH line, and be sure to 'finish off' the slurred RH crotchet clearly on the 2nd beat of b.16, before you leap up to 'lean' again on the tied upbeat to b.17.

bb.25 – 64   After the first double bar continue to emphasize the tied upbeats, first in the LH and then in the RH from the upbeat to b.29, steadying yourself by also 'leaning' on the *RH* slurred crotchets on the 1st beat of bb.25 – 8, and on the *LH* minims on the 1st beat of bb.29 and 30. In order to keep steady again after the second double bar, feel the 1st beats clearly and accurately, whether in the LH (bb.41, 42, 44, etc.) or the RH (bb.43, 47, etc.). Lead off firmly therefore ('taking over' from the RH upbeat quavers), with firm LH *staccato* crotchets in b.41, letting the RH detached offbeat quavers follow evenly and relatively lightly as the LH 'goes to' a firm crotchet third on the 1st beat of b.42. Then let the RH quaver figure in b.42 'go to' a firm 1st beat of b.43, immediately 'taking over' again with the LH *staccato* crotchets on the 2nd

82

and 3rd beats, and so on. Give a firm LH lead from bb.49 – 64 (only momentarily 'taking over' with the RH in b.62). Underpin the RH quaver figures with resonant, sustained dotted minim chords on the 1st beats of bb.50 – 2 etc.

From bb.65 – 8 give firm 1st beats with the RH and LH alternately. Lead *bb.65 – 111* off with smooth inner LH crotchets from the upbeat to b.69, over the sustained pedal point A, letting the RH offbeat detached quavers again follow relatively lightly. Take time to 'point' the interrupted cadence at bb.87 – 8, coming to a resonant 'stop' on the diminished 7th chord. This is followed by an extraordinary cadenza-like passage from the upbeat to b.89 through to b.102. Balance the insistently syncopated RH tied upbeats, with a firm LH on the 1st beat of bb.89 – 92 and 95 – 6 (reversing the procedure from the upbeat to b.99). Give full value to the tied dotted minim chords (bb.93 – 4). Count the rests (bb.102 – 3) and resume the 'normal' pulse smartly with the triplet upbeat to b.104. Spread the RH chords snappily in bb.104 – 5, and go on to end in immaculate time. Once rhythmic stability has been achieved, do avoid giving the impression of a dogged adherence to the beat, and enjoy and convey the exuberance of this movement to the full.

No. 40 in E flat major
(Hob. XVI/25)

First movement – Moderato (8)*

This is an audacious and dynamic movement, a worthy successor to the first movements of Nos. 30, 31 and 33.

The movement opens rousingly, even aggressively. Set a firm and very *bb.1 – 7* *moderato* crotchet pulse, bearing in mind the elaborate figurations to come.

Lead off with a resounding RH line, and follow the detailing of the RH in meticulous time in bb.1 – 2 over strongly supportive LH octaves. Do not shirk the abruptness of the RH *staccato* quavers, nor the fierceness of the LH detached crotchet octaves through b.2. Articulate the contrapuntal dotted rhythm figures through bb.3 – 5 with military precision. Give a firm tied crotchet C on the 1st beat of b.3, and feel that the LH dotted rhythm figure 'goes to' the slurred quaver on the 2nd beat; then feel that the RH dotted rhythm figure 'goes to' a firm tied crotchet on the 3rd beat, and so on. Keep a steady crotchet pulse through b.6 as you articulate the RH descending demisemiquavers 'rattlingly' over a steady LH semiquaver scale (feeling that the LH is 'leading' here), and then run up the RH scale to arrive on the top G precisely on the 4th beat of the bar. (The descending LH semiquaver scale could be either detached or legato, as you feel inclined – the essential is that it is steady.) Detach the RH quavers on the 1st beat of b.7 and time this bar meticulously, *feeling* the dotted semiquaver rest on the 2nd beat. The RH fourth at the end of the bar could be felt either as a rather fierce 'stop' at the end of b.7, in tune with the prevailing temper of bb.1 – 7, or, on the other hand, as an upbeat to the more gracious phrase from b.8.

Find a warmer tone for the melody line from b.8 (though still with vigorous *bb.8 – 14* undercurrents), over evenly pulsating LH semiquavers. Feel the implied 'lean' on the tied B flat on the 2nd quaver pulse of bb.9 and 10, and co-ordinate the upward scale neatly with the LH semiquavers. 'Lean' on the treble tied quaver on the 1st beat of b.11, and 'flick' the hemidemisemiquaver figure lightly and clearly towards the tied quaver on the 2nd beat, and so on, over perfectly even LH semiquavers. After the abrupt *staccato* cadence in b.12, give the crotchet rest on the 2nd beat its full value before the fierce restatement of the opening motif in C minor. Be sure to 'feel' the crotchet rest on the 2nd beat of b.13 and then 'lean' again on the tied top D of the spread chord on the 3rd beat. Place the LH B natural precisely on the 4th beat of the bar, and then keep a steady crotchet pulse as you follow the more gracious RH sextuplet curves.

bb.15 – 27   Launch purposefully into b.15 with a clear B flat chord, returning to a further firm chord on the 1st beat of bb.16 and 17. Take care to keep a steady crotchet pulse through the insistent demisemiquaver figurations here with the help of steady and cleanly phrased LH fragments, and 'trumpet out' the RH semiquaver sixths and thirds through the second half of bb.15 and 16 with a brassy sound. In bb.18 – 19 co-ordinate the descending demisemiquaver scales neatly with precisely timed LH offbeat semiquaver chords. From the middle of b.19 show the slightly syncopating, 'rocking' effect of the offbeat slurred semiquavers alternating between the hands, without losing the sense of your steady crotchet pulse. Control the descending LH broken octaves leading into b.22 by showing the quaver pulse with the fifth finger on the lower F, and then D, as you 'go towards' the strong 1st beat of b.22. In b.22 phrase the RH sixths and thirds brassily again over the insistent reiterated LH semiquavers. Drive on towards a strong spread diminished 7th chord on the 4th beat of b.23, giving this chord its full value and feeling its implied syncopated emphasis. Then time the quick scale to arrive on the top E flat precisely on the 2nd beat of b.24, also timing the remainder of this bar carefully. Give the RH demisemiquaver and LH semiquaver pattern in bb.25 – 6 a 'rumbling' effect (similar to passages in Mozart's D minor Concerto), and end the section in lively style and in immaculate rhythm. Observe the RH slurs and rests precisely in b.26 over steady LH quavers, support the RH demisemiquavers through b.27 with accurately placed LH quaver chords, and end the section with a clear detached high quaver third.

bb.28 – 71   The impressive and extended development section brings an extraordinary series of adventures. Show the 'rocking' effect of the slurred offbeat semiquavers again, starting from a meticulously timed RH upbeat to b.29. At bb.30 and 31 be sure that the LH leads off emphatically, as it restates the opening motif in octaves, and that the LH rhythm is not disrupted by the RH's high semiquaver leap from the 2nd beat of these bars. Practise slowly and absolutely rhythmically 'hands separately' at first. When you put 'hands together' ensure that the LH continues to 'lead' through these two bars, and *not* the other way about. Then following the violent 'stop' in C major at b.32 (which in fact pitches us into F minor), drive on vigorously and in steady rhythm from b.33 towards b.39, where Haydn suddenly veers back to the 'warm' melody of b.8. But this calmer moment is soon disrupted by urgent repetitions of the rising demisemiquaver scale figures, leading to the fierce unison scales and wild dotted rhythms of bb.43 and 44 ending with defiant quaver C's on the 3rd beat of b.44. Make sure here that the hands are perfectly co-ordinated, with the utmost rhythmic vigour. Articulate the demisemiquaver and semiquaver passage-work from b.45 rhythmically and with absolute clarity, but with an almost dogged onward drive as you build up towards the half-close in b.50 on what appears to be the dominant of G minor, but which in fact throws us without warning back into the recapitulation. Be particularly careful to time the LH demisemiquaver fragments precisely through bb.45 – 7, feeling that each is 'going to' a clear quaver on the 2nd, or 4th beat of the bar. Support the RH with firm LH octaves on the 1st, 2nd and 3rd beats of b.48 as it plunges down to a firm quaver D on the 3rd beat. Then feel that the *LH semiquavers* and *not* the RH demisemiquavers are 'leading through' to the emphatic 'stop' on the 3rd beat of b.50. Feel the implied, syncopating little 'surges' in both hands up towards the B flats on the last quaver pulse of b.48, and up again towards the B flats on the 4th quaver pulse of b.49, and also to the RH B flat and LH G on the 12th and 16th semiquaver pulses of b.49, and the 4th semiquaver pulse of b.50. In bb.58

and 68 shoot up the rapid scales, in each case arriving on the top note on the 2nd beat of the bar.

Second movement – Tempo di Menuet (6)

This movement proceeds in strict canon, with the RH leading in the first section, and the LH in the second. However interesting this experiment may have been to Haydn himself, most players will find it a sad letdown after the adventures of the first movement. Practise carefully 'hands separately' in short sections, and then when you put 'hands together', ensure that each hand has equal importance and clarity.

bb.1 – 44　　Lead off with a clear ornamented upbeat, feeling that this is 'going to' a firm 1st beat of b.1. These ornamented upbeats can be interpreted throughout: Immediately establish your clear minuet pulse with the three steady descending RH crotchets in b.1. Be sure that the LH 'follows on', perfectly matching the RH, and without disturbing the steadiness of the RH crotchets. It is particularly important to the rhythmic impulse that you feel each clearly ornamented upbeat is 'going to' the subsequent 1st beat. (Treat the appoggiaturas on the 1st beat of bb.2, 3, and 4 as firm crotchets.) Similarly let the LH upbeat fifth 'go to' a firmly slurred crotchet fifth on the 1st beat of b.5 as the emphatically defined RH dotted rhythm figure takes off on the offbeat to 'go to' a firm tied crotchet on the 1st beat of b.6, and so on. Shape the LH crotchet thirds smoothly through b.8 up to a resonant slurred third on the 1st beat of b.9, ready for the RH semiquaver scale to take off in a neat *crescendo* up to the high quaver on the 3rd beat. Then feel that the upbeat third is 'going to' a clear dotted crotchet third on the 1st beat of b.10 as the LH scale follows on, and so on. 'Join in' confidently with the LH on the offbeat in b.12, to make a more emphatic *crescendo* up to the 4th beat. Be sure to 'finish off' the LH dotted quaver precisely in b.14 ready for the LH to lead on confidently into the second section from a clear upbeat to b.15. Give the LH dotted rhythm thirds in b.23, the matching RH thirds in b.24, and similarly the dotted rhythm figures through bb.31 – 5, a bright brassy sound. Be particularly careful to keep a steady crotchet pulse through bb.31 – 6. As always in such instances, think of each semiquaver as the 'upbeat' to the subsequent main beat, rather than as the 'tail-end' of the previous beat.

No. 41 in A major
(Hob. XVI/26)

First movement – Allegro moderato (8)*

This Sonata has another delightfully original first movement, less spectacular than the first movement of the previous Sonata in E flat, but glowing with invention – rhythmic elaboration alternating with warm lyricism.

bb.1 – 10　　The rhythmic patterns of the opening bars are like steps in a formal dance. Set a steady *moderato* crotchet pulse. From a neatly timed LH upbeat 'go to' a clear detached quaver on the 1st beat of b.1, and then give the descending detached figures in either hand in b.1 a bright 'woodwind' colour. In b.2 time the RH meticulously over steady LH chords. Be sure to 'feel' the quaver rest on the 4th beat of b.2, before entering again with a precisely timed *LH* upbeat. Be careful that the rhythm does not flounder in bb.3 – 4. Keep the LH quavers very steady through b.3, feeling the 1st, 2nd and *4th* crotchet beats clearly *within* these quavers. 'Flick' the RH demisemiquaver figures lightly down from the top notes, and balance yourself rhythmically by making a little extra emphasis on the RH demisemiquaver figure falling on the 3rd beat (when the LH has a quaver rest). Then in b.4 feel that the RH is 'leading', while also taking care to place the LH offbeat quaver chords immaculately. Observe the rests precisely through these two bars and then lead on with a clear upbeat to b.5, following on with a confident RH triplet 'upbeat' to the 3rd beat of the bar. In the first half of bb.6 and 7 feel that your neatly articulated figures are 'going towards' singing RH dotted quavers and LH dotted crotchets on the 3rd beats (and similarly to the RH slurred crotchet on the 3rd beat of b.8.). In b.9 ensure that you sustain the treble dotted crotchet E on the 3rd beat, and then incorporate the turn smoothly into the melodic line as you 'go to' the slurred crotchet on the 1st beat of b.10. Maintain a *steady* and supportive LH through these bars (6 – 10).

bb.11 – 29　　From bb.11 – 14 introduce a smooth, more mellifluous tone as you shape the three separate lines with equal care, giving the RH tied minims in both the upper and inner parts sufficient tone to sing through their full duration. Study each line separately here. Then continue to follow the two RH lines smoothly through bb.14 – 18, listening acutely to the varying intervals over even LH semiquaver broken octaves. Treat the grace notes in b.19 like acciaccaturas that are not too clipped. Then 'lead' in bb.20 – 1 with neatly placed LH quaver chords on the crotchet beats, and 'flick' the RH demisemiquavers up to lightly emphasized tied quavers so that the overall rhythmic effect is of even quaver beats alternating between the hands. Keep a steady pulse as these RH figures become more bird-like and screeching through bb.21 and 22. Place the LH quaver chords *firmly* on the 1st and 2nd beats of b.22 and go up to a ringing treble detached E on the 4th *quaver* pulse. Then 'rip up' to the dotted semiquaver B on the 6th *quaver* pulse in immaculate time, and feel, as the trill runs through the 4th beat of the bar, that you are making a steep *diminuendo* towards the warmly lyrical fragment beginning on the 1st beat of b.23. Go very *legato* here as you shape the RH line expressively, listening to the subtle clash of the RH appoggiatura A natural on the 3rd beat against the A sharp in the LH semiquavers. 'Open out' towards a leisurely pause on the 3rd beat of b.24, and then follow the relaxed RH octave line smoothly from the upbeat to, and through, b.25, 'leaning' on the slurred crotchets on the 1st and 3rd beats, over evenly placed offbeat LH quaver chords. In b.26 be sure that the first of the two RH demisemiquavers is placed *on* each quaver pulse, and does not anticipate it, and make a brisk 'skipping' effect as you come clean *off* each *staccato* quaver. Then follow the leisurely line of the RH sextuplets smoothly through to the double bar.

bb.30 – 38　　The development, like that of No. 40, is extended and wide-ranging, but rhythmically more complex. In b.30 keep steady, being quite clear, as in b.3, exactly where the crotchet pulse falls. Let the demisemiquaver figures *crescendo* upwards from the upbeat to b.31 and then be sure to 'feel' the quaver rest on the *2nd* beat of b.31. Feel the triplet sequences from the middle of b.31 as a 'linking' passage, leading to the melodic passage beginning with the RH quaver F sharp on the 3rd beat of b.33. Practise from here at first without the ornaments so that you fully absorb the rhythm and shape of the melody line. Then incorporate the ornaments smoothly, making sure that the evenness of the LH sextuplets is never undermined. Feel the rests like 'breathing points' in a vocal line, and play this passage with all the eloquence you can muster. It is 'correct' here, and certainly easier, to allow the RH demisemiquavers (as on the upbeat to b.34, and through bb.36 – 7) to coincide with the relevant LH triplet note. On the other hand, players may find a slight 'shortening' of some, at least, of these notes more expressive.

bb.39 – 82　　Arrive resonantly on the chord of C sharp on the 1st beat of b.39, and then be careful to keep a steady crotchet pulse through bb.39 and 40. 'Lead' clearly with the LH, 'pointing' the LH semiquavers purposefully, and keeping the RH relatively light as you descend towards a firm LH quaver octave on the 1st beat of b.41. In b.41 and in the *first* half of b.42, the rhythmic effect is the same as that of b.20. Then from the *second* half of b.42, through b.43 and the first half of b.44, show that the demisemiquaver figures fall *on* the quaver pulse (as in b.26). From the middle of b.44 follow both the upper and inner RH lines smoothly, listening to the changing intervals, as at bb.14 – 18. Through the sequential passages from bb.47 – 55 ensure that all long and tied notes in either part are held for their full value. This long passage of RH part-writing (bb.44 – 55) must move smoothly and expressively, yet with a purposefully 'ongoing' feeling over very even LH broken octave semiquavers. Make an overall *crescendo* as the pitch rises towards bb.49 – 50, and then gradually subside towards b.55. In bb.55 – 7 (compare with bb.6 – 8) Haydn 'borrows' a figure from the recapitulation. Notice, after the pause in b.59, how the recapitulation opens on the upbeat to the *3rd* beat of the bar rather than to the 1st, and then, having omitted the figure which he 'borrowed' (bb.55 – 7), the rhythmic pattern 'rights' itself at b.65.

Second movement – Minuet and Trio (Al rovescio) (4)

Al rovescio merely means 'in reverse', in other words, in the second half of both Minuet and Trio, the first half is played backwards. Despite the neatness of the trick, the whole affair looks somewhat dull on the page, and indeed can sound dull. On the other hand, if treated in a formal, very stylized manner with carefully controlled sound effects, it can sound quite charming. Thus, although the notes are simple enough to play, the piece really requires the skills of an experienced player.

bb.1 – 20   There are many different ways of articulating the 'plain' notes. Try giving the treble line a smooth light tone and playing the LH crotchets (and the inner RH crotchets in b.4) in a lightly detached 'stepping' style. Then you could slur the high B's on the 1st beat of bb.8 and 9 with a warm 'lean', down to the third on the 2nd beat. Alternatively you could detach *all* the RH crotchets, or slur those on the 1st beat of bb.3 – 5. In any event, lead off with a lightly singing RH dotted minim sixth, and feel the little 'climb' up to a further lightly singing dotted minim on the 1st beat of b.4 and up again to b.6, and finally up to the high B's on the 1st beat of bb.8 and 9. Similarly give the inner dotted minims (bb.3, 5, 6 and 7) a light sustained tone. Set a steady crotchet pulse immediately in the LH through b.1, supporting the RH right through to b.8 with your neatly 'stepping' crotchets and 'leaning' a little on the minim sixths on the 1st beat of bb.8 and 9. Keep the LH crotchets going like a little pendulum through bb. 6, 10 and 11. Then detach the chord in both hands on the 1st beat of bb.12 and 13, and make a clear emphasis on the chord on the 2nd beat, perhaps slurring the treble crotchet on the 2nd beat up to the high B's. Then gradually curve the line down again towards b.20.

Trio

bb.21 – 44   The Trio could perhaps have a sturdier tone. Be sure to give the firm dotted minim chord its full value through b.21. Then play the thirds on the upbeat to, and the 1st beat of, b.23 in a clear detached style. *Feel* the silent 2nd beat of b.23 and shape the 'answering' phrase very precisely. Place the LH crotchets also very precisely on the 2nd beat of bb.25 and 26, and slur the RH thirds neatly up to the 1st beat of bb.26 and 27. Support the RH with resonant LH dotted minim chords through bb.28 – 30, and again through bb.35 – 7.

Finale – Presto (5)

This tiny bustling movement is more tricky than it at first appears. It sets a considerable test of steadiness.

bb.1 – 8   Set a clear crotchet pulse *before* you start, and make it plain that you are starting on the upbeat. Let the brightly articulated scale descend to a firm RH dotted crotchet on the 1st beat of b.2 balanced by neatly placed LH quaver chords. Then feel that the RH is 'taking off' again on the upbeat to b.3 (supported by a clear LH upbeat quaver and then crotchet) to 'go to' a firm slurred crotchet on the 1st beat of b.4, and so on. Take care to co-ordinate the vigorous unison scale perfectly from the upbeat to b.7, and come to a clear 'stop' on the unison crotchets on the 1st beat of b.8.

bb.8 – 26   Then take a quick 'breath' on the quaver rest before leaping up to the high upbeat to b.9. From bb.9 – 13 be sure to sustain the lower LH line and to phrase the inner LH line clearly beneath the clear-running RH semiquavers. Support the RH descending scale with firm LH octaves from the upbeat to, and through, b.14, and carry the RH scale through to a very definite detached crotchet on the 1st beat of b.15. Be very careful to keep steady in bb.15 – 18 by feeling the crotchet pulse securely on the 2nd beat of b.15 (the LH *staccato* quaver E), on the 1st and 2nd beats of b.16 (the LH semiquaver E and the quaver A sharp) and on the 1st beat of b.17 (the RH quaver D), and so on. Keep steady again in b.22, giving full value to the slurred crotchet and quaver, thus poising yourself to start the descending scale in tenths precisely on the upbeat to b.23, rather than 'falling into it'. Articulate this scale as brightly as possible, 'going to' firm quavers on the 1st beat of b.24. Then time the detached quaver chords accurately, 'going to' a strong LH crotchet D on the 1st beat of b.25, and end in lively style with no *rallentando*, descending to ringing unison crotchets on the 1st beat of the final bar.

Among the next six Sonatas, Nos. 42 – 47, published as a group in 1776, there are several works, and in particular first movements, of outstanding interest.

No. 42 in G major
(Hob. XVI/27)

This is a splendid work as a whole for players of Grade 5 – 6 standard. There is nothing, strictly speaking, that is too demanding for Grade 5 players, but because the long passage of Alberti semiquaver accompaniment through the development section could be tiring for a young hand, the first movement has been listed under Grade 6.

First movement – Allegro con brio (6)*

bb.1 – 24   This is a marvellously invigorating movement. Set a brisk but not reckless crotchet pulse, 'con brio' (taking into account the turns in b.1), and lead off from a clear quaver upbeat 'going to' a firm 1st beat of b.1. Give an upward lift to the ornamented RH line towards the 1st beat of b.2. Then place the repeated quaver D's cleanly (rather than letting them slurp into each other), over neatly phrased LH thirds, with the feeling of 'going towards' the 1st beat of b.3. Take care also to support the RH with neatly placed LH chords on the upbeat to, and the 1st beat of, b.6, and to articulate the LH quavers clearly beneath the steady RH crotchets in b.7, 'going' in both hands to firm crotchets on the 1st beat of b.8. Be sure to *feel* the 2nd beat of b.8 on the quaver rest. Then time the descending unison quavers from the upbeat to b.9, and the triplet semiquaver descending figures from the upbeat to b.11, meticulously, sounding jaunty (or mock-serious, as you feel inclined), not ponderous. Give four brisk notes to

the short shakes in b.9, starting on the upper note: Slur the RH

semiquaver couplets neatly in b.13, and then give bb.17 – 20 a more sustained and lyrical tone, 'leaning' warmly on both the RH D sharp and the tied E in b.18 (and similarly in b.20) over warm-toned LH chords. 'Snap' the perky RH acciaccatura, and the demisemiquavers *on* the quaver beats (*not* anticipating them) in b.21. (Play the acciaccatura and quaver just like the demisemiquaver/dotted quaver figures.)

Be sure to 'finish off' neatly in both hands on the 2nd beat of b.24, then *bb.24 – 58*   from the upbeat to b.25, set off with an exuberant rhythmic swing which carries right through the remainder of the exposition. Articulate the two RH melodic fragments brightly from the upbeat to bb.25 and 27, over lively Alberti semiquavers. The LH broken octaves (bb.30, 32 and 34) are awkward for small hands. (Practise them

at first in plain octaves, if possible, and then in a dotted rhythm: ♪. ♪ ♪. ♪ and

♫♫♫ ♫♫♫). Hold fast to your crotchet pulse here and, keeping the ascending RH

quavers perfectly steady, feel that the LH broken octaves 'go to' firm crotchets on the 1st beat of bb.31, 33 and 35, otherwise these intervening bars (31 etc.) are bound to be unsteady. Follow the details of RH slurs and *staccatos* over 'keen' LH semiquavers through bb.36 – 41, and 'go to' and 'lean' well on the slurred crotchet A sharp on the 1st beat of b.41. Then be careful to keep a steady crotchet pulse through b.42, and 'come in' purposefully with the LH quaver upbeat to b.43. Feel the racy, slightly syncopating effect of the slurred ornamented upbeats to bb.44 and 45, etc, over your rhythmic and vigorous LH Alberti semiquavers, carrying off these bars with joyous buoyancy. Help yourself to keep steady through bb.52 – 4 by placing the LH quaver figures precisely, and end the section with bright clear RH quaver chords over clear LH broken octaves. You could either *crescendo* towards a ringing crotchet chord on the 1st beat of b.57, or, perhaps more stylishly, *diminuendo* to *piano*.

After the double bar, with the change to the minor, the music takes a more *bb.59 – 143*   serious turn. Establish the urgent forward drive with purposeful, detached RH quavers, supported by unflaggingly rhythmic LH semiquavers. A long stretch of rapid Alberti bass such as this is often difficult for inexperienced players. Practise slowly and rhythmically, and also practise in dotted rhythms:

♪. ♪ ♪. ♪   and   ♫♫♫ ♫♫♫

see also Introduction. From bb.58 – 71 always feel that the RH quaver figures are 'going to' firm crotchets on the 1st beats of the subsequent bars. Then from the upbeat to b.72 drive on resolutely with lively detached, but rock-steady, RH quavers. Listen acutely to the downward harmonic progressions of the LH from b.80, and then expand a little through b.85 towards a firm dominant 7th chord in b.86, poising yourself through the pause for the return to the opening theme in varied form. From bb.98 – 106 Haydn cannot resist returning to the determined mood of the development. Keep very steady through b.97, so that you do not 'fall into' the 1st beat of b.98. (Feel that the *LH quavers*, rather than the RH triplets are 'leading' downwards here.) Then let your detached RH quavers ascend to a ringing dotted quaver on the 2nd beat of b.99, and go on again through b.100 towards a resonant dotted crotchet sixth on the 1st beat of b.101. Then articulate the reiterated RH figures precisely from the upbeat to b.102 as you lead back towards the continuation of the recapitulation proper from the upbeat to b.107.

Second movement – Minuet and Trio (5)

The gracious Minuet, mainly in a flowing triplet rhythm, has few problems.

Lead off with a clear RH ornamented crotchet (playing the turn *on* the beat) *bb.1 – 14*   over a firm LH crotchet third. Then feel the 'lift' up to the high G as you bring in the triplets in immaculate time. Support the RH with precisely placed

LH crotchets from the upbeat to b.2, and feel in both hands that you are 'going to' the 2nd beat of b.2, playing the RH crotchet thirds and LH crotchets here as if they were slurred. Then support the RH with a firm LH dotted minim on the 1st beat of b.3. Feel the RH triplets are 'going to' the slurred minim on the 1st beat of b.4, and then 'bring in' the LH triplets cleanly on the 2nd beat, letting them 'go down to' another firm third on the 1st beat of b.5. Feel the 'lift' up to the RH diminished 5th on the 2nd beat of b.7. Then show the implied emphasis on the tied RH crotchet A on the 2nd beat of bb.9 – 12, taking particular care to place the LH crotchet chords precisely in these bars. Feel that your curving triplets through b.13 are 'going to' a warmly slurred minim on the 1st beat of b.14, taking care to give the RH and inner LH minims and the crotchets their full value here before leading on into the second section.

bb.15 – 42   Support the RH from b.15 with perfectly steady, evenly running LH triplets. Keep a steady crotchet pulse through b.17 as the RH triplets take over from the LH in a graceful curve. 'Lean' expressively on the slurred quaver on the 1st beat of bb.19 and 20, ensuring that the LH triplets remain steady through this cross-rhythm effect. Take care to keep a steady crotchet pulse again as the neatly shaped repeated figures ascend from b.29, drawing out a little towards the pauses at b.32. Then pick up the tempo briskly from b.33. Show the implied slight emphasis on the tied inner LH upbeat to b.39, ensuring that this note is sustained through the 1st and 2nd beats of b.39.

Trio

bb.43 – 66   Feel the more serious tone of the minor Trio as you lead off in b.43 with a singing RH minim. Then show the 'lift' up to the high second quaver of bb.44 and 46 as you shape these quaver fragments expressively. Support the RH through bb.43 – 6 with warm-toned LH thirds, showing the decisive upward leap to the 2nd beat of bb.43 and 45. Then take particular care to place the LH chords in immaculate time beneath the RH trills in bb.47 and 48. Start these trills on the upper notes (C and D respectively) and do not try to cram in too many notes – twelve notes,

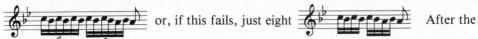 or, if this fails, just eight After the

double bar the reiterated bassoon-like LH broken octaves bring an extra sturdiness and resonance to bb.51 – 4. Treat the grace notes on the upbeat to bb.52 – 4, and from the upbeat to, and through, b.57 like not too clipped acciaccaturas, and then 'lean' on the longer, crotchet appoggiatura A on the 1st beat of b.58.

Finale – Presto (5)*

Let this movement be as merry as possible. The material of the first two sections is varied in each of the following sections. There are no serious rhythmic problems – the essential is to keep steady, never losing sight of the crotchet pulse. Set a realistic tempo therefore, bearing in mind the coming semiquaver figuration.

bb.1 – 25   There are various possible ways of articulating the RH. Detach the upbeats to bb.1, 3, etc, then you can either detach the quavers in bb.1 and 3, or slur the first two and detach the third and fourth. (In bb.73 and 75 Haydn himself slurs the first *three* quavers.) Through bb.5 – 6 the quavers could either be detached or slurred (or again the first pair could be slurred and the second pair detached). In any event, whichever pattern you choose, do define your slurs and *staccatos* cleanly, and be sure throughout the movement to support the RH with immaculately placed and steady LH figures. Leading in with your neat detached upbeat, support the RH with a firm crotchet third on the 1st beat of b.1, and then feel that you are 'going to' a firmly slurred crotchet on the 1st beat of b.2. Then 'finish off' the RH neatly on the quaver on the 2nd beat of b.2, ready to lead on with the detached upbeat to b.3, and so on. It is particularly important throughout that you 'finish off' each phrase cleanly, and lead on with a perfectly timed upbeat as at bb.4, 8, 10, 12, etc. Feel the 'lift' from the quaver upbeat to the quaver on the 1st beat of bb.9 and 11, and then let the descending quaver figures 'go to' firm slurred crotchets on the 1st beat of bb.10 and 12 over neat LH quaver fragments.

bb.25 – 48   Articulate the ascending semiquavers in b.25 towards a bright detached quaver D on the 2nd beat. Support the RH semiquavers with firm LH crotchets on the 1st beats of bb.29 and 30. In bb.37 and 38 let the RH semiquavers 'go to' a firm crotchet on the 2nd beat, and then feel the onward lead of the *LH* quaver upbeat to the 1st beat of the subsequent bar. Phrase the LH fragment from the upbeat to b.39 smoothly, and listen to the sustained tied inner G falling to the F sharp on the 2nd beat of b.40.

bb.49 – 152   'Rattle out' the RH semiquavers (bb.49 – 72) over immaculately placed detached LH thirds (bb.50 – 1) and quavers (bb.53 – 6 and 57 – 63, etc.).

Articulate the LH fragment neatly up to the crotchet on the 2nd beat of b.52, ready to lead on in a poised manner with the RH upbeat to b.53. Be particularly careful to 'point' the quavers on the 2nd beat of bb.57, 58, 59, 60, etc. so that you avoid 'falling into' the upbeats to the subsequent bars. Note Haydn's slurs from b.73, indicating a more *legato* feeling. Find a new, more serious tone colour for the minor section from the upbeat in b.81. Place the slurred offbeat LH quavers carefully in bb.90 – 2 beneath the warmly slurred RH crotchets. Resume the major scamper (supported by a perfectly rhythmic and clear Alberti LH) from b.105. However you may have articulated the quavers initially, it is more effective to play them here in a 'keen' detached style. Avoid unsteadiness in bb.112 and 115 by again 'pointing' the LH quaver on the 2nd beat of each of these bars (and similarly the *RH* quaver in b.137 and the LH quaver in b.139). In bb.141 and 142 be sure to show the 2nd beats securely on the RH G sharp and A sharp respectively, where the LH has a rest.

No. 43 in E flat major
(Hob. XVI/28)

First movement – Allegro moderato (8)*
This is a powerful and eventful movement. Take heed of the indication *Moderato* (bearing in mind the occasional sextuplet passages to come, as at bb.46 – 7 etc, and the tricky RH ornamentation, bb.11, 45 – 6, etc.) and set a decisive and steady crotchet pulse.

bb.1 – 8   Lead off boldly with a full-toned RH tied crotchet B flat, and vigorously articulated semiquavers, over very rhythmic and energetic LH detached quavers. Let these LH quavers ascend towards a firm crotchet on the 1st beat of b.2 as the RH detached quavers 'take over' to ascend to another firm tied B flat on the 1st beat of b.3, and so on. Let the RH 'go to' a clear quaver E flat on the 1st beat of b.4, and then feel that the evenly reiterated RH sixths are 'going to' a singing slurred seventh on the 1st beat of b.5, with the LH seconds following on evenly, and in turn 'going to' the slurred second on the 1st beat of b.6. From the middle of b.7, 'snap' the RH demisemiquavers smartly *on* the quaver beats, against very steady LH quavers. 'Finish off' the phrase with a clear LH crotchet placed almost with a 'plonk' on the 2nd beat of b.8, and be sure to *feel* the crotchet rest on the 3rd beat, before leading off again with the RH in b.9.

From the upbeat to b.11, keep the awkward RH trills on the quavers neat

bb.9 – 28   and short: [music notation] or [music notation] over firm and steady LH

crotchets (likewise at bb.45 – 6 and 48 – 9). Feel that the RH figures through b.11 are 'going to' a strong dotted crotchet on the 1st beat of b.12, as the LH also 'goes to' a resonant minim (take care also to place the inner LH crotchet E flat clearly on the 2nd beat of b.12 beneath the held RH dotted crotchet). Then let the RH run clearly to, and 'lean' well upon, the slurred crotchets on the 1st beat of bb.13 – 15 over neatly placed LH quaver thirds, and come to a clean 'stop' on the 2nd beat of b.16. 'Lean' again on the tied crotchets on the 1st beat of bb.17 and 19 over neat LH thirds, and shape the RH semiquavers clearly up to the quaver on the 4th beat of bb.18 and 20. Then balance yourself by placing the LH upbeats to bb.21 and 22 neatly, 'going to' firm thirds on the 1st beats of bb.21 and 22 to support your RH semiquavers. *Crescendo* through the ascending scale in b.22 towards a ringing quaver B flat on the 1st beat of b.23, and 'skip' briskly down through b.23. The awkward RH figures with the turns in thirds (bb.25 – 6 and 27 – 8) will need careful, slow and rhythmic practice. 'Lean' on the RH dotted crotchet thirds on the 1st beats of bb.25 and 27, and then be sure to mark the 2nd beats of these bars clearly in the LH. (To help a clear execution of the turns, the lower note of the upbeat thirds (C) and the lower note of the thirds on the 1st beat of bb.26 and 28 (D) can be taken with the LH.) Then keep steady in bb.26 and 28 by placing the detached repeated LH quavers precisely on the crotchet beats, with the equally carefully placed RH detached quaver thirds following steadily.

bb.29 – 58   From bb.29 – 35 let the treble melody line sing out buoyantly over even and steady but 'ongoing' LH repeated quaver chords. 'Draw out' b.36 a little as you move towards the *Adagio* and pause (bb.37 – 8), and then resume the tempo smartly with the slurred quavers on the upbeat to b.39. Take care to time the ascending triplets through the 3rd beat of b.42 to arrive on a ringing tied crotchet B flat precisely on the 1st beat of b.43, balanced by a meticulously placed LH quaver third and crotchet. 'Go to' a firm RH tied crotchet B flat on the 2nd beat of b.46, and then move into the RH triplets with an easy swing, steadied by firm LH crotchets. (Take particular care to place the LH third accurately on the 3rd beat of bb.46 and 49 beneath the tied treble B flats.) Support the RH through bb.51 – 4 with firm and accurately placed LH quaver-crotchet B flats, and 'snap' the demisemiquaver figures energetically again in bb.53 and 54. 'Point' the LH quaver on the 2nd beat of b.55, and make a tiny break, so that you don't 'fall into' the subsequent detached quavers. Treat the RH grace notes here like acciaccaturas. Break off as if in mid-flight on the 2nd beat of b.56, *feel* the crotchet rest on the 3rd beat of b.56 and end the section in perfect time.

bb.59 – 83   Set off with renewed vigour into the development. Listen to the smoothly ascending inner LH quaver line through b.61, and to the sustained seventh through b.62, beneath the snapped RH figures. Listen acutely also to the subtle resonances of b.63 as the syncopated RH line descends smoothly over the even LH lines, and then articulate the RH and LH figures energetically again through bb.64 – 7. Then from bb.68 – 77 balance the sound carefully between the hands to avoid undue shrillness through this urgent passage of high-pitched writing. As at bb.4 – 5, feel that the reiterated quaver figures in either hand are 'going towards' the slurred minims on the subsequent 1st beats. You could either make a *diminuendo* or a *crescendo* as you 'draw out' through b.76 towards the pause at b.77. Place the lower F of the diminished 7th arpeggio precisely on the 3rd beat of b.81 (taking the four demisemiquavers with the LH) and *crescendo* towards a singing tied treble C on the 1st beat of b.82, and then steady yourself with an accurately placed LH quaver and crotchet. (These two bars appear more complicated than bb.42 – 3, on account of the 'uneven' arpeggio figure.)

bb.84 – 155   Let the RH descend in grandly improvisatory style through bb.84 – 5 over a resonant tied LH D flat chord, again keeping the RH trills neat and short, and then control the brilliantly whirling RH triplet and sextuplet passage-work through bb.86 – 8 with a sustained LH through b.86, and then with powerful and rhythmic LH detached crotchets through bb.87 – 8. Drive on resolutely, maintaining a taut crotchet pulse, towards the 'written out' pause on the dominant 7th at b.96, in preparation for the start of the recapitulation in b.98. Do not shirk the jagged persistence of the 'snapped' demisemiquavers from b.91. Keep steady with the help of clear and firm LH quaver-crotchet figures in bb.89 – 93 (as at bb.51 – 4) and with firm LH quaver octaves through b.94. Be sure that in b.140 you arrive on the B flat crotchet octave precisely on the 2nd beat of the bar, and then count a full crotchet rest.

Second movement – Minuet and Trio (5)*
This Minuet and Trio is of special charm, spare in texture, with a delicate poise, and with subtle interplay between the hands.

bb.1 – 32   Lead in with an immaculately timed ornamented upbeat 'going up to' a clear detached (not spiky) crotchet on the 1st beat of b.1. Then be careful to place the LH crotchet third precisely on the 2nd beat ready for the RH to lead on in perfect time with the next ornamented upbeat, and so on. The turns on the upbeats can either be placed *on* the beat, or more easily, *anticipating* the beat (see the opening of Sonata No. 20). Then let the RH triplets descend easily but rhythmically towards a warmly slurred crotchet on the 1st beat of b.4. Listen to the sustained upper and lower LH lines from the upbeat to b.5 beneath the varied figures of the RH and then, from b.8 through to the double bar allow the triplet lines to 'take over' from each other evenly, as they alternate between the hands. Feel that the LH triplets in b.8, beneath a singing RH tied dotted minim, are 'going to' a clear crotchet F on the 1st beat of b.9. Then 'take over' confidently with the RH on the 2nd triplet quaver of b.9, to go on in turn to a singing dotted minim on the 1st beat of b.10, and so on. Take care to 'finish off' the LH neatly with the quaver on the 2nd beat of b.12, ready to lead on with the upbeat into the second section, finding a more serious tone colour here as you turn into the minor. Then returning to the major, keep a steady crotchet pulse as the RH triplets ascend through bb.17 – 20 with the help of immaculately placed, detached crotchets in the LH. Make sure that the triplet scale in tenths is smoothly co-ordinated up to the 1st beat of b.31.

Trio
bb.33 – 48   Do not make the mistake, in view of the foregoing triplets, of thinking that the RH three-quaver upbeat to the first bar of the Trio (and the subsequent upbeats to bb.34 and 35) are also triplets. 'Lean' expressively on the slurred RH crotchets on the 1st beats of bb.33 and 34, placing the LH thirds smoothly and neatly. Then continue the RH line smoothly through to b.40 over immaculately shaped LH fragments. Throughout this Trio, feel the wistful and serious charm of the quiet chromatic inflections, and listen acutely to the little hushed diminished 7th arpeggio as it descends from the RH upbeat group to b.45 towards the sustained lower dominant at b.46. Listen again to the inflections of the RH line as it curves smoothly above even inner LH crotchets over this tied B flat through bb.46 – 7.

Finale – Presto (6)*
The Finale is in a variation form on a rather similar plan to that of the previous Sonata, but it is, if anything, even more engaging, always on the brink of laughter. Set a realistic

crotchet pulse, as fast as is safe, bearing in mind the semiquaver figuration (bb.23 – 44 and 107 – 128).

bb.1 – 22   'Lean' lightly on the slurred quaver upbeats to bb.1 and 2, 7 and 8, etc, and also on the slurred LH offbeat quavers (observing the rests precisely in either hand), thus creating an amusing rocking, syncopated effect in these bars. Then observe the further syncopated effect in bb.3 – 5, 9 – 11, etc, showing the implied 'lean' on the syncopated RH crotchets over the continuing neatly slurred offbeat quavers. Take care, however, amidst all this rocking and leaning, not to lose the sense of your basic crotchet pulse. Keep steady between bb.5 and 6 where the RH quaver upbeat is tied, by lightly marking the 1st beat of b.6 in the LH (and similarly at bb.20 – 1 and 49 – 50). Take care to 'finish off' neatly with the LH quaver in b.12, and then perhaps 'open out' the tone a little as you lead off sprily into the higher register with the slurred upbeat to b.13.

bb.23 – 72   Leading off from a lively detached upbeat to b.23, carry off the semiquaver arpeggio patterns of the first variation with the utmost rhythmic verve. Keep steady in bb.23 – 4 and 29 – 32, etc. by 'pointing' the LH detached quavers (E flat in b.23, B flat in b.24, etc.) clearly on the 2nd beat of these bars, so that you don't 'fall into' the upbeats to bb.24, 25, etc. Again in bb.25 – 8 and 39 – 42 keep the RH figures in place by keeping an even and steady line in the LH. In the second variation (from b.45) 'flick' the triplet upbeats, with a twittering bird effect, down to lively *staccato* quavers on the 1st beat of bb.45 and 46, 57 – 60, etc, and be sure to place the LH offbeat quaver chords neatly in these bars. Then make a quite different, bassoon-like sound in the lower register as you 'go down' to the *crotchets* on the 1st beat of bb.51 and 52. Savour the unexpected C flat octave in the LH (on the 1st beat of b.53) and then follow the syncopated RH line smoothly over even 'step-like' LH octaves. Sustain both the inner and lower LH lines warmly from the upbeat to b.61, and also feel the lightly syncopating effect of the implied emphasis on the RH tied quavers in bb.61 – 3. End the section with brightly detached RH quaver sixths and LH quavers.

bb.73 – 172   Find a more subdued tone colour for the minor moment, from the upbeat to b.73. In contrast to the 'normal' slurred style you could detach the unmarked quavers from the upbeat to b.87. Then 'draw out' the sustained bars (91 – 4) observing the multiple pauses, in a progressive *rallentando* effect, before dashing off again with the upbeat to b.95. 'Rattle out' the RH semiquavers from b.107 with all the brilliance you can muster, keeping control of the rhythm with a firmly placed LH, and with tiny accents on the first note of each group of four RH semiquavers (particularly on the 2nd beat of bb.107 – 8, 113 – 14, 119 – 22, etc, when the LH is silent). It is easy to be unseated between bb.141 and 152 if ever you lose sight of the crotchet pulse. Shape the slurred LH thirds in bb.141 – 2 and 147 – 8 graciously and without hurry, and lightly mark the 1st beat of bb.146 and 152 in the LH, beneath the tied RH quaver thirds.

No. 44 in F major
(Hob. XVI/29)

First movement – Moderato (8)*

This is another exciting and original movement. Players lacking the courage to commit themselves to the thrills and spills of its bizarre rhythmic landscape and wild changes of mood had better pass on. Once more, bearing in mind the rhythmic intricacies to come (see bb.15 – 20 etc.), heed Haydn's indication *Moderato* and set a firm and very steady crotchet pulse.

94

bb.1 – 14   In b.1 project the march-like figure forthrightly, with precisely timed detached RH chords over steady ostinato repeated detached LH quavers. Then feel the more sustained quality of the RH answering phrase (bb.2 – 3) observing the articulation of the RH precisely. Place the *staccato* bass 'march' fragment solidly in b.4. Follow the curves of the more yielding treble solo phrase from the upbeat to b.7, then 'lean' warmly on the emphasized slurred RH quavers from the upbeat to bb.8 and 10, placing the LH offbeat chords lightly. These *forte-pianos* indicate melodic emphases, not jerky bumps. Then *crescendo* through b.13 towards the wide-leaping *staccato* quavers in b.14. 'Pluck' these quavers vigorously as you plunge forcefully downwards to the low G and pause.

bb.15 – 31   In the rapid ascending arpeggio figures like screeching birds (bb.15 – 16 etc.) and in the menacing reiterated detached single notes and thirds in bb.21 – 3, Haydn (not for the only time, and however fortuitously) recalls the idiosyncratic sound effects of Scarlatti. Work out the rhythm of bb.15 – 16 etc. by tapping or clapping out at first the quaver beats (and then, when you have absorbed the rhythm, the *crotchet* beats) and mentally fitting in the rapid notes. Then, 'feeling' the quaver rest at the beginning of b.15, zip up to a strong top C as fast as a *glissando*, making sure that you arrive on the top C's exactly on the 2nd and 4th crotchet beats of the bar. Help to keep steady by placing the two LH detached quavers very precisely on the 4th and 5th quaver beats of the bar. Execute these figures with glittering brilliance of tone. Then be sure to 'snap' the RH demisemiquavers *on* the quaver beats at the end of bb.16 and 17. Drop to *piano on* the 2nd quaver of b.21, and *crescendo* in tautly controlled tempo with 'plucked' quavers, then semiquavers, towards a strong LH diminished chord on the 1st beat of b.24, making a further *crescendo* through brilliant ascending RH triplets towards a ringing *staccato* D on the 3rd beat. Then, as in several of his 'dramatic' first movements (see Nos. 30 and 33), Haydn defuses the tension by ending the exposition with more formal passage-work. Poise yourself therefore at the beginning of b.25, after the leaping *staccato* quavers, to follow the semiquaver curves of the RH gracefully, placing the LH figures smoothly but with absolute precision through to the double bar. End the section quietly with neat, clear triplet figures over precise LH quaver chords.

bb.32 – 90   Exploit the drama of the development section, though without becoming too Beethovenian. Trumpet the chords of the 'march' fragment (bb.32 – 4, and 37) with a ringing clarion sound (perhaps spreading the big chords on the 1st beats, at any rate in the LH) and keep the LH quavers going resolutely. Then in contrast, give the low RH thirds (bb.35 – 6) a warmer, horn-like quality. Listen through bb.39 and 42 to Haydn 'worrying' at the naturals and flats, with 'snapping' acciaccaturas over smooth and resonant supporting LH thirds. From b.44 underpin the RH with strongly resonant sustained LH semibreve chords, taking care to keep a steady crotchet pulse as the RH curves magisterially up to and down from the highest notes of each improvisatory broken chord figure. Then plunge down to a resonant bass minim A on the 1st beat of b.49. Through bb.54 – 5 feel that the amazing, exultant, wide-leaping *staccato* quavers are plunging upwards and downwards in continuous wide 'arcs', rather than in isolated 'plonks'. Then, having dropped to *piano* again on the first of the RH quavers in b.56, drive on in tautly controlled rhythm in a gradual *crescendo* towards the start of the recapitulation at b.60. For once Haydn leaves his recapitulation more-or-less alone. This time, however, in contrast to the end of the exposition, *crescendo* through the 'extended' b.89 towards *forte* final chords.

Second movement – Adagio (6)
In contrast to the first movement, the Adagio moves with measured expressive solemnity.

To set a tempo, try playing from the middle of b.6, and find a tempo at which the LH semiquavers and RH demisemiquavers of b.7, and the detached RH demisemiquaver scale of b.8, flow comfortably and naturally, to lead easily into the long melodic passage beginning in b.9. There should then be plenty of time for the ornamentation in bb.1 and 2, etc. to fit into the melodic line in a leisured manner.

bb.1 – 8   Practise bb.1 and 2 at first without ornaments. Time the RH figures carefully over immaculately placed LH quaver thirds or single notes (which occur, as will be seen, regularly *on* the crotchet beats). Observe the RH rests precisely, but at the same time try to show that the RH is moving in overall melodic curves, rather than in a series of disjointed fragments. When you add the ornaments, place them *on* the beat, incorporating them smoothly and graciously into the overall melodic line (rather than, as so often happens, 'clamping' them on in a series of fraught clusters). Then in bb.3 – 4 phrase the RH thirds smoothly over even LH offbeat semiquavers. Feel, again, a wide melodic curve from the crotchet third on the 1st beat of b.3, up to the dotted quaver third on the 2nd beat. Keep a steady crotchet pulse as the RH moves into demisemiquavers at b.5. 'Finish off' the RH demisemiquavers down to a quiet but clear bass quaver B flat on the 2nd beat of b.6, and then enter with a singing ornamented crotchet on the 3rd beat. Slur the RH demisemiquaver couplets neatly through the second half of b.7 over smoothly phrased inner and lower LH lines. Finish off the RH scale with delicate, not spiky, *staccatos* in b.8.

bb.9 – 36   From b.9 phrase the treble line expressively, in a 'vocal' manner over an easy-moving, even, demisemiquaver Alberti LH. Observe all RH rests, feeling these like 'breaths'. But at the same time do phrase mentally *over* the rests. Thus, in b.9 lead off with a singing dotted quaver C, and then do not feel that the melody line stops dead on the E natural on the 2nd beat, but mentally carry the melody on in a continuous curve up to the offbeat high C, as a singer would. Do not dab vaguely at the offbeat detached semiquavers through b.11 but let them 'speak' expressively as you make an overall *crescendo* towards b.12. Then take time to 'point' the interrupted cadence in the middle of b.12. Do keep the LH semiquavers moving in an even, quietly rhythmic flow right through from b.9 to the middle of b.13. Feel, as always in such circumstances, that the eloquent RH line is fitting in with this steady yet 'ongoing' LH, and *not* the other way about. On the 1st beat of b.14 be sure to give the treble ornamented tied crotchet D its full value, 'feeling' the held 2nd crotchet beat of the bar, like a 'written-out' pause. Show the continuous RH line from the high demisemiquaver C near the middle of b.15, right down to the low 'horn-like' cadential chords in b.16. Through bb.19 and 20 you could either *crescendo* or *diminuendo* towards the half-close at b.21. In either case feel that the RH 'is going on down' to the LH crotchet D on the 3rd beat of b.21. At b.27 continue the RH slurs through the bar.

Third movement – Tempo di Menuet (6)
This movement, of a rather sober cast, takes the form of variations on the first two sections, with an intervening 'Trio-like' minor episode (from bb.19 – 45).

bb.1 – 18   Time each ornamented upbeat immaculately, with the feeling of 'going up to' a clear and definite detached quaver on the 1st beat of bb.1, 3, etc. Give six notes to each trill (starting on the upper note, and including the 'turn':

). In each instance ensure the smooth transition from the upbeats to the subsequent 1st beats by using the second finger and thumb respectively on the 'turned' ending to the trills (B natural and C), and then going up to the fourth or fifth finger on the 1st beat of b.1 (and the fifth on the 1st beat of bb.3 and 5). Then establish your precise minuet tempo securely as the detached RH quavers descend in perfect time towards the warmly slurred crotchet on the 1st beat of b.2. Support the RH with warm-toned and accurately placed LH thirds. Be sure to 'finish off' neatly in both hands with the quaver on the 2nd beat of b.2 (and in all similar instances e.g. bb.4, 8, 53, etc.) and then to show the semiquaver rest before leading on in immaculate time with the next ornamented upbeat. Follow the contrapuntal writing smoothly from b.5, letting the RH 'lead' clearly into b.5, with the LH quavers following on evenly and going towards a firm minim B flat on the 1st beat of b.6, and so on. (Ensure that the syncopated RH B flat and tied upbeat A are perfectly co-ordinated with the 4th and 6th LH quavers in b.5.) Let the LH lead off boldly from the upbeat to b.9, with the RH quavers 'entering' smoothly in the 4th quaver pulse of the bar. Finger this upbeat: 3 2 3 2 3 5 3, or if you must, take it with the RH! In this case be careful to 'take over' neatly, and without a bump, with the LH, on the B flat or the A in b.9. Listen acutely to the striking intervals between the hands as the quavers curve through bb.9 – 10. Here, as so often in this movement, the quality of sound is distinctly 'woodwind'. Then take care to maintain your steady minuet pulse as you run up the little scale flourishes through bb.13 – 14.

bb.19 – 45   Lead into the minor section gravely with even upbeat quavers. Then listen acutely again to the expressive and concentrated interplay between the hands as the RH 'goes to' a singing dotted crotchet on the 1st beat of b.19,† the LH 'following on' to go to a singing dotted crotchet third on the 2nd beat, and the RH going to a singing tied upbeat to b.20, and so on. Lead off with the LH from the upbeat to b.27, and be careful to sustain the inner and lower LH lines from the upbeat to b.30 through to b.32. Lead up to the *tenuto* and pause in b.40 through an implied slight *rallentando*, resuming the tempo from the upbeat to b.41 for the little passage of improvisatory play on the minor tonic (bb.41 – 4).

bb.46 – 100   From b.46, as you move into the easy-flowing triplets of the first variation, do be careful to preserve the steady minuet pulse (and similarly when you move into the semiquavers of the second variation at b.72). It is easy to lose the pulse at bb.50 – 1 (the varied version of bb.5 – 6). Lead off with a singing treble tied C on the 1st beat, then 'take over' the crotchet pulse in the LH from the 2nd beat, letting the treble line follow smoothly in cross-rhythm. Feel that the LH triplets in b.50 are 'going to' a firm LH minim B flat on the 1st beat of b.51, with the RH triplets similarly 'going to' the minim on the 1st beat of b.52. (Follow similar 'leads' in bb.76 – 9.) Feel the implied emphasis on the tied RH crotchets on the 2nd beats of bb.54 and 55, and similarly on the tied *LH* crotchet in b.56. Keep steady from bb.90 – 3, 'leading' with clear LH quavers in b.90, and similarly with the *RH* quavers through bb.91 – 2. Time the penultimate bar precisely, 'snapping' the slurred demisemiquavers neatly *on* the quaver beats, and coming cleanly *off* each dotted semiquaver, and end in immaculate time.

†NOTE: If you have the new Associated Board selection of 23 Sonatas, in which this Sonata is included, both first-time and second-time bars are counted. This creates a discrepancy in bar numberings from b.19 onwards.

No. 45 in A major
(Hob. XVI/30)

First movement – Allegro (7)

Although there is less drama and excitement, and this movement is of much lighter weight, both in texture and from a technical point of view, than the first movements of the two previous Sonatas, there is still no let-up in Haydn's ceaseless flow of invention and experiment. Set a bright march-like tempo, imagining a quick 'step' to the quaver pulse.

bb.1 – 16   Lead off from a clear and neatly timed upbeat figure, and play the opening bars lightheartedly, but with the utmost precision and clarity. Support the RH with clearly placed LH quaver thirds on the 1st and 2nd beats of b.1. Let the RH 'go to' a clear detached quaver on the 1st beat of b.2, and then take care to time the LH offbeat quaver chords, and the RH fragments immaculately as the hands alternate through bb.2 – 4. In b.5 keep the RH dotted rhythm in place with steady LH quaver sixths. 'Go to' firm unison crotchets on the 1st beat of b.8, and *feel* the quaver rest on the 2nd beat. Then following all these dotted rhythms, show the contrasting evenness of the rising *legato* semiquavers from the upbeat to b.9. Support the RH with a warmly sustained LH tied minim fourth on the 1st beat of b.10. From the upbeat to b.13 play the detached 'horn-call' figures with military precision. 'Finish off' clearly with the quavers on the 1st beat of b.16, and take care to *feel* the silent 2nd beat before leading on with the upbeat to b.17.

bb.17 – 60   Lead purposefully through b.20 towards firm slurred crotchets on the 1st beat of b.21 and take care to 'finish off' cleanly in both hands on the 2nd beat of the bar. Then leading on from a clear RH quaver upbeat, phrase the RH semiquaver line smoothly through bb.22 – 5 over a warmly sustained LH. Lead into b.26 from a clear LH quaver upbeat; and then be careful not to thump out the reiterated patterns from b.26, but *listen* to every inflection of the *legato* LH semiquavers beneath the even pulse of the RH quaver seconds or thirds, making a gradual overall *crescendo* towards b.33. Listen to the inner sustained minim through b.33, and feel that the LH semiquaver line is 'going to' the tied minim E on the 1st beat of b.34. Then feel that the inner LH semiquavers are 'going to' the inner tied G sharp on the 1st beat of b.35, and listen to the sustained LH notes as the RH continues its line through bb.35 – 6. Then from b.38 lead off in the LH with sharply 'plucked' *staccato* quavers, following with evenly placed (and also *staccato*) relatively light RH semiquavers. Go very *legato* with the unison semiquavers at b.47, feeling tiny, light syncopating 'surges' up to the B's on the 2nd *quaver* pulse of bb.47, 48, 51 and 52. Keep the descending broken sixths smooth and steady through b.49, and steady yourself with a firm LH crotchet and quavers in b.50. Articulate the 'horn-calls' again exuberantly from b.55, ending the section with sharply defined little semiquaver flourishes. Alternatively you could play the 'horn-calls' in a distant *pianissimo*, and end the section quietly.

bb.61 – 153   From b.69 keep a taut rhythm as you pursue the development of the material from bb.38 – 46, again leading clearly with the LH. From b.79 keep the alternating upper and inner semiquaver phrases running smoothly, always feeling that each of these is 'going to' a singing minim on the 1st beat of the subsequent bar. Keep steady throughout this passage (bb.79 – 84), with the help of firm lower LH minims and even inner LH quavers. From b.85 lead up in a gradual *crescendo* towards the pause on the dominant 7th (of F sharp minor) at b.96, listening particularly, through this passage, to the changing RH intervals. Articulate the unison semiquavers resonantly from b.97. Then from b.103 you could either *crescendo* towards the dominant chord on the 1st beat of b.108, or alternatively make a gradual *diminuendo*. In either case be sure to *feel* the silent 2nd beat of b.108 before launching back into the recapitulation with a perfectly timed upbeat.

Near the end of the recapitulation (from b.154) lead up in a resonant *crescendo*
bb.154 – 83   towards the dominant 7th flourish at b.162, observing the pauses *on* the 1st
beat *and* over the rests. The dramatic C sharp major chords, followed by a quiet cadence, announce the startling interlude (rather than the slow movement) from b.165. You could either carry the sustained RH melody in continuous sweeping lines over a buoyantly 'plucked' LH arpeggio accompaniment; or alternatively play this passage in a quietly expressive, contemplative manner over gently detached LH quavers. In either event make your effect with conviction, with a degree of freedom which is, however, governed by the steady but persistently 'onward' impetus of the LH quavers. Allow yourself to 'go with' the natural curves of the melody line. 'Lean' on a singing tied minim on the 1st beat of b.165, and on the long appoggiatura on the 1st beat of b.166, and then feel the 'lift' up to, and implied emphasis upon, the dotted crotchet on the 2nd beat of b.167, and the tied crotchet on the 2nd beat of b.169, and so on. End the section with perfectly timed chords in the low register.

The *Tempo di Menuet* (7)* (or 6 for older players), is in the form of a theme and variations, in which Haydn's treatment of his material is unfailingly delightful. As there is no clear division between the movements of this Sonata, the Vienna Urtext Edition numbers the bars continuously through the work.

Establish a clear minuet tempo in the RH (note Haydn's direction *cantabile*)
bb.184 – 99   and place the occasional LH fragments precisely. In the theme, and
throughout each variation, feel that the first phrase is 'going to' the slurred 1st beat of the second bar (b.185) and similarly that in the third bar (b.186) you are 'going to' the 1st beat of the fourth bar (b.187). Do be careful to place the LH slurred crotchet precisely on the 2nd beat of b.185, and the two LH detached crotchets equally precisely on the 2nd and 3rd beats of b.187. Then feel the gentle implied melodic and rhythmic emphasis on the tied crotchets on the 2nd beat of bb.188 and 189 (and similarly in bb.196, 197, 204, 205, etc.), being particularly careful to place the LH slurred crotchets accurately on the 3rd beat of these bars, beneath the tied RH. Ensure that the minuet rhythm is maintained with perfect poise through each variation.

In Variation 1 show the smooth 'lift' up to the quaver on the 4th *quaver*
bb.200 – 63   pulse of bb.200 and 208. And in b.210 'lift' again to the high crotchet E
as you shape the syncopated RH curve smoothly over even LH crotchets. In Variation 2 let the LH 'lead', phrasing the warm-toned inner melody line smoothly over sustained lower dotted minims, with the RH quavers following evenly on the offbeat in bb.217 and 219, etc. Be sure to 'feel' the held 3rd beat in bb.220 and 221, and to co-ordinate the scale figures in thirds smoothly here. In Variation 3 let the curving semiquaver lines alternate evenly between the hands. Feel that the RH semiquavers in b.232 are 'going to' a singing slurred minim (E) on the 1st beat of b.233, and that the LH semiquavers in b.233 are 'going to' the crotchet on the 1st beat of b.234, and so on. Practise the expressive individual lines of Variation 4 separately, sustaining all the long notes warmly, and listen acutely to the interplay of the three lines (or four, from b.260) when they are put together. Again feel that each smooth quaver fragment is 'going to' the minim on the 1st beat of the subsequent bar.

Variation 5 is disconcertingly difficult to time. Work out the rhythm to begin
bb.264 – 79   with away from the keyboard. Feel the rhythm slowly in quaver beats at
first, then when you count in crotchets, ensure that you arrive on the detached

treble quaver (A in b.264 and D in b.266) precisely on the *2nd* crotchet beat of these bars, and that you place the uppermost note of the little descending scale (C sharp in b.264, B in b.266) precisely on the 3rd beat. Time bb.265 and 267 equally carefully, 'leading' with a singing treble minim, and allowing a full crotchet rest in the LH on the 1st beat. Then 'lead' on the 1st beats of bb.268 – 70 with singing *LH* slurred minims, while also feeling the implied emphasis on the RH dotted crotchets on the *2nd* beat of bb.268 and 269. Do not be caught out by the 'ordinary' (non-triplet) semiquavers in bb.270, 273 and 275. Be sure that the LH quaver coincides exactly with the first RH semiquaver in bb.272, 274 and 276, and also be very sure to feel the silent 2nd beat in bb.273 and 275. Take time to absorb these rhythmic niceties so thoroughly that you can forget about *counting*, and toss this variation off with grace and spirit.

After Variation 5, the beginning of Variation 6 will sound slow. Hold fast, bb.280–311 however, to the minuet pulse as you listen to the resonance of the low RH melody line, against the gruff but clear bass fragments (bb.1 – 4). Do not panic at b.284 – there is plenty of time for the run within the crotchet pulse. Make sure that you arrive on the dotted crotchet F sharp precisely on the 2nd beat of the bar, feeling the usual 'lean' on this note, and steadying yourself with a clear LH crotchet on the 3rd beat. Let the widely-spaced LH quaver lines of bb.289 and 291, and the RH quaver line of b.292 curve expressively up towards singing dotted minims on the 1st beats of the subsequent bars. Treat the grace notes (bb.290 and 297 – 8, etc.) like gentle, not too 'snapped' acciaccaturas. Listen to the inflections of the LH quavers in bb.305 and 307 beneath singing RH ornamented slurred minim thirds. In general, allow a freer feeling through this final variation (though always within a stable crotchet pulse), and finish with neat chords in the last two bars precisely in tempo.

No. 46 in E major
(Hob. XVI/31)

First movement – Moderato (7)

This is a lively and pleasant movement, though less striking than the first movements of its neighbouring Sonatas. Set an easy crotchet pulse that will accommodate the predominant sextuplet figuration without any feeling of hurry.

Lead off warmly and smoothly with the treble melody in thirds (following bb.1 – 8 the parts clearly when they 'divide' in the second half of b.1). Follow on, entering neatly on the offbeat, with an equally carefully shaped LH line, being sure to hold the tied upbeat quaver B over the bar line and through its full (minim) duration in b.2. Finish off the first phrase neatly, allowing a full crotchet rest on the 4th beat of the bar, as you prepare to lead off similarly again with the RH in the lower register, on the 1st beat of b.3. Lead off at the beginning of b.5 with a singing tied crotchet E, and then keep the flowing sextuplet lines in place with neatly but quietly interjected LH offbeat octaves.

Lead off yet again in the RH with a sustained treble dotted crotchet on the bb.9 – 16 1st beat of b.9, and phrase the wide leap of the LH fragment in thirds as if in a wide curve. (It is interesting to note that in b.3 of Sonata No. 47, the RH is identical with the RH here in b.9.) 'Finish off' the RH demisemiquaver/semiquaver figure neatly in b.10, and be sure to 'feel' the semiquaver rest on the 6th quaver pulse of the bar, and then to 'come in' on the offbeat triplet with a perfectly co-ordinated unison scale figure. Leap up calmly (rather than lurching up in a panic – there is plenty of time to 'get up there'!) from a firm RH low quaver F sharp on the 1st beat of b.11, to resume the 'delayed' melody line with the syncopated treble crotchet F sharp, steadying yourself with a clear LH quaver third on the 2nd beat. Let the LH upbeat sextuplet 'go down to' a firm crotchet B on the 1st beat of b.13. Then through bb.13 and 14 follow the RH sextuplet and triplet curves smoothly over precisely placed detached LH quavers, feeling that these LH quaver fragments are 'going to' firm crotchets on the 1st beats of bb.14 and 15. Go to, and lean well upon the slurred RH crotchet (F double sharp) on the 3rd beat of b.15 (and 'lean' similarly on the 1st and 3rd beats of b.16) over neatly placed LH offbeat chords.

bb.17 – 24 Set off with a clear quaver chord on the 1st beat of b.17, and then listen to the gracious interplay of the sextuplet and triplet figures between the hands, within an even crotchet pulse. In bb.17 and 18 take care to co-ordinate the 'entry' of the RH semiquavers precisely with the LH slurred quaver and crotchet. Arrive on a clear RH crotchet on the 1st beat of b.21 as you shape the LH broken chord down to a clear *quaver* on the 2nd beat before leaping up, again without panic, to place the high LH quaver D sharp in perfect co-ordination with the 'entry' of the RH triplets. Listen to the resonance of the tied inner RH upbeats to the 1st and 2nd beats of b.23, as you move towards a clear, spread quaver chord on the 3rd beat, and end the section with a clear B major arpeggio, neatly finished down to the bass quaver on the 3rd beat of b.24.

bb.25 – 65 In the development section feel the forward impulse and urgency of the reiterated RH three-quaver and slurred crotchet figures in bb.29, 30 and 31, over very even LH triplets. Feel in each of these bars that the three quavers are 'going towards' the slurred crotchet on the 3rd beat, 'leaning' well on this slurred crotchet, and do observe the quaver rests at the beginning of bb.30 and 31 (like 'breathing' points). Build up the dynamics towards b.32 (letting the LH triplets 'go to' a firm quaver chord on the 1st beat of b.32), and then continue the *crescendo* with strong LH chords, 'drawing out' the treble line after the 3rd beat in a *rallentando* towards the ornamented minim in b.33. Give the appoggiatura a good crotchet value, and give full value to the whole chord as well as to the pause effect of the minim rest. From the middle of b.36 the music takes another more serious turn. Follow the sustained LH lines resonantly, and then continue to support the RH with a strong octave line from b.38, as you listen to all the inflections of the RH triplets, building up the dynamics towards the half-close on the dominant at b.41. Steady yourself here, 'feeling' the quaver rest on the 4th beat of the bar before coming in on the offbeat, to lead into the recapitulation with a perfectly timed RH sextuplet run. Be sure that this upbeat run 'goes up to' a *firm* third on the 1st beat of b.42, letting the LH come in smoothly to run up to an equally firm B on the 2nd beat. In b.44, phrase the chromatic variant of the opening figure with 'sliding' smoothness.

Second movement – Allegretto (6)(O)*

This short movement, a sort of *moto perpetuo* of quavers in strict three-part writing, of pervasive, lightly hypnotic effect, is probably more suited to the older player at Grade 6. Those familiar with it cannot fail to be reminded of Scarlatti's Sonata in B minor (Kp. 87). Although the Scarlatti piece is in four parts, the atmosphere of this *Allegretto* and the style of the part-writing, sometimes widely spaced, sometimes moving in very close harmony, is extraordinarily similar. Set a stable but easy-moving crotchet pulse. Study the parts separately, following the gracious melodic curves of the phrases as smoothly as possible, in continuous onward motion.

bb.1 – 24 Sustain the RH dotted minims warmly through bb.1, 2 and 3 showing the 'entry' of the inner RH part in b.2 as you establish the even quaver movement in the LH. Shape the two RH lines carefully through bb.4 – 6, ensuring that in the treble line the dotted crotchet E on the 2nd beat of b.4, the minim A sharp on the

2nd beat of b.5, and the minim B on the 1st beat of b.6 all have sufficient tone to sing through their full duration. Note also and listen to the inner tied crotchet upbeat (E) to b.5, and the inner tied quaver upbeat (also E) to b.6. Similarly ensure that the treble crotchet line and inner RH syncopated line (bb.19 – 21) move evenly and smoothly. Allow the dynamics to undulate gently with the rise and fall of the phrases. Feel a rise, then, up to the treble dotted crotchet E on the 2nd beat of b.4, falling a little towards the end of b.6. Then start the new phrase clearly on the 1st beat of b.7, to rise towards b.12, and so on. Note the steeper 'climb' of the treble line from the crotchet D on the 1st beat of b.16, through elaborate crossing of the parts, up to the high quaver D on the 2nd beat of b.18 as the LH proceeds downwards in an even scale. Then let the two upper lines curve easily down towards the low ending of the first section, supported by a quietly resonant LH through bb.21 – 4.

bb.25 – 47   Lead off in a rather fuller tone from b.25, sustaining the upper tied minim D warmly as the inner voice moves towards a singing tied minim on the 2nd beat of b.26, and so on, listening acutely to this interplay between the upper voices, above the continuing procession of curving LH quavers, through to b.32. Then, from b.39 continue to shape the upper parts (now joined by a fourth voice) expressively over the long dominant pedal point as you move towards the quiet dominant chord at b.47, ready to spring straight into the Finale.

Finale – Presto (6)

This Finale, in variation form, is based on an epigrammatic, lively folk-like tune. It is more tricky than it at first appears. It is essential to absorb the rhythm of bb.1 – 16 thoroughly, and to preserve it all through the variations.

bb.1 – 32   Set a smart but steady crotchet pulse. Lead off from a bright detached quaver upbeat, and define the detailed articulation of the RH quavers clearly; the ornamented *slurred* quavers, followed by two *detached* quavers in bb.1 and 2, the slurred quaver couplets in b.3, etc. Be sure that these RH figures are supported by an immaculately and firmly placed LH. Take care to 'finish off' each phrase clearly in the LH down to the crotchet or quaver on the 2nd beat (as in bb.4, 8, and all similar instances through the variations) so that you are poised to lead on clearly with the subsequent RH quaver upbeat. Note Haydn's *tenuto* in b.8. In bb.9 – 13 the same RH detailing as bb.1 – 2 can be assumed. From b.17 'rattle out' the RH semiquavers, again over a clear, and precisely placed LH. Again detach the two RH quavers sharply in bb.17, 21, 22, etc. Be particularly sure to 'finish off' the LH neatly down to the quaver B on the 2nd beat of b.20.

bb.33 – 64   In the more *legato* variation from b.33, note the *different* detailing: the first *three* quavers in bb.33 – 4 etc. are slurred, and in b.33 the fourth is *staccato*.

But feel, in contrast, the implied emphasis on the tied treble quaver upbeat to b.35. Place the LH crotchet thirds firmly in b.35, feeling the further implied emphasis on the inner LH tied upbeat to b.36, and then also 'lean' on the treble slurred A sharp on the 1st beat of b.36. Make a little *rallentando* towards the pause on the dominant 7th chord in b.44, observing the sustained lower LH B through b.43. In the minor variation from b.49, establish a clear and vital LH, marking the crotchet beat in the semiquavers with a little accent with the fifth finger on the 2nd beat of the bars as well as the 1st (particularly when the RH is silent on the 2nd beats, as in bb.49 – 50 etc.), and likewise in the *RH* semiquavers from b.57. Carry off this whole section with maximum *brio*, and feel that your brassy-toned RH chords are 'leading' through bb.49 – 56, and vice-versa through bb.57 – 64.

Carry on from b.73 to the end with high spirit. From bb.73 – 80 'rattle out'
bb.65 – 101   the RH semiquavers, again over a firm and perfectly timed LH. From b.81
establish a clear and rhythmic Alberti LH. Practise this in dotted rhythms

 (see also Introduction for hints on practising Alberti basses).

In bb.82, 84, etc, feel the racy implied emphasis on the RH crotchet octaves on the 2nd
beat, in perfect co-ordination with your very rhythmic LH. Play the RH octaves (bb.85 – 8
and 93 – 6) boldly and jauntily. 'Go down' firmly and without panic to the LH A and
E on the 1st beat of bb.87 and 88 respectively (and 95 and 96). It is effective to make
a *diminuendo* (but not a *rallentando*), from the upbeat to b.97, down to a *pianissimo*
chord on the 1st beat of the penultimate bar, and then to end with two bold *subito forte*
chords.

No. 47 in B minor
(Hob. XVI/32)

First movement – Allegro moderato (7)*
The first movement is as uncompromisingly fierce and defiant as that of No. 40 in E flat
major. But this movement, while equally or even more powerful in impact, with an
unremitting rhythmic drive from first note to last, is both shorter and less technically and
rhythmically complex.

Set an incisive *moderato* crotchet pulse, and give the ornamented RH minims
bb.1 – 12   on the 1st and 3rd beats of b.1, and the dotted crotchet on the 1st beat of
b.2, a full, strong tone (placing the ornaments clearly *on* the beat), accompanied by vigorous and very rhythmic 'plucked' LH quavers. Time and shape these LH
semiquaver figures carefully in b.1 so that you make it clear that the 2nd and 4th beats
of the bar fall on the D, and C sharp respectively. Treat the ornament on the 1st beat
of b.2 either like those in b.1, or (as given in some editions) as a turn. This forceful opening
theme opens out, from the upbeat to b.3, into a more *cantabile,* but still resonant, treble
melody. Let the LH 'go down to' a firm crotchet D on the 3rd beat of b.2 while at the
same time 'finishing off' the RH cleanly on the quaver B. Then make it clear that the
three quavers (F sharp) are the upbeat group to b.3. Play these repeated quavers in a barely
detached style, so that they 'speak' (rather than slurring into each other), as they 'go towards'
a singing dotted crotchet on the 1st beat of b.3. Then in b.3 keep a smooth RH line, and
ensure that the RH ornaments and dotted rhythms do not disrupt the even placing of your
LH offbeat chords. Come clean *off*, and *feel* the quaver rest on the 4th beat of b.4. (No
one but Haydn, surely, would throw us with an interrupted cadence four bars into an
'important' first movement!) Compare this phrase with bb.9 – 10 in the first movement
of the previous Sonata, No. 46. The RH line of b.3 here is identical to that of b.9 in No. 46.
But in No. 46 the phrase does the expected thing, and returns in the subsequent bar to
its temporary 'base', C sharp minor. 'Point' the interrupted cadence therefore in b.4, and
be sure to come *off* cleanly so that you *feel* the silent 4th beat before leading on with a
clear treble upbeat to b.5. Shape the more yielding solo lines from here in gracious curves,
feeling that you are 'going to' a warmly slurred crotchet on the 3rd beat of b.5 supported
by warm-toned LH slurred thirds. 'Finish off' cleanly in both hands on the 4th beat of
bb.5 and 6 so that you lead on clearly with the RH upbeat to bb.6 and 7. Then 'go' more
resolutely towards a stronger slurred crotchet chord on the 3rd beat of b.7 as you *crescendo*
towards the restatement of the opening motif. Arrive on firm unison crotchets on the 3rd
beat of b.8, and poise yourself on the silent 4th beat ready to set off again. Show the
insistence of the sharply articulated, reiterated dotted rhythm figures through b.10, and

their increasing jaggedness from the end of b.11. Keep your rhythm intact through these bars with the help of a firmly placed and 'ongoing' LH. Support the RH with a carefully placed slurred broken octave on the 2nd *quaver* pulse of b.11, and with a firm LH line from the upbeat to b.12. 'Finish off' cleanly with the quavers in both hands, and *feel* the crotchet rest on the 4th beat as you prepare to launch into b.13.

bb.13 – 28 Give a strong D major LH chord (perhaps spread) on the 1st beat of bb.13, 14 and 15, and then 'catch' the subsequent LH quaver D with the fifth finger and hold it right through each bar. Alternatively (and I personally find that this works better), change quickly on this second quaver D from thumb to fifth finger. 'Come in' clearly with the RH to join in with the LH on the 2nd quaver pulse of b.13. Pursue the LH quaver lines and slurred RH semiquaver figures resolutely, feeling that the LH is 'leading', and show the 'churning' effect as you return towards the strong D major chord on the 1st beat of bb.14 and 15. Then from b.15 hold the LH D right through to b.17. From the middle of b.17 and through b.18 feel that the semiquavers 'open out', and relax a little (though without getting slow). It is effective to make a *decrescendo* through b.18. Then from b.19 resume the onward drive in a *crescendo* towards the 1st beat of b.22. Feel that the RH quavers are 'leading' through b.19, and that the LH quaver line 'takes over' the lead from b.20. There is an awkward moment in the middle of b.21. Make a little break in the LH quaver line as you leap up to the high G on the 4th quaver pulse, and place the LH *over* rather than *under* the RH as you play the LH quaver G and F sharp. Keep a steady pulse through this bar as you proceed towards a firm LH crotchet and RH quaver A on the 1st beat of b.22. Then take care to continue in a steady crotchet pulse as you swing into the more formal and graceful triplet and sextuplet figuration. Make a little break after the quaver A on the 1st beat, and 'bring in' the triplets confidently on the high D. Support the RH with a firm and carefully placed LH crotchet on the 3rd beat of b.23. Slur the RH semiquaver couplets cleanly over a *steady* LH quaver line through b.25 and the first half of b.26. Be sure to 'go to' a definite quaver chord on the 3rd beat of b.26 so that you don't 'fall onwards' into the second half of the bar. It is these last three bars of the exposition (and similarly bb.68 – 70) that are perhaps the most difficult to keep steady. Be very conscious of the sense of the crotchet beat as you lead on from the sixth quaver pulse of b.26, imagining that the LH semiquaver intervals are slurred. Then support the RH with very definite LH quavers at the end of b.27 and end the section with clearly placed detached RH chords 'going to' a ringing D major chord on the 3rd beat of b.28.

bb.29 – 70 The relentless onward drive is resumed in the development section, but with another more relaxed interlude from the middle of b.34. Let the treble melody sing eloquently here over even LH semiquavers, and feel the implied melodic emphasis on the tied treble upbeats to bb.35, 36 and 37. At b.38 show the increased intensity given to the opening motif by the octave doubling of the LH *staccato* figures. In b.40 let the vigorously slurred LH offbeat broken octaves 'buoy along' the treble reiterated fragments. Listen to the smooth descending LH line through bb.41 – 2 beneath the RH dotted rhythms. From b.43, where they are 'doubled', the dotted rhythms grow increasingly vicious and jagged. Let the RH really 'bite' as it plunges downwards towards the start of the recapitulation in b.48 over strong sustained dominant notes in the LH. Maximize the effect of this passage by treating the RH figures as if they are slurred, so that you come *off* each *staccato* demisemiquaver and (see Haydn's staccatos in bb.41 – 2) and *drop* the hand onto each subsequent quaver (similarly in *both* hands through bb.43 – 5), which

perforce causes a more 'biting' accent on the quavers:  (Some

editors favour a *diminuendo* as you descend towards b.48, in my view an effect completely at variance with the forceful intent of this passage.) Note and 'point' the varied touches in the recapitulation; the strong unison progression towards the dominant crotchets in b.54; the tonic pedal point through bb.63 – 3; and be careful to time the diminished 7th arpeggio precisely in b.66 so that you arrive on a definite high quaver B exactly on the 3rd beat of the bar.

Second movement – Minuet (Tempo di Menuet) (5)*

The lines of the Minuet are elegantly shaped, and the texture open and clear. As is so often the case, Haydn reserves his expressive intensity for the minor (Trio) section.

bb.1 – 22 Set off with a clearly articulated upbeat, and be sure to time the unaccompanied dotted-rhythm figures accurately on the 1st beat of bb.1, 3 and 5, feeling a 'lift' up to, and implied emphasis upon, the tied crotchets on the 2nd beat of these bars. Do place the LH crotchet chords or single notes neatly, particularly the sixth on the 3rd beat of b.1 beneath the tied RH. Start the trills on the upper notes,

using eight notes or, if this feels too scrambled, just six

'Finish off' neatly with the crotchets in both hands on the 2nd beat

of bb.2, 4, etc, ready to lead on with a poised RH upbeat to bb. 3, 5, etc. Then feel the implied 'lean' on the slurred LH augmented fourth upbeats to bb.6, 7 and 8, and be sure that *both* the repeated RH quavers on the 2nd beat of bb.6 and 7 are detached. All but the very experienced will be tempted to take the 1st beat of b.5 (and more particularly b.17) with the LH. (If you *must* do this, ensure that you do not forego the implied emphasis on the tied crotchet on the 2nd beat, which occurs *naturally* when the upward leap is taken with the RH. But it is far better to take the leap with the RH – composers create intervals like this not at random, but because they *want* the effect of the wide span.) Time this 1st beat precisely, without skimping the value of the dotted quaver, then allow just an extra fraction of a second as you leap up calmly and confidently, not lurchingly, to a warm-toned upper tied crotchet. *Listen* to the sustained LH sixth beneath the RH semiquavers through b.8. Then lead off into the second section as you turn into the minor, in a rather fuller tone. 'Point' the more expressive intervals through bb.11 – 13, and then support the RH semiquavers through bb.14 – 16 with a warmly sustained LH line.

bb.23 – 40 From b.23, in effect a minor Trio, Haydn reverts to the mood of the first movement with a positively aggressive forward drive. Give full value to the firm crotchet upbeat, then stress the 1st beat of bb.23 and 24 in both hands (recalling the 'churning' effect in the first movement, bb.13 – 15), as you pursue the LH quaver and RH semiquaver figures energetically. Then 'pluck' the *staccato* quavers vigorously in tautly controlled rhythm through bb.25 and 26. Maximize the tension of this movement by giving the feeling that the 'brakes' are on, controlling, though not dragging back the onwards impetus. Preserve this taut rhythmic control after the double bar, where a menacingly snaking reiterated semiquaver figure in the RH complements the active quaver lines of the LH. Drop the tone to *piano* from the upbeat to b.31, and then *crescendo* steeply towards the 1st beat of b.34. Feel that the resolute LH crotchets are 'leading' from b.37, and end the section with defiant LH and RH crotchets on the 1st and 2nd beats of b.40.

Finale – Presto (8)*

The Finale is dominated by an urgent reiterated quaver figure which immediately sets its tone of demonic energy. This figure is tossed around contrapuntally in combination with a descending five-quaver/crotchet figure which first appears in the LH, from the upbeat to b.6.

Set a rock-steady crotchet pulse *before* you start. You will find that a tempo
bb.1 – 13   which allows the passage from b.39 to sound frenetic, yet tautly controlled,
is the right one for the movement as a whole. Make it clear that you are starting
on the upbeat, and 'pluck' the reiterated quavers energetically through b.1. Then show
the precise detailing of RH slurs and *staccatos*, also taking care to place the LH slurred
fragments accurately on the upbeat to, and 1st beat of, bb.3, 4 and 5. From the upbeat
to b.6 'join in' actively with the LH descending *staccato* figure, feeling that this figure
'goes down' to a firm crotchet on the 1st beat of b.7. Then from the upbeat to b.8 show
the 'entry' of the opening figure clearly in the LH and then again in the RH from the
upbeat to b.10. Come to a clear half-close on the 1st beat of b.13, and then *feel* the quaver
rest on the 2nd beat before darting off again on the upbeat to b.14.

In contrast to the activities of the RH, phrase the LH thirds smoothly from
bb.14 – 39   the upbeat to b.16. Come clean *off* in mid-air in b.18, and do have the courage
to give full value to the 'written out' pause from the end of b.18, coming
in again precisely on the upbeat to b.21. Feel the hectic 'slide' of the chromatic octaves
from the upbeat to b.23 (and 27) and steady yourself with the LH octave fragment in
b.24. Then keep a firm hold on the crotchet pulse as the RH and LH fragments alternate
between bb.24 and 37. Observe all rests and be particularly careful to place the LH offbeat
fragments accurately. Go as *legato* as possible in the RH from b.28, then follow suit in
the LH from b.29. Keep yourself perfectly steady from b.29 by always feeling that the
RH upbeat quaver is 'going to' a clear dotted crotchet on each 1st beat, with the LH similarly
'going to' a clear crotchet on each 2nd beat. Then continue the RH *legato* through to
b.37, placing the LH fragments with special care as you make a very little *ritenuto* into
b.37. Poise yourself on the pauses to hurtle off again on the upbeat to b.38.

From the upbeat to b.40, let the LH quaver octave figures *crescendo* upwards
bb.39 – 193   towards a firm crotchet on the 1st beats of bb.41, 43, etc. against the hectically
'buzzing' RH semiquavers. Support the RH with firmly placed crotchet chords
on the 1st beats of bb.46 and 47, and with rock-steady quaver chords through bb.49 – 50.
From bb.63 – 7 keep your brilliantly articulated reiterated RH semiquaver figures in place
with firm LH chords. Break off in mid-air again at b.69. After the double bar follow
the contrapuntal workings energetically. From b.80 let the alternating inner LH, and RH
repeated quaver figures 'go to' firm minims on the 1st beat of each subsequent bar, over
steady and resonant lower LH minims. Again be sure to give full value to the 'written
out' pause (bb.94 – 5) and then lead off incisively with the LH from the upbeat to b.96.
Then be sure to sustain the lower LH minims (bb.99 and 100 and 103 and 104) and listen
to the discordant effects from the upbeat to b.98, through b.99, and to the sharp clash
of the RH and LH upbeats to bb.100 and 104. Practise this passage (bb.98 – 104), snail-
slow, so that you fully absorb these raucous discords aurally. From the upbeat to b.106
let the LH octaves *crescendo downwards* towards the crotchets. Keep the RH semiquavers
going furiously, through to b.123, supported by urgent but steady LH chords. Build the
dynamics as the hands move apart in contrary motion from b.147 towards a powerful-
toned pause on the dominant at b.150 as you gather yourself for the final wild lap. Support
the RH with ferociously 'plucked' LH crotchets from the 2nd beat of b.161 through to
b.164. End the movement with unabated defiance and without the hint of a *rallentando*.
Do not panic at the sight of the RH octaves, from the upbeat to b.185. Paradoxically,
if you feel that the *LH* quavers are 'leading' (from the upbeat to b.185) you will keep
steadier, and feel more confident with your RH octaves. And the more positively you leap
up to the octave G on the upbeat to b.187, the less likely you are to fluff it!

This movement is not, strictly speaking, technically too difficult. It is a matter of maintaining its furious drive, within a firm crotchet pulse from first note to last. This does not mean a continuous *forte* − it is far more effective to drop the tone, for example after the pause at b.37, gradually building up again from b.40 (or alternatively to *diminuendo* to *pianissimo* at b.37, and start *forte* from the upbeat to b.38), and to drop to *piano* after the double bar, and again after b.123. But the dynamic possibilities are limitless, and no two performances of this wild gallop can, or should, come out the same. And we must *feel*, not merely 'sit through' the hectic silences or dramatic pauses (see Introduction). Studied effects will administer the kiss of death, and we must rise to every occasion with spontaneous and unfettered spirit.

The next five Sonatas, Nos. 48 − 52, were published in 1780, along with No. 33 in C minor (which had been written in 1771). The set was dedicated to the sisters Katherina and Marianna Auenbrugger, whose musicianship Haydn greatly admired.

No. 48 in C major
(Hob. XVI/35)

First movement − Allegro con brio (7)*
The rhythmic patterns of this popular movement are, for Haydn, unusually straightforward, some might say monotonous. Indeed John McCabe † gives this movement a decisive 'thumbs down'. While taking his points, I still feel that it gives an attractive introduction to Haydn, particularly to a young student not yet capable of grappling with the complexities of the more dramatic and adventurous first movements. And for this reason it will, for better or worse, maintain its appeal. While there is nothing here technically beyond a Grade 6 standard, the movement is long, and the extended triplet passages, particularly for the RH in the development section, can be tiring for a young hand. It has therefore been listed under Grade 7.

bb.1 − 7 Set a lively crotchet pulse with an overall two-in-the-bar feeling, and start with the utmost brightness, and at the same time with perfect neatness, as if taking steps in a formal dance. Lead off from a clear and immaculately timed upbeat, and feel the *sforzato* upbeat to b.2 as a firm rhythmic 'lean' not as a harsh bump, as you slur this note (treating the grace note as an acciaccatura) down to the *staccato* 1st beat of b.2. Study the first eight bars carefully, so that you fully absorb the rhythmic sense of the implied (or stated) upbeat emphases, which is so important to the impetus of the movement as a whole. Thus there is an implied slight 'lean' on the upbeats to bb.1, 3 and 5, an *indicated* and definite emphasis on the slurred upbeat to b.2, and further implied emphases on the slurred upbeats to the 2nd main beat of b.5, and on the upbeats to the 1st and 2nd main beats of b.6. Articulate the RH repeated *staccato* crotchets clearly, though not too sharply, or they will lose their melodic quality. Support the RH with carefully placed crotchet thirds on the 1st beat of bb.1 and 2, and 'point' the detached RH crotchets, and LH crotchet chords precisely through b.3 with the feeling of 'going to' the dominant chord on the 1st beat of b.4. Take care to *feel* the crotchet rest on the 2nd main beat (or 3rd crotchet beat) of b.4 so that the upbeat to b.5 is perfectly timed.

bb.8 − 35 From b.8 practise the LH triplets alone, slowly at first, until they run easily, evenly and rhythmically. (It is a good plan to set your overall tempo from that at which you can negotiate this triplet passage comfortably; in other words, beware of starting too fast.) When the hands are put together here, despite the

†John McCabe, *Haydn Piano Sonatas* (BBC Music Guides).

feeling of greater freedom created by the flowing LH triplets, continue to articulate the RH just as neatly as you have done in the first eight bars. Be sure that your demisemiquaver upbeat to b.11 does not disrupt the evenness of the LH. Feel that the RH is fitting in with your even LH, and not the other way about. From bb.16 – 19 be sure to sustain the lower pedal point C as you phrase the inner LH minim line smoothly, continuing to 'lean' on the slurred RH upbeats to both the 1st and 2nd main beats of bb.17 – 19. From bb.20 – 32 do not allow the turns (placed *on* the upbeats) to disrupt the general rhythm, nor the evenness of the LH triplets. Make a slight accent on the first notes of these turns to give the required 'leaning' effect. Arrive on clear crotchets on the 1st beat of b.32, and do count the rests, and time and co-ordinate the ascending unison dotted rhythm, then triplet, flourishes accurately, making a *crescendo* up to the crotchets on the 1st beat of bb.33 and 34 respectively. Then come to a decisive half-close on the dominant of G major, and once more be sure to give full value to the rests.

bb.36 – 67   'Lean' again on the RH upbeat to bb.37 and 38, and on the upbeats to the 1st and 2nd main beats of bb.39 and 40, as you *crescendo* upwards towards the 1st beat of b.41. Then phrase the RH solo octaves smoothly as you continue the *crescendo* through bb.42 – 3 and drop to *piano* as indicated on the 1st beat of b.44. Keep steady (feeling your overall two-in-the-bar) as you 'lean' (*pianissimo*) on the slurred LH upbeats to bb.46 – 8, while continuing to place your RH figures immaculately. Then, from the upbeat to b.51 when the LH 'takes over' in earnest, be sure that your RH triplets remain perfectly steady, and are not disrupted by the extra 'lean' on the slurred *forte* LH upbeats. Support the RH scale in b.60 with a firm LH minim chord on the first beat. From b.63 it is effective to make a gradual *diminuendo* (but on no account a *rallentando*) towards the double bar.

bb.68 – 170   Proceed resolutely towards the important sounding half-close and pause at b.71, from which you leap off into F major instead of the expected A minor.
     'Take over' confidently with the RH triplets on the 1st beat of b.79. From the upbeat to b.80 again feel the extra 'lean' on the LH upbeats (and again, as from b.50, without disrupting the RH triplets). Thereafter build the tone gradually through this powerful modulating passage towards the sustained pedal point at b.94. From the upbeat to b.84 support the RH triplets with a firm LH crotchet line, and from b.91 with resonant LH octaves. After b.94 you can either 'drive on' purposefully, or alternatively 'unwind' a little towards the sustained dominant 9th chord at b.100. In either event 'draw out' b.99 in a *rallentando* towards b.100. Allow plenty of time for the sustained pause, and for the expressively slurred *adagio* crotchet sixths. Take up the *tempo primo* in b.101, and then allow another little *rallentando*, leading to a further pause on the dominant 7th in b.103. Having set off into a 'normal' recapitulation from the upbeat to b.104 (show the different 'timbre' of the lower register here), Haydn suddenly bursts into the minor at b.111. Articulate your semiquaver upbeats clearly up to the G on the 1st beat of bb.112, 114 and 116, and again do not let the LH triplets be disrupted by the cross-rhythm effect. Later, at b.151, the recapitulation is interrupted by a sudden *fortissimo* diminished 7th chord. Spread this chord resonantly (at least in the LH), and allow time through the pause for the shock to register, and for some of the sound to die before continuing in tempo, but *piano*, into the coda. This time Haydn does not mark the repeated crotchets with a *staccato*. Perhaps he wanted a quiet, more veiled colour here, in contrast to the *forte* from the upbeat to b.161. In the last three bars follow the downward plunging *forte* RH thirds forcefully through to the final chord with no *rallentando*.

Second movement – Adagio (5)
This is a quiet, free-flowing and rather bland movement. To set the tempo, find one at

which the melody and semiquaver accompaniment from b.9 will flow comfortably and graciously, with an overall slow two-in-the-bar swing, and then time the first eight bars to this tempo.

bb.1 – 9 Lead off with a warm-toned spread chord and shape the overall undulating curves of the melodic line expressively through the first four bars, over carefully placed and warmly supportive LH chords. Detach the *staccato* quavers in bb.1 and 2 gently and not spikily, in a 'speaking' style. Again, detach the LH quaver chords in bb.1 and 2 gently, and not sharply. Deliver another, perhaps fuller-toned chord on the 1st beat of b.5, and then time the dotted rhythms precisely over the sustained LH lower C and an evenly descending LH inner quaver line. Then phrase the RH semiquavers in b.7 gracefully, over warm-toned LH octaves on the 1st and 4th crotchet beats, showing the 'vocal' curve up to and down from the high D on the 4th beat. Feel that you are 'going to' a sustained chord on the 1st beat of b.8, and be sure to give full value to the RH dotted crotchet, and to the crotchet rest on the 4th beat of this bar.

bb.9 – 21 From b.9 shape the curving RH melodic line smoothly over an even Alberti LH. Again in b.12 detach the RH semiquavers gently and not spikily. In b.13 'go towards' a warm *sforzato* octave B flat on the 2nd main beat. In b.14 observe the RH semiquaver rests, feeling these like little 'breaths' as you phrase the offbeat semiquaver and ornamented fragments expressively, while *listening* to the line and to the inflections of the continuingly even LH semiquavers. Let the LH 'go to' a rather resonant semiquaver on the 1st beat of bb.15 and 16 to balance the 'entry' of the RH on the offbeat. Give the *legato* RH thirds from the second half of b.17 and through b.18 a warm, horn-like quality (over even LH crotchet octaves in b.18). Let the LH 'go to' a firm crotchet octave on the 1st beat of b.19 to support the resonant RH triplet figuration. 'Go to' a warm-toned RH tied crotchet on the 1st beat of b.20, taking care to place the LH octave F precisely on the 2nd crotchet beat beneath the tied F, and then phrase the RH thirds in b.20 smoothly down towards a sonorous low cadence in b.21.

bb.22 – 42 Shape the RH fragments eloquently in bb.22 and 23, and be careful to keep the LH semiquavers steady and even through the second half of these bars.

From b.24 feel the gently heightened intensity of the music. Let the rising RH detached quavers in b.25 once again sound melodic rather than spiky, and 'lean' warmly, not aggressively, on the RH syncopated *sforzato* tied quavers in b.26. Note the RH slurred semiquavers in b.27, which are again slurred in their ornamented form in b.28. Try to fit in four notes, lightly and clearly, on the trills in b.28, starting on the upper note, and leaning slightly on that first upper note: Then treat the subsequent grace notes like acciaccaturas, gentle and not too clipped. Do ensure that your RH is supported all the way from b.22 to b.37 with even and smooth LH Alberti semiquavers. Allow a little 'give' as the descending LH semiquavers lead you back, through the second half of b.29, towards the shortened recapitulation, from b.30.

Finale – Allegro (6)*

This is another popular movement. Give it a neat 'stepping' rhythm, like a fast minuet. It is essential throughout that all LH chords and figures (which in most instances keep the RH in place, and *not* the other way about), are placed with absolute precision, and that the predominant dotted rhythm figures are perfectly timed, never degenerating into triplets.

bb.1 – 25 'Lean' on the RH tied crotchets on the 1st beat of bb.1, 5, etc, and ensure that these tied crotchets are given their full value, by placing the LH chords exactly on the 2nd beat of the bars. Then articulate the RH dotted rhythm figures with perfect precision, and place the RH crotchets precisely through bb.2 and 6, feeling the 'lift' up to the crotchet on the 2nd beat. 'Lean' lightly on the RH slurred quavers in b.3, over the smooth lower LH line and sustained inner G. Then 'flick' the slurred RH semiquaver figures in b.7 in carefree fashion (but in immaculate time) supported by neat LH crotchet chords on the 1st and 3rd beats. Be sure to give full value to the crotchet rests on the 2nd and 3rd beats of b.8 before either returning to the beginning, or leading on from b.9. The dotted rhythm figures in alternating hands between bb.13 and 17 are apt to be unseating for inexperienced players. Practise 'hands separately', preserving a steady crotchet pulse. Try to feel each semiquaver as an 'upbeat' to each subsequent dotted quaver (representing the crotchet beat) rather than as the 'tail end' of each crotchet beat (see Introduction). Feel that the RH dotted rhythms in b.13 are 'going to' a firm crotchet 1st beat of b.14, and similarly that the LH dotted rhythms in b.14 ('led in' by a clear LH crotchet upbeat) are 'going to' a firm minim third on the 1st beat of b.15, and so on. Support the LH with firm and perfectly steady RH crotchets in bb.14 and 16, and 'draw out' b.16 a little towards b.17. Give full value to the jokey pause at b.17, and then resume the tempo immediately.

bb.26 – 53
Bb.30 – 8 are also rhythmic danger areas. 'Finish off' the RH phrase neatly with the three crotchets through b.29, then lead off boldly with the LH with a firm tied crotchet on the 1st beat of b.30 (and similarly at b.34). Feel the *crotchet* pulse and particularly the 1st beats securely in the LH, through the dotted rhythms of bb.30 – 2 and the triplets of bb.34 – 6, and support the LH with rock-steady, immaculately placed RH thirds from the 2nd beat of bb.30 and 34. Steady yourself in b.33 with firm LH crotchets and even RH triplets, ready to launch off again *fortissimo* with the LH on the 1st beat of b.34. Be careful to keep a steady crotchet pulse again from bb.39 – 46. Enter clearly with the LH on the 1st beat of b.39 beneath the sustained RH sixth, be sure to 'feel' the held 2nd beat, and 'go down' to a firm sustained minim on the 1st beat of b.40 as you also 'join in' clearly with the treble. Enter clearly again with the inner LH part on the 2nd beat of b.40, and 'go down' to a firm inner crotchet G on the 1st beat of b.41 over the tied lower E. Then let the RH go on over firm LH crotchet thirds, and similarly, 'come in' again with the LH on the 2nd beat of b.42 beneath firm *RH* crotchet chords, and so on. Revert to your 'formal' minuet style at b.46.

bb.54 – 97
From b.54 introduce a sturdier feeling with a more solid tone. Phrase the RH crotchet lines smoothly from bb.54 – 7, and practise the LH at first in octaves (if the hand is big enough) and then in these dotted rhythms:

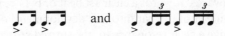

Then from bb.58 – 61 support the curving RH quavers with a firm LH. From b.62 ensure that the RH quaver lines and dotted minims alternate smoothly between the upper and inner lines over even LH quavers. Feel that the upper quaver line in b.62 'goes to' the dotted minim B natural on the 1st beat of b.63, and that the inner RH quaver line in b.63 'goes to' the dotted minim G in b.64, and so on. Be sure to *feel* the held beats through the tied minim at bb.68 – 9, in effect a 'written out' pause. Then after the pause at b.86, make the most of the little variations: 'creep' in with the triplets following the pause, point the repeated RH quavers through b.88, and shape the chromatic quavers through b.89 with sliding smoothness. Burst into *forte* at b.91, and keep a steady crotchet pulse as the RH alternates between triplets and dotted rhythms, with the help of accurately placed LH chords. 'Go down' confidently to the LH third on the upbeat to b.93, and also to the RH crotchet D on the 1st beat of b.93. End with bright clear *forte* chords.

110

No. 49 in C sharp minor
(Hob. XVI/36)

First movement – Moderato (8)*

The first movement, compact and full of event, both rhythmic and harmonic, is particularly fine. Characterized by mercurial changes of mood, it warrants, and indeed requires, the closest study. Establish a steady *moderato* crotchet pulse, bearing in mind the elaborate figuration to come.

bb.1 – 11   Launch in with bold unison C sharp quavers, and co-ordinate the hands precisely through the rapid demisemiquaver turn, and vigorous and very rhythmically 'plucked' *staccato* quavers through b.1. Feel that the demisemiquavers are 'going up to' a very definite detached quaver on the 2nd beat of the bar. This pithy opening statement is answered in a more yielding dialogue between the hands (bb.2 – 4). Carry the opening *forte* through to the 1st beat of b.2, and then observe the sudden *piano* on the second quaver of the bar. Then feel that the RH repeated quavers (played in an even, barely detached, 'speaking' style) are 'going to' the ornamented crotchets on the 3rd beat of bb.2 and 3; and similarly feel that the graciously phrased LH slurred quaver thirds are 'going to' the crotchet thirds on the 1st beat of bb.3 and 4. Then 'open out' expressively into b.5 and arrive on a clear crotchet chord on the 1st beat of b.6. *Feel* the 2nd beat on the quaver rest, and then 'snap' the RH dotted rhythm figures smartly in a descending *crescendo* towards b.7, placing the demisemiquavers *on* the quaver beats and not anticipating them. Count carefully in b.9, 'feeling' the held 2nd beat, and giving the low *sforzato* dotted unison crotchet its full value. Then 'pluck' the ascending *staccato* quavers clearly, 'lean' on the quaver appoggiaturas on the 1st beat of b.10, 'feel' the held 2nd beat, and zip up the scale to arrive at the top quaver B exactly on the 3rd beat of the bar. Then feel that the reiterated LH quavers and RH semiquavers are driving on towards a firm crotchet chord on the 1st beat of b.11, and then *feel* the rests through the remainder of the bar. Alternatively you could make a *diminuendo* through b.10 towards a quiet chord on the 1st beat of b.11.

bb.12 – 33   Phrase the RH lines smoothly through bb.12, 13 and 14 and, having practised them first carefully on their own, fit in the LH scale interjections neatly, feeling that the scales in b.12 and b.13, precisely co-ordinated with the RH quavers, are each 'going to' a firm crotchet on the subsequent 1st beat. Then follow the longer contrary motion lines of both hands in *crescendo* through b.15 towards the 1st beat of b.16. Return 'inwards' towards a clear 1st beat of b.17 ready to lead on in a poised manner from the 2nd quaver of the bar into the 'development' of the figures of bb.2 – 4. 'Lean' firmly on, and give a clear resonance to, the slurred *sforzato* chords in both hands through the concentrated harmonic progressions of bb.20 and 21. Then from the quaver upbeat to b.22, feel an easing out into the subsequent *dolce legato* phrase. 'Lean' lightly on the RH slurred quaver octaves in b.23, observing the rests precisely, over light, carefully placed LH quaver chords. Then 'lean' on the RH and LH minims on the 1st beat of b.24, and time this bar carefully, *feeling* the held 2nd beat, and 'flicking' the upbeat demisemiquavers down towards a firm diminished 7th chord on the 1st beat of b.25. Treat the grace notes in b.25 probably like acciaccaturas (although you may disagree with this when you compare this passage with b.87) as you descend boldly, keeping a perfectly steady crotchet pulse towards the resonant *sforzato* minim octaves in b.26 (being very sure to give these their full value). Then hold fast to the crotchet pulse again through bb.27 – 9; these can be rocky moments for the relatively inexperienced player. It will help if bb.27 – 9 are practised at first *slowly*, but in perfect time, substituting plain octaves for the broken octaves. Support the RH with firm LH crotchet octaves on the 1st and 3rd beats of b.27, and again with firm chords on the 1st and 2nd beats of b.28, and 'join in' confidently with the LH broken octaves on the 3rd beat of b.28 and the 1st beat of b.29. Come off cleanly to *feel* the silent 2nd beat of b.29 on the quaver rest, articulate the high RH demisemiquaver figure and detached quavers vigorously, and then rip up to ringing RH *staccato* crotchets in b.30, enjoying the exuberant screech of these RH figures, supported by firm LH detached chords. Then end this section, from the upbeat to b.31 to the double bar, with neat and formal precision, feeling the slightly syncopating effect of the offbeat slurs alternating between RH and LH in bb.31 and 32 and finishing with immaculately placed *pianissimo* chords in b.33.

bb.34 – 64   Move on from the three *forte* chords at the end of b.40 in a further *crescendo* towards a resonant dominant 7th crotchet chord on the 3rd beat of b.41.

Mark the dramatic silence here with a full crotchet rest, resuming in an echoing *piano* in b.42 before moving on again into *forte* towards a further dramatic stop and silence in b.43, this time with pauses. The development moves on with driving impetus through a concentrated series of modulations. Go to, and 'lean' well on the RH slurred crotchets on the 1st and 3rd beats of bb.48 – 50, and be sure to place the offbeat LH quaver chord figures precisely here. Set off from b.51 with very steady LH quaver figures beneath evenly pulsating RH semiquavers. Observe how the LH rests on the 4th beat of bb.51 – 4 (when accurately implemented!) serve to heighten the rhythmic tension. Then follow the long build-up from b.55 through to b.64, keeping a taut rhythmic control. You can either make an overall *crescendo,* or *diminuendo* a little from about b.60 and *crescendo* again from the 2nd beat of b.62. From bb.55 – 61 listen to all the inflections of the RH semiquavers over the sustained lower LH line, and evenly placed inner offbeat LH quaver figures. Keep the LH quaver chords rock-steady through bb.62 – 3 as you drive on towards the stentorian dominant chords at b.64, leading towards the start of the recapitulation.

bb.65 – 97   As he so often does, Haydn varies his recapitulation daringly. Note from bb.68 – 71 the persistent, Beethovenian, contrapuntal 'development' of the 'gracious' slurred figure in thirds (see bb.2 – 4), and from the upbeat to b.73 the jagged and lengthy extension of the 'snapped' dotted rhythm figure (see b.6). Do remember to 'snap' the demisemiquavers *on* the beat, and to continue this effect through bb.75 – 7. Keep a steady crotchet pulse from the upbeat to b.73 with the help of firmly and precisely placed LH offbeat octave figures. Then from the middle of b.74 through to b.77, keep the rhythm under control by keeping the LH quavers rock-steady (feeling the subdued tension of these bars). From bb.84 – 6 Haydn extends the material of bb.23 and 24 into a cadenza-like passage. 'Draw out' the RH semiquavers over the sustained tied LH third as you move through the second half of b.85 towards the pause on the high tied crotchet A. Descend in a further *rallentando* towards the second pause (on the B sharp). Then 'feel' a brisk *a tempo on* the rest on the 1st beat of b.87, and enter again confidently with the broken octaves on the 2nd beat. Bb.89 – 95 are an extended version of bb.27 – 31. Make a broad curve up towards the high broken octave E on the 6th *quaver* pulse of b.91, and down again to 'finish' neatly on the 1st beat of b.93. Then *feel* the silent 2nd beat and articulate the RH demisemiquaver 'turns' clearly in b.93, letting each 'go to' lively *staccato* quavers, over accurately placed, firm LH quaver chords, as you *crescendo* towards b.94. Play the three quaver chords on the 2nd and 3rd beats of b.94, and the 1st beat of b.95 with ringing clarity. Then end, as at the close of the exposition, with neat formality.

Second movement – Scherzando (Allegro con brio) (6)

This bright and open-textured movement is, in contrast, quite straightforward. It is, in effect, a set of variations, with two minor sections. The harmonic 'ground' remains more-

or-less constant through the major variations. Study the LH with particular care therefore, since its rhythmic stability is essential throughout to the poise of the RH.

bb.1 – 16 Set a lively, dance-like, but very precise crotchet pulse, and realize from the outset the rhythmic importance of the implied 'lean' on the slurred upbeat figures to bb.1, 3, 8, etc. 'Lean' well therefore on the opening dotted quaver, being careful to give this its precise value. Then 'flick' the demisemiquavers clearly and lightly down to the quaver on the 1st beat of b.1. Articulate the RH neatly through b.1 over precisely placed LH quaver chords, and 'go to' a clear quaver chord on the 1st beat of b.2. Come off to show the quaver rest, ready to 'lean' again, this time with both hands, on the 2nd beat, felt as the *upbeat* to b.3. Detach the quavers precisely in both hands through b.3 as you move neatly inwards towards a clear dominant chord on the 1st beat of b.4. Then from the upbeat to b.5 proceed briskly towards the double bar, supporting the RH with rock-steady LH quaver chords. 'Lean' with a little extra emphasis on the upbeat to b.15, and then in b.15, 'flick' the triplet in perfect time down to the 2nd beat.

bb.17 – 35 Introduce a sturdier tone at the change to the minor from the upbeat to b.17, and make a purposeful *crescendo* towards the *sforzato* chord on the 2nd beat of b.20. Be careful to co-ordinate the vigorous unison figures precisely from the upbeat to b.23, feeling the implied 'lean' on the quavers on the 2nd beats of bb.23 and 24. Then from the 2nd beat of b.26, *crescendo* again towards a strong sustained six-four chord at b.28, 'carrying on' the *crescendo* again in the RH to the high quaver A 1st beat of b.29. See how the varying lengths of the sections give a 'kick' to the movement: the first parts of the two minor sections (bb.17 – 22 and 51 – 6) deviate from the 'normal' eight-bar sections in each having only six bars; and at bb.31 and 65, bb.1 – 4 are thrown in again, and the final section is extended to ten bars.

bb.35 – 94 From the upbeat to b.35 articulate the RH semiquavers athletically over a perfectly steady LH. Let the LH quavers in b.37 ascend smoothly to the tied minim E on the 1st beat of b.38, and be sure to *hold* this note through to the 1st beat of b.40 as you shape the line of the inner LH crotchets evenly beneath the continuingly determined, but perhaps smoother RH semiquavers. From the upbeat to b.43 you could play the RH semiquavers in a clear, tinkly style, returning to the 'athletic' manner from the upbeat to b.47. Take care to keep a steady crotchet pulse through the second minor section, particularly from the second half of bb.52 and 58. Ensure that the semiquavers alternate evenly between the hands, making it quite clear where the main beats fall, i.e. on the LH semiquaver A on the 2nd beat of b.52, on the RH B on the 1st beat of b.53, and so on. Support the RH semiquavers with firm LH chords as you *crescendo* from bb.61 – 4. Note the *legato* phrasing from the upbeat to b.69. Listen to the clash of the LH D sharp and RH E and D natural as the LH quavers rise smoothly (as at b.37) through b.71. This is an awkward little corner – finger the LH thus:

Do not lurch upwards in a panic at b.82; avoid hurrying the RH semiquavers through the 1st beat, and then allow a tiny natural break as you leap up to a confident high semiquaver E on the 2nd beat. Be careful to co-ordinate the scale in tenths perfectly (bb.90 – 1) feeling the implied *crescendo* up to the top notes (E and C sharp) and down again. End with bright clear chords.

Third movement – Minuet and Trio (Moderato) (6)*
The minor Minuet (which would perhaps be appreciated by an older player before Grade

6) is outstanding. Haydn uses the 'formality' of the minuet structure to poignantly expressive effect. Do not, however, allow yourself to be so carried away by the beauty of your playing that you lose sight of the fundamental 'step' of the minuet rhythm!

bb.1 – 8   The LH downward leaping crotchet thirds in bb.1, 5, etc. (or upward, as in bb.9, 13 and 15) give a masculine feel to the structure. Play these clearly and firmly (but not lumpily), with *equal* tone and *not* as if slurred. Give the tied RH crotchet on the 1st beat of each of these bars sufficient tone to sing over the 2nd beats. Then be absolutely sure to place the second LH third precisely on the 2nd beat, thus giving a little rhythmic springboard for the RH semiquaver line to run up to the 1st beat of b.2. Be sure also to take the LH crotchet third *off* on the 3rd beat of b.1. Let the repeated detached (not spiky) G sharp crotchets 'speak' in b.2, and feel that they are 'going to' the warmly slurred F double sharp on the 1st beat of b.3, supported by a quietly resonant LH. Note the *tenuto* over b.4, and be sure to give this dotted minim chord its full value. Do define the rhythmic difference clearly in the RH between bb.1 and 5, and 'bring in' the semiquavers precisely on the 4th *quaver* pulse of b.5 rather than slurping in, in a vague imitation of b.1.

bb.9 – 31   From b.9 show the overall continuity of the phrases, and the 'onward' feeling of the melody line right through to the end of b.23. Listen to the tied inner LH D natural 'resolving' to the minim C sharp on the 2nd beat of b.11, and 'come in' clearly with the LH thirds on the 2nd beat of b.12. Feel the detached quavers in b.14 like forward-moving 'steps' and not isolated plonks. Treat the crotchet rest on the 2nd beat of b.19 like a 'breath' point and then 'come in' impulsively with the semiquavers on the upbeat to b.20 with the feeling of moving on urgently (though without hurrying) towards the dramatic syncopated diminished 7th *sforzato* chord on the 3rd beat of b.20. 'Point' the interrupted cadence here, and then feel the Mozartean pathos of bb.22 and 23, as you lead back towards the restatement of the opening figure (which this time might be played more quietly and tenderly).

bb.32 – 55   The major Trio is equally beautiful. Give a warm tone to the horn-like opening RH phrase in thirds, and to its complementary LH line, entering on the 1st beat of b.33. 'Lean' on the slurred RH minim thirds on the 1st beat of bb.36 and 38 over smooth slurred bass octaves. From the upbeat to b.40 listen acutely to the sustained LH lines beneath the expressive curves of the RH. Lead off after the double bar with a singing RH G sharp, and then phrase the rising chromatic RH line with gliding smoothness through bb.45 – 6. From b.50 listen acutely again to the beautiful inflections in both hands, and end the section quietly, in immaculate time.

No. 50 in D major
(Hob. XVI/37)

This must be the best known of all Haydn's Sonatas. Indeed, the first movement epitomizes the popular view of Haydn — brisk, bright and uncomplicated. A far cry from this are the drama and passion of the first movements of Nos. 33 and 40, the expressive warmth of No. 58, or the splendour of No. 62, to name but a few.

First movement — Allegro con brio (8)*

bb.1 – 16   Establish a realistic crotchet pulse at which you can safely negotiate the coming semiquaver passage work. Set the mood of exuberant vitality with a bold and bright, but not heavy. opening chord, with a 'snapped' acciaccatura. Play the three repeated RH D's in lively *staccato*, then slur the ornamented quavers on the 3rd and 4th beats (over similarly slurred LH thirds) as you 'go towards' a further bright chord on the 1st beat of b.2. Play the ornaments in bb.1 and 2 [musical notation] if you can manage it, otherwise [musical notation] as in bb.5 and 6. Show the syncopating effect of the slurred offbeat quavers and inner offbeat RH crotchets in b.3 and 'finish off' the LH up to a clear crotchet A on the 3rd beat of b.4, with the RH figure 'going on down' to finish the phrase on a neat quaver on the 4th beat. Define the RH quavers brightly again over spanking LH semiquavers through bb.5 and 6. Let the LH 'go to' a firm crotchet G on the 1st beat of b.8, and then 'finish off' the RH sixths clearly down to a strong crotchet sixth on the 3rd beat of b.8. Feel an implied *forte* (or *sforzato*) on the 1st beat of b.9, followed by a *subito piano*, and then drive on in an overall *crescendo* towards the half-close on the dominant in b.16. Enjoy one of Haydn's characteristic 'churning' effects here as, with lively detached LH quavers and immaculately articulated RH semiquavers, you 'return' towards implied *fortes* on the 1st beats of bb.10, 11 and 12. 'Rattle out' the RH semiquavers over increasingly lively (but steady) LH quavers through bb.13 and 14. Then be careful to co-ordinate the unison scale immaculately, making a *crescendo* up towards the top D's on the 3rd beat of b.15. End the passage with firm dominant chords, and come clean *off* to give full value to the rest on the 4th beat of b.16.

bb.17 – 40   Show the more delicate texture from b.17, but without letting the rhythm flag. Articulate the RH semiquaver figures neatly, observing the quaver rests, over very steady LH thirds. From bb.19 – 26 the rhythm will flounder unless you hold fast to the crotchet pulse. From the second half of b.19 through to b.21 keep the alternating LH-RH-LH figures in the thirds rock-steady, letting the LH quaver thirds 'go to' a firm crotchet third on the 3rd beat of bb.19 and 20. Lead off clearly with the RH quavers in bb.22 and 24 over cleanly articulated ascending LH broken thirds, and then support the *RH* semiquavers with a *firm LH* from the middle of these bars. Feel in each of these two bars that the LH semiquavers are 'going to' a firm minim B on the 3rd beat. 'Rattle out' the semiquavers with maximum vitality and clarity in both hands through bb.26 and 27, making a bright sharp accent on the 1st and 3rd beats of the bars. Support the RH semiquavers through bb.28 and 29 with sustained lower minim E's and evenly placed LH inner offbeat quaver fragments. Let the LH 'go to' a firm LH B flat minim chord on the 1st beat of b.30, keeping a steady crotchet pulse as the semiquaver flourish alternates between the hands, and go up to a ringing quaver F on the 3rd beat of b.31. Then give full value to the quaver and crotchet rests in the second half of b.31. Many a nervous performance has disintegrated at b.32. Lead off forcefully with the LH octave D sharp, and, while articulating the RH semiquavers very clearly, continue to feel that the LH is 'leading', with firm and steady quaver octaves as you descend towards a strong minim octave E on the 1st beat of b.33. 'Pluck' the RH, then the LH ascending quavers vigorously and rhythmically through bb.33 – 4, and 'go to' a strong dominant 7th chord on the 3rd beat of b.34 (giving this chord and trill its full value). Keep a steady crotchet pulse too through bb.35 – 8, placing the quaver chords and 'feeling' all quaver rests precisely, and being careful to co-ordinate the RH semiquaver and LH quaver figures immaculately in b.37. End the section in lively style with an immaculately timed dotted rhythm figure in b.40.

bb.41 – 52   To remain steady is indeed often the problem in this movement. Bb.41 – 6 are further danger points. Practise *slowly*, and very rhythmically 'hands separately' here, and when the hands are put together, be sure that the LH 'leads' and that its steadiness is not disrupted by the activities of the RH. Let the LH quavers 'go to' a firm crotchet on the 3rd beat of bb.42, 44 and 45. Then ensure that the RH quavers remain perfectly steady through the second half of these bars, with the LH 'leading in' again clearly on the quaver upbeat to bb.43, 45 and 46 in perfect co-ordination with the RH. From the middle of b.46 shape the sustained upper and inner RH lines smoothly over immaculately clear and rhythmic LH scale figures. At the beginning of this passage the semiquavers in the low register can sound very muddy on the modern piano unless they are perfectly articulated. Help the awkward LH passage from the middle of b.49 and through b.50 by making light, sharp accents with the thumb on the first semiquaver of each group of four, letting your even RH lines keep you steady here. Again in b.51, accent the inner RH semiquavers similarly, steadying these with firm LH and upper RH crotchets.

Crescendo purposefully through b.52 towards the 1st beat of b.53. Then
bb.52 – 103   underpin the RH with resonant sustained LH minim chords on the 1st and
3rd beats of bb.53 and 54, with the feeling of 'going to' a yet more powerful chord on the 1st beat of b.55. Do keep the sense of your steady crotchet pulse through the improvisatory RH semiquavers (particularly in bb.55 – 7 where the RH has no help from the LH on the 3rd beat of the bar). Let these RH semiquavers in b.55 plunge down towards a strong LH semibreve octave E sharp on the 1st beat of b.56, and then drive on towards a further strong LH octave on the 1st beat of b.57. Carry the B minor flourish up to a ringing quaver B on the 4th beat of b.57. Be sure that you do not cut b.58 short, but give a 'boost' to the RH trill with a firm LH dominant 7th chord on the 3rd beat of the bar. Maintain the utmost rhythmic vitality between bb.65 and 79, where Haydn expands exuberantly on material from the exposition. Through bb.71 – 2 help to keep yourself steady by placing the RH crotchets clearly on the 4th beat of b.71 and the 1st beat of b.72. In b.100 (compare with b.37) be careful to co-ordinate the semiquaver figures in tenths with perfect precision within a steady crotchet pulse.

Second movement – Largo e sostenuto (5)(O)*

The slow movement has a nobility and tragic power out of all proportion to its mere nineteen bars. It has the motion of a slow sarabande. Set a slow and very measured **3/4**. You will find it best to count in quavers at first.

Start with a full, spread *sostenuto* chord, and then feel the slight implied
bb.1 – 9   'lean' on the 2nd beat of b.1, thus giving the upper melodic RH dotted crotchet
F sufficient tone to sing over the 3rd beat, while also listening carefully to the movement of the inner parts. Be sure to 'point', and to sustain, and *listen* to all long and tied notes through their full value – the tied inner RH D from the 1st beat of b.2 (while savouring the 'clash' of the lower LH B flat against the tied inner LH seventh), the tied inner LH G on the 2nd beat of b.2, and the tied lower LH A on the 1st beat of b.3, etc. (Details of these ties vary in different editions.) Be very precise, even deliberate, with the dotted rhythms, always feeling the semiquavers (e.g. in b.1), the triplet demisemiquavers (e.g. in bb.2 – 3) and the demisemiquavers in b.6, and so on, as *upbeats* to the subsequent crotchet or quaver beats rather than as 'tail-ends' to the previous beats (see Introduction). Indeed, Professor Robbins Landon suggests that, in keeping with the Baroque character of the movement, these figures should be *double dotted*.

This 'sharpening' of the rhythm adds immensely to the clarion quality of the texture, and to the 'bite' and majestic impact of the music. Note the *tenuto* on the 2nd beat of bb.4 and 9, and be sure to give these minim chords their full value. Spread the big dominant 7th chord on the 2nd beat of b.7 with a full and unhurried tone, likewise the subsequent spread LH chords, while 'leaning on' the upper RH slurred quaver thirds from the upbeat to b.8. Maximize the intensely expressive, laden, discord/resolution effect here of the slurred thirds 'against' the spread LH crotchet chords.

bb.10 – 19   Lead off into the second section in a clearer, less sombre tone with the major chord on the 1st beat of b.10. Continue to listen to all inner as well as outer moving parts, particularly in bb.12 – 13. Then show the suspenseful effect of the quaver rests in bb.13 and 14, feeling these like 'breaths'. Play the repeated fragments expressively here, carrying out the echo effect from the upbeat to b.15 with a *really pianissimo* sound. Then give more tone to the upbeat dominant 7th chord on the 3rd beat of b.15, implying a *crescendo* through this one chord towards the tremendous E flat major spread and tied chord on the 1st beat of b.16. Be sure to give this chord its full value, 'feeling' the held 2nd beat, and then let the melody line 'fall' in a smooth *decrescendo* towards the quiet reiterated dominant chords. Listen to the fading sound of the final chord through the pause before moving straight into the Finale.

Finale – Presto ma non troppo (Innocentemente) (6)

Set and maintain a smart **2/4** pulse, and play this movement with the utmost gaiety.

bb.1 – 20   Lead in with a lively detached upbeat, then 'lean' on the slurred RH crotchets (or dotted quaver) on the 1st beat of bb.1 – 4, over neatly placed LH offbeat quaver thirds. Then, from the upbeat to b.6, articulate the RH figures cleanly over continuingly neat LH quaver chords. Take care to *feel* the quaver rest on the 2nd beat of b.8, and similarly bb.20, 22, 26, 28, etc, so that in each instance you are poised to lead on with the subsequent clear upbeat. Lean well again on the slurred RH crotchets on the 1st beat of bb.9 and 10, and on the dotted quaver on the 1st beat of b.11. Then 'flick' the demisemiquavers in b.11 lightly and snappily down to the F sharp on the 2nd beat. Do keep yourself steady through bb.1 – 20 by placing all the LH offbeat chord figures with immaculate precision, also observing all LH rests equally accurately. Burst into *forte*, on the upbeat to b.13, and continue to 'lean' on the slurred crotchet thirds (or sixth) on the 1st beat of bb.13 – 16. Do not allow the rhythm to be disrupted by over-heavy LH octaves, and avoid getting ponderous here, thinking rather of a mock-important strutting.

bb.21 – 60   Play the detached *forte* chords in bb.21 – 2 and 25 – 6 like a jumping game or dance, 'pointing' the interrupted cadences. Then *feel* the silent 2nd beat of bb.22 and 26 as you poise yourself to lead on with the upbeats to bb.23 and 27, to play the *piano* fragments in immaculate time. From the upbeat to b.31 phrase the *legato* quaver lines smoothly and equally in either hand. 'Finish off' the RH phrase neatly on the 2nd beat of b.34, allow a tiny natural break, and then let the *forte* RH upbeat in semiquaver thirds 'go to' a firm RH quaver third on the 1st beat of b.35. If absolutely necessary the lower notes of this quick RH figure in thirds can be taken by the LH. From the upbeat to b.36 let the LH 'skip' down towards a firm crotchet B flat on the 1st beat of b.37, supported by rock-steady RH detached ascending quaver chords, and then articulate the high RH figures with immaculate clarity. (You could either play this repeated RH 'skipping' figure *forte* or *pianissimo*.) Then *feel* the quaver and crotchet rests, and finish the section neatly, in perfect time.

bb.61 – 80   'Rattle out' the little RH semiquaver figures with spanking clarity in bb.61, 65, 69 and 70, 'going to' bright detached quavers on the 2nd beat of these bars. Keep steady through these sections by always preserving the sense of the precise crotchet pulse, and by always placing the LH figures accurately. Be sure that the LH 'leads' in bb.63 – 4 and 67 – 8, with the RH offbeat detached quavers following relatively lightly. Let the LH 'go to' a firm crotchet on the 1st beat of bb.64 and 68, and then slur the RH offbeat thirds neatly in b.64. Be particularly careful to 'point' the 2nd beats of the bars clearly in the RH (in bb.61, 62, 65, 66, etc.) where the LH has a quaver rest on those 2nd beats.

bb.81 – 121   Lead off clearly with the RH from the upbeat to b.81, letting the *LH* follow relatively lightly this time with the detached offbeat quavers. 'Lean' on the RH slurred thirds on the 1st beat of bb.82 and 84, dovetailing the LH broken octaves neatly. Do not lose your tempo as you make a gradual *diminuendo* from bb.87 – 93. The jokey, simulated *rallentando* effect would be spoilt by an *actual rallentando*. From b.102 practise the LH slowly and rhythmically, with a sharp light accent on the first of

each group of two semiquavers. Practise also in dotted rhythms: and

(as has been said elsewhere, a rapid Alberti bass such as this often floors the inexperienced player; see also Introduction). When the hands are put together, ensure that you 'lean' on the slurred RH 1st beats as before, and that the hands are perfectly co-ordinated, taking particular care to 'match' the LH semiquavers with the detached RH upbeat to bb.103, 104, etc. Be careful to keep steady at bb.110 – 11, continuing to lean on the slurred RH 1st beats, and timing the LH semiquaver fragments precisely. Be sure that you do not clip the 2nd beats short in these bars, causing you to 'fall into' the upbeats to the subsequent bars. Go from b.114 to the end in a final burst of exuberance with a strong and rhythmic RH over brightly articulated 'whirling' LH semiquavers. Note the held bass minims from bb.118 – 20, and end with emphatic but bright-toned chords. (Note: Henle give a *da capo* at the end of b.40, ending at b.20, and thus creating a twenty-bar discrepancy in the bar numberings from b.40 onwards.)

No. 51 in E flat major
(Hob. XVI/38)

First movement – Allegro moderato (8)*
As has been said above, the delights of Haydn's music lie not so much in his basic material as in the astonishing versatility of his imagination in building upon it – in effect his capacity for development. We could be forgiven, in the course of a browse through the Sonatas, for taking a look at the first page of this first movement and passing on – it does not look particularly promising. In fact, though, Haydn is on one of his wildest inventive sprees, hardly giving the player time to grasp one idea before leaping on to the next. It follows that the maintenance of a clear, unifying crotchet pulse is all-important.

bb.1 – 4   When setting your tempo, take a look at the demisemiquaver runs of bb.10 – 11, and accept the caution 'Allegro *moderato*'. Practise the first four bars at first without the ornaments, until you have fully absorbed their rhythmic shape. Stride in with a broad-toned RH line in a realistic and rock-steady crotchet pulse, and in bb.1 and 2, feel that you are 'going to' the slurred crotchets on the 3rd beats of each of these bars. Also observe the effect of the slurred quaver couplets on the 1st and 2nd beats of b.2. Shape the LH with equal care. Place the LH offbeat quaver fragments neatly in b.1, and feel that the LH upbeat quavers 'go to' firm slurred crotchets on the 1st beat of bb.2 and 3. Then in bb.3 – 4, time the RH dotted rhythm figures with immaculate precision, over smooth and firm LH crotchets in b.3, and from the upbeat to b.4, over neatly placed LH offbeat chords. Be sure that your short, quick shakes or turns in b.3

 do not 'hold up' your rhythm.

bb.5 – 12 'Take over' clearly from the rising LH upbeat quavers with a *firm* RH dotted quaver on the 1st beat of b.5. In bb.5 – 8, while preserving virtually the same LH figures, Haydn is already 'worrying' at the RH material from bb.1 – 4. Note his syncopated emphasis on the RH offbeat quavers in b.6, and then see how he turns the dotted rhythms from bb.3 and 4 into even semiquaver figures on the 1st and 2nd beats of b.7, and then into 'flicked' demisemiquaver/semiquaver figures. (Be sure that you 'snap' the first of these two demisemiquavers smartly *on* the crotchet beats and do not anticipate them, bringing the hand *off* on the *staccato* semiquavers.) In the second half of b.8 he introduces a quirky repeated quaver figure in the RH, and then plays about with it through b.9 over quietly insistent reiterated LH quaver figures in thirds (keep these very steady). *Crescendo* through the second half of b.9 ready to launch into the brilliant demisemiquaver runs of bb.10 – 11. Make these runs as exuberant and virtuosic as possible, supported by resonant LH crotchet chords on the 1st and 3rd beats, making a little *crescendo* up to and down from the top note of each curve (i.e. up to the B flat and to the G in b.10, and up to the C in b.11). Finish off the passage with reckless (but perfectly timed) unison dotted rhythm figures, giving full value to the rests at the end of b.12.

bb.13 – 28 At b.13 Haydn seems to be about to embark on a more melodic and lyrical 'development' of the opening theme. But he breaks off again in b.14 with the repeated quaver figure from b.8, leading into a *legato* semiquaver figure which he takes through a momentarily 'serious' development through bb.16 – 18. In b.16 let the RH line 'go to' the treble crotchets F and E on the 3rd and 4th beats, as you also, from the middle of this bar, follow the inner, then upper (b.17) semiquaver line smoothly and expressively over the sustained LH lines. At b.19 there is a flourish of B flat major chords. 'Finish off' neatly in both hands in b.18 and *feel* the rest on the 4th beat, taking care to give this its full crotchet value. Then play the RH grace notes *before* the 1st beat of b.19 exactly like the subsequent demisemiquaver 'upbeat' to the 2nd and 3rd beats. Count carefully here, and give this flourish a ringing clarion quality, sustaining the treble dotted quavers, but giving the LH chords only their exact quaver value. Then 'lean' lightly on the RH slurred dotted semiquaver upbeats to the 1st, 2nd and 3rd beats of b.20, and 'flick' the hemidemisemiquavers lightly down to the *staccato* quavers, precisely synchronized with the neatly placed LH quaver chords. Then 'go to' a firm singing RH dotted crotchet E flat on the 3rd beat of b.20, over a warmly resonant LH treble third. Shape the LH lines smoothly from the middle of b.20 (easing out a little towards the decorated pause on the 3rd beat of b.21) and again from the middle of b.22, as you tail the *pianissimo* treble line away towards the middle of b.24, over the sustained LH dominant 7th chord. Give full value to the rests before bursting in with the brilliant demisemiquaver runs of bb.25 – 6, supported with strong LH crotchet chords, on the 1st and 3rd beats. Be sure to come clean *off* the high quaver at the end of b.26. Be careful not to upset the pulse by cutting short the double trill on the 1st and 2nd beats of bar 27. (In other words, be sure to 'feel' the 2nd beat of the bar as you trill.) These last two bars of the exposition are not easy to time, and to play accurately. Practise slowly until you have fully absorbed the rhythm and can play the chords with brisk precision.

bb.28 – 49 Haydn launches purposefully into the development section, taking the figures from bb.8 – 9 down into a low register. But this idea dissolves again into thin air at b.31. You could either go *subito piano* here, or 'tail off' the very end of the unison scale in the previous bar. Then from b.35 he really does embark on a serious contrapuntal development of the semiquaver figure from b.7 (itself, as we have seen, a variant of the RH dotted rhythm figure of b.3). Study the parts carefully here, as you would the voices of a fugue. When necessary, in the interests of smoothness of the treble line (although not at the expense of continuity in the inner RH line), you can take some of the RH inner line notes of bb.35 – 8 with the LH: e.g. the inner semiquaver F on the 4th beat of b.35, and in b.36 the inner crotchets on the 1st and 2nd beats and the semiquaver E flat on the 4th beat; likewise in b.37, take the slurred inner crotchets on the 1st and 2nd beats, and of course the semiquaver E flat on the 3rd beat with the LH. The LH will anyway have to take the last four inner semiquavers of b.37, and the inner quaver line through bb.38 and 39. Work all this out carefully, and mark in clearly these and any other notes you decide to take with the LH. In the first half of b.35 feel that the semiquaver line is 'going towards' the slurred crotchet E flat on the 3rd beat, and then that the inner semiquavers from the middle of the bar 'go to' the inner slurred crotchet A flat on the 1st beat of b.36, and so on. At the same time follow the sustained lower LH line smoothly and resonantly (and in bb.38 – 9 the inner quaver line, ensuring here that the tied quavers are fully sustained over the subsequent beats). Then drive on purposefully from the middle of b.40, and then, having dropped to *piano* on the upbeat to b.43, build up the dynamics again towards b.45. Exploit the Beethovenian resonances of b.45 fully in both hands, and let the bass upbeat thirds 'go to' a strong LH third on the 1st beat of b.46, as a 'springboard' for the 'flicked' RH demisemiquaver figures in b.46. (Make these figures *more* 'snappy' and insistent than those in bb.7 – 8.)

bb.49 – 76   Haydn uses the recapitulation as the excuse for further flights of exuberant 'development'. Make the most, first, of the joke *piano* 'false start' in b.48, and then *crescendo* steeply up the scale towards the start of the recapitulation proper at b.49. Be careful to keep a steady crotchet pulse from the middle of b.52, where Haydn exploits the 'flicked' figure (see bb.7 – 8 and 46 – 7) with Beethovenian persistence. Be sure as before to 'snap' these figures *on* the beat, and keep steady by 'feeling' and showing, that here they always fall on the *crotchet* pulse, balanced by immaculately placed LH quaver chords. Keep the *staccato* 'upbeat' semiquavers relatively light, stress the *first* of the two demisemiquavers, and come *off* smartly on the *staccato* quavers. As the RH ascends like an agitated bird, build the dynamics towards the powerful LH *fortissimo tenuto* dominant 7th chord, and cadenza-like RH run (bb.55 – 6). Pause exaggeratedly on the 3rd beat of b.56, and then flick the upbeat demisemiquavers jauntily down to the 1st beat of b.57. Control your sharply defined RH dotted rhythm chords with rock-steady LH quavers as you *crescendo* through b.58. Then, from b.59 the runs of bb.10 and 11 are extended over several extra bars. Muster and maintain your most brilliant articulation here, as you 'rattle out' these scale figures over implacably steady LH chords. From the middle of b.63 support the buzzing RH demisemiquavers with resonant lower LH dominant pedal point minims and resolute inner quavers as you 'churn' vigorously towards ringing dominant chords in b.65. Be careful to co-ordinate the 'doubled' *pianissimo* figures neatly in b.71. Feel that each demisemiquaver run 'goes to' each *staccato* quaver. Do have courage to *wait* through b.72 before you burst forth for the last time. It should be added that Howard Ferguson in his notes in the Associated Board Edition takes a rather different view of this movement. For example, he interprets the demisemiquaver runs (bb.10 – 11, 25 – 6, etc.) as *cantabile* rather than 'brilliant'. This suggests a comparatively leisurely tempo. Others like myself, on the other hand, who see these runs as exuberant eruptions, will adopt a rather brisker tempo.

The welter of material makes this a difficult movement for any but an experienced artist to bring off, in the sense of *performance* on a platform. But for the player who can follow Haydn's inventive exuberance with some of his own spirit of adventure, there is immense fun to be had.

Second movement – Adagio (6)*
In this profoundly felt movement Haydn exploits the registers of the keyboard in a bold, orchestral, and as in the first movement, sometimes Beethovenian manner. It is the kind of grandly contoured music that will 'play itself', providing that you establish and maintain a really secure, slow **6/8** swing. (Try playing from the middle of b.9, through to b.13, and find a tempo at which the melody line 'moves', rather than 'sticks', over the flowing sextuplet accompaniment.)

bb.1 – 6 Lead off in the RH in a warm, resonant tone. Be sure that the upbeats to bb.1 and 2, etc, are read accurately as demisemiquavers and *not* semiquavers.

Feel the slow **6/8** surely, therefore, before you begin, and then feel that your perfectly timed demisemiquaver upbeats are 'going to' a warmly slurred dotted quaver on the first beat of b.1. Support the RH line with carefully placed and smoothly slurred quaver thirds in the LH, and then feel a buoyant upward lift from the RH quaver B natural up to the diminished 7th on the 5th quaver pulse. Interpret the *staccato* in a detached 'speaking' manner, as you place these quavers *equally* (perhaps with a *short* touch of pedal on each), avoiding any tendency towards a slurred effect. Then *feel* the semiquaver rest as you poise yourself to lead on with the upbeat to b.2. From the upbeat to b.3 shape the longer melodic phrase with the utmost expressiveness incorporating the ornaments smoothly, and supporting the RH with carefully balanced and warm-toned LH chords. Be sure to time the demisemiquaver triplet upbeat to b.6 accurately. While shaping each melodic fragment carefully as an entity, and observing all rests precisely, do at the same time phrase mentally *over* the rests so that you feel an overall sequence of melodic curves through these first bars, rather than a series of disjointed fragments.

bb.7 – 13 Then follow the long and eloquent overall melodic line from the upbeat to b.7 through to b.13, feeling the sense in which the phrases 'overlap' and lead on in the middle of b.9. 'Sing' for all you are worth from here, and interpret the *sforzato* on the 2nd beat of b.10 as a strong melodic 'lean', creating not a bang but an effect of intense yearning. Similarly, 'go to' a strongly melodic, not harsh, *fortissimo* chord in the middle of b.11, and feel your full-throated tone 'going on' to the chord on the 1st beat of b.12, before making a *decrescendo* towards b.13. Feel the 'onward' movement of the LH semiquaver accompaniment from the middle of b.9, though without altering your basic pulse. Place the 'orchestral' sounding detached *piano* thirds immaculately in b.13 (and b.26).

bb.14 – 45 In bb.14 and 15 (where Haydn begins an elaborated re-statement of the first thirteen bars) be sure to use a separate pedal for the spread treble chords, thus giving the feeling of slight detachment from the previous lower chord (as in bb.1, 2, etc.). Phrase the demisemiquaver scale figures gracefully through bb.18 – 19. Do not panic at the sight of the runs in bb.19 and 27 – the first, starting immediately after the quaver, fits easily into the slow quaver pulse (lean a little on the quaver, then think of the notes as hemidemisemiquavers and place the grace note figure at the beginning of b.20 *on* the beat). The second and longer run (b.27) could, if necessary, be divided between the hands, taking the B flat, C, D and E flat with the LH, and this time you will need to allow a little 'give' in the pulse – be sure that you 'go up to' a *clear* dotted quaver third on the 1st beat of b.28. From bb.29 – 31 follow the sustained lower LH line evenly, shaping the inner semiquavers smoothly, as you place the detached RH chords accurately, with a melodic, not spiky touch, and again avoiding any tendency to 'slur' them. In b.33 and in the beginning of b.34 (in a further, elaborated version of the main theme) phrase the slurred RH demisemiquavers eloquently, and then shape the demisemiquaver line graciously, again taking care to place the LH slurred thirds carefully. Go resolutely towards the interrupted cadence at b.42, 'easing' a little on the upbeat, and allow a generous pause. Then feel that the curving RH demisemiquaver line is 'unwinding' as you *decrescendo* towards a *pianissimo* in the penultimate bar. Listen to the eloquent low RH crotchet F sharp from the last beat of b.43 resolving smoothly to the G on the 1st beat of b.44. Avoid muddiness by articulating the hushed bass demisemiquaver accompaniment with immaculate clarity in b.44 beneath your smooth RH chords, and end with the quietest possible, but at the same time definitely placed chords, poising yourself on the pause, ready for the *attacca*.

Finale – Allegro (5)(O)

The tiny Finale is like a rather brisk, strutting Minuet.

bb.1 – 28   Lead off with a lively detached RH upbeat, 'going to' a firm slurred and ornamented 1st beat of b.1, placing the turn clearly *on* the beat. 'Follow on' confidently with the LH detached 'step-like' octaves from the 2nd beat of b.1. Then observe the slurred effect of the RH quavers on the 1st and 2nd beats of b.2. Players struggling with these first eight bars will readily agree with H.C. Robbins Landon's reference to the 'excessive ornamentation' of this movement!† As always, learn the notes *without* the ornaments. If four quick notes starting on the upper note, i.e.

 (b.2, and similarly in b.3) are too much, use acciaccaturas instead:

 In any event, place the ornaments snappily *on* the beat without

disrupting your crotchet pulse, and rely on the stabilizing support of your rock-steady LH crotchet octaves. Take care to 'finish off' the LH cleanly on the 2nd beat of b.4 (and similarly in bb.8, 12, etc.) so that you are ready to lead on with a clear upbeat to the subsequent bar. Similarly underpin the widely curving quavers through bb.6 and 7 with the steadily 'stepping' LH octaves. Then from the upbeat to b.9, adopt a more yielding tone as you slur the RH quaver couplets neatly over a smoothly phrased LH crotchet line. Show the piece of contrapuntal writing at bb.13 – 15, 'entering' clearly with the LH on the 2nd beat of b.13. Do not disrupt the rhythm by trying to cram too many notes into the quick trills on the 1st beat of bb.17 and 18. Start on the upper note, and allow six notes *including* the 'turn', with the feeling that the trills are 'going to' the high slurred

quavers on the 2nd beats: If this fails, just take a four note turn.

Lead off clearly with a steady RH from the upbeat to b.21, and then phrase the syncopated RH line smoothly over even and very steady LH crotchets. From the upbeat to b.25 lean jauntily on the syncopating offbeat slurred quavers in either hand without losing the sense of the 'normal' pulse.

bb.29 – 50   The A flat major 'trio' section is more formal and minuet-like. Lead off from a clear crotchet upbeat and 'go up to' and 'lean' on the RH minims on the 1st beat of bb.29 and 33. From bb.29 – 36 do take care to place the

†*Haydn: Chronicle and Works,* Vol. 3 (Thames & Hudson).

LH chords precisely, beneath your neatly shaped and articulated RH. From b.37 continue to phrase the RH figures neatly over a sustained dominant pedal point and smoothly shaped inner LH line. From b.43 follow the three lines clearly and smoothly, practising *slowly*, parts separately at first. Be sure to enter cleanly with the inner line on the upbeat to b.44. (You could take the inner crotchet A flat on the 3rd beat of b.44, and the inner slurred crotchets on the 1st and 2nd beats of b.45 with the LH.) Be sure to sustain the tied inner pedal point A flat from the upbeat to b.47, 'retaking' it on the 1st beat of b.48.

No. 52 in G major
(Hob. XVI/39)

First movement – Allegro con brio (7)*

This movement, a theme and variations, is based on the 'Scherzando' second movement of the Sonata in C sharp minor (No. 49), but here the heightened emphases (see the *sforzato* upbeats) and the 'toy band' dotted rhythms bring more of a sense of fun, even of the absurd, to this movement than to its companion movement. On account of the rather taxing passage in dotted rhythm (bb.53 – 75) it has been listed under Grade 6, but older players with a good sense of rhythm could perhaps enjoy it at an earlier stage.

bb.1 – 16 Establish and maintain a smart, march-like crotchet beat, imagining a very brisk step to each quaver pulse. Lead in with an immaculately timed RH upbeat. 'Lean' well on (rather than banging) the *sforzato* dotted quaver, and then 'flick' the demisemiquavers neatly down to a clear detached quaver on the 1st beat of b.1. Practise this effect carefully, since the timing and emphasis of these upbeat figures are vital to the overall rhythmic impetus. Articulate the RH with military precision through b.1, supported by immaculately placed LH detached quaver chords. 'Finish off' the phrase neatly in both hands on the 1st beat of b.2, and *feel* the quaver rest, then 'lean' again on the RH slurred figure on the 2nd beat of b.2, and the 1st beat of b.3, over perfectly steady LH quavers. (These LH quavers could be detached, *legato* or slurred – the essential is that they are steady.) From the upbeat to b.5 articulate the RH line crisply, over light but rock-steady LH detached quaver chords. From the 2nd beat of b.10 and through b.11, co-ordinate the RH dotted rhythms perfectly with your steady LH quavers. Then 'lean' on the LH, RH, LH *sforzato* dotted quavers from the 2nd beat of b.12 (keeping the 'plain' quavers in the LH on the 1st beat of b.13, and the RH on the 2nd, *rock-steady* again) so that you get a perfectly timed alternating 'lean' on each crotchet beat. Support the RH in b.14 with a resonant LH minim C.

bb.17 – 36 The minor variation, from the upbeat to b.17, has a more *legato* feeling. In b.17 phrase the syncopated RH thirds smoothly over even LH crotchets, and then feel the implied warm emphasis on the tied upper crotchet G on the 2nd beat of b.18. In b.19 treat the grace notes like light and not too clipped acciaccaturas, supported by your smooth LH line. In bb.21 and 22 feel the *sforzato* 'lean' on the syncopated RH crotchets warmly and smoothly, not aggressively, over smooth and resonant LH crotchet thirds. Note the inner RH tied quaver upbeats to the 2nd beat of bb.25 and 27, and from bb.25 – 30 also phrase the inner LH fragments smoothly over the sustained lower tied minims. From b.31 go ultrasmoothly up the chromatic scale towards the 'lean', on the *sforzato* upbeat to b.33.

bb.37 – 52 From the upbeat to b.37 swing easily into the sextuplets without altering your crotchet pulse, and let the RH sextuplets run in easy curves over your steady LH quaver chords. Lead off cleanly with the LH detached quavers from the middle of b.38, letting the offbeat triplets follow relatively lightly. Then at the beginning of the next section, 'take over' from the RH sextuplet upbeat with a *clear* LH triplet on the 1st beat of b.45, and continue to 'lead' with the LH through to b.48. From the 2nd beat of b.48 make a clear 'alternating' effect, as from the 2nd beat of b.12.

bb.53 – 79   Convey a new, more martial feeling (though *piano* at first) as you move into the minor dotted rhythms from the upbeat to b.53. If you are uneasy with dotted rhythms, prepare for this long passage by practising five-finger exercises, scales, etc, in dotted rhythm. Always maintain an even quaver pulse, and think of the demisemiquavers as upbeats 'going to' the subsequent dotted semiquavers, rather than as 'tail ends' to the *previous* dotted semiquavers. It is essential to keep the demisemiquavers short and light, avoiding the frequent tendency to degenerate into triplets (see also Introduction). When you put 'hands together', it is vital that the LH quavers remain rock-steady. Feel that the RH dotted rhythms are fitting in with the LH quavers, and *not* the other way about. From the upbeat to bb.63 and 65, phrase the inner LH quaver line smoothly over the sustained lower B's, without letting your (*piano*) RH dotted rhythms get sloppy. Treat the *forte* passage from the upbeat to b.67 with mock, strutting importance, and do not get too heavy and ponderous. Plunge forcefully down to the crotchet B's on the 1st beat of b.75, allowing a slight *rallentando* as you descend, and making a generous pause on these resonant unison B's.

bb.80 – 105   Phrase the *legato* semiquaver upbeats to bb.80, 82 and 84 smoothly (in conscious contrast to the previous dotted rhythm upbeats) and slur the RH semiquaver couplets neatly in b.82. Follow the curves of the RH broken octaves smoothly from the 2nd beat of b.84. From the upbeat to b.92 phrase the chromatic semiquavers smoothly in either hand (the 'alternating' effect again). Give full vent to the sudden rumbustuous outburst from the upbeat to b.96, and let the RH plunge down athletically to the F sharp on the 1st beat of b.98 and the upbeat to b.99 over the sustained LH C. Allow the sound to die a little through the pause before resuming the smart march tempo on the upbeat to b.100. End with bright, clear chords.

Second movement – Adagio (6)(O)

This is an expressive, spacious, easy-flowing movement, which would suit older players at about Grade 6. Choose a tempo at which the melody line from b.8 will flow comfortably over the easy-moving LH sextuplets.

bb.1 – 7   Lead off with a full-toned and generously spread C major chord, incorporating the B smoothly in the upward spread towards a singing dotted quaver C.

Then feel an overall melodic curve from the C, down to the semiquaver G and up to the treble G on the 2nd beat, and then 'tail off' down to the detached quaver B on the 3rd beat over smoothly slurred LH thirds. *Feel* the dotted semiquaver rest precisely so that the demisemiquaver upbeat to b.2 is perfectly timed. Then in b.2 articulate the RH dotted rhythm figures neatly but smoothly over a smoothly shaped LH quaver fragment. Be careful to time the RH precisely in b.3, again over steady and smooth LH quavers. Feel the hemidemisemiquavers here as 'upbeats' to the subsequent dotted semiquavers, rather than as 'tail-ends' of the previous beats, and feel that the RH is fitting in with the *steady* descending LH quavers, and *not* the other way about. From the 3rd beat of b.3 shape the RH expressively through to b.5. 'Lean' warmly, not aggressively on the syncopated tied quaver C in b.4, and then feel that the demisemiquavers are 'going towards' the slurred dotted quaver on the 1st beat of b.5. Support the RH with a warm-toned LH, listening acutely to the two lines as the inner voice enters on the upbeat to b.4 and taking particular care to place the inner crotchet F securely on the 3rd beat of b.4 beneath the tied RH C. 'Finish off' neatly in both hands on the 2nd beat of b.5, and then place the rising LH quavers clearly, feeling these as an upbeat group, leading on up to a further full-toned chord on the first beat of b.6. Treat the ornament here as a five-note turn fitting into the space of the fourth semiquaver (there is plenty of time for this at this leisurely tempo).

bb.8 – 22   From the upbeat to b.8 move serenely into the new melody line over the gentle swing of the LH semiquaver sextuplets. It is best in b.8, in accordance with traditional practice, to let the demisemiquaver B coincide with the sixth LH semiquaver D, feeling this RH note as the 'upbeat' to the high semiquaver B on the 2nd beat. Leap up in a poised manner to this high B and then let the semiquavers descend in a gently detached, not spiky, manner towards the long appoggiatura and leisurely trill in b.9. 'Free' runs, as in bb.9 and 11, invariably cause consternation among inexperienced players. While advanced players in such instances find their own groupings which they will vary at will, it helps the less advanced if they can follow more or less regular groupings initially, until they gain the confidence to manage such runs more spontaneously. In b.9, where the run has ten notes, 'stop' the trill neatly on the 3rd beat, and then fit two RH notes to each LH semiquaver; the first note of the run (G) will thus coincide with the second LH semiquaver (C) of the sextuplet group. At b.11, imagine (or, to begin with, *play*) a *third* group of LH sextuplets – this time there are only eight notes in the run, so the first note of this run (F sharp) will coincide with the *third* semiquaver of the imagined LH group. (In both bb.32 and 34 there are again ten notes in the runs – the first note will therefore again coincide with the second note of the LH sextuplet, real in b.32, and imagined in b.34.) In order that all this shall sound as uncontrived as possible, let the first note of each run 'drift' in very quietly, following on smoothly from the singing ornamented long notes in bb.9 and 32

(and from the crotchet in b.34), and moving in a light *crescendo* towards a singing top note on the 1st beat of the subsequent bar. Returning to b.10, follow your singing treble dotted quaver C with a graceful curve of semiquaver triplets, observing the slurs and *staccatos* neatly, but gently and not spikily. Then in bb.12 and 13 listen to the eloquent interplay between the LH and the inner RH semiquaver lines beneath a smooth and warmly singing treble line. Feel that the LH sextuplets are 'going to' the slurred crotchets on the 2nd beat of bb.12 and 13, and that the inner RH sextuplets are 'going to' the inner RH crotchet (B) on the 1st beat of b.13. Note the *tenuto* applied to the treble line through bb.14 – 15, and 'sing' for all you are worth here, balancing the treble carefully with the sustained lower LH line and the inner slurred crotchets, and the smoothly shaped offbeat inner sextuplets. In b.15 show the eloquence of the inner crotchet E flat on the 2nd beat, slurred down to the A (small hands will have to take the E flat with the RH, or the beauty of the ninth above the held bass D will be lost). In b.16 let the slurred detached RH thirds 'enter' over a *firm* LH crotchet third on the 1st beat, and descend easily and without hurry towards a warm *tenuto* third on the 3rd beat of the bar, as you bring the LH arpeggio up to take the lead with the LH detached quavers at the beginning of b.17. Be sure to give full value to the sonorous interrupted cadence at b.20, even if the wait on the minim feels interminable − it will help if you imagine sextuplets running through the bar. Then in b.21, following on from a firm LH minim octave, endeavour to give the treble octave line a beautifully smooth curve. Count carefully through b.22, taking care to place the LH quaver chord precisely on the 2nd beat. In the first-time bar slur/detach the LH thirds as in the RH in b.16.

    Going into the second-time bar find a new, more serious tone colour for
bb.23 − 63 the change to the minor, and shape the undulating treble line expressively
    over even, flowing LH semiquaver sextuplets. At b.28 follow the LH semiquaver line smoothly, beneath a warm-toned RH minim third, up towards a singing crotchet C on the 3rd beat and then listen acutely to the inflections of the RH through b.29 over the sustained LH. Take care not to 'snatch' at the high triplet semiquaver third in b.41, but rather allow a tiny natural break as you leap up calmly, as if in a wide arc, from the third on the 2nd quaver pulse of the bar. The remarkable feature of this movement is the improvisational cadenza from b.48. Build up the tone through b.46 with resonant LH crotchet chords and carefully balanced RH offbeat sextuplets, towards the long six-four chord in b.47. Then shape the relaxed and easy-flowing lines smoothly. Co-ordinate the curving scale figures in tenths graciously through b.49, and from bb.50 − 3 listen to all the inflections of the undulating RH line over warmly sustained broken chord figures in the LH. Follow the interplay of the RH/LH figures in thirds from the upbeat to b.54. Feel that the upbeat treble thirds are 'going to' a resonant tied crotchet third on the 1st beat of b.54, and then that the LH thirds are similarly 'going to' the crotchet third on the 2nd beat, and so on. Then listen to the inflections of the treble triplets and sextuplets over resonant LH thirds through bb.55 − 6, and over a smoothly singing LH quaver line from the upbeat to b.57 as you move in *crescendo* towards the 'spread out' six-four chord effect in b.58, slowing progressively towards the pause. Then through b.59, avoid cutting the long, double trills short by 'feeling' the crotchet pulse moving within them. 'Tail' the trills off gracefully through the 'turned' semiquaver ending in order to get the LH down to the lower C in b.60 without a bump. Resume the *tempo primo* gently, and avoid snatching at the high C in the penultimate bar. Imagine that it is lightly slurred up from the A on the 1st beat and 'ease' up to it as a singer would, allowing just a little 'give' in your otherwise continually even-flowing LH sextuplets.

Third movement − Prestissimo (8)*

This must be the most intoxicatingly high-spirited of all the finales. The faster it can go the better, short, of course, of risking loss of clarity or rhythmic stability. It is essential at the outset (and through most of the movement − see the exceptions below, bb.17, 47, 95, etc.) that the *LH* gives a perfectly secure rhythmic foundation for the activities of the RH.

    Lead off smartly, therefore, with lively but very steady LH detached thirds,
bb.1 − 16 to establish a secure **6/8** two-beat pulse. 'Lean' on the RH offbeat slurred
    broken octave quaver figures in bb.1 − 3 (though lightly and without holding up the main beat), and play the RH semiquaver/quaver figures in bb.1 and 2 as if they are also slightly slurred (many editions do anyway supply a slur), 'flicking' the hand *off* on the *staccato*. Do master the rhythmic sense of these first bars thoroughly − they set the pulse, and the spirit of the whole movement. Then lead off again in the LH from the 2nd beat of b.3 with smooth and even octaves beneath the clearly articulated RH as you

'go towards' the *sforzato* on the 1st beat of b.5. Hang on to your secure **6/8** pulse as you feel the 'kick' of Haydn's uneven phrase lengths, and 'random' repetitions of phrases or portions of phrases between bb.1 and 16. 'Finish off' cleanly with clear octaves on the 1st beat of b.7, and then underpin the sharply articulated RH with firm LH thirds again on the 2nd beat of b.7 and the 1st beat of b.8. From the 2nd beat of b.8 support the immaculately defined RH figures with neatly shaped LH fragments. From the 2nd beat of b.12 show the typical 'churning' effect of the RH semiquavers and LH chords over the lower dominant 'drone' (D) as you *crescendo* towards the brassy dominant chords at b.16.

bb.17 – 43   Then lead off keenly with the *RH* at b.17, phrasing the LH fragments just as you did the corresponding *RH* fragments in bb.1 – 3. Be particularly careful to keep your RH chords perfectly steady here. 'Rattle out' the RH semiquavers with maximum vitality over lively but steady LH quaver fragments through bb.23 – 6. Detach the first three LH quavers in bb.23 and 24 with the feeling of 'going to' a firmly slurred quaver on the 2nd main beat. Then support your RH with *firm* LH crotchets, then chords, in bb.26 – 8, dash upwards through b.29 feeling that the detached LH quavers are 'leading', and go on to 'lean' well on the six-four chord on the 1st beat of b.30. From the upbeat to the *2nd* beat of b.31, drop the dynamics (but not the forward impulse) as you phrase the upper and lower lines smoothly in a rather 'veiled' style, listening to the quiet inner 'drone' D. Open out again through b.34, feeling the implied, slightly syncopating emphasis on the tied RH quaver upbeats to the *2nd* beat of b.34, and to the *1st* beat of b.35, over steady and resonant LH dotted crotchets. Let the RH run down to a clear quaver E on the 1st beat of b.36, and then feel a buoyant 'lift' up to the treble *staccato* quaver third in b.36 rather than making a wild upward snatch. Then keeping a steady two-in-the-bar pulse, let your LH quaver octaves 'lead' downwards towards a firm dotted minim on the 1st beat of b.39. From b.41 tail away the sound breezily and nonchalantly down to the double bar. Be sure to *feel* the rests securely here as you poise yourself to lead off clearly with the LH as you either return to b.1 or continue into b.44.

bb.44 – 68   Lead off again with the LH from the 1st beat of b.44, and switch the 'lead' smartly to the RH on the 1st beat of b.47. From the 2nd beat of b.51 continue to 'lead' with evenly sustained treble dotted crotchets over a busy inner line, and neatly placed LH offbeat quaver broken octaves. Then again switch over the 'lead' to the LH quaver thirds from the 2nd beat of b.53 – there is a delicious sensation here of running *almost* out of control downhill. From bb.61 – 3 keep control of the tricky RH chords by marking the main beats with a light accent. Practise these bars slowly and very rhythmically, and underpin your RH with clear and steady, detached LH quavers. This passage will seem easier if you feel that these LH quavers, and not the RH chords, are 'leading'. In bb.64 – 5 'rattle out' the LH 'whirring' semiquavers beneath *firm* RH chords. Similarly through bb.66 – 7, control the RH semiquavers with firm lower LH dotted crotchets, and precisely placed inner LH offbeat quavers.

bb.69 – 121   The main technical difficulty arises from bb.70 – 7, when the original RH figures occur in double notes. Treat these as described for bb.1 and 2, as if slightly slurred, with the hand coming *off* on the quaver thirds, which must, as elsewhere, be treated as *staccato*. Do be sure that the LH gives a firm and very steady rhythmic 'lead' throughout this passage. Bb.71 – 4 are particularly treacherous – show the *2nd* beat of these bars clearly with the thumb, on the upper notes of the LH broken quaver octaves, and be careful to place the wide-leaping RH quaver thirds accurately. 'Pluck' these leaping thirds rather than whacking wildly at them; and to avoid the inevitable sense of panic here it is helpful to feel these RH thirds as 'upbeats' to *strong LH* crotchets on the 1st beats of the subsequent bars, rather than as 'tail-ends' to their own bars. Then let the LH continue to 'lead' you, from b.75 back to the beginning of the reprise in b.79. Disappear into *pianissimo* at the end without a hint of a *rallentando*.

No. 53 in E minor
(Hob. XVI/34)

This is one of the most popular of Haydn's Sonatas. In comparison with those of some of the first movements of the previous Sonatas, Nos. 30, 33, 40 and 44 to name but a few, the patterns of this first movement are relatively uncomplicated. And both in spirit and in texture, all three movements are comparatively lightweight.

First movement – Presto (7)*

bb.1 – 8   This tightly-knit movement is dominated by an urgent arpeggio figure. Set a taut **6/8** pulse, not too fast, bearing in mind the semiquaver passage-work to come. 'Pluck' the LH *staccato* rising quaver figures with extreme precision, conveying their feeling of suppressed energy and excitement, and always giving the feeling that these figures are 'going up to' the quavers on the 2nd beats of the bars. Phrase the more soothing RH slurred answering fragments smoothly. From the upbeat to b.4 the 'soothing' figures take over. Phrase the slurred RH quaver sixths smoothly down towards a warmly sustained dotted crotchet sixth on the 1st beat of b.4, and let the LH quavers rise smoothly towards the dotted crotchet on the 2nd main beat, ensuring that these alternating RH and LH tied dotted crotchets sing over the subsequent beats. Then, from b.6 continue to shape the reiterated RH fragments and the carefully dovetailed offbeat LH fragments neatly as you *diminuendo* with a little *rallentando* towards the pause at b.8.

bb.9 – 29   From b.9 build up the tone towards the *forte* octave version of the opening *staccato* figure at bb.14 – 15. Here (in bb.14 and 15) feel that you are making a little *crescendo* towards the top note of each *staccato* octave figure, so that a firm and accurately placed quaver octave on the 2nd beat of each of these bars gives a rhythmic springboard for the brightly articulated RH semiquaver answering figures. Similarly, in the varied sustained form of the arpeggio figure from bb.16 – 18 (and again in the development section) feel that you are *crescendoing* towards the upmost note of each sustained broken chord. Then from the upbeat to b.17 let the RH answering figures 'go to' firm slurred crotchets on the 1st beat of each subsequent bar. From bb.19 – 21 'rattle out' the treacherous RH semiquavers over lively and very rhythmic detached LH quavers. Feel that the LH quavers are 'leading' here, in a rhythmic sense, and *not* the other way about, and let the first three quavers in bb.19 and 20 'go to' the quaver on the 2nd main beat. Then 'take over' confidently with the RH on the 1st beat of b.22 and drive on vibrantly towards b.26. 'Go to' a clear RH semiquaver D and LH quaver F sharp on the 2nd main beat, and then be careful to co-ordinate the scale passage accurately (bb.26 – 7). *Crescendo* through the second half of b.26 towards a clear RH semiquaver F sharp on the 1st beat of b.27, in order that the LH can enter on the offbeat without a bump. *Crescendo* again towards the high D's on the 1st beat of b.28, and then let the lively 'plucked' quavers descend in perfect time towards the 1st beat of b.29.

bb.30 – 45   Use the pause at b.29 to poise yourself for the more pliable second subject material. Give a firm but quiet bass octave on the 1st beat of b.30 and let the RH thirds and sixths rise as smoothly as possible through bb.30 – 1, with the LH thirds dovetailing in neatly on the upbeats to bb.31 and 32. Then phrase all three, then four, lines very smoothly through bb.32 – 5, feeling that you are 'going to' the sustained six-four chord on the 1st beat of b.34. Show the implied emphasis on the treble tied crotchet (D) in b.32, and on the tied quaver upbeat (C) to b.33. Here, and in the extended version of the passage (bb.38 – 41), study the parts separately, and when they are all put together listen as carefully to the inner and lower parts as to the treble. Play the RH quaver chords through b.40 in a just detached, 'speaking' manner. 'Rattle out' the RH semiquavers again from b.42 over the vigorous and very rhythmic reiterated LH crotchet/quaver figures, and finish off the section in b.45 with exuberant, detached treble thirds.

bb.46 – 127   Set off very quietly in the major at the start of the development, and then draw out a little towards the pause at b.50. From b.53 Haydn takes us through a closely reasoned modulatory passage based on the material of bb.16 – 18. Build up the tone gradually, perhaps dropping it a little after b.60, to build up again towards b.64. Play the passage as expressively as you will, though without losing the rhythmic momentum. Listen acutely to the harmonic resonances of the LH, and the inflections of the RH as you show the interplay between the rising LH figures and the offbeat RH semiquavers 'going to' the slurred crotchet on the 1st beat of each bar. From bb.64 – 7 the RH passage is a varied version of the passage at bb.19 – 21, and is equally treacherous.

In both instances practising in dotted rhythms will help: [musical rhythm notation] and [musical rhythm notation] etc. (see Introduction) and do remember to let the LH quavers 'lead' with the feeling of 'going to' firm crotchets on the 2nd beat of the bars. From the middle of b.67 let the buoyant RH melody 'take over' to lead exuberantly into a version of the opening material (from b.71) in which the hands are reversed, and which in turn drives on to the sustained pause on the dominant in b.78. Take care not to overbalance in b.70, and thereby 'fall into' b.71. Let the LH semiquavers 'go to' a clear quaver F sharp on the 2nd main beat of b.70, and then treat the RH quavers as the upbeat to b.71. From b.109 Haydn launches into a kind of coda, expanding on the material from the close of the exposition. Set off from here with renewed vigour, but keep the headlong rush towards b.124 under taut rhythmic control, always feeling a secure two-in-the-bar pulse. Feel that the LH 'leads' in bb.109 – 10, and 112 – 13, with the RH briefly 'taking over' in b.111, and again from b.114. Support the RH semiquavers with firm LH crotchet octaves in bb.120 – 3. It is effective to make a *diminuendo* through the last four bars towards a *pianissimo* ending. Be sure, however, to begin the *diminuendo* only *after* you have arrived, with full vigour, on the unison tonic on the 1st beat of b.124. Then tail away the sound with no *rallentando,* placing the treble octaves in the last bar with neat finality, as *pianissimo* as possible.

Second movement – Adagio (6) (O)
The slow movement is, in contrast, a florid, but rather dull Adagio. It does, however, give good opportunities for studying the refinements of *cantabile* phrasing. Set a leisurely 3/4 pulse at which the demisemiquaver figuration will flow easily and without a sense of hurry, and make the most of the movement by treating it like a vocal aria, imagining, in every instance, how a singer would shape the curving melodic phrases.

bb.1 – 8   Give the RH dotted quavers on the 1st beat of each of the first six bars (and the minim in b.7) sufficient tone to sing through their full value, and to join smoothly, ideally to float almost imperceptibly into the subsequent triplet demisemiquaver 'turns'. If the dotted quavers are not given sufficient singing tone the 'turns' will inevitably cause a 'bump'. Balance this RH line carefully, with sustained and perfectly timed but never overpowering LH chords. Play the *staccato* quavers in b.1, and semiquavers in bb.3 and 5 in a gently detached 'speaking' and not spiky style, showing the 'vocal' curve up to and down from the quaver D on the 3rd beat of b.1, the semiquaver E on the 3rd beat of b.3, and the high semiquaver D on the 4th *quaver* pulse of b.5, and so on. Then let the demisemiquavers in bb.2 and 4 ascend in a gradual *diminuendo*, tailing the sound away gracefully towards the upper quaver on the 3rd beats. Feel the *forte* (or *sforzato*) emphasis on the tied treble minim (b.7) as a warm melodic 'lean', merging smoothly into the *perdendosi* chromatically descending semiquavers. Be particularly careful to place the inner LH thirds accurately and quietly on the 2nd and 3rd beats of this bar, over the sustained lower LH D.

bb.8 – 20   Take care to place the low LH crotchet G accurately on the 2nd beat of b.8 so that the upbeat demisemiquaver arpeggio leading into b.9 enters in perfect time. Rise to singing high D's on the 1st beats of bb.9 and 11, and take care to place the LH quaver chords gently and accurately in these bars. In b.12 feel the implied emphasis on the detached syncopated RH G sharps, and on the tied quaver upbeat to b.13, over very steady LH partly-tied crotchet chords. Follow the 'vocal' curves of the flowing demisemiquavers smoothly through bb.13 – 16, over carefully balanced supporting LH chords. Allow the trill to run easily, not hectically, through b.17, and do not be so preoccupied with it that you allow the crotchet pulse of the supporting LH chords to be disrupted, and thus to shorten the bar. Do not, in panic, see a long trill such as this as an interminable line of black notes, but rather feel the crotchet or even the quaver pulse moving steadily within it. From b.19 follow the melodic line smoothly and sonorously downwards, feeling that the line is 'going on', down to the bass D on the 2nd beat of b.20.

bb.21 – 49   Lead into the development in a rather more positive tone. Through bb.25 – 9 feel the presence of the crotchet pulse (and within it the quaver, though without obvious accents) so that the demisemiquaver passage-work alternates evenly in smoothly undulating curves between the hands. Then make a slight *rallentando* into the *piu adagio* at b.30. 'Lean' a little on the pauses on the 3rd beat of b.30, and the 1st beat of b.31, and as at b.20, feel the melodic line dropping down to the bass D in b.31, allowing a full, slow rest before taking up the *tempo primo* in b.32. Let the demisemiquavers expand through bb.41 – 2 in improvisatory style. Then let the LH join in smoothly from the upbeat to b.43 and take the 'lead' as you move in a warm-toned and not aggressive *crescendo* towards the six-four flourish and interrupted cadence (bb.44 – 5). Time this flourish accurately so that the bass D and the treble appoggiatura G leading into the trill, fall exactly on the 2nd beat of b.44. As at b.17, be sure to give this bar its full value, feeling that the LH dominant 7th chord gives the trill a 'boost' as you go towards the interrupted cadence. Then count carefully through the declamatory, recitative-like chords (bb.45 – 6). From the upbeat to b.47 listen to the horn-like quality of the *piano legato* RH thirds, and end quietly and perfectly in tempo, ready for the *attacca subito*.

Finale – Vivace molto (Innocentemente) (6)*

This Finale has an irresistible and infectious gaiety. Let it go as fast as is consistent with clarity and rhythmic security but, having set your tempo, be sure that you maintain a secure crotchet pulse from first note to last.

bb.1 – 18   Practise the Alberti LH slowly and carefully until you can manage it with perfect light evenness and clarity, always marking the beat with a light accent

with the fifth finger. Practising in dotted rhythms will help:

and ♪ ♪♪♪ ♪ ♪♪♪ (see also Introduction). Be particularly careful to keep this LH steady when it plunges downward at bb.12 – 13, and to *listen* to the LH bass notes

130

from here through to b.18. Set off in the RH with a clear detached upbeat 'going to' a firm dotted quaver on the 1st beat of b.1, and thereafter meticulously follow all details of RH slurs and *staccatos*, particularly the slightly 'syncopating' slurred upbeats to the 1st and 2nd beats of b.3, and to the 1st beat of b.7 etc. Observe the quaver rests accurately in bb.2 and 6 etc. Slur the quavers on the 1st beats of bb.10 and 12 dashingly down to the sevenths, and go boldly down to the crotchet D sharp on the 1st beat of b.16. When you put 'hands together' practise slowly, until your rhythm feels absolutely secure, and there is perfect co-ordination between the hands. Take particular care, in the interests of rhythmic security, to *feel* the 2nd beat of the bar securely in the LH when the RH has a quaver rest on those 2nd beats (e.g. in bb.2, 6, 10, 12, etc.).

bb.19 – 76   At the turn into the major after the second double bar, with the loss of the stabilizing effect of the LH semiquaver pattern, it is easy for the pulse to become rocky. Feel the crotchet pulse consistently therefore, particularly when (as in bb.19, 21, 23, 24, etc.) the LH is silent on the 2nd beat. Help yourself throughout these two major sections by placing all LH figures clearly and very precisely (particularly the quaver A's on the 2nd beat of bb.20 and 34 which give a rhythmic springboard to the ascending RH scales). From the middle of b.36 let the RH scale curve clearly up to the B on the 2nd beat of b.37, and then feel that the line is 'going on down to' a strong LH quaver on the 1st beat of b.38, rather than stopping in mid-air at the end of b.37. At b.46 'go' firmly to the syncopated treble *sforzato* crotchet C without disturbing the rhythm of the LH. At b.66 make a controlled and decisive downward leap with the LH to the B on the 2nd beat of the bar without disrupting the steadiness of the leaping, detached RH quavers, as you 'drive on towards' the half-close and pause at b.68.

bb.77 – 136   Support the RH with light but 'keen' LH semiquavers as you launch into the major again from b.77. Again feel the syncopating effect of the slurred quaver upbeats to the 1st and 2nd beats of bb.89 and 97, and let the descending RH scale *crescendo* dashingly towards the unison B's and pause in b.92. In the last section, from b.101 'point' all the racy little variations: show the emphatic emphasis on the RH syncopated *sforzato* crotchet in b.110; play the chromatic quavers in b.117, and the semiquavers in b.119 with 'sliding' smoothness; and articulate the repeated-note figures in bb.127 and 129 with pinpoint sharpness. There are different schools of thought as to how to deal with such a series of rapid repeated notes: some advocate changing the fingers, some do not, while most players adopt either method according to the circumstances. In any event, the essential here remains the same: feel that you are 'going through' the repeated notes in a *crescendo* towards a strong slurred quaver on the 1st beats of bb.128 and 130, starting therefore relatively lightly from the first note of the series. Balance the implied syncopation on the tied RH quaver upbeat to b.133 by marking the LH 1st beat of b.133 accurately. In b.134 feel that you are 'going to' a strong LH quaver octave on the 1st beat of b.135, and end with an emphatic unison double octave.

The three two-movement Sonatas, Nos. 54 – 6, were dedicated to Princess Marie Esterházy. As H.C. Robbins Landon puts it: 'These are gentle and sophisticated works which really seem to be destined for a lady's hand.'†

No. 54 in G major
(Hob. XVI/40)

The two movements of this little work are sheer enchantment (perhaps older players would enjoy the first at around Grade 6).

First movement – Allegretto innocente (7)*
This first movement consists of two variations on a major theme, separated by two sections in the minor, the second a varied version of the first.

bb.1 – 24   Feel a gentle, but very secure **6/8** swing within yourself before leading in with a perfectly timed quaver upbeat, and let the RH melody move expressively, but easily over quiet and steady LH chords through bb.1 – 2. Place the RH grace note (played like a gentle, not too clipped acciaccatura), and the turn *on* the beat. Try to incorporate these ornaments smoothly, feeling each one as part of the melodic line, rather than as a clamped-on excrescence. Play the detached quavers in b.2 in a quietly 'speaking', not spiky manner, with the feeling of 'going towards' the crotchet on the 2nd main beat. Then, from the upbeat to b.3, follow the lines as carefully in the LH as in the RH, observing all slurs, and again detaching the occasional *staccato* quavers gently as in b.2. Feel the *sforzatos* in bb.3, 4, 7, 9, 10, etc, as warm melodic 'leans', not bumps. Be sure to listen to, and give full value to, the inner RH dotted crotchets (b.3), the lower LH tied dotted minim G (bb.6 – 7), the RH inner tied crotchet G from the 2nd beat of b.6, and the inner LH tied quaver upbeat to b.8. Lead into the second section in a fuller tone from the upbeat to b.9 (second-time bar), and give the LH thirds a horn-like quality here. Let the RH detached repeated quavers 'lead', in a rhythmic sense, through bb.12 – 13, giving these a 'speaking' and again, not spiky quality, supported by smoothly slurred, and carefully placed LH offbeat thirds. Reverse this process in the *pianissimo* echo (bb.14 – 15) letting the *LH* quavers 'lead'. Then gather the tone again with a firm lower LH tied D on the 2nd beat of b.15 as you approach the half-close on the 1st beat of b.16, allowing a full, not harsh tone to sustain the dotted minim chord through the pause. Listen as the sound of the chord fades, then let the little grace note 'upbeat' figure move lightly towards an *a tempo* return to the opening phrase in b.17. Incorporate the turns as smoothly as possible with the RH melody line in sixths from the upbeat to b.22, placing the grace note figure again *on* the beat in b.22. As will be evident, there is an immense amount of detail to be attended to in this movement.

bb.25 – 36   'Finish off' clearly with the crotchet chord on the 2nd beat of b.24, and either lead back with a full-toned upbeat to b.9 or, making a tiny break, lead on with the *piano* quaver upbeat to the minor section. Place the detached RH quavers delicately in bb.25 – 6 over equally accurately placed *piano* LH offbeat quaver chords. Feel the RH quaver rests as little breaths, the phrase increasing in intensity as it rises towards the syncopated *sforzato* upbeat to b.27. 'Lean' on the treble tied quaver of this upbeat chord (as also on the 'upbeat' to the 2nd beat of the bar), yearningly, not harshly, being careful to sustain these melody notes over the LH and inner RH crotchets placed quietly and accurately on the subsequent main beats. Move on with increasing intensity to the end of b.28, before dropping to piano on the 1st beat of b.29. After the

†*Haydn: Chronicle and Works,* Vol. 2 (Thames & Hudson).

double bar, in bb.31 and 32 note that the RH offbeat quaver figures are *slurred*. While the ascending detached quavers of bb.25 and 26 conveyed an underlying urgency, conversely the slurred quaver figures here give a feeling of quiet resignation. Lean warmly again on the syncopated treble tied quaver upbeats to the 1st and 2nd beats of b.33, listening to the quiet inner RH sevenths (A) against the upper tied G's on those 1st and 2nd beats. Then 'go towards' a full-toned tied diminished 7th chord on the 1st beat of b.34, *listening* as you release the inner RH F sharp and lower C on the 2nd beat (as well as all the notes of the LH chord) while retaining the treble C and the inner RH E flat. Listen acutely also to the subtle resonances of b.35: the tied treble upbeat from the previous bar, and the tied treble and tied inner LH 'upbeat' to the 2nd beat, the inner RH tied E flat, and the lower LH sustained dotted crotchets. In b.36 note also the beautiful effect of the resolution of the suspended 9th in the LH (small hands take the A with the RH).

bb.37 – 60   Following these subtle minor refinements and inflections, resume the major theme in its first variation (from the upbeat to b.37) with absolute simplicity, listening to the smooth and graceful interplay of the flowing semiquavers, within your perfectly steady 6/8 pulse. Phrase the RH thirds smoothly and expressively through bb.40 – 1 over smoothly curving LH semiquavers. In bb.48 – 9 be careful to keep steady, again letting the repeated RH quavers 'lead' in a rhythmic sense, and fitting in the LH offbeat semiquaver figures evenly. Similarly, let the LH quavers 'lead' through b.50 with the feeling of 'going to' a resonant bass D on the 1st beat of b.51. Then let the RH broken chord figure descend in improvisatory style. Leap up without snatching towards a full-toned tied dotted crotchet E on the 1st beat of b.52, to be 'joined' by the LH as it rises towards the dotted crotchet F sharp on the 2nd main beat. Let the sound die a little through the pause, then let the demisemiquaver upbeat run lightly down to the 1st beat of b.53. At b.59 let the treble and LH quaver lines 'lead' smoothly with the inner RH syncopated line following evenly and relatively lightly.

bb.61 – 72   The yearning intensity of the first minor section is heightened in the varied version from b.61 by the 'sighing' slurred RH semiquaver figures (bb.61 and 62). 'Go to' a singing high dotted quaver C on the 1st beat of b.63, timing the downward scale to run clearly on to the firm LH diminished chord placed precisely on the 2nd main beat of the bar. Also be sure to place the following RH syncopated *sforzato* chord precisely on the 5th *quaver* pulse of the bar, and then lead off firmly with the LH third on the 1st beat of b.64. Let your beautifully shaped and articulated RH demisemiquaver arabesques in this bar fit in with accurately timed and smooth LH thirds, rather than the other way about. Then place the further *sforzato* syncopated crotchet chord firmly on the 5th quaver pulse of the bar. Place the 'normal' LH chords and the syncopated RH octave and seventh firmly again in b.65, and then note the sudden *piano* on the slurred 1st beat of b.66. These complex rhythmic effects between bb.63 and 65 will need to be carefully worked out, even by experienced players, and physically *felt* and absorbed into the system. 'Lean' on the RH slurred *sforzato* semiquavers and LH thirds from the upbeat to b.69, and then descend with full-toned RH broken octaves through the first half of b.70, over smooth inner LH quavers above a warmly sustained lower F sharp. Then make a gradual *diminuendo* through b.71 towards precisely timed *pianissimo* offbeat unison octaves in b.72.

bb.73 – 99   Phrase the RH slurred semiquavers neatly in bb.73 – 4 over a continuingly steady LH. Take care not to overbalance in b.76, but let the LH run fit in with smooth, firm and steady RH thirds, and *not* the other way about. Let the RH scale *crescendo* gently up to the treble third on the 2nd main beat of b.77. From the tied upbeat to b.78 phrase the treble line graciously over a smooth inner LH line above the sustained lower LH G, treating the treble grace notes like gentle acciaccaturas and feel the implied emphasis on the tied LH inner upbeat to b.80. Listen particularly to the shifting resonances through b.79 as the RH line moves in syncopation with the LH, and the tied inner LH crotchet G resolves to the F sharp in b.80 over the lower LH dotted crotchet D. From the upbeat to b.81, let the LH thirds provide a smooth and warm-toned foundation for your neatly slurred, then detached, RH semiquavers as you crescendo towards b.84. Lean well on the *forte* RH broken octave slurred semiquavers on the main beats of b.84, and similarly on the slurred demisemiquaver figures in b.85, and the slurred semiquavers in bb.86 and 87. Do not hammer the insistent repeated semiquavers, nor play them too spikily, but rather let them 'speak' and support this active and high-pitched treble through bb.84 – 8 with firmly placed LH slurred offbeat quaver thirds. Then let the sound die away through the *calando* towards the pauses in bb.90 and 91. Spread the *forte* chords in b.94 generously, and in b.95 time the brilliant run to arrive at the top D to coincide with the resonant bass chord precisely on the 2nd main beat. Feel the detached semiquavers in the last two bars like little receding steps, and end with a full tonic spread chord exactly on the 2nd beat of the last bar.

Second movement – Presto (7)*
This movement is characterized by hectic changes of mood. Rhythmic security is vital, so set a brisk but sane crotchet pulse, bearing in mind the prolonged semiquaver passage-work from b.56, and the wild syncopated effects from bb.69 – 71.

bb.1 – 10 Haydn rattles off merrily in b.1, only to veer disconcertingly into momentary seriousness in a brush with C major (bb.2 – 3) on the way to the dominant at b.4. 'Lean' on the RH dotted quaver on the 1st beat of b.1, then 'flick' the demisemiquavers back to the quaver G on the 2nd beat over neat and perfectly rhythmic mettlesome LH quaver thirds. Balance the RH rest in b.1 by lightly marking the 3rd beat of the bar in the LH. Then feel that you are 'going to' a firm slurred 1st beat of b.2 in both hands, and similarly that the reiterated quavers from the middle of b.2 are 'going to' a firm 1st beat of b.3. Then let the RH leap decisively up to an emphatic syncopated *sforzato* crotchet A in b.3, over steady LH crotchet thirds. Maintain the sense of the crotchet pulse as the unaccompanied RH dashes down b.4 towards a firm 1st beat of b.5. 'Rattle out' the RH semiquavers through bb.8 – 9 (making a little 'surge' up to and down from the A on the 2nd beat, and the G on the 4th beat of each bar) over steady and very rhythmic LH quaver chords as you *crescendo* towards the reckless *sforzato* RH-LH 'plonks' on the dominant in b.10.

bb.11 – 24 At b.11 Haydn plunges into B flat major. Keep your rhythmic balance from bb.11 – 14 with the help of perfectly timed LH thirds, always feeling the quaver thirds as upbeats, 'going to' firm crotchet thirds on the 1st and 3rd beats of the bars. (Be particularly careful to place the crotchet thirds firmly on the *3rd* beats, where the RH has a rest.) Articulate the first figure of b.11 vigorously (the opening RH figure in reverse) and then 'pick out' the RH offbeat repeated quaver figures sharply, always with the feeling of 'going to' the dotted quavers on the 1st beats of bb.12, 13 and 14. Articulate the unison figures energetically in b.14, ending with a bit of a 'plonk' again on the 3rd beat. Then catch your breath on the crotchet rest ready to 'start again' in b.15. Be sure to come clean *off* the quaver on the 2nd beat of b.18, count the rests carefully, and then let the demisemiquaver/*staccato* quaver figures 'skip' down in perfect time towards the 1st beat of b.20. 'Feel' the dotted quaver rest on the 2nd beat of b.20 and 'flick' the demisemiquavers lightly in both hands down to a firm 3rd beat. Then (keeping your balance with *steady* repeated RH C's in the second half of this bar), likewise 'flick' the LH upbeat demisemiquavers down to a *firm* LH third on the 1st beat of b.21.

bb.25 – 49

Turning into the minor at b.25, create a beautifully expressive *legato* in the alternately moving LH and RH lines, though without losing your rhythmic momentum. Lead off with the LH in b.25, and again from the upbeats to bb.29 and 33, with the RH following on evenly. Show the rise of the RH line towards a singing, high treble third on the 2nd beat of b.27 (and b.31), and then let the syncopated RH line descend smoothly over even LH crotchets. The RH 'leads' briefly from the upbeat to b.35, the LH 'taking over' again on the 1st beat of b.36. Then let the RH lead off again into b.37 from the *forte* upbeat semiquavers, and build up the tone in both hands towards the unison diminished 7th flourish through b.40. Descend towards resonant crotchet D sharps on the 1st beat of b.41, then *feel* the quaver rest on the 2nd beat before playing the solo 'echo' in a distant *piano*, perhaps making a little *rallentando* towards the 1st beat of b.42. Then *feel* the silent beats again, and shape the RH three-quaver figure neatly while feeling the the LH is 'leading' into b.43 from the upbeat crotchet D sharp. Let the detached quavers alternate evenly between the hands through b.43, and then feel that the RH is 'leading' into b.44. From here slur the RH quaver-crotchet figures smoothly, with the LH broken octave offbeat figures following evenly (observing the rests precisely) and listen to the subtle colour of the chromatic downward step in the LH (b.46) as you pass from E minor, through A minor and D major on the way back to the reprise in the tonic at b.49.

bb.49 – 68

From bb.53 – 60 articulate all RH semiquaver passage-work racily over rock-steady LH quaver chords. Practise the awkward b.61 slowly and rhythmically (always 'practising through' to the 1st beat of b.62). Steadiness here depends on the firm and accurate placing of the LH crotchet C on the 3rd beat of b.61, and the minim D on the 1st beat of b.62. Avoid snatching at the RH treble E – let the RH go down to a clear semiquaver A on the 3rd beat, perfectly co-ordinated with the LH crotchet C, and then allow a little natural break as you leap confidently up to the high E. (Unless you really must, avoid taking the easy way out by taking the semiquaver A on the 3rd beat with the RH, which would weaken the effect of the upward leap.) Then support the descending RH broken octaves with a firm LH crotchet D on the 3rd beat of b.62. Feel that these broken octaves are 'going to' the strong dotted crotchet on the 1st beat of b.63, and keep steady by marking the 4th beat of b.62 (feeling this as the *upbeat* to b.63) with a light accent with the RH thumb on the B. Practise in plain octaves until you feel rhythmically secure.

bb.69 – 83

In bb.69 – 71 leap up giddily to the high syncopated *sforzato* crotchets over vigorous and perfectly steady Alberti LH semiquavers. Balance these high *sforzato* crotchets by taking particular care to place the *3rd* LH beat of these bars accurately, particularly in b.71 where the LH jumps down to the E flat. The joyous recklessness of these bars depends absolutely on this steady LH. If the LH falters you will collapse in a heap. Practise the 2nd half of b.72 in plain octaves as in the *RH* in b.62, feeling here that you are descending to a *firm* bass G on the 1st beat of b.73. In b.74, having 'leaned' on the slurred 1st beat in both hands and come *off* cleanly on the 2nd beat, make it clear that the first treble broken octave is an 'upbeat' to the 3rd beat of the bar (and likewise in b.75). Keep your balance here with steady LH quaver chords, 'going to' firm crotchet thirds on the 1st beats of bb.75 and 76, and 'flick' the Papageno-like demisemiquaver runs lightly down to *staccato* quavers. Count the rests carefully in bb.76 – 7, then 'flick' the runs down to the *staccato* quavers with a 'skipping' effect. Underpin the tricky RH semiquavers in b.79 with firm and steady LH crotchets. Drive on through bb.80 – 2, and end with a wild downward flourish towards a clear LH quaver on the 3rd beat of the last bar. Alternatively, you could *diminuendo* to a *pianissimo*, but in either event, end in exact tempo without a hint of a *rallentando*.

No. 55 in B flat major
(Hob. XVI/41)

First movement – Allegro (8)*

Although it is not difficult in a strictly technical sense, this splendid, closely reasoned movement is considerably demanding rhythmically. Set a realistic and very secure tempo, bearing in mind the extensive triplet figuration to come. It is absolutely essential throughout that you feel the overall two-in-the-bar pulse.

bb.1 – 24   Set off with a resonant chord, perhaps spread in the LH as well as the RH, 'feel' the held 2nd crotchet beat, and then 'skip' down the scale cleanly and rhythmically towards a singing dotted crotchet on the 1st beat of b.2. Place the LH slurred thirds carefully and with a warm tone (listening to the minor inflection) and note that the RH 'upbeat' to the *3rd* crotchet beat of this bar consists of two *semiquavers*, as opposed to the *demisemiquaver* upbeats to the 4th crotchet beat and to the 1st beat of b.3. Time this bar carefully, with the feeling that you are 'going up to' the tied crotchet on the 1st beat of b.3. Go to, and 'lean' warmly on the syncopated RH minims in bb.4 and 5, supported by also warmly sustained LH fragments. 'Shake out' the descending semiquaver run in b.6 rhythmically and exuberantly over a strong, sustained LH dominant 7th chord, and continue into b.7 with a precisely timed RH dotted rhythm line over steady LH crotchets, noting that here the dotted rhythms are sustained and not 'skipping'. Feel the silent 2nd and 3rd beats of b.8. Time the semiquaver upbeat group to b.9 crisply (treating the grace note like an acciaccatura). Keep steady through the series of dotted rhythm figures from bb.9 – 19 by preserving the sense of the steady overall two-in-the-bar pulse. As always in such instances, feel the semiquavers as 'upbeats' to the subsequent dotted quavers, rather than as 'tail ends' of the previous beats (see Introduction). 'Lean' well on the RH slurred minim chords on the 1st beats of bb.10 and 12, and place the LH interjections neatly in these bars. Be sure to sustain the lower B flat tied upbeats to bb.14 and 16, through to bb.15 and 17 respectively, and keep the 'skipping' RH in place with an evenly phrased inner LH crotchet line through these bars (and likewise through b.17, with accurately placed LH detached quaver chords). Shape the RH quaver line smoothly through b.19 (interpreting the offbeat *sforzando* as a warm melodic 'lean') with the feeling of 'going to' the slurred minim on the 1st beat of b.20. 'Finish off' neatly in both hands on the 3rd beat of this bar, and *feel* the silent 4th beat. Then 'flick' the demisemiquaver upbeats vigorously up towards clear and strong dotted crotchets on the main beats of b.21, and the 1st beat of b.22, and 'place' the big 'offbeat' LH chords strongly, rather than banging them or, as well as making an ugly sound, you will overbalance your two-in-the-bar pulse. Let the RH scale descend confidently through the second half of b.22 towards a clear dotted crotchet E natural on the 1st beat of b.23. Then take care to place the LH offbeat chords quietly and neatly beneath the precisely timed RH as you go towards a warmly slurred RH crotchet F sharp on the 1st beat of b.24.

bb.24 – 55   Feel the silent 3rd and 4th beats of b.24 once more as you poise yourself to launch into the buoyant, almost vehement melodic passage from the semi-quaver upbeat to b.25. Support the RH through to b.40 with lively but perfectly even LH triplets. 'Lean' ardently on the syncopated *sforzato* dotted crotchets in bb.25, 27, etc, and incorporate the ornaments smoothly into the melodic line, never allowing either the *sforzatos* or the ornaments to disrupt the flow of the LH triplets. Be careful to preserve your sense of the overall two-in-the-bar pulse (particularly in bb.25, 27, 28, 29, 30, 32, 34, etc, where the RH either is held or has a rest, by marking the 2nd main beat (or 3rd crotchet beat) lightly in the LH. Detach the RH crotchets on the 1st beats of bb.32 and 34, the better to define the 'lean' on the *sforzato* minims. Support the RH solo triplets in bb.31 and 33 with firm LH minims on the 1st beats. Keep the RH trills short and light in bb.35 and 36 and through bb.38 – 9, feeling that the ornamented RH is fitting in with the *even LH triplets* here, and not the other way about. Give these

trills six notes including the turn: Let the RH demisemiquaver/

staccato quaver figures 'skip' through bb.40 – 1 (moving smoothly into triplets in the second half of b.41), again supported by firm LH crotchets on the 1st beats. Keep your smooth RH chromatic scale figures in place through bb.43 – 5 with accurately placed LH crotchet chords. Run up to a ringing high quaver F on the 2nd main beat of b.46, allowing a tiny break as you leap down, clearly showing the unison crotchet B naturals as the *upbeat* to b.47. It is easy for the rhythm to get rocky from b.47. Be sure that you do not cut short the 2nd main beat of b.47 (with the trill) as you poise yourself to let the LH 'take over' the dotted rhythm in b.48. Feel your two main beats steadily through b.48 and support your LH with clear detached RH octaves placed accurately on the 3rd and 4th crotchet beats as you 'go to' firm *sforzato* dotted minims in both hands on the 1st beat of b.49. Also be sure to 'feel' the held 2nd main beat (or 3rd crotchet beat) in b.49, and then keep the *RH* dotted rhythms in place through b.50 with even *LH* crotchets. Treat bb.51 – 3 similarly, and end the section in *piano* with even RH triplets over quietly placed LH thirds.

From the point of view of the player the development section is comparatively
bb.56 – 151 straightforward. Feel the serious intent of the *forte* plunge into D flat major at b.56, and then play the dominant 7th echo very quietly and evenly before setting off high-heartedly in E flat major at b.60. Let the LH thirds 'lead' quietly but firmly from the 1st beat of b.65 in a *crescendo* down towards the *forte* minim third on the 1st beat of b.66, with the RH offbeat triplets following evenly and relatively lightly. From b.68 follow the exuberant modulations of the long melodic passage with the utmost rhythmic vitality. Go *piano* perhaps at b.73, then build up the dynamics again towards b.82, and 'skip' down through bb.82 – 3 in a bright, not heavy *forte,* taking care to co-ordinate the unison figures through b.83 with diamond-cut precision. Lead through b.84 into b.85 with steady LH crotchet octaves and then take care to keep steady as you follow the triplet interplay between the hands. Feel that the RH chromatic fragment, 'following on' evenly from the bass octave on the 1st beat of b.85, is 'going to' the crotchet C on the 2nd main beat of the bar, and similarly that the LH fragment is 'going to' the crotchet G on the 1st beat of b.86, and so on. Build up the dynamics with lively RH triplets over firm LH dominant 7th chords through bb.92 – 3, and then from b.94 expand the triplets in cadenza-like style over the sustained dominant 7th chord. Draw out the descending quavers (*calando*) and poise yourself on the pause on the E flat before setting off into the recapitulation at b.97. For once Haydn does not vary his recapitulation to any great extent. Support the high pitch of the RH from b.121 with full-toned LH triplets. Leap down boldly allowing the slight natural break, from the previous high F to the trill on the 1st beat of b.143 (starting the trill with a firm upper note D) and do give this semibreve trill its full value, giving it a 'boost' with a firm LH dominant 7th chord on the 2nd main beat of the bar. End in a 'disappearing' *pianissimo* with hardly a hint of a *rallentando*.

Second movement – Allegro di molto (7)
This short and tightly-knit movement is also not too difficult in a technical sense, except in the passage of quick LH thirds near the end. But its contrapuntal figurations need careful study, and an absolutely stable 2/4 pulse must be maintained from first note to last.

Practise each section carefully 'hands separately'. Let the detached upbeat
bb.1 – 9 quaver 'go to' a firm RH tied minim B flat on the 1st beat of b.1, and follow on with a neatly articulated LH figure, 'going to' a firm crotchet F on the

1st beat of b.2. Detach the RH quavers neatly in b.2, feeling that they, in turn, are 'going to' the tied minim third on the 1st beat of b.3, with the LH semiquaver scale figure following on evenly, and so on. This sense of the lines 'following on' from each other is essential to the rhythmic impetus of the first two sections, and indeed of most of the movement. Be sure that the long tied notes, e.g. the minim B flat on the first beat of b.1, and the minim third on the first beat of b.3 are given enough tone to sing through their full duration. Feel the implied emphasis on the tied treble upbeat to b.7, and listen to this note singing over the bar line as you place the inner RH and LH notes precisely on the 1st beat of b.7. Take care to 'finish off' each section or phrase cleanly (e.g. in bb.8, 16, 30, etc.) so that you lead off again clearly with the subsequent upbeat.

bb.9 – 30   Bb.9 – 16 are of a more *legato* character, though equally contrapuntal. From the upbeat to b.9, feel the lightly syncopating effect of the slurred offbeat quaver-crotchet figures in either hand, without losing the sense of the crotchet pulse. Then ensure that the syncopated treble line, bb.14 – 16 (feeling the implied emphasis on the high crotchet G in b.14) moves smoothly over even LH, and inner RH lines. From the upbeat to b.17 follow the restatement of the first eight bars in reversed hands, leading off firmly with the LH. Then from the 'upbeat' to the *2nd* beat of b.24, lead off again with the *RH*, following clearly and steadily with the LH thirds from the upbeat to b.25. Feel that these RH upbeats are 'going to' firm tied crotchets on the *2nd* beats of bb.24, 25 and 26 (and similarly that the LH upbeats are 'going to' firm tied crotchets on the *1st* beats of bb.25, 26 and 27), as you *crescendo* upwards to the high F on the 2nd beat of b.26, letting the LH continue *its crescendo* to the 1st beat of b.27. Then, preserving a steady crotchet pulse, *decrescendo* downwards and finish the section in immaculate time.

bb.31 – 70   The first five bars of the minor section again suggest a more *legato* character. Ensure that the RH tied minims sing over to the 1st beats of bb.32 and 34 as you articulate the LH figures neatly. Then from b.36 'rattle out' the RH semiquavers over lively but rock-steady LH detached quavers. Lead firmly and smoothly with the sustained RH lines from b.48, following evenly with the LH offbeat semiquaver figures, and then let the *LH* take the lead from the 2nd beat of b.51. Mark the syncopated *sforzatos* in either hand in b.54, and then, in one of Haydn's typical 'churning' effects, 'return' to the *sforzatos* in bb.56 and 58, with 'buzzing' RH semiquavers over even inner RH quavers and a resonant sustained dominant pedal point.

bb.70 – 121   Keep a steady crotchet pulse through bb.70 – 3, ensuring that the semiquaver passage-work alternates evenly between the hands, and likewise from b.100.

From the upbeat to b.100 feel that each offbeat semiquaver upbeat figure in each hand 'goes to' a precisely placed quaver on the subsequent main beat. To negotiate those awkward little LH semiquaver figures in thirds, from the upbeat to b.116, feel similarly that they are 'going up to' firm tied crotchets on the 1st beats of bb.116 – 18, and similarly that the treble semiquavers are 'going up to' firm tied crotchets on the *2nd* beats, so that you feel a secure crotchet pulse alternating between the hands. Let the semiquavers start lightly from each offbeat in either hand, making a little upwards *crescendo* towards each tied crotchet. Having negotiated these hurdles, keep steady as the RH scale runs down through b.118, and support the RH through b.119 with neat detached LH quaver thirds. Arrive on a firm 1st beat of the penultimate bar in both hands, place the LH dominant 5th squarely on the 2nd beat, and end with a clear RH crotchet sixth and snappy 'so there' LH quavers.

No. 56 in D major
(Hob. XVI/42)

First movement – Andante con espressione (8)
The rhythmic complexities of this extensively ornamented variation movement are considerable. The task is to count accurately and to maintain the continuity of the gentle *andante* tempo while incorporating the ornamentation graciously with the melodic lines. To set a tempo it will be well to turn to b.21, the first variation, and then to b.90, and settle on a speed at which the triplets, and then the demisemiquavers will flow easily and sound neither sluggish nor hurried.

bb.1 – 8 Count out the rhythm of the first eight-bar section – it is a good plan to do this away from the piano, clapping or tapping out the steady crotchet or even the quaver pulse, and singing, speaking, or just imagining the rhythmic figuration within the *physical* feeling of your crotchet pulse. Be sure that all the small variations in the note values are understood, and pay particular attention to the values of the upbeats: e.g. note that the opening upbeat is a semiquaver; the upbeat to b.2 is a demisemiquaver triplet, preceded by a dotted quaver rest, and therefore fits into the space of the last semiquaver of the bar; whereas the demisemiquaver upbeat to b.3 is preceded by a simple quaver rest on the 3rd beat of the bar and therefore occupies the time value of a whole quaver. Lead off from your clear semiquaver upbeat towards a precisely timed dotted rhythm figure in b.1 (like a little march figure) over neatly placed LH quaver thirds. (Articulate this dotted rhythm figure with equal precision each time it recurs, e.g. in bb.9, 13, 21, 41, etc.) Then, 'feeling' your silent 3rd beat, go from the quick demisemiquaver triplet upbeat to a firm slurred dotted quaver on the 1st beat of b.2. 'Feeling' your silent 3rd beat again, 'go to' and 'lean' upon, the slurred *sforzato* quaver on the 1st beat of b.3. Time this bar carefully, slurring the RH *sforzato* quavers warmly *on* the 2nd and 3rd beats, and savouring their 'clashes' with the LH quavers a seventh below. Here, and throughout the movement, do observe all *sforzatos* as melodic 'leans' and not as harsh bumps or bangs. Also, while observing all rests meticulously, do at the same time phrase mentally over the rests so that you show an overall melodic line rather than a series of stops and starts. Lead on in a full tone from the *forte* upbeat into b.5, supporting the ornamented treble with resonant LH chords. From the upbeat to b.6 (let the 'written out' turn *anticipate* the dotted semiquaver here, and at the beginning of b.5) feel the onward impulse towards the *sforzato* RH tied crotchet and LH dotted crotchet third falling on the 2nd beat of the bar. Take care to give these their full value, and then, from the upbeat to b.7, slur the RH semiquaver couplets neatly over the smoothly slurred LH quavers.

bb.9 – 20 Lead off emphatically with the LH from the upbeat to b.9, and then dovetail the slurred semiquaver figures neatly in alternating hands within your steady crotchet pulse. 'Go to' a resonant slurred LH crotchet F sharp on the 2nd beat of b.11, and lead on into b.12 with a firm LH line beneath smoothly shaped RH thirds. Time the ascending upbeat run to b.18 to fit into the space of a crotchet, landing perfectly in time on the C sharp on the 1st beat of b.18, again supporting the ornamented treble with resonant LH chords.

bb.21 – 40 As you move into triplets in b.21, do take care to maintain your steady crotchet pulse, letting the LH triplets 'follow on' confidently from the RH detached quaver on the 2nd beat of this bar. Phrase the treble line expressively through bb.26 – 8 over sustained and equally expressive inner and lower LH lines. Keep steady as you revert to 'plain' semiquavers again at b.29, and dovetail the slurred semiquavers neatly as at bb.9 – 10, in reversed hands. Divide the upbeat run to b.35 mentally into two groups of six notes, and you will find it fits into the crotchet pulse more easily than you think. Keep steady again as you move into demisemiquavers from the upbeat to b.38, and support the treble line yet again with resonant LH *sforzato* chords through bb.38 – 9.

bb.41 – 61   Feel the stronger, more martial character of this minor variation. Lead in from a strong RH semiquaver upbeat to b.41 and let the RH lead on resolutely from the upbeat to b.42 and through bb.42 – 3, the LH triplets following on in an easy but vigorous flow. Conversely, feel that the sustained LH line is leading through bb.44 – 5. Then shape the curving RH semiquavers expressively through b.46 – 7 over a smooth LH line, and make a gradual *diminuendo* towards the end of b.48, taking care to 'finish off' the LH graciously down to a clear quaver F on the 3rd beat of b.48. Give a clarion sound to the dotted rhythm figures alternating between the hands from the upbeat to b.49, and then let the LH thirds lead on smoothly from the upbeat to b.51. Give a firm LH lead again from the upbeat to b.53, and keep the active treble offbeat figures under control with a rock-steady LH line through bb.53 – 4. Follow the old convention of letting the LH semiquavers coincide with the last triplet of the 1st and 2nd beats of b.53. From the 2nd beat of b.54 take the detached triplets up to a clear quaver A on the 3rd beat, and then make a smooth echo effect in b.55. Then support the improvisatory RH triplets through bb.56 – 7 with resonant bass octaves. From the upbeat to b.59 move purposefully through the concentrated dotted rhythm progressions towards the *sforzato* pause on the dominant 7th at b.61, in this 'linking' passage leading towards the resumption of the gentler movement of the 3rd variation, from the upbeat to b.62.

bb.62 – 105   Count carefully through bb.70 – 1. Run down from a firm tied treble D on the 1st beat of b.70 to arrive on the lower quaver D exactly on the 2nd beat of the bar; and similarly from the high tied D on the 3rd beat to arrive on the tied E exactly on the 1st beat of b.71. Then let the detached LH quavers 'lead' through b.72 with the RH offbeat semiquavers following relatively lightly. Phrase the RH line sonorously from the low upbeat to b.75, supported with resonant LH crotchet thirds through b.75, and lead on with smooth LH quavers through b.76, letting the syncopated RH line follow evenly. Note that the demisemiquaver upbeat to b.90 is *not* a triplet, and preserve the sense of the crotchet pulse through bb.90 – 2 (though without obvious accents) as the demisemiquaver passage-work flows evenly between the hands. Show the RH emphasis on the tied syncopated semiquaver E in b.95 over the sustained LH fourth. In b.97 phrase the LH demisemiquaver run gracefully beneath a sustained RH slurred minim third. Be sure to give the 'plain' crotchets and the dotted quaver rest their full value in b.101. Finally, 'lean' on the *sforzato* treble tied crotchet A and LH six-four chord on the 1st beat of the penultimate bar, letting the chromatic sextuplet semiquavers 'fall' in *decrescendo* in a *perdendosi* effect towards the *pianissimo* ending. Once you have conscientiously done all your counting, do try to rise above the dots and lines, to seek the overall shape and tenor of the music beneath the deluge of ornamentation. (The other *andante con espressione* first movement, of No. 58, is, however, more original, and at the same time infinitely more expressive.)

Second movement – Vivace assai (7)

From the point of view of the player this is one of Haydn's least happy experiments. The opening repeated eight-bar section sets out two figures, the first consisting of *legato* broken thirds in quavers, the second, a little semiquaver descending and ascending pattern. These figures, neither of which is immediately appealing, become increasingly tedious as they are tossed around contrapuntally through the remainder of the movement. (This, of course, is a personal view. Others may agree with John McCabe, who finds it 'a cunningly worked little piece' and that 'its intricacy is delightful'!†)

bb.1 – 45   Set a brisk but steady crotchet pulse, lead off clearly from the slurred quaver upbeat, and phrase the descending RH broken third quavers smoothly through bb.1 and 2. Then from b.3 articulate the RH semiquavers neatly over rhythmic reiterated LH quavers. Let the three parts 'enter' smoothly in turn on the upbeats to bb.9, 10 and 11, and then follow the parts clearly through to the 1st beat of b.13. From b.13 pursue the interplay of the semiquaver figure between the hands with perfect clarity, maintaining a steady crotchet pulse. Be sure to observe the quaver rests precisely in either hand so that the RH 'enters' clearly on the quaver upbeat to b.14, and the LH similarly on the upbeat to b.15, and so on. In b.19 let the descending LH semiquavers 'go to' a firm crotchet D on the 2nd beat of the bar, and likewise let the tricky RH descending thirds 'go to' a firm crotchet D on the 1st beat of b.20, and so on. Shape the lines smoothly again from the upbeat to b.26, through to b.28. From the upbeats to bb.33 and 35, support the RH semiquavers with lively and rhythmic LH quavers, feeling that these LH quavers are 'going down to' a firm crotchet on the 1st beat of bb.34 and 36. Similarly, underpin the RH semiquavers through bb.40 – 1 with rock-steady detached LH quavers. 'Take over' with the *RH* quavers in b.42 (taking care to avoid 'falling into' this bar), and again with the LH quavers in b.43. 'Point' the interrupted cadence dramatically at bb.44 – 5.

bb.46 – 101   Then from the upbeat to b.46 pursue the contrary-motion working out of the original quaver figure cleanly. From the upbeat to b.50 let the syncopated treble line follow smoothly over the even inner RH crotchet and LH quaver lines. Then 'take over' the inner RH line cleanly with the LH from the upbeat to b.52, through to b.55, over the long sustained lower dominant. Show the LH 'entry' clearly on the upbeat to b.56, and similarly the entry of the inner RH line and the treble on the upbeats to bb.57 and 58 respectively. Feel the crab-wise movement of the RH fourths through bb.58 – 9, and draw out towards generous pauses on the 1st and 2nd beats of b.60. Then set off from the upbeat to b.61 in a bright *a tempo*, in further contrapuntal workings-out of the semiquaver figures. From b.88 support the RH scale figures with firm LH crotchet chords (likewise in reverse from b.92). Play the detached quaver chords through bb.95 – 6 in a bright springy manner, and end in immaculate time, in *piano* as indicated.

No. 57 in F major
(Hob. XVI/47)

We will pass over the first movement of this sonata (8). With its almost continuous, and uncharacteristic, exercise-like patterns of scales and broken thirds, it can have little appeal to players. For notes on the second and third movements, see Sonata No. 19.

No. 58 in C major
(Hob. XVI/48)

First movement – Andante con espressione (8)*

This expansive and profoundly expressive movement takes the form of loosely constructed variations, fantasia-like in their freedom of expression and ornamentation, upon an already extensively ornamented theme. Haydn exploits the registers of the piano in a rich, orchestral manner, the melodic line moving freely between treble and bass clefs (see bb.1 – 4, 11 – 21,

†*Haydn Piano Sonatas* (BBC Music Guides).

etc). As in the slow movements of Nos. 53 and 59, treat the melodic line in a 'vocal' manner, shaping the curving phrases (whether in soprano or bass) as a singer would. Establish a broad and secure **3/4** pulse. Try the opening phrase (bb.1 – 2, and similarly bb.11 – 19) and then the semiquaver passage-work from bb.33 and 37, and the triplet and demisemiquaver figuration (bb.58 – 60 and 61 – 2 respectively). Then find a tempo at which the opening phrase 'moves', and the semiquaver and triplet passages do not sound sluggish, but on the other hand the demisemiquavers (bb.61 – 2) flow evenly and without a sense of hurry. This music is far from easy to hold together. The marvellously subtle and varied inflections of the writing combined with considerable rhythmic complexities, challenge the performer at every turn, and necessitate the unifying presence of a stable overall crotchet pulse. This is particularly important in order that the onward impulse is maintained through the frequent and protracted silences to which John McCabe has drawn attention.† Concert artists, when they do perform this movement, tend to take it, I believe, far too fast. It is an *andante con espressione*, not an exhibition of brilliant demisemiquaver runs.

bb.1 – 10   Project the bold, upward contours of the opening phrase in a carrying, singing *forte* over resonant LH chords. In b.1 feel the melodic curve through the turn, and up to the slurred crotchet E on the 2nd beat, then feel that you are 'going to' the slurred 1st beat of b.2, and 'tail off' this slurred crotchet B up to the quaver G on the 2nd beat as Haydn has indicated. The second phrase (bb.3 – 4) is, as will be seen, an elaborated version of the first. Time the runs carefully in b.3 (and similarly in b.6), to fit into the 2nd beat of the bar. Practise these runs at first in two groups of four and five notes until you gain sufficient confidence to phrase the nine notes as a whole, in *crescendo* towards the 3rd beats, and then be careful not to hurry the 3rd beats of these bars. Show that the third phrase (from b.6) reaches the top of its overall dynamic curve with the high C on the 2nd beat of b.7 as you *crescendo* towards a singing, high tied crotchet here over a resonant LH chord. Then tail the sound away through the descending gently detached sextuplet semiquavers towards the interrupted cadence in b.8. Place the detached quaver chords neatly through b.9 like quiet steps, in further *diminuendo* towards the *pianissimo* close on the spread dominant chord on the 1st beat of b.10. Do give all rests their full value, taking care to *feel* the silent 3rd beats in bb.2, 4, 5, etc, and in all similar instances in the variations. But at the same time try to phrase mentally *over* the rests, so that you create a feeling of continuity, showing the immense span of Haydn's melodic line from the opening low G up to high C in b.7, rather than proceeding in a series of stops and starts. Pay close attention too to Haydn's detailed dynamic signs, noting the new freedom in the use of *crescendo*, and 'tailing off' *decrescendo* markings.

bb.11 – 26   Find a new, strong tone colour as you move into the minor at b.11, and then tail the sound away through bb.12 and 13, resuming the broad tone in b.14, and so on. Let the treble line sing freely through bb.11 – 12 while also showing the inner line of descending thirds (taken by the LH) over a strong sustained bass G. At b.14 where the LH has the upward leaping melodic line, do not immediately decide to take the A and F sharp with the RH. The upward 'heave' of the LH automatically produces the implied emphasis on that slurred A, an emphasis which would have to be contrived if the notes were taken with the RH, which anyway has to 'concentrate' on its own sustained resonances. Show the inner RH slurred dotted minim C held from the 1st beat of b.14, descending to the B on the 2nd beat of b.15, beneath the upper sustained D. Do not panic at the sight of the run in b.20: there is plenty of time for the fourteen-note run within the two crotchet beats. Make an even *crescendo* as you run calmly up towards

†*Haydn Piano Sonatas* (BBC Music Guides).

a clear detached semiquaver C exactly on the 3rd beat of the bar. Through b.23 incorporate the turns smoothly in the melodic line as you *crescendo* towards the *sforzato* 1st beat of b.24 over steady and resonant LH crotchet chords.

bb.27 – 55   At b.27 lead off in a finely expressive, strong tone into the minor variation, 'following on' equally resonantly with the LH in b.28. From b.33 feel that the line descends from the high RH F sharp right down to the bass G in b.36. From b.37 let the semiquaver lines curve and flow easily between the hands within a steady crotchet pulse. Feel that the RH semiquaver line in b.37, 'following on' from a clear LH crotchet third on the 1st beat, is 'going to' a singing minim C on the 1st beat of b.38, with the LH semiquaver line following on to 'go' in turn towards a singing dotted minim third on the 1st beat of b.39. Support the RH semiquavers with resonant LH dotted minim chords through bb.42 and 43. Let the LH scale curve up in *crescendo* towards the *sforzato* crotchet on the 3rd beat of b.47 beneath smooth RH thirds (and similarly in reversed hands in b.48). Feel the *sforzatos* here, as elsewhere in the movement, as warm melodic 'leans', and not as harsh bumps. Then expand the RH semiquaver line in improvisatory style over resonant LH chords, and tail the sound away gradually from b.53 down towards the low *pianissimo* G on the 1st beat of b.55.

bb.56 – 97   Keep a steady crotchet pulse through the curving RH triplets (bb.58 – 60) and then the demisemiquavers (bb.61 – 2) always over warm supporting LH chords. Time the graceful arabesques carefully through bb.64 – 5. From b.73 let the RH melody line sing expressively and resonantly over warm-toned LH semiquavers as you *crescendo* upwards. Avoid the possible tendency to stickiness here by feeling the 'onward' movement of these evenly pulsating LH semiquavers. Keep a steady pulse at b.82 as the LH swings into sextuplets beneath a full, singing treble melody line. Articulate the RH rising scale in detached thirds boldly through b.89, swooping back to a resonantly melodic dotted crotchet B on the 1st beat of b.90. At b.93 articulate the diminished 7th flourish clearly within the 1st beat, showing the curve up to and down from the high C sharp, and arriving on the quaver E neatly on the 2nd beat. Preserve the sense of the crotchet pulse as you ascend through b.94, noting, though without obtrusive accents, that the 2nd beat falls on the D, and the 3rd beat on the A.

bb.98 – 135   On the 1st beat of b.100 be sure that the LH 'takes over' the melody line clearly from the RH in the previous bars, and continues to sing out in *crescendo* through bb.100 – 1 over the rising RH semiquavers. Swing easily into the sextuplet rhythm at b.103 over steady LH crotchet chords. Support the RH with a powerfully resonant, but not banging, LH through bb.106 – 7, and then plunge down the scale in b.107 towards a strongly sustained tied E flat on the 1st beat of b.108. Let the LH enter *piano*, as indicated, on the 2nd beat of this bar; then follow the 'delayed' upward curve of the melody line through bb.109 – 10. Play the *staccato* semiquaver scale in b.111 (and the downward curve in b.112) in an easy, detached and not spiky style. Time bb.114 – 16 carefully, matching the urgency of the RH ornamented and partly syncopated melodic line with equally intense (but steady) chords in the LH. From the upbeat to b.117 feel the high treble offbeat *sforzatos* again as melodic emphases and not bumps, supporting the melodic line with a strong and sustained LH chord on the 2nd beat of b.116. Then follow the curving RH line smoothly as it 'unwinds', descending in *diminuendo* through bb.118 – 19 and ascending again in demisemiquavers, easing out into the broad major final section. Note the RH detailing in b.126, and feel that these sextuplets are 'going to' a firm treble third on the 1st beat of b.127. Then 'follow on' evenly with the LH semiquaver sextuplet, 'going' in turn towards a clear detached quaver B flat on the 2nd beat. Allow the sound to fade through the pause on the interrupted cadence in b.129, and then 'lean' on the slurred crotchets on the 1st beat of bb.130 and 131 over very even LH semiquavers. Let the LH 'go to' a resonant slurred dotted minim F on the 1st beat of b.132, and *listen* as this note resolves to the minim E on the 1st beat of b.133 beneath even RH semiquavers before the final *pianissimo* chords.

Second movement – Rondo presto (8)*

bb.1 – 30   This is a movement on a grand scale. From the point of view of the player it is quite an endurance test. It needs to go at a spanking tempo, and there is no let-up from first note to last, as Haydn's ideas tumble after each other in a hectic, boisterous chase. Set a brisk, but stable crotchet pulse, lead in from lively detached upbeat quavers and articulate the slurred RH figures cleanly in bb.1 and 2 over immaculately placed LH crotchet chords. Observe the LH rests precisely in bb.2 and 3, as the slurred RH chromatic upbeat quavers lead 'keenly' on into bb.3 and 4. Bring the RH cleanly off after the quaver on the 1st beat of b.6, ready to set off again with the detached upbeat quavers to b.7. Then feel the syncopating effect of the implied emphasis on the slurred upbeats to bb.9 and 10. Enjoy the 'slither' of the descending sixths leading into b.11, and then support the *detached* RH sixths with neat LH quavers. Take care to 'finish off' the LH neatly in b.12 ready either to lead back to b.1 or to lead onwards with clear detached LH quaver thirds on the upbeat to b.13, 'following on' equally clearly with the RH from the upbeat to b.14, and so on. Let these detached upbeats 'go to' firm slurred quaver thirds on the 1st beats of bb.13, 14, etc, and then underpin the sharply articulated RH figures with lively but rock-steady LH detached quavers from the upbeat to b.17. Keep a steady crotchet pulse as you pursue the 'busy' detailing in either hand from the upbeat to b.25, as Haydn expands on the material of the opening phrase. Allow a tiny break as you leap up to the octave on the upbeat to b.27 poising yourself for an instant for the little run of RH octaves and LH thirds.

bb.31 – 53   Feel the mock seriousness of the stentorian LH chords from b.31. Then make the most of the jokey tension of the 'worrying' of the semiquaver fragment from the upbeat to b.37 (as if the record has got stuck), and of the downhill lurch from the upbeat to b.41 down to b.45, keeping yourself steady here with very rhythmic, mettlesome detached LH quavers. From b.45 follow the detailing of the RH and inner LH lines with equal care and clarity over the sustained dominant pedal point, tailing away to disappear into thin air at b.52. Then *feel* the two crotchet rests securely before darting off again from the upbeat to b.54 (and similarly at bb.91 – 2, etc.).

bb.54 – 91   From the upbeat to b.58, phrase the LH chromatic fragments smoothly beneath your cleanly articulated RH, and similarly in reversed hands from the upbeat to b.60. Support the RH with resonant LH chords from the upbeat to b.62, and from the upbeat to b.64 'rattle out' the unison semiquavers with cleanest articulation, making sure that the hands are perfectly co-ordinated. Then keep a steady crotchet pulse as the chromatic octaves veer upwards recklessly in alternating hands from the upbeat to b.71. From bb.73 – 9 underpin your 'churning' RH semiquavers (avoiding any tendency to 'hang on' with the fifth finger) with a very firm and steady LH line. Keep the RH semiquavers steady again as they 'rattle' down towards clear quavers on the 1st beat of bb.85 and 87, over light but very rhythmic tremolo bass broken octaves. Then let the RH disappear into thin air again at b.91.

bb.92–263   From b.122 note the more legato LH giving a different and more subdued tone colour to the beginning of this minor section. Do, however, avoid muddiness by continuing to articulate the RH clearly though quietly in this low register (particularly the 'growly' semiquavers through bb.125 – 8 and 137 – 9). Maintain the rhythmic tension of this eerie passage with smooth though clear and perfectly rhythmic LH quavers. Slur the RH quavers cleanly from the upbeat to b.131, and let the RH semiquaver figures 'go up' to a sharp detached quaver on the 2nd beats of bb.133, 135 and 139. Burst in with the *forte* detached thirds on the upbeat to b.143, and build up the tone from here over firm LH crotchet octaves towards the syncopated sustained RH *sforzato* third in b.145 (and again from the upbeat to b.149). 'Come in' smoothly on the 2nd beat of bb.145 and 151 with the legato LH chromatic fragments. From the upbeat to b.155 define the busy contrapuntal treatment of the opening fragment clearly in either hand, keeping the RH thirds perfectly steady as the LH 'takes over' this fragment in earnest from the upbeat to b.158. Feel the Beethovenian character of the persistent reiterated LH chords as the RH in turn takes over the same fragment from the upbeat to b.162. Then be sure to sustain the dominant pedal point as the RH turns upwards from b.166 over the even inner LH line. Tail away the sound to end this section with *pianissimo* treble seconds at bb.171 – 2. From the upbeat to b.258 articulate the *piano* LH fragment neatly beneath a sustained RH minim third (and similarly in reversed hands from the upbeat to b.260). Then phrase the final LH fragment vigorously, supported by clarion RH chords, without a hint of a *rallentando*.

No. 59 in E flat major
(Hob. XVI/49)

Haydn wrote this work for Marianne von Genziger, wife of the physician to Prince Nicholas Esterházy. Haydn enjoyed an especially warm and affectionate friendship with her and her family, and as his letters show, he was able to open his heart freely to her. She was a woman of charm and culture, and, it appears, an able pianist.

First movement − Allegro (8)*
This is one of the finest of Haydn's mature first movements. But, though on an imposing scale, it is much less virtuosic than that of the final Sonata in this key (No. 62). It has the motion of a fast minuet (see also remarks on the Finale of Sonata No. 33 in C minor). Immediately establish therefore a clearly defined and very stable three-in-the-bar pulse.

bb.1 – 24   It is on the pithy semiquaver opening motif and its more *legato* answering phrase that the movement is built. Lead off with clear RH slurred semiquavers, 'going to' a clear detached quaver on the 1st beat of b.1. (Always feel these semiquavers as a very definite upbeat group 'going to' the quavers on each subsequent 1st beat, i.e. of bb.2, 5, 6, etc.). Take care to place the detached LH quaver thirds clearly and *equally*, on the 1st and 2nd beats of bb.1 and 2, etc, with a virile rhythmic spring, so that there is no tendency towards slurring. Then let the three upbeat quavers rise smoothly towards a firm *sforzato* slurred treble crotchet on the 1st beat of b.3, supported by an almost equally firm LH chord, and in contrast let the next three quavers descend relatively lightly in a detached style in both hands towards a clear RH dotted quaver and LH crotchet on the 1st beat of b.5. 'Rattle out' the RH semiquavers from the upbeat to b.9 (supported by a resonant LH chord on the 1st beat of b.9), feeling the dynamic curve up to the B flat on the 2nd beat of the bar, and then down towards a resonant slurred crotchet B natural on the 1st beat of b.10. 'Lean' lightly on the slurred RH quavers in b.11, and 'finish off' the phrase neatly down to the low detached E flat on the 3rd beat of b.12. Then, as you lead off again with the RH quaver upbeat B flat, feel the more legato character of the passage from bb.13 – 24. Let each quaver upbeat 'go up to' a singing tied minim as you *crescendo* upwards towards b.19 over very even offbeat LH quaver figures. Be sure to continue to feel the crotchet pulse steadily or you may tend to get progressively faster through this ascending passage. Keep steady too through bb.20 – 2, not losing your sense of the crotchet pulse, despite the temporary **6/8** effect created by the syncopated *sforzatos* falling on the 4th quaver pulse of these bars. Feel these *sforzatos* as strong melodic 'leans' in either hand, not as harsh bangs, also listening to the reinforcing sound of the sustained inner RH tied dotted crotchet C's. Make the third *sforzato* (in b.22) the most emphatic, then 'ease out' towards the sustained pause in b.24 before setting off in tempo from the upbeat to b.25.

bb.25 – 36   Be sure again to place the LH quaver thirds with that clear rhythmic 'spring' in bb.25 – 7, and take particular care not to hurry the little RH descending semiquaver scale figures leading into bb.26 and 28. The Alberti LH from bb.28 – 36 must provide a taut, virile and absolutely stable foundation for the activities of the RH. Practise this LH slowly and rhythmically, always marking the first note of each group of four semiquavers with a light firm accent. Practise it also in dotted rhythms:

♩. ♪ ♩. ♪ and ♪♫♫ ♪♫♫ (see also Introduction). Do work at this passage with a

metronome if necessary (both 'hands separately' and 'hands together'). The least threat of rhythmic insecurity is destructive to the confidence of the player and the ease of the listener. Let the RH scales (bb.28, 30 and 32, and similarly in the development, bb.84, 86, etc.) run up keenly, in *crescendo,* and in perfect co-ordination with the LH, towards a ringing slurred or dotted crotchet on the 1st beat of the subsequent bars, and descend with lively detached quavers towards the slurred quavers on the 1st beat of bb.30 and 32. Bb.33, 34 and 35 – 6 are rhythmic danger areas. Be sure that you continue to mark the crotchet pulse in the *LH* with a light accent, particularly the *2nd* beat in b.33 and the *3rd* beat in b.34, so that the pulse remains steady beneath the held treble dotted crotchet C in b.33, and the treble trill in b.34. End the high RH turn with an exultant *staccato* quaver on the 2nd beat of b.35. 'Skip' also off the 3rd beat of b.35 (C) as you 'go to' a firm slurred crotchet B flat on the 1st beat of b.36, *keeping all this lively RH figuration in place with your continually steady Alberti LH.*

bb.37 – 64   Continue to keep a steady crotchet pulse through the lighter figuration of bb.37 – 41, and again through the hand-crossing in bb.42 – 9. Feel here that the RH is swooping up and down from bass to treble in continuous arcs, with the three ascending detached quavers in bb.42 and 44 'going to' ringing dotted crotchets on the 1st beats of bb.43 and 45. Keep steady again here, where the RH has a rest or is held (bb.42 – 6 and 48) by feeling the *2nd* beats securely in the LH. Practise the RH carefully and rhythmically from the upbeat group to b.47 through to the 1st beat of b.48, letting the demisemiquavers 'flick' down to exactly timed quavers on the 2nd and 3rd beats of b.47. Then co-ordinate the RH figures with your steady LH in *slow* practice. Following the exuberant RH flourish through bb.48 – 9, let the detached quavers alternate evenly between the hands in a *diminuendo* down towards the expectant silence of bb.52 – 3. Give full value to the rests and then time the mysterious reiterated quavers precisely in either hand like distant horn calls, always 'going to' sustained dotted minims. Then 'open out' through the chromatically descending LH crotchet line in b.57 towards the affirmative spread six-four chord on the 1st beat of b.58. From bb.60 – 3 shape the 'close' legato treble and inner LH quaver lines with equal care over the sustained lower tied B flat. Then 'open out' again through the smooth RH thirds in b.62, and keep your clear detached LH octaves steady through b.63 as you go towards a ringing dominant crotchet chord on the 1st beat of b.64.

Shape the concentrated three-part writing smoothly at the beginning of the
bb.65 – 107 development. Practise carefully '*parts* separately' here. Then when you put
the three lines together, listen acutely to the movement of the more sustained
RH treble and inner lines over the curving LH quavers. Listen particularly to the tied treble
notes singing over the bar lines (bb.67 – 8, 68 – 9, etc.) and to the sustained inner notes
(the dotted crotchets on the 1st beat of bb.68 – 70, the dotted minim on the 1st beat of
bb.72 – 3, and the tied minim on the 2nd beat of bb.74 – 5). Show the important inner
LH ascending quaver upbeat figures to bb.77 and 79, ensuring that each of these 'goes
to' a firm singing minim E flat on the 1st beats of bb.77 and 79, over the sustained pedal
point G. Set off on the long passage of development from the upbeat to b.81 with brimming
vitality held within a taut rhythmic pulse, feeling the continuous onward impetus through
to b.107. Be careful to place the RH reiterated quaver upbeat figures to bb.97, 101, etc.
precisely, with the feeling of going 'keenly' but steadily towards the dotted crotchets on
the 1st beat of the subsequent bar (placing the grace note figures emphatically *on* these
1st beats). Ensure here that the RH quavers are precisely co-ordinated with your perfectly
rhythmic LH, again keeping steady by showing the *2nd* beat of the bar in the LH in bb.95 – 8
and 100 – 2. 'Rattle out' the RH semiquavers from bb.103 – 7 over vigorous LH chords.
This is another rhythmic danger area. Feeling, as always, your steady crotchet pulse, be
sure to 'go up to' clear, and slightly emphasized treble C's on the *2nd* beats of these bars.
This will give a further onward impetus to the rhythm, at the same time keeping you steady
and also helping you to time the reiterated *LH* quaver upbeat figures to bb.106 and 107
accurately. Feel that these upbeat figures are 'going to' a firm fourth and fifth on the
1st beat of bb.106 and 107 respectively. Be sure to come smartly *off* the crotchet chord
at the rest on the 2nd beat of b.107.

Following this dramatic silence, Haydn develops the mysterious reiterated
bb.107 – 31 figure in masterly fashion, with strikingly Beethovenian orchestral colour.
Be sure to separate these figures with accurately timed rests, feeling the spatial
effect of the widely distanced echoing treble and bass (bb.108 – 9 etc.). Feel also the different
'colours' of the varying RH intervals, minor thirds, major seconds, etc, and particularly
of the arresting diminished 7ths (bb.112 – 13). From the upbeat to b.117 show the increasing
intensity (following the inner parts as carefully as the treble and lower lines) as the sustained
and strongly syncopated chords approach the anguished outburst of the *forte* diminished
7th chords of bb.122 – 3, with their *piano* echoes in bass and treble (bb.123 – 6). After
this high drama, Haydn typically, and quite perkily gathers up the threads again. Using
the opening broken third motif in the RH and the reiterated quaver figure in the LH,
he rises from b.126 towards a cadenza-like run over a dominant 7th chord, leading back
towards the recapitulation. Hold the high F at b.31 through a substantial pause, over a
resonant LH dominant 7th chord. Then run freely down to the lower F and back up to
the topmost note of each curve, the C, the B flat, and the G, before dashing down the
chromatic scale towards the two deliberate quavers, B flat and A natural leading to a
resonant long slurred A flat. Allow a generous pause again, and then pick up the tempo
smartly from the upbeat to b.132.

Characteristically again, at bb.181 – 2 Haydn defuses the previous seriousness
bb.132–218 of the reiterated quaver figures with chirpy chromatic grace notes (treat these
like acciaccaturas). Be sure to lead off clearly with the LH from the upbeat
to b.196. Then, keeping a steady crotchet pulse, 'take over' with the RH broken octaves
(from the upbeat to b.199) as you *crescendo* through bb.199 – 200, keeping the offbeat
LH chords relatively light. Come clean *off* as if in mid-flight at the end of b.200, and
give full value to the silence in b.201 before leading off again quietly with the RH quaver

upbeat to b.202. Take care to keep steady from here to the end. Let the descending quaver figures follow on evenly in either hand through bb.203 – 6. Then play the ascending chromatic quavers with creeping smoothness in the LH and RH through bb.206 – 7. 'Lean' well on the RH minim chords on the 1st beat of bb.210 and 212. Then 'take over' with the LH and lead through bb.211 and 213 with quiet detached quaver chords, with the RH offbeat fourth following steadily and relatively lightly. Support the RH with resonant LH chords from b.214 and time your brilliant scale through the penultimate bar to arrive on a ringing high crotchet G precisely on the 1st beat of the final bar. (You will get a better sound on this final note if you finger the last three notes 3 1 *3* rather than 3 4 5.)

Second movement – Adagio e cantabile (8)*

This fine and expressive movement could perhaps be enjoyed by older players at Grade 7. Writing to Marianne von Genzinger, Haydn said of it: 'It has a deep significance, which I will analyse for you when opportunity affords'. Approach the outer sections like long vocal arias, imagining in every instance how an accomplished singer would curve the phrases, and incorporating the ornaments smoothly into the melodic line over a sustained and supportive LH.

bb.1 – 16   Set a leisurely but stable **3/4** pulse, finding a tempo at which the extensive ornamentation does not sound rushed, but which 'moves' sufficiently for the movement never to become 'sticky'. Try the melodic passage from bb.17 – 26. If you are too slow, the reiterated quaver accompaniment will immediately sound plodding. If, on the other hand, you are too fast, the passage will lose its grave expressive quality, and sound almost jaunty. Let the opening RH D sing so that it merges smoothly into the subsequent turn, and time the dotted rhythm figures cleanly in bb.1 and 2 over a sustained lower B flat and smoothly sustained inner LH line. 'Tail' the RH away towards a gently detached quaver F on the 2nd beat of b.2, rather than coming off it with an abrupt bump. 'Lean' on the slurred quavers through b.3, feeling the offbeat *sforzatos* like melodic emphases, not bangs, again over smoothly sustained LH lines. 'Open out' the tone through b.7, and then let the line 'fall' in *diminuendo* from the warmly sustained dotted crotchet G on the 1st beat of b.8 as you 'come back' towards b.9. Through bb.9 – 16 the RH is a varied and further ornamented version of the first eight bars, over an identical LH. It cannot be too strongly emphasized that the LH must always be phrased and listened to with the greatest care, to give a smooth and sustaining foundation for the increasingly elaborate RH. In b.14 'tail away' the RH again towards the 2nd beat, as in b.6. Detach the *staccato* figures gently and melodically in b.15, not spikily (and similarly in bb.19, 33, 34, etc.). While shaping each two-bar sub-phrase carefully and expressively (i.e. bb.1 – 2, 3 – 4, etc.) endeavour to show the overall continuity of line through these first sixteen bars. Breathe, and phrase mentally over the rests at the end of bb.2 and 6, etc, and in bb.4 and 8 feel the 'overlap' on the 4th *quaver* pulse of the bar as one phrase ends and at the same time 'leads on' into the next.

bb.17 – 56   Bring a new and fuller tone colour as the melody line moves to the lower register at b.17, supported by sustained lower dotted minims and even inner LH repeated quavers. Feel the steady but 'ongoing' impulse of these inner quavers, particularly if, as often happens, things are by now getting a bit sticky. Place the detached quavers steadily, in a 'speaking' manner in either hand through b.19. Then let the low LH quaver line *crescendo* through b.20 towards a yet fuller tone as you move into the minor on the 1st beat of b.21. But return immediately to *piano* as indicated, and then support the melody line in a gradual *crescendo* towards the 1st beat of b.26 with even and increasingly resonant LH quaver chords. Then let the RH semiquaver and demisemiquaver line 'unwind' upwards through b.26 towards the return of the opening theme. At bb.31 – 2 listen to the inner LH line. Then feel the 'ongoing' movement of the LH upbeat group leading into b.33, and similarly of the detached RH repeated quavers and descending LH thirds leading into b.34. At b.37 the material from b.17 returns in elaborated form. Phrase the slurred RH demisemiquaver figures lightly and graciously through b.39, taking care also to place the intervening LH quavers neatly and quietly. In bb.43 – 5 keep the agitated RH offbeat semiquavers in place with steady LH quavers. (Compare the heightened intensity of this passage with the 'straight' version, bb.23 – 5.) Keep a steady crotchet pulse from b.47 and realize that the graceful arabesques here are a further elaborated variation on the material of the opening bars. Support the RH offbeat figures through b.49 with clear and steady LH quaver chords and treat the RH grace notes

like demisemiquavers thus: Listen again to the inner LH line bb.51 – 2,

and count carefully in b.54, as you learn to skip easily down the slurred and detached demisemiquaver figures.

bb.57 – 81 Give full expression to the dramatic power of the middle section. Follow the dynamics from bb.57 – 66, feeling in addition an implied *crescendo* through b.64 towards the *forte* at b.65. Let the LH sweep from bass to treble in continuous melodic arcs (rather than in disjointed fragments) over even but expressive 'waves' of RH sextuplets. Note that the slurred crotchets on the 1st beat of bb.58 and 60 are 'tailed off' to *piano* quavers. From b.66 (second-time bar) feel the overall continuity of the melodic line as the expressive intensity rises towards b.72, over continuously even and supportive LH sextuplets. Although it is doubtless correct here to conform to the convention of letting the RH semiquavers or demisemiquavers (bb.66, 67, 68, etc, and, of course similarly the LH semiquavers in b.57 etc.) coincide with the last LH sextuplet of the group, some freedom to create an occasional semi-cross-rhythm effect does add to the expressiveness of this section. Continuing the melodic line smoothly, most players will go through a gradual 'unwinding' from b.72, in *diminuendo* towards a *pianissimo* ascent to the high quaver F on the third beat of b.75 (although there is a case for continuing in *forte* right through to the bass F on the 3rd beat of b.76, and on again towards the *sforzato* chord of b.78, and the high E flat in b.79, only then unwinding in *diminuendo* through the descending quavers towards a *piano* return to the reprise in b.81). If you do make a *diminuendo* up to the high F in b.75, place the low F quietly but firmly on the 1st beat of b.76, and then *crescendo* towards a resonant *sforzato* chord of b.78. Go on in the RH up to a full singing dotted crotchet E flat, and then ease out in a *diminuendo* towards b.81.

bb.81 – 124 Allow the sextuplet semiquavers to flow in easy curves from bb.83 – 8 over your smooth and sustained LH. Let the LH upbeat quavers 'go up to' a resonant crotchet F on the 1st beat of b.92 beneath a singing tied RH third, and then give a strong onward lead into b.93 with the three descending LH quavers. 'Lean' on the RH tied E flat on the 1st beat of b.95, and then co-ordinate the rising diminished 7th arpeggio evenly with your steady LH quaver thirds. Leap up boldly from the ornamented upbeat to a ringing high tied D flat on the 1st beat of b.97, again keeping yourself steady with firm and evenly placed LH quaver chords. Do not panic at the sight of the scale in b.101 – there is plenty of time to fit this into the steady crotchet pulse given by the LH detached quaver thirds, then leap up calmly, as if in a wide curve, to the high E flat on the 6th quaver pulse of the bar, rather than snatching at it. In b.105 detach the treble repeated semiquavers again gently so that they 'speak' as you 'go towards' the quaver on the 1st beat of b.106. The interrupted cadence and the dramatic dominant 7th chords at bb.108 – 9 herald a cadenza-like passage. You can 'point' the interrupted cadence (bb.107 – 8) by approaching it either in a resolute *forte* or in a *diminuendo*. Then you could spread the *forte* minim chord in b.109, at least in the LH. Let the RH line flow freely in improvisatory style over the sustained dominant 7th chord from b.114 (again this will sound better spread), tailing away the sound towards another interrupted cadence at bb.117 – 18. (Shape the chromatic LH quaver line expressively here as it rises to 'meet' the RH.) Let the RH scale plunge boldly down from the spread C minor chord to the detached quaver F on the 3rd beat of b.119, and then move towards the end serenely and quietly, with hardly a hint of a *rallentando*. Show the inner RH chromatic fragment from the upbeat to b.122, echoing the previous upper RH fragment an octave higher, and end with perfectly placed *pianissimo* chords.

Finale – Tempo di Minuet (6)*

Although this delightful Finale is less demanding than the other two movements, inexperienced players often find themselves floundering rhythmically. In order to maintain a secure minuet rhythm, it is essential to keep a steady LH, always preserving a stable crotchet pulse. Do also, throughout the movement, feel the rhythmic importance of the *upbeats*, being sure to give each one its due value and weight.

bb.1 – 25 Ensure at the outset that the LH slurred quaver couplets are perfectly steady and even, while at the same time giving a 'keen' onward impulse. Lightly but definitely 'lean' on the opening RH slurred upbeat, being very sure to give this its full crotchet value, and then place the detached quavers cleanly and not too spikily on the 1st and 2nd beats of bb.1 and 2. Feel a similar 'lean' on the ornamented upbeats to bb.2 and 5, allowing the turn to *anticipate* the dotted quaver on the 3rd beat here. Then show the curve of the triplets, from the upbeat to b.3 up to the high C on the 1st beat of b.3 and down again towards the 1st beat of b.4. Do feel that the RH cross-rhythm triplets are fitting in with your steady LH quavers, and *not* the other way about. Feel, if anything, an even more pronounced 'lean' on the RH upbeat to b.6. Articulate the dotted rhythms precisely in b.7, over a clear, supporting LH, and finish the section neatly, allowing a full crotchet rest. Then lead off again clearly with the LH triplet upbeat towards a firm LH quaver on the 1st beat of b.9, from which the RH triplets follow on evenly, kept steady by your even detached LH quavers as you 'go to' the 1st beat of b.10. Then 'come in' again with the LH precisely on the 3rd beat of b.10. Phrase the LH thirds smoothly from the upbeat to b.13, again giving a stable foundation for the curving RH triplets. Treat the grace note before the semiquaver upbeat to b.21 as an acciaccatura.

bb.25 – 60 Phrase the descending RH thirds smoothly from the upbeat to bb.25 and 27 (being sure again to give these upbeats their full crotchet value) and then place the repeated detached quaver chords neatly and formally. Descend from a firm high ornamented upbeat (E flat), in an energetic triplet scale through bb.29 – 30, over resonant LH chords, and then underpin the RH with firm 'step-like' LH crotchet octaves. Phrase the LH lines smoothly from the upbeats to bb.33 and 35, as the hands move apart in contrary motion. Feel the exuberance of the ringing high detached C's in bb.37 and 38 over the sustained lower RH C's and vigorous LH triplets. Starting from a full crotchet upbeat, hold firmly to the crotchet pulse through the ascending and descending triplet-semiquaver-triplet scale (bb.45 – 7) supported by resonant and perfectly timed LH octaves. Show the dynamic curve of this scale up to the top G near the end of b.46, and down again through b.47.

bb.61 – 115 Find a different, *pianissimo* tone colour for the minor section from the upbeat to b.61, and do not allow the semiquaver upbeats (to bb.65 – 7) to disrupt the stability of the LH triplets as you *crescendo* determinedly towards b.67.

Keep steady again through bb.69 – 72, where the rhythm can get very rocky. Hold fast to your crotchet pulse as the hands alternate, and be careful not to clip the LH quaver rests in these bars, thus shortening the 2nd beats and causing you to 'fall into' the upbeats to the subsequent bars. Give a full tone to the RH triplets in bb.73 and 74, marking the *sforzato* emphases on the 1st beats, over resonant LH dotted minim chords, and supporting the RH with a strong inner LH line through bb.75 – 7. Let the RH triplets 'open out' in improvisatory style over the sustained LH dominant 7th chord through bb.85 – 6, with a *diminuendo* and a little *rallentando* at the end of b.86 as you ease back into the reprise. Let the RH upbeat 'go up to' a firm quaver on the 1st beat of b.95 (like the LH upbeat to b.9, and again to b.97). Keep steady again from b.111 to the end, letting the LH triplets rise to a definite and accurately placed quaver on the 2nd beat of these bars. It is effective to make a *diminuendo* towards the 1st beat of the penultimate bar, and then a little *crescendo* in the LH towards the strong, bright, final detached chords.

The last three Sonatas, often known as the 'English Sonatas', were composed during Haydn's second visit to London in 1794 – 5. The order of even these final Sonatas appears to be debatable and varies in different editions, but the Vienna Urtext Edition ends fittingly with the E flat major, grandest of all Haydn's piano works. They were written for Therese Jansen, later Mrs Bartolozzi, who, judging from the style of the C major and the E flat Sonatas at least, must have been an accomplished pianist with a turn of virtuosity.

No. 60 in C major
(Hob. XVI/50)

First movement – Allegro (8 +)*

While less overtly virtuosic than the first movement of No. 62, this movement is equally bursting with thematic and rhythmic originality, with dizzy changes of mood and style almost from bar to bar. Although the texture is mainly light and transparent, it requires considerable agility and above all a secure sense of rhythm. A unifying sense of a stable crotchet pulse is vital – with the continual crossing of the beat with syncopating slurs and the frequent fragmentary interplay between the hands, there are numerous pitfalls for the unwary or unsteady player. Set your crotchet pulse realistically, therefore, bearing in mind the RH demisemiquaver 'turns' from the upbeats to bb.8, 11, etc, and the RH slurred semiquaver thirds, bb.34 – 6 etc. This is one of the few Sonatas which is fairly frequently performed. Eager, presumably, to show their paces, players often take this movement at a terrific speed. If you do likewise, you will succeed not only in driving a steamroller over this stunning display of the quirks of Haydn's astonishing mind, but you will also trivialize his breathcatching moments of warmth, passion and fierceness.

bb.1 – 19   The sparse, downward-leaping *staccato* opening theme is extraordinary: feel it not merely as sprightly, but as conveying a taut anticipatory tension. Lead off with immaculately timed 'plucked' detached quavers through bb.1 – 2, and then see how Haydn immediately starts to amuse himself, 'rocking' the rhythm with syncopating slurs alternating between the hands from the upbeat to b.3. In bb.4 – 5 the RH rhythm is 'normalized' with its slurs falling *on* the beat, while the offbeat slurred quaver couplets continue in the LH. Follow these details with immaculate precision, 'leaning' lightly on the slurred quavers and ensuring that these slurred figures are neatly dovetailed and co-ordinated between the hands (always preserving the sense of your steady crotchet pulse) as you *crescendo* towards the pause on the *sforzato* third on the 3rd beat of b.6. 'Draw out' fractionally towards this *sforzato* third, allow a generous pause, and then maximize the shock of the *forte* chords in b.7 by showing the *silence* at the end of b.6 (observing that the second pause is over the final quaver *rest* in this bar and not over the quaver itself). Spread these three chords exuberantly on the first three beats of b.7, with a short touch of pedal to give an added ring to each (but be sure that it *is* only a touch, so that the clear quaver rests are given their full value). Then articulate the RH 'turns' lightly and cleanly on the upbeats to the 1st and 3rd beats of b.8, giving them the same overall slurred feeling as the upbeats to the 1st and 3rd beats of b.3, and steady yourself with neatly placed LH offbeat detached chords. In b.9 be careful not to hurry the LH semiquaver figures. Continue to 'lean' on the slurred RH offbeat figures, and be sure that you do not put a false emphasis on the first LH semiquaver (D), but make it clear that the LH enters on the offbeat, and 'goes to' the C natural on the 2nd beat (and similarly that the LH semiquavers in the second half of the bar 'go to' the F on the 4th beat). Then, from the upbeat to b.11, continue to articulate the RH upbeat 'turn' figures with immaculate precision, over very even and steady LH inner semiquavers and lower quavers. Be sure that *both* the RH quavers (B), on the 1st beats of bb.11, 12, and 13 are detached, and then, in contrast, 'go to', and lean upon, the slurred quavers on the 3rd beats of bb.11 and 12. Let the RH 'go to' a clear detached quaver on the 1st beat of b.15, and then *crescendo* towards a ringing treble *sforzato* on the 3rd beat. Give this dotted quaver its full value, and descend in perfect time towards a smoothly phrased RH fragment in thirds in b.16. Take care in this bar to phrase the rising LH semiquaver figure equally smoothly. Then follow the 'busy' alternating figures in either hand cleanly and rhythmically, 'leaning' slightly on all slurred figures and observing all rests precisely. 'Finish off' the low unison *piano* fragments in b.19 neatly, and in perfect time.

bb.20 – 53   Lead off clearly with the LH from b.20 as the opening theme reappears in octaves in the dominant. Give these LH quaver octaves a slightly longer, less sharply 'plucked' quality than those in the RH in b.1 (and b.30). Ensure that the LH continues to 'lead' through to b.24, with the RH semiquavers curving freely but evenly in the treble, with the certain feeling that the RH is fitting in with the LH, and not the other way about. Show the more legato phrasing of b.23, shaping the inner LH line warmly and smoothly from the tied upbeat, over the sustained lower D. Keep steady in bb.26 – 7, keeping the crotchet pulse in sight through the cross-rhythm effect of the slurred semiquaver couplets. Then *diminuendo* gracefully through the ascending dominant 7th arpeggio, towards the quietly sustained slurred minim thirds in b.29. Lead off vigorously again with the RH in b.30, and this time ensure through bb.30 – 1 that the *LH* semiquaver figures fit in with the *RH*. Negotiate the awkward little LH run in thirds in b.32 by starting lightly on the offbeat, and making a little *crescendo* up to a definite quaver third on the 4th beat. Follow the upper and lower LH lines smoothly through b.33 beneath clear semiquaver curves in the treble. The passages of RH slurred offbeat couplets in thirds from bb.34 – 6 are not as difficult as they look if they are performed exactly as indicated – 'lean' slightly on each slur, bringing the hand *off* on each *staccato*, thus creating a down-up movement of the hand on each couplet. Be sure also to 'kick-off' with a definite first semiquaver in the *LH* at b.34, and then keep the LH semiquavers moving in a *perfectly even* pulsation, to give a steady foundation for the activities of the RH. Keep the LH semiquavers continuously even, and even smoother (though with an onwardly propelling feeling) as, from b.37, Haydn suddenly expands into a passage of warm and sustained lyricism. Follow the upper and inner RH lines with a warm tone, feeling the eloquent *sforzato* 'leans' (not bumps) on the minim chords on the 3rd beats of bb.38 and 40. Then instantly spring back into the brisk and busy mood at b.42, with bright-toned spread quaver chords. Time the RH dotted rhythm upbeat to b.43 neatly over the even slurred LH quaver couplet. Be sure to keep a steady pulse as you swing into the sextuplet upbeat group to b.44, and then keep the reiterated RH sextuplet figures in place from the upbeat to b.45 with neatly placed and steady, yet 'ongoing' LH detached thirds. In b.46 let the LH D major arpeggio *crescendo* up to a definite quaver on the 4th beat beneath an easy-running treble trill, which in turn 'goes to' clear detached quavers on the 1st beat of b.47. Skip down the little scale at the end of b.47 (treating the grace notes as acciaccaturas) towards a singing tied F sharp on the 1st beat of b.48, and then let your neat and clear staccato scale *crescendo* towards the high D on the 1st beat of b.49. Then, in contrast, phrase the scale in b.50 smoothly, with the feeling that you are making an 'arc' from a singing tied F sharp on the 1st beat up to the high B, rather than snatching at and 'bumping' that B. From bb.47 – 50, do be sure once again that the LH gives a perfectly steady foundation for the RH. Phrase the alternate *piano* and *forte* fragments cleanly and rhythmically through bb.51 and 52, and end this section with bright, clear chords.

The long, but tightly-knit development is much less rhythmically complex *bb.54 – 101* than the outer section. Do not be faint-hearted in exploiting its changing moods, by turn passionate, vehement and tenderly lyrical. Let the LH lead off clearly, though *piano*, in b.54 as the opening theme appears again, to be answered by the RH in b.56. The LH semiquaver scale in b.56 leads up into a semiquaver fragment in the second half of the bar, which is then 'developed' through bb.57 – 8. Show the 'entry' of the RH clearly on the upbeat to b.57, and of the LH on the 'upbeat' to the 3rd beat. Then, from the 3rd beat of b.60, when the opening theme appears yet again in the LH (more solidly, in crotchets this time), be sure that the RH figuration (treating the trills here, and through bb.64 – 5 like the 'written-out' turns in bb.11 – 14) fits in with the *LH* rhythm and not the other way about. Feel the intensity at b.66 as Haydn, suddenly brushing with the minor, leaps up to the sonorous *sforzato* high F, and then unwinds gradually down to the dominant of A flat major in b.72. The 'Open Pedal' instruction (bb.73 – 4, and again at bb.120 – 4) has been the cause of much scholarly controversy. It seems that Haydn's intention was for the damper to be off: in other words, for the sustaining pedal to be *on*. Similar indications are to be found in some Beethoven Sonatas, and obviously effects which were acceptable on the much lighter earlier instruments would not be tolerable with the heavier sonorities of the modern piano. Treat this instruction, therefore, with caution, using the soft pedal and half-pedalling effects at the discretion of your own acutely listening ear, to create a veiled, distant and rather mysterious effect (see also Appendix 2 of this Volume 3 of the Vienna Urtext Edition). Then from b.76 feel the onward propelling impetus of the offbeat LH *sforzato* detached quaver thirds as they build up in a fierce and Beethovenian *crescendo* towards b.80, beneath also 'ongoing' but very steadily pulsating RH semiquaver broken octaves. Continue the onward impetus by slurring the offbeat quavers buoyantly up to the 3rd beat of b.80 and the 1st beat of b.81; and then with the aid of a touch of pedal, continue this effect through bb.81 – 2, still in *crescendo,* towards the 1st beat of b.83. Then show the contrasting warmth as you go *piano* on the 3rd beat of this bar. From here shape the sustained RH lines smoothly, and with intense expressiveness over even LH semiquavers. Renew your *crescendo* from b.85 towards the forceful resonances of b.86, and on again towards the E major chord on the 1st beat of b.89. Then the 'busy' passage (bb.89 – 90) is fiercer here in the minor than at bb.16 – 17. Then from b.92 pursue the further passage of improvisatory development with maximum vitality, exploiting the dynamics, and the darting upward and downward changes of register to the full. Tail away the sound, but in perfect time, towards the tiniest *pianissimo* on the 1st beat of b.94, feeling the rests as expectant onward-looking points, rather than as silent 'holes' in the texture. *Crescendo* again through b.94, towards a ringing *sforzato* dotted crotchet on the 1st beat of b.95, and then whirl confidently into the RH sextuplets on the 3rd beat, over firm LH chords. Then, from the upbeat to b.99, build up towards the ringing dominant 7th chords at bb.100 – 1, heralding the start of the recapitulation.

Even now Haydn has not run out of ideas. He extends the sequences of 'turns'
bb.102 – 50 into a passage of improvisatory semiquavers from b.116, plunging down to a forceful low bass half-close on the dominant at b.119. Be sure to *feel* the silent 4th beat ready to lead off with the LH in *pianissimo* in the treble from b.120 in an elaborated version of the 'Open Pedal' passage. Go ultra-*legato* here, following the three lines clearly and smoothly, this time with a 'tinkly' and even more distant sound. Do not cut short the resonant trills in b.129 in your anxiety to 'get back' to the LH C on the 1st beat of b.130. It may however be easier, and stronger in effect, if the LH 'takes over' the RH trill on the D on the 2nd beat of the bar, the *RH* then taking the higher trill on the B on the 3rd beat. Do not, however, try to avoid the necessary and *intended* 'break' as the LH leaps downwards. Pedal the trill, and leap down confidently to a *strong* LH C on the 1st beat of b.130, to give a good 'kick-off' once again for the RH figures.

Second movement – Adagio (7)*
(The Vienna Urtext Edition also gives the first version of this movement, which was published in 1794 as a single piece. See Appendix 1.)

Treat the curving lines of this spacious and expressive movement like a vocal aria (rather in the manner of the slow movement of No. 59), always supported by carefully placed and balanced LH chords and figures. Establish a tempo that allows the rhythmic figures of the first eight bars to flow comfortably within the slow but easy swing of a steady crotchet beat. This tempo must also accommodate the descending demisemiquaver octaves (bb.20 – 1) without sounding hectic, and the semiquaver passage (bb.24 – 30) without a feeling of dragging.

Spread the full-toned opening chord generously up to a singing tied crotchet
bb.1 – 8 F, and then time the RH figures accurately in gracious curves over warm-toned supporting LH chords. Be careful to place the LH chord precisely on the 2nd beat of b.1 beneath the tied RH F (and similarly in bb.3 and 5). 'Tail away' the sound from the end of b.1 as indicated as you shape the first phrase down toward the quaver C on the 2nd beat of b.2. Then *feel* the quaver rest before leading on with the demisemiquaver upbeat group towards a further singing crotchet on the 1st beat of b.3. Similarly *feel* the quaver rest at the end of b.4 before leading on from b.5. But at the same time phrase mentally *over* these rests (as also on the 4th quaver pulse of b.7) so that you create a sense of melodic continuity through the first eight bars. If you actually *breathe* on these rests, this sense of continuity will occur naturally and demonstrably. Feel the melodic line curving from b.5 right down towards a strongly singing (not banged) *sforzato* minim C sharp on the 2nd beat of b.6, taking care to give this minim its full value, while also feeling the sense in which this note 'leans onward' towards the crotchet on the 1st beat of b.7. Do not panic at the sight of the 'free' run in b.7 (and b.40) – there is plenty of time for this within the slow pulse. Some editors give a *crescendo* to the top of the runs. Try, however, the far more subtle effect of a *diminuendo*, as if the run is slurred from the low D up to the lightly 'lifted' quaver D at the top. In any event, time both of these runs to arrive on the top quaver on the 2nd beat of the bar, which in practice will mean starting the run approximately on the 2nd quaver pulse of the bar, or a little before if necessary. Then, giving a firm LH crotchet seventh on the 3rd beat of b.7, time the slurred RH demisemiquaver couplets neatly, feeling the *sforzatos* as melodic emphases rather than bumps as you 'go towards' and lean well upon the slurred crotchets on the 1st beat of b.8. Be sure to 'finish off' neatly in both hands with the quavers and to *feel*

once more the semiquaver rest, and then treat the five rising semiquavers as an upbeat group to b.9.

bb.9 – 33   Let these semi-*staccato* rising notes 'speak' rather than sounding spiky, as you 'go up to' a singing tied crotchet A on the 1st beat of b.9. Then shape the treble line expressively, while also listening to the inner LH semiquaver fragments, as they 'go to' singing tied minims on the 2nd beats of bb.9 and 10, over the sustained lower dotted minims. Note the LH *sforzato* offbeat semiquavers, and feel these, as with all *sforzatos* in this movement, as warm melodic 'leans', and not as harsh bumps or bangs. Follow the movements of all the parts resonantly through b.11, and feel the implied 'lean' on the tied RH semiquaver upbeat to b.12. Move easily but steadily into the flowing demisemiquaver figuration from the 2nd beat of b.13 (though taking care to give full value to the *semiquavers* through the 3rd beat). Support the RH with carefully placed LH chords on the upbeat to, and the 1st beat of, b.14 (and b.16). Take care to *feel* the semiquaver rest on the 4th *quaver* pulse of b.14 so that the emphasized *semiquaver* 'upbeat' to the 3rd main beat is perfectly timed (and similarly in b.16). Be careful to time b.17 accurately, supporting the RH with a firm and steady LH through from the 3rd beat of b.16. Feel that the RH line through b.17 makes a wide curve up to the high dotted quaver F on the 2nd *semiquaver* pulse, and down again to the appoggiatura and trill. Do not let the trill 'run dry', nor cut it short, but let it run easily, not hectically, feeling the supporting 'boost' given by the inner LH crotchet chord on the 3rd beat of the bar. 'Stop' the trill quietly approximately on the 6th quaver pulse of the bar so that the grace note, taking its semiquaver value or a little less, can 'fall' graciously to the crotchet on the 1st beat of b.18 as the LH leads on in a steady pulse. In bb.18 and 19 let the detached descending RH scales (and in bb.20 and 21 the descending octave scales) descend in a leisurely and gracious style over the LH accompaniment of even inner semiquavers and lower quavers. Feel that these descending scales are fitting in with your steady LH rather than the other way about, or the octaves are bound to get hectic and the whole passage will collapse in a heap. Feel that the RH through bb.18, 19 and 20 is 'going to' the slurred *sforzato* semiquaver on the 1st beat of bb.19, 20 and 21, savouring the sharp, yet warm dissonances between RH and LH. Time b.22 carefully. Play the RH quaver octave and sixth steadily so that they are placed *equally* rather than slurred. Then fit the ascending diminished 7th arpeggio cleanly into the 2nd beat, place the bass quaver G accurately and quietly on the 3rd beat, and let the neatly timed ornamented upbeat 'go to' a clear crotchet sixth on the 1st beat of b.23. Let the RH semiquaver line enter smoothly in b.24 over a resonant bass E flat, and then follow the expressive part writing evenly (this is a 'development' of the passage from b.9) as it moves with increasing warmth and intensity over a resonantly sustained lower LH line, towards bb.29 and 30. 'Lean' expressively on the *sforzato* minim thirds beneath smooth and evenly 'turning' RH semiquavers, feeling the onward impetus (though without hurrying) of these emphasized 2nd beats. Typically, in b.31 Haydn defuses the emotion of this passage, letting the RH dissolve into easy-running demisemiquavers moving towards the half-close on the dominant 7th minim chord in b.33. Ease out a little through the chromatic run through the 3rd beat of b.32, and then be sure to give this dominant 7th chord its full value, if not more, as you poise yourself for the restatement of the opening theme in b.34.

bb.34 – 63   Again, in b.35 there is plenty of time for the eighteen-note run (divide it mentally into triplets within two nine-note groups) within the 3rd beat of the bar. Think of the run as an 'upbeat' ascending towards a clear, high, tied crotchet F on the 1st beat of b.36. 'Tail off' the RH broken octaves in b.37 to 'go down' lightly to the upper quaver G on the 2nd beat. Then *feel* the semiquaver rest, making it clear that the LH broken octaves enter on the offbeat with the 3rd beat of the bar falling on the upper B natural. The 'free' run in b.40 is, as will be seen, a little longer than the one in b.7, and may therefore have to be started a fraction earlier. In bb.42 and 43 let the LH semiquaver line curve up as smoothly as possible beneath the steady and expressive RH lines. Then let the treble semiquavers curve easily through b.44 above warmly sustained LH thirds. Listen carefully to the upper and inner RH lines through b.45 over the sustained LH tied dotted minim. Compare this passage, from b.42, with those from bb.9 and 24, and show the very different textural and expressive quality of each. Give a beautiful 'horn' quality to the low, echoing fragment in thirds taken up by the RH from the upbeat to b.47. Take time to span the 'widened' upward leap in b.52 (compare with b.17). Allow the natural break as you leap up confidently as if in a wide arc, rather than snatching upwards in an uncontrolled lurch. Through bb.56 – 8 let the syncopated RH octave line flow smoothly and expressively from a singing high dotted quaver octave F, over an even and steady LH accompaniment, listening also to the smooth upward movement of the LH through bb.57 – 8. 'Fade' the sound as you rise through the first half of b.58. *Listen* to the quaver silence, and to the quiet LH quaver third, and the high RH sixth and pause. Then play the improvisatory arpeggio gracefully, to arrive on the high C on the 2nd beat of b.59. *Feel* the quaver rest and place the low C quietly on the 3rd beat of b.59. Then 'go to' and lean well upon the slurred crotchet sixth on the first beat of bb.60 – 2 over the quietly resonant lower LH tonic minims and expressively shaped inner LH fragments. Show the upward curve up to the C on the 3rd beat of b.60, and again towards the D natural on the 3rd beat of b.61 as you move in *diminuendo* towards the *pianissimo adagio* ending.

Finale – Allegro molto (7)*

Complications about bar numbering can arise with this movement. In the Vienna Urtext Edition (and in Peters) the repeats are written out, while in Henle both sections are repeated, giving first- and second-time bars for each section. Bar numbers here follow the Vienna Urtext Edition, with bar numbers for Henle given in brackets.

bb.1 – 48   The headlong jocularity of this scherzo-like movement anticipates Beethoven in its sudden lurches, stops and starts. (As John McCabe has pointed out – 'the derivation from minuet style can be demonstrated by playing the main theme at a normal steady minuet pace'.†) Set a brisk **3/4** pulse with an overall feeling of one-in-the-bar, and set off busily from a lively crotchet upbeat. Detach the LH thirds and RH repeated crotchets brightly in b.1, and articulate the RH figures sharply in bb.2 and 3 (treating the grace notes like 'snapped' acciaccaturas) over firm LH dotted minim chords. Feel a little *crescendo* towards the 1st beat of bb.5 (and 7). Then break off cleanly, giving the rests in bb.5 and 7 their full value, before hurtling on towards the jolting *forte* 'stop' at the end of b.10, and subsequent pause. Enter *piano* again on the upbeat to b.12, and then *crescendo* over rhythmic LH chords through bb.14 – 16 towards the 1st beat of b.17. Show the syncopating effect of the LH slurred upbeats to bb.17 – 20, beneath lively but even RH quavers, and then let the *legato* LH thirds plunge downwards in *crescendo* from the 2nd beat of b.20. Let this passage sound as if you are almost, but not quite, running out of control downhill, with the RH quavers plummeting down to end with a bump on the 1st beat of b.24.

bb.49 – 184   It is effective to let the lower and upper lines move inward from the upbeat
(25 – 92)   to b.49 (25) in a smooth, more 'sliding' style. Shifting this fragment up to a higher octave on the upbeat to b.52 (28), Haydn worries at it with

†*Haydn Piano Sonatas* (BBC Music Guides).

156

Beethovenian persistence. Then from the 2nd beat of b.57 (33) he plunges downwards
again with the smooth LH figure in thirds, towards a sturdy but brief foray into D minor
from b.62 (38). Pursue the subsequent stops and starts courageously as Haydn *diminuendos*
to a half-close on the dominant of G minor, b.68 (44) and of C major again at b.71 (47),
before opening out into the exuberant *tutti* at b.75 (51). Deliver ringing, spread, RH minim
chords on the 1st beats of bb.75, 77, 79 and 80 (51, 53, 55 and 56) over busy, but even
LH quavers and lower crotchets. Through this passage (bb.75 – 81 (51 – 7)) avoid 'falling
into' the 1st beat of each bar (particularly of those bars with the spread minim chords)
by feeling the 3rd beat of the previous bar as an *upbeat* rather than as the 'tail-end' of
'its own' bar. Then make a sliding broken octave effect in bb.82 – 3 (58 – 9), treating the
grace notes like snapped acciaccaturas again, and pursue the further series of stops and
starts, ending in a *rallentando* towards the pause in b.94 (70). Pick up the tempo briskly
again from the upbeat to b.95 (71) as Haydn veers upwards towards a restatement of the
tutti passage in a higher octave. The Vienna Urtext Edition gives a *piano* ending to this
section at b.116 (92), and to the end of the movement, while Henle and Peters suggest
a *crescendo* to *forte*. In either event end without a hint of a *rallentando*, disappearing
into thin air if in *piano*, and with bright, clear chords if in *forte*.

No. 61 in D major
(Hob. XVI/51)

First movement – Andante (7)*

As has already been said, there is no such thing as a 'typical' Haydn first movement.
Nothing, particularly in comparison with the technical and rhythmic gymnastics of the
first movements of Nos. 60 and 62, could be more unexpected than this *Andante* movement,
free in form but uncomplicated in its rhythmic patterns. It is also compact in an expressive
sense, with nothing of the wild and lightening changes of mood that characterize the first
movements of Nos. 60 and 62. It divides into three sections, the second and third sections
(from bb. 44 and 88 respectively) each starting off with lightly varied versions of the material
of the first eight bars. Feeling an overall two-in-the-bar pulse, set a tempo at which the
cantabile octave melody from b.11 will flow easily and serenely over its accompanying
triplets.

bb.1 – 10 Lead off with resonantly singing RH minims, placing the grace notes
confidently *on* the beat in the manner of spread chords. Support the RH
with firm and meticulously measured LH octaves on the 2nd and 4th crotchet
beats of b.1. Feel that the RH is 'going to' the minim on the 1st beat of b.2, and then
time the LH triplet precisely to 'go down to' a firm crotchet D on the 2nd main beat,
ready for the RH to lead on into the answering phrase with a precisely timed upbeat to
b.3. Then time the RH dotted rhythm figures meticulously, supported by an even LH
crotchet line and quietly resonant dotted minims on the 2nd crotchet beat of b.3 and the
1st of b.4. 'Finish off' this phrase cleanly on the 2nd main beat of b.3, and then *feel* the
crotchet rest on the 4th beat as you poise yourself to lead off again with resonant RH
minims in b.5. Take care here that the 'ornamented' LH does not disturb the steadiness
of the RH. Feel the LH two-semiquaver figures in b.5 as 'upbeats' to the 2nd and 4th
crotchet beats, and similarly feel the single semiquaver in b.6 as the 'upbeat' to the 2nd
crotchet beat. Carry the RH line up to a clear crotchet on the 2nd main beat of bb.8 and
9. Then *feel* the rest on the 4th crotchet beat of b.8, and similarly the dotted quaver rest
in b.9, so that the strong, onward-leading upbeat to b.10 is precisely timed. Shape the

descending triplet arpeggio in a full tone through b.10 over a firm LH six-four chord, and then 'ease' a little through the last beat of the bar as you prepare to open out into the long, Schubertean melody in octaves from b.11.

   Let this melody flow in long, *cantabile* lines over perfectly even LH triplets.
bb.11 – 25 Here the question arises as to whether the RH semiquavers (bb.12, 16 and
   18) should follow the older convention and coincide with the third note of the triplet, or be played as written. No final answer can be given, and while most pianists will comply with the old rule, the melody line is perhaps more eloquently 'pointed' if the semiquaver falls just *after* the third note of the triplet. Pedal this passage lightly, changing the pedal on every beat so that even over the first two crotchet beats of bb.11 and 15, for example, when the harmony remains the same, the sound is never allowed to build up and 'thicken'. This particularly applies in b.13, where a light separate pedal allows the semi-*staccato* octaves to 'speak' instead of blurring into each other. Let the RH 'go to' a warmly slurred minim sixth on the 1st beat of b.14, and *listen* to the LH rising to the crotchet A on the 2nd main beat of this bar as you prepare to 'ease' the descending RH line back into the octave melody. *Crescendo* towards b.19, and then be careful to keep steady as the full-toned RH arpeggio figure descends towards b.20 supported by a resonant LH dotted minim and crotchet chord. Then taking up the octave melody again, feel that you are 'going on' towards a warm 'lean' on the singing tied minim octave on the 1st beat of b.21. There is no need to panic at the sight of the triplet octaves here – these are not difficult to manage at this relaxed *Andante* tempo provided that the LH triplets remain perfectly steady. Feel that the RH octaves are fitting in with the steady LH triplets and *not* the other way around. Poise yourself here by marking the 2nd main beat of the bar lightly in the LH, and let the RH octaves descend evenly in a relaxed style in perfect co-ordination with the LH towards the 1st beat of the subsequent bar. 'Go to' and 'lean' even more warmly on the tied minim octave A sharp on the 1st beat of b.23, and then feel that you are curving, rather than lurching, up to the high quaver octave E. Poise yourself here with a fractional 'vocal' hold on this high octave before the octaves descend evenly again. Let the melody line expand through b.24 towards a sustained slurred minim 6th on the 1st beat of b.25, listening, as in b.14, to the LH curving up towards a clear crotchet E on the 2nd main beat of this bar.

   Place the detached RH crotchets in a 'speaking', not spiky manner in bb.26
bb.26 – 39 and 27. Let the LH 'go to' a firm crotchet third on the 1st beat of b.28,
   and 'enter' clearly and confidently with the RH on the high offbeat triplet C sharp. Support the RH with firm LH chords on the upbeat to, and the 1st beat of, bb.29 and 30 as you 'enter' again each time on the high RH offbeat triplet. Allow a slight natural break in each case as you leap up, and make little melodic 'leans', not bumps, on the descending offbeat slurred *sforzatos* through b.29. Continue to support the descending RH triplets through bb.30 – 1 with smooth and resonant LH crotchet thirds. Bb.34 – 5 are a rhythmic danger point. 'Go to' a clear RH quaver and LH crotchet third on the 1st beat of b.34, and then, again making a fractional break in the RH, 'enter' cleanly with the high third on the 2nd quaver pulse. Proceed similarly in the second half of the bar, and then allow a greater and more deliberate break as you leap up to the high C sharp in b.35. Support the RH with firm LH octaves, feeling thet the LH is holding the rhythm here. Let the LH semiquaver octave definitely coincide with the RH triplet here (see bb.100 – 1) and feel the semiquaver-cum-triplets in the nature of upbeats 'going to' the strong crotchets on the 2nd main beat of b.34 and the 1st of b.35. Then keep steady through b.35 as you 'join in' confidently with the LH, maintaining the *sense* of the steady pulse despite the slightly syncopating 'skipping' effect of the offbeat slurred triplets. Place the

repeated semi-*staccato* sixths in the second half of bb.39 and 40, and the low crotchet A's in b.41 like neat 'steps' in a formal dance, supported by immaculately even LH triplets. Then let the RH triplets open out in *crescendo* through bb.42 – 3 towards the restatement at b.44. Take care again at b.48 to keep steady through the further ornamentation of the opening motif. Let the LH 'go down to' a clear quaver on the 2nd and 4th crotchet beats, and take equal care with the precise timing of the 'spread chord' RH figures. Let the RH 'go to' a firm crotchet on the 1st beat of b.49, with the LH 'following on' with a neat scale up to the crotchet B on the 2nd main beat. Take care to time the alternating scale figures precisely through bb.51 – 2, and open out the tone as the high quavers 'go on up' through the second half of b.52.

    Find a new and more serious tone colour as you turn into the minor at b.54.

bb.54 – 111   Then, keeping a steady crotchet pulse, shape the LH and RH lines of 'development' vigorously from b.56, building up the tone towards b.62. Practise the LH alone (and similarly the RH from b.60) and be sure that you work out a sensible fingering for each hand. Support the RH triplets with firm LH chords through bb.62 – 4 and with a resonant LH octave line through bb.65 – 6. Feel the heightening intensity of the music as you rise towards the diminished 7th harmony on the 1st beat of b.70, and again towards b.72. Then perhaps 'wind down' a little through bb.73 – 5 and build the tone again through the doubled triplets of bb.75 – 7 towards the dominant 7th flourish leading back to the final restatement from b.80. Hold fast to your overall two-in-a-bar pulse through bb.85 and 87. Let the LH scale 'carry on' from a firm RH quaver on the 1st beat of b.85, to run down to a clear quaver on the 2nd main beat, with the RH scale similarly running down to a clear dotted crotchet on the 1st beat of b.86. While b.87 is, of course, rhythmically easier, do be sure that you 'take over' confidently with the LH scale on the 2nd main beat, and similarly with the RH scale on the 1st beat of b.88. Compare bb.90 – 2 with bb.39 – 40, and show the more woodwind-like colour of the bare fourths at bb.90 – 2 as opposed to the warmer sixths at bb.39 – 40. Move in *diminuendo* from b.106 towards a *pianissimo* ending, showing the subtle inner LH inflection to the B flat on the 2nd main beat of bb.108 and 109.

Second movement – Presto (7)*

This extraordinary movement bears some resemblance to the Finale of the previous Sonata, though here Haydn is tempestuous rather than high-spirited, and more uncompromisingly Beethovenian – there is little trace of eighteenth-century elegance in the persistent *sforzato* syncopations and snaking chromatic progressions. As with the Finale of No. 60, there are problems with bar numberings. The Vienna Urtext Edition repeats the first section (23 bars), but gives a written-out repeat of the second section. (Henle gives two repeated sections with first- and second-time bars, but this does not affect the numberings below. Peters, on the other hand, writes out both repeats, and their bar numberings are given in brackets.)

bb.1 – 23   Set a brisk but secure crotchet pulse with (as in the Finale of No. 60) an overall feeling of one-in-the-bar. Feel the 'onward' push given by the *sforzato* upbeat (and similarly by the recurring *sforzato* upbeats to bb.5, 7, 9 and so on), and then shape the upsweeping first phrase quietly and smoothly, but very rhythmically, with a feeling of taut, suppressed, anticipatory tension, rising in a little *crescendo* towards b.3. Finish the phrase off cleanly to clear unison crotchets (taking care that the three quavers in b.3 do *not* sound like a triplet) on the 1st beat of b.4, and then *feel* the crotchet rest on the 2nd beat, ready to 'push' onwards with the *sforzato* upbeat to b.5. Show the implied emphasis on the partly tied *RH* upbeats to bb.5 and 7 (although these ties are not shown in Henle) as well as on the *sforzato* LH upbeats, and maintain the sense of the clear crotchet pulse in the LH (while showing the further 'crossing' of the beat with the slurred LH crotchet couplets, bb.5 – 6 and 7 – 8) beneath the sustained RH. From the upbeat to b.9 be sure to sustain the tied inner RH upbeats between the active outer lines, as you crescendo upwards through the tiered *sforzatos* towards the 3rd beat of b.13. From b.15 listen to the sustained lower dominant pedal point. Show also the emphasis on the 'normal' beat with firm *sforzatos* on the 1st beats of bb.18 and 20, keeping the RH lines and inner LH lines moving as smoothly as possible here.

A subdued moment, from the upbeat to b.24 (47) is quickly disrupted by more syncopated upbeats, leading through the ascent to the fierce syncopated *sforzato* chord and pause on the 2nd beat of b.33 (56) (with a further 'cross-accent' on the 2nd beat of b.32). Be sure to sustain and *listen* to all tied LH notes and chords through to their full value between bb.25 (48) and 31 (54). Return to *piano* on the upbeat to b.34, and then rise in a further *crescendo* towards b.41, again feeling the onward propelling effect of the upbeat *sforzatos*, first in the bass, and then in the treble. Then over a sustained LH dominant 7th chord, hurtle down from b.41 (though maintaining an iron control of the pulse) showing the stabbing RH upbeat accents, and taking care to co-ordinate the *sforzato* 'entry' of the LH on the upbeat to b.45 (68), as you press on towards the restatement of the opening figure at b.46 (69). Show the implied emphasis on the tied LH upbeats to bb.64 – 6 (87 – 9), 'crossing' with more implied emphases on the *2nd* beats in the RH. Steady yourself by 'going to' a firm RH minim third and LH slurred crotchet on the 1st beat of b.67, and then show the lashing LH *sforzatos* on the upbeats to bb.68 – 71 (91 – 4) and 73 – 5 (96 – 8), against the partly tied and also accented RH upbeats. Whether to end the movement *forte* or in a steep *decrescendo* to *pianissimo* from the *sforzato* 1st beat of b.144 (167) is debatable. In either event carry out your effect with conviction, and end as clearly as you began with hardly a hint of a *rallentando*.

bb.24 – 147
(47 – 170)

No. 62 in E flat major
(Hob. XVI/52)

First movement – Allegro (8 +)*

This is the most imposing and virtuosic of all Haydn's Sonatas. The first movement, fantasia-like in the range of its rhythmic and pianistic figuration, belongs to that select band among the great works of music, of such grandeur and immutability of design that you feel an inevitable and unquestionable progress from first note to last.

A glance at the pages shows the scope of Haydn's brilliant exuberance, and the need to provide rhythmic stability with a steady overall crotchet pulse.

bb.1 – 6

When setting a tempo, therefore, take into account the extensive demisemiquaver and dotted rhythm passage-work, and realize that here 'Allegro' must be interpreted in the sense of 'lively', and that the crotchet pulse must perforce be 'Moderato'. Declaim the magisterial opening chords with a ringing clarion sound, spreading not only the first chord, but the LH of all the chords in bb.1 and 2, excepting perhaps the semiquaver chord in b.1. Do count out the dotted rhythms accurately, neither double dotting nor 'tripletizing' the rhythm. Keep the awkward descending demisemiquaver upbeat to b.2 relatively light, and feel that it is 'going towards' the upper D on the 1st beat of b.2. Most people find the best fingering for the four demisemiquavers is 3 2 1 4, with the fingering $\frac{3}{2}$ on the RH 1st chord of b.2. Be sure to *feel* the silent 4th beat of b.2, and to time the dotted rhythm figures equally carefully in the *piano* 'echo' (b.3) over neatly placed LH quaver chords – inexperienced players will almost invariably lose the tautness of the rhythm here. 'Feel' the silent 4th beat of b.3 (and the 2nd and 4th beats of b.5) and come in accurately with the offbeat semiquavers, showing the slurred effect of these figures in either hand as they move inwards in contrary motion towards the detached quavers. From the upbeat to b.5 you can take the lower part of the semiquaver figures, and the scale in thirds with the LH, descending in *diminuendo* in strict tempo towards a warmly singing, though *piano*, tied RH crotchet E flat on the 1st beat of b.6.

bb.6 – 19 From b.6 create a perfectly rhythmic and buoyantly singing melody line, supported and propelled along by evenly pulsating semiquavers. Give the long tied notes (e.g. the E flat on the 1st beat of b.6 and the C on the 1st beat of b.7) sufficient singing tone to sound over the subsequent beats, and feel the demisemiquaver figures as 'upbeats' 'going to' the subsequent crotchets or dotted quavers (rather than as 'tail ends' to the previous beats). Make a slight swell through the second half of b.7 towards the slurred crotchet on the 1st beat of b.8. Then place the detached chords accurately on the 3rd and 4th beats of b.8 as you poise yourself for the trumpeting restatement of the opening chords in the higher register at b.9. Shoot down the scale from a strong high C placed exactly on the 4th beat of b.9, and try to fit the groupings of the scale into the natural crotchet pulse with the help of a firm LH dominant 7th chord on the 1st beat of b.10. It is technically helpful, as well as musically convincing if you feel that you are making a *crescendo* downwards towards a strong bass E flat on the 3rd beat of b.10, taken with the LH. Nervous players are often amazed by their own brilliance here, if they can but let themselves go, and really *rip* down the scale, focusing their attention towards the low E flat, rather than on the actual notes of the scale. Then leap up, in a poised manner, to lead off with the *piano* LH melody on the upbeat to b.11. Phrase this melody line perfectly rhythmically (as in the RH in bb.6 – 8) beneath even and steady RH semiquavers. Be particularly careful to keep steady as the inner LH melody continues over the sustained lower pedal point F from b.14, and also listen acutely here to the melodic and harmonic inflections of the continuingly even RH semiquavers. In b.16 keep a steady crotchet pulse in the smoothly phrased LH thirds as the RH swings into sextuplets, in *diminuendo*, in preparation for the *subito forte* restatement in the dominant at b.17. Support the scale passages through bb.18 – 19 with firm LH chords and make a *crescendo* towards the top note of each scale (the semiquaver F) with brilliant demisemiquavers, poising yourself on this high F as if applying an instant brake, so that you can control the pulse of the descending *semiquavers*. (Help yourself by consciously playing the LH crotchet chord accurately on the 3rd beat.) No more than a quick three-note ornament is practicable in the second half of b.19, delivered with a slur-*staccato* effect thus:

bb.20 – 26 Follow the part-writing carefully through b.20, keeping the LH line and each of the RH lines as smooth as possible, and letting the tied crotchets sing over the subsequent beats. This bar is far from easy to phrase smoothly – practise it not only 'hands separately', but parts separately. Do not then hurry through bb.21 and 22 in your relief at their simplicity, but follow the contours of the RH semiquavers and the sustained LH lines evenly and expressively. Continue to keep these semiquavers moving evenly and do not allow the fundamental crotchet pulse to be disrupted by the syncopated LH *sforzato* quaver chords on the upbeats to the 1st and 3rd beats of b.23 and to the 1st beat of b.24 (these chords are often spread, at least in the LH). Articulate the RH demisemiquavers through bb.24 – 5 with all possible brilliance (showing the curve up towards, and down from the three high G's in b.24 and to the high C and the F in b.25), keeping steady with the help of clear and accurately placed LH quaver chords in b.24, and of a strong minim chord on the 1st beat of b.25. Apply a sharp 'brake' again on the 3rd beat of b.25, to avoid the tendency to hurry through the actively plucked *staccato* semiquavers through the second half of b.25 and the first half of b.26.

bb.27 – 33   Preserve your crotchet pulse intact as you launch into Haydn's wild rhythmic spree at b.27. Tovey calls this 'the most hilarious tune in the world'. 'Finish off' the previous phrase with a clear quaver chord on the 1st beat of b.27, and *feel* the dotted semiquaver rest as you poise yourself for a perfectly timed demisemiquaver 'upbeat' to the 2nd beat of the bar. These slurred demisemiquavers must be 'snapped' like acciaccaturas and the hand 'flicked' off the *staccato semiquavers* so that the demisemiquaver rests occur naturally, creating an exultant, skipping effect. Master this effect by inventing your own exercise in other keys and note combinations (also in both hands, in preparation for Haydn's 'doubled' version of this figure in bb.46 – 7 and 69). Practise the LH alone too, in strict time, and then when you put 'hands together', control the RH with accurately placed LH *staccato* quaver chords in bb.27 – 8, and then from the middle of b.28 with the more sustained LH lines. Feel that the RH is fitting in with your rock-steady LH, and *not* the other way about. From the middle of b.29 (taking care not to 'fall into' the 3rd beat of the bar, by poising yourself on the RH demisemiquaver rest before the RH demisemiquaver 'upbeat' to the 3rd beat) articulate the RH demisemiquavers and detached repeated semiquavers with 'rattling' clarity over even and steady LH semiquavers. Let the LH 'lead' with clear quaver octaves through the second half of b.30 (again taking care not to 'fall into' the 3rd beat of the bar) and then with smoothly phrased and steady crotchet octaves beneath the 'buzzing' RH demisemiquavers as you *diminuendo* through b.31 towards the *piano* bass octave F on the 1st beat of b.32. Go *pianissimo* in the RH here, and then make a steep *crescendo* through the second half of this bar towards the B flat chord on the 1st beat of b.33. (It is helpful to take the lower RH note of this chord (B flat) with the LH.)

bb.34 – 43   Time b.34 carefully, like b.3, and then pursue the contrapuntal treatment of the semiquaver figure in detached thirds clearly in either hand from the upbeat to b.35. Keep steady as you descend through the first half of b.36 towards a firm slurred crotchet chord on the 3rd beat of the bar. There are various possible fingerings for this awkward descent, and players must work out which suits them best. But do not lurch blindly downwards – leap up confidently from a firm RH third on the 1st beat of the bar, to a strong high fourth, allowing a tiny natural break, and then 'feel' the 2nd beat of the bar, and also feel that you are 'going towards' a 'lean' on that slurred 3rd beat. Count calmly through bb.37 and 38, feeling the stillness of the minim octaves in b.38, before you burst forth again in b.39. Keep the LH tremolo in place with bright-toned and accurately placed RH quaver chords in b.39, and similarly, control your glittering RH demisemiquavers with firm, clear detached LH quaver chords in b.40, and lively but steady LH quaver octaves, then chords in bb.41 – 2. The ascending RH demisemiquaver passage in b.41 is far from easy.   Practise it in dotted rhythms:

and   etc. (see Introduction) and above all be sure to let your clear and steady ascending *LH* quavers (within a firmly held crotchet pulse) control the RH and *not* the other way about. Let the treble quavers 'take over' from the 3rd beat of b.42, and make a sharp *diminuendo* towards the neat *piano* quaver chords that end the exposition.

At the beginning of the development give full value to the suddenly still and
bb.44 – 60 anticipatory chords and pause (as Haydn slides us, astonishingly, to the
dominant of C major), before launching again into the 'hilarious' theme.
You may feel that the wait at bb.44 – 5 is interminable – it will not be if you *listen* to
the intervals, *feeling* the crotchet pulse within the chords, and again *listening* to the fading
sound through b.44. Take care to co-ordinate the hands precisely as the LH 'joins in'
enthusiastically on the semiquaver 'upbeat' to the 2nd beat of b.47. 'Rattle out' the RH
semiquavers vigorously again through bb.48 – 9. Then abruptly change tack as you 'go
to' and 'lean' ardently upon the syncopated crotchet octave B flat on the 2nd quaver pulse
of b.50, and let the RH octave line sing warmly but smoothly over the LH tremolo through
b.50. Let this LH tremolo 'go to' the D major third with the sustained bass D on the 1st
beat of b.51, and then shape the undulating and mainly contrary-motion semiquaver lines
of both hands in a 'close' legato through to b.55. Feel tiny 'surges' up to and down from
the uppermost notes as you shape the melodic curves (e.g. in the RH up to E natural and
then the E flat in b.52, and up to the E flat again in b.53; and in the LH up to the C
in b.52 and up to the E flat twice in b.53, and so on; this slightly syncopating effect needs
careful practice 'hands separately'). Then descend to a *pianissimo* at the beginning of b.56,
opening out again in a steep *crescendo* towards another fervent 'lean' on the *sforzato* fourth
on the 3rd beat of b.57. Sustain the melodic treble minim C ringingly here, and listen keenly
to this treble melody line as well as to the inner RH line through to the middle of b.58
over even LH semiquavers. Then phrase the slurred LH melodic fragments cleanly as they
swoop between the higher and lower registers beneath steady RH semiquavers, always
feeling the implied 'lean' on the dotted quavers, and 'tailing' away the sound towards
the quaver. Feel that these fragments progress in continuous 'arcs', rather than in isolated
stops and starts, listening at the same time to the inflections of the evenly pulsating RH
semiquavers. If you use the pedal, give just a short light touch on each dotted quaver only,
so that you always show the quaver rests.

Support your brilliant RH demisemiquaver passage-work through bb.61 – 2
bb.61 – 79 with firm LH crotchet chords. Make a *subito piano* on the 1st beat of b.63,
and then let the LH quavers *crescendo* downwards beneath buzzing RH demisemiquavers towards a resonant bass F sharp minim octave on the 1st beat of b.64. Then
from the 3rd beat of b.64 let the RH (then the LH) demisemiquaver figures 'whirl' with
the utmost glitter and brilliance, supported by bright, clear (not heavy) quaver chords in
the other hand. This is another difficult passage, where practising in dotted rhythms will
help. Following the emphatic half-close on the apparent dominant of C at b.67, Haydn
throws us instead into E major, where the 'hilarious' theme is 'developed' at first quietly,
and then in a more jolting and Beethovenian manner. The mood changes almost from
bar to bar though, and more serious, smooth LH thirds enter under the skipping RH on
the 3rd beat of b.71, followed by a fragment of the melody from b.5, from the upbeat
to b.73. (Be sure that the LH 'takes over' this melody line smoothly from the upbeat to
b.74.) *Diminuendo* as indicated through to b.77, then let the descending RH broken chord
figure cascade downwards in a vigorous *crescendo* through b.78 towards the beginning
of the recapitulation in b.79. Be careful here to show the three LH semiquavers as the
upbeat leading into b.79, rather than 'falling into' the E flat chord.

Do not snatch at the high B flat following the chord on the 1st beat of b.95,
bb.79 – 116 but rather allow the inevitable and natural slight break as you leap up from
the *firmly* played RH semiquaver G. Haydn torments us by altering the RH
demisemiquaver pattern from the 3rd beat of b.113. It is not more difficult, however,
than the passage at b.41, providing that you make a clear (but not heavy) accent on the

repeated notes, i.e. the first note of each group of demisemiquavers, relying for rhythmic security as before on your steady LH quavers. As at the close of the exposition, it is effective to *decrescendo* through the second half of the penultimate bar towards *pianissimo* unison crotchets (treating the jokey grace notes as acciaccaturas) ending with bright and vigorous final chords.

Second movement – Adagio (8 +)*

The impact of this 'Adagio' is almost as great as that of the first movement. Its effusions of rhythmic and melodic figuration and ornamentation (which test the rhythmic sense even of experienced players) must, as in the first movement, be held together within a fundamentally steady pulse. Set a slow and measured **3/4** pulse, and help yourself at first by counting in quavers within the crotchets. Try bb.7 and 8, and then bb.21 and 22, and find a tempo at which the semiquaver triplets (bb.7 – 8) flow easily and comfortably, and at which the demisemiquaver triplet figures (bb.21 – 2) 'trip' downwards, neither feeling hurried nor sticky.

bb.1 – 8   Lead off in a quiet but warm tone in the RH and inner LH lines over quietly sustained lower dotted minims, co-ordinating the dotted rhythm immaculately in either hand. In bb.1 and 2 feel the RH melodic curve up to and down from the crotchet on the 2nd beat of the bar (and similarly the 'lift' of the inner LH line up to the minim A). To give the necessary onward-moving impulse, always feel the demisemiquavers as 'upbeats' to the subsequent beats, rather than as tail ends to the previous beats. Then through b.3 feel the melodic curve up to the *3rd* beat of the bar. Follow the smooth treble line up to this 3rd beat, but note the inner RH and LH dotted semiquaver rests on the 1st and 2nd beats. While shaping these three individual phrase curves, do also feel the *overall* curve of this noble melody line from b.1 up to the 3rd beat of b.3 and down again towards the 2nd beat of b.4, and do not be afraid to give a fine resonance to the chords as you *crescendo* through b.3 (and again through bb.6 – 7). 'Finish off' the phrase carefully in b.4, *feel* the RH semiquaver rest and poise yourself neatly on the emphasized semiquaver third before descending in perfectly timed triplets towards the restatement of b.1. (Note that this emphasized third in b.4 is a 'plain' semiquaver, not a triplet, and feel it as the 'upbeat' to the little triplet 'run'.) Master the rhythm of b.7 thoroughly before adding the ornaments. Then place the broken chord grace notes *on* the beat in the manner of a spread chord and place the second grace note figure *on* the second triplet, making in effect a five-note 'turn', and maintaining the overall stability of the triplet group.

bb.8 – 18   Listen to the curve of the LH triplets through b.8 as you prepare either to return to b.1, or to lead on into b.9. Then feel the heightening intensity from the diminished 7th chord on the 1st beat of b.9, as you *crescendo* towards the *fortissimo* chords of b.10 (giving these chords a full, ringing, but not harsh resonance). Curve down again in *diminuendo* towards b.13, but ensure that the RH A sharp sings over the 2nd beat of b.12, listening to the 'clash' of this A sharp with the lower LH sustained B, and also to the expressive 'resolution' of the slurred inner LH crotchet E to the minim D sharp. Be sure also not to hurry these 'plain' notes through this bar. Play the semi-*staccato* upbeat scale to b.14 in a gently detached, not spiky style, and then let the repeated

RH B's in decreasing note values 'speak' over the steadily continuing LH melody line in sixths as you *crescendo* towards the chord on the 3rd beat. Then starting the scale figure almost at once after the chord, ensure that you arrive at the top of the scale with a ringing dotted quaver octave, precisely on the 1st beat of b.15. Rise to a ringing minim chord on the 2nd beat of b.16, and end the section quietly, in perfect time.

bb.19 – 25   Delineate the stark ascending minor dotted rhythm unison figures forcefully up towards the 1st beat of b.20. Then plunge down to a powerful *sforzato* dominant 7th chord on the 2nd beat, and run up the scale to arrive at the top E as nearly as possible on the 3rd beat of the bar. It is more stylish, as well as less unnerving, to make a *diminuendo* rather than a *crescendo* up the scale, so that it 'disappears', rather than arriving with a bump. Then time b.21 carefully, letting, as said before, the demisemiquaver triplet figures 'trip' down easily over steady detached LH semiquaver thirds. Bb.23 – 4 will need especially careful timing, particularly the initially confusingly placed run of b.24. Do, of course, practise *without* the runs until you have absorbed the skeleton rhythm. Then start the first RH run in b.23 approximately on, or a little before, the 2nd quaver pulse, and start the subsequent double run and the LH run in b.24, almost *immediately* after the preceding quaver. Make sure that you arrive on the unison semiquavers C precisely on the 3rd main beat of b.23. Then place the semiquaver chord precisely on the 6th *quaver* pulse, and 'go to' and lean well on the RH slurred minim sixth on the 1st beat of b.24 over a carefully placed bass quaver. Then *feel* the LH rest on the 2nd quaver pulse, run up neatly to the high quaver on the 4th quaver pulse, and then synchronize the RH and LH precisely on the 3rd main beat. Providing that you hold fast to your steady quaver pulse, you will find that these runs 'fit in' surprisingly easily. (Some editions may place the runs slightly differently, but the 'authentic' layout is that given in the Vienna Urtext Edition, Henle, and Peters.)

bb.25 – 54   Lead off clearly with the LH in b.25, beneath steady and 'speaking' RH semidetached repeated semiquavers, as you *crescendo* towards b.26. Then take over the 'lead' clearly in the RH on the *sforzato* dotted quaver D sharp on the 1st beat of b.26. Maintaining a resonant tone, underpin the RH dotted rhythms through bb.26 – 7 with rock-steady LH semiquaver chords. Through b.26 feel the RH hemidemisemiquaver figures as 'upbeats', 'flicked' cleanly towards the subsequent dotted semiquavers. In b.27 again feel the demisemiquavers as 'upbeats', and then place the grace notes *on* the beat like strong acciaccaturas. Do feel through bb.26 – 7 that the RH is fitting in with your steady LH and *not* the other way about, and maximize the extreme rhythmic tension of this section of the development (bb.25 – 32) by maintaining an iron control of the rhythm. Take care to give the unison octave crotchets on the 1st and 2nd beats of bb.30 and 31 their full value, listening to their dark resonances and to the jagged bite of the dotted rhythms in these bars. Tail the rising diminished 7th arpeggio off, leaving it in 'mid-air', and give the rests here their full value or more as you poise yourself to move into the recapitulation. 'Point' all the little decorative differences as they occur. Phrase the chromatic triplets with gliding smoothness in bb.37 and 38. Time the long arpeggio in b.39 so that the top note (E) falls on the 4th *quaver* beat of the bar, and the shorter one in b.40 so that the bass quaver B, taken with the RH, falls precisely on the 3rd crotchet beat. In b.43 let the broken octave hemidemisemiquavers again go with a clear 'flick' to the dotted quavers on each main beat, supported by resonant LH crotchet thirds, in this poignantly expressive variant of bb.11 – 12. Let the diminished 7th arpeggio 'fall' freely from a strong chord on the 2nd beat of b.48, and then enter again quietly and precisely on the 1st beat of b.49. Take care to 'finish off' the RH phrase with a quiet but clear quaver sixth on the 2nd beat of b.50. Then feel the low semi-*staccato* quavers (taken with the RH) like distant, mysterious drumbeats, and listen to the marvellous effect as the inner LH melodic fragment enters sonorously on the 1st beat of b.51. Let the steady drumbeats 'go on' towards a resonant minim on the 1st beat of b.52, and take time (*listening* to the resonance of the sustained LH dominant 7th chord) to play the final treble fragment with the utmost expressiveness, ending with quiet but deliberate chords. Mastering the complex rhythms and ornamentation of this great movement is, need it be said, only the preparatory groundwork for the greater task of seeking the musical unity and expressive content of the music.

Finale – Presto (8 +)*

There is no let-down in the Finale. Haydn is at his most wildly exuberant, and the pace is relentless, with hectic turns of mood and rhythm every few bars. Take your tempo from the maximum speed at which you can manage the treacherous semiquaver passage from bb.18 – 28, and let your crotchet pulse be as lively as is safe.

bb.1 – 28 Make it clear that you are starting on the upbeat, and launch into the sharply defined repeated quavers with a feeling of suppressed but bursting vitality, 'going to' a strong slurred crotchet on the 1st beat of b.2 over a quiet but sustained lower LH tied E flat minim. Co-ordinate your RH, and 'ticking' repeated inner LH quavers precisely over these sustained pedal E flat points and, never losing sight of the crotchet pulse, avoid the tendency to clip short the 2nd crotchet beats of the bar and thus to 'fall into' the subsequent 1st beats. Feel the breathless expectancy of the silent pause at b.8 before launching off again with the reiterated quavers, exactly in tempo. After the 2nd pause, burst forth with the *forte* LH quavers from the *sforzato* upbeat to b.17, synchronize the vigorous entry of the RH semiquavers precisely with the LH upbeat to b.18, and then steady yourself with a strong LH crotchet octave on the 1st beat of b.18 beneath your glittering RH scale. Feel that your LH is 'leading' through to b.28, so that brilliantly whirling RH semiquavers are being controlled by very lively and rhythmic detached LH quavers, and *not* the other way about. Keep these LH quavers rock-steady, and feel as if there is a little *crescendo* towards the quaver on the *2nd* beats of bb.19 – 22 (to the E flat in b.19, and to the F in b.20 etc.). This not only keeps you steady, but also boosts the rhythmic drive of the passage. Also feel the sharp little 'surge' in the RH up to the A flats on the 2nd beat of bb.20 and 22. Practise the RH in dotted rhythms:

[musical rhythm notation] and [musical rhythm notation] etc. (see Introduction) and also practise co-ordinating these rhythms with your steady LH quavers.

bb.28 – 56 From the upbeat to b.29, the mood changes abruptly. Come to a clear 'stop' with the unison crotchets on the 1st beat of b.28, *feel* the silent 2nd beat, and then shape the treble line very smoothly and expressively (though without any slackening of the rhythmic impetus) over a sustained lower LH line and even inner LH quavers. 'Go up to' a strongly singing tied E flat on the 2nd beat of b.34, and then leap boldly up to a ringing syncopated high crotchet F in b.36, preserving your rhythmic balance by keeping the LH quavers perfectly steady. Then shape the RH descending syncopated melodic line smoothly over continuingly even LH quavers. Seize the instant change of mood again from the upbeat to b.45 with the first of the series of sharply syncopated *sforzato* upbeats (but phrase the LH chromatic fragment smoothly from the upbeat to b.47, incorporating the *sforzatos* with a kind of 'push'). Then keep steady as the battering *fortissimo* chords burst out from the upbeat to b.49, feeling that these are 'going to' the 'stabbing' slurred *sforzato* RH augmented fourths and LH fifths on the 1st beat of b.50. Reiterate this slurred *sforzato* chord with equal force on the 1st beat of b.51 but perhaps with more warmth on the 1st beat of *b.52*, as you prepare to ease out towards the sustained and suddenly contemplative pauses in bb.55 and 56.

bb.57 – 102   Then pick up the tempo from the upbeat to b.57, and phrase the inner RH quaver line smoothly from b.60 between the sustained treble, and LH tied minims, 'joining in' clearly with the treble from the 2nd beat of b.61. From b.65 articulate the semiquaver figures evenly between the hands with immaculate clarity, keeping steady by preserving the sense of the crotchet pulse, and particularly of the 1st beats. *Crescendo* gradually from b.69 and descend abandonedly, though without losing control of the pulse to the low F and pause taken by the RH at b.77. From the upbeat to b.78 keep the 'picking' LH repeated quavers perfectly steady to avoid being thrown off balance by the jerking RH *sforzato* upbeats (and likewise in reversed hands from bb.86 – 90). Feel that the detached *LH* quavers on the main beats are 'leading' through bb.83 – 4. 'Rattle out' the RH semiquavers over lively, detached, and very rhythmic LH quavers from b.91 as you *crescendo* towards the bright, spread, detached quaver chords of bb.95 and 96. Then from the upbeat to b.98 phrase the RH thirds smoothly over even and *legato* semiquaver 'trills' (and similarly in reversed hands from the upbeat to b.100), making a *diminuendo* to *pianissimo* towards the 1st beat of b.101, and ending with a ringing crotchet chord. Alternatively you could dash onwards to the double bar in a continuing *forte* playing the RH, then LH, quaver thirds in spanking *staccato* against the *legato* 'trills'.

bb.103 – 45   Be sure to *feel* the crotchet and quaver rest at the end of the exposition so that you are ready to launch into b.103 from a clear detached upbeat. Follow the detailing of the RH slurs and *staccatos* over firm LH octaves through bb.103 – 4, and then from the upbeat to b.105, follow the contrapuntal workings with immaculate clarity. From the upbeats to bb.107, 109 and 111, launch off each rising quaver fragment from a bold *sforzato* upbeat as you *crescendo* upwards towards b.112. Then 'unwind' to *piano* as the phrase descends towards b.118, shaping the treble and LH lines expressively while keeping the inner repeated quavers continuously 'ticking'. Then burst into a *subito forte* at b.118. Set off again ebulliently from the upbeat to b.123 in Haydn's brief development of the opening phrase, which soon shoots off into a passage of brilliant semiquaver runs. Keep the RH under control here with firm, perfectly placed LH chords. Be careful always to *feel* the crotchet pulse on the *2nd* beat of the bars where the LH has a quaver rest (bb.130 – 5), or when the LH dotted crotchet chords are sustained over the 2nd beats (bb.136 – 7). Always feel also that the LH quaver upbeats (to bb.131 – 8 and to bb.143 – 5) are 'going to' firm chords on the subsequent 1st beats.

bb.146–309   From b.146 Haydn embarks on an extended development of the passage from bb.69 – 77. Articulate the semiquavers in this Scarlattian passage with all the glitter you can muster, building up the dynamics again towards the wild plunge down to the bass notes at b.170. From the upbeat to b.171 we have another extended version of a corresponding earlier passage (from b.45). After the *fortissimo* chords of bb.179 – 80 poise yourself to place the high, echoing RH thirds neatly from the upbeat to b.181. Give full value to the rests and pause (bb.184 – 5) and then from the upbeats to bb.186 and 188, phrase the LH quaver fragments smoothly in a rather ruminative manner, supported by quiet even thirds in the RH (and similarly in reversed hands from the upbeats to bb.190 and 192). Then from the high *sforzato* upbeat to b.194 (allowing a natural break as you leap cleanly up) 'open out' towards bb.195 – 6, treating the treble B flat in b.195 like a long appoggiatura and spreading the sustained dominant 7th generously through b.196. *Listen* to these chords through the pauses, and then lead on from the upbeat to b.198 as if in a continuous *rallentando* towards bb.202 – 3. Play out the *adagio* chromatic quavers in a resonant sighing tone, and *listen* as the sound of the long chord in b.202

fades before playing the decoration in an expressive *piano*. Then poise yourself through another long pause, to launch with renewed vigour into the recapitulation. Take care not to 'fall into' b.291, but 'brake' yourself with a vigorous LH *sforzato* upbeat and then let the RH trill run easily and relatively quietly, avoiding the tendency to let it 'take over' and sabotage the activities of the LH. End with immaculately placed, clarion-toned crotchet chords.

Quite apart from its technical demands, players find this a difficult movement to hold together – it is certainly a considerable test of vitality and stamina. Do, above all, try to preserve the sense of a stable, overall crotchet pulse through thick and thin. It is Haydn's extraordinary achievement that he is able to organize his wildly diverse rhythmic patterns and volatile changes of mood here, as in the first movement, into a logical and compelling unity.

MISCELLANEOUS PIECES

Capriccio in G major
(Hob. XVII/1) (8)

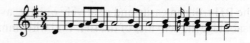

This is a substantial piece, in the form of free variations on a folk song theme, which appears contrapuntally, and with various accompanying figurations interspersed with long, and often startlingly free modulatory and improvisatory passages. This freedom is the more remarkable in that the piece was written as early as 1765 (though not published until 1788), and despite its early origin, appears to have been intended for the fortepiano rather than the harpsichord. The original song concerns itself with the news that eight people are required to accomplish the delectable task of castrating a boar!

Eahna achte müassen seyn,	It takes eight of you,
Wann s'an Saubärn wolln schneidn.	if you want to castrate a boar.
Zwoa voran, zwoa hintn,	Two in front and two behind,
Zwoa schneidn, zwoa bindn.	two to cut and two to bind.

To the player unfamiliar with Haydn's style, this piece may at first seem dull, and the sheer expanse of its 368 bars is indeed daunting. But for those who persevere there is much to enjoy in its many surprising twists and turns, which take us through at least two passages of striking impact and power (bb.165 – 89 and 247 – 63).

bb.1 – 23 Note the *moderato* and set a sensible, steady **3/4**, bearing in mind the extensive semiquaver scale passages and triplet figuration to come. Lead off from a clear crotchet upbeat and play the 'song'-theme in a simple straightforward 'peasant' style, supported by a sturdy LH, in a jolly kind of jogging motion. Treat the double appoggiatura on the 1st beat of b.4 and the LH appoggiatura on the 1st beat of bb.7 and 9 like acciaccaturas. 'Finish off' the LH cleanly down to the low crotchet G on the 2nd beat of b.5. Then 'enter' with a chunky RH third on the upbeat to b.6, and make a vigorous 'churning' effect with the RH thirds as you 'go to' a firm 1st beat of each of bb.6 – 9, over resonant, drone-like LH minim D's, with an overall onward impetus towards the grand LH and RH pauses in b.9. Then take up the tempo precisely, on the upbeat to b.10. 'Finish off' the theme firmly with the unison G's on the 1st beat of b.14, then leap up cleanly and articulate the RH triplet figures (bb.14 – 15 and 18 – 23) and the slurred 'ordinary' quavers (bb.16 – 17) neatly and precisely, supported by a clear and perfectly placed LH. Be particularly careful to place the LH fifth firmly and accurately on the 1st beat of b.15, where the RH has a crotchet rest, and show the implied firm emphasis on the tied inner upbeat to b.16 (and similarly to b.20). Execute the RH turns smartly and clearly on the 1st beat of bb.20 – 2, ensuring that they do not delay your clear triplet descending scales which must 'fall' from a firm fifth finger placed precisely on the 2nd beat of these bars. Keep steady here with the help of a firm LH.

bb.23 – 39 'Finish off' the RH ornamented slurred crotchet cleanly on the F sharp on the 2nd beat of b.23 before entering vigorously (even clumpingly) with the theme in the LH line on the upbeat to b.24. From here to b.32 practise carefully 'hands separately'. Feel the implied emphasis on the (again drone-like) RH inner tied upbeats to bb.25 and 26. When you put 'hands together' do ensure that your LH 'lead' is not disrupted by the activities of the RH. Run up the RH scales clearly and vigorously through bb.29 – 32, dropping to a clear detached quaver A on the 3rd beats over your sturdily 'churning' LH thirds. You could either drive on in tempo and stop on a knife-edge in b.32, or alternatively 'draw out' gradually through bb.31 – 2. In either event do have courage to *wait* through the written out pause at bb.33 – 4 before 'stomping' in again on the upbeat to b.35.

bb.39 – 61   Let the ascending RH scales in b.39 (and 41 and 43) 'lead into' the line of descending crotchets in the next bar, creating an overall melodic curve, supported by even LH quavers in b.40 etc. Then take over the 'lead' clearly in the LH with the ascending scale starting on the 2nd beat of b.45. In bb.46 – 7 and 48 – 9 keep your supporting RH quavers very even and relatively light, so that they neither swamp nor disrupt the descending LH crotchet line. Then from b.49 let the *RH* scales 'go to' a clear and firm quaver appoggiatura on the 1st beat of bb.50 – 3, supported and steadied by firmly placed LH crotchet sixths and fifths. The negotiation of bb.53 – 61 represents a considerable balancing act! Practise carefully 'hands separately', showing all implied emphases clearly. Note and feel the implied emphasis on the RH tied semiquaver/crotchet A on the 3rd beat of b.53, while letting the scale 'go on up to' a firm upper slurred crotchet C on the 1st beat of b.54. (Editions vary regarding the tying of the inner LH upbeat (D) to b.54, but if, as in the Vienna Urtext, you tie this note, give it a corresponding implied emphasis.) Then feel a *strong* implied emphasis on the tied RH thirds on the upbeats to bb.55 – 61. At the same time let the LH ascending scales through bb.54, 56, etc. *and* also the LH upbeat trills to bb.56, 58, etc. 'go to' very definite crotchets on the 1st beat of each subsequent bar beneath these held RH thirds. This will help to counteract the insistent urge you are bound to have, when you put 'hands together', to 'resolve' the RH thirds on the 1st beat of bb.55 – 61 instead of holding them over to the 2nd beat. Give the LH trills six notes, starting on the upper note and including the 'turn':

bb.61 – 84   The theme enters again in the treble on the upbeat to b.62, this time in the minor. Be careful in bb.63 and 64 to phrase the LH inner offbeat quaver fragments neatly over the sustained lower line, and do not let the third quaver (E) 'hang over' the 3rd beat of these bars. From bb.72 – 84 Haydn 'develops' the opening motif of the theme in a protracted sequence of RH dotted rhythms over a sustained LH. Articulate these RH dotted rhythm figures with immaculate precision, feeling that the RH is fitting in with your rock-steady LH and *not* the other way about. Keep the semiquavers relatively light with the feeling of 'going to' the subsequent longer note. As always in such instances, it is helpful to think of the semiquaver as the 'upbeat' to the subsequent dotted quaver or tied crotchet, as the case may be, rather than as the 'tail-end' of the previous beat. Do practise the LH carefully alone, sustaining the two lines as smoothly as possible. Feel the implied emphasis (this helps steadiness) on the inner tied or untied minim on the 2nd beat of bb.72, 73, 75, 76 and 78 – 83.

bb.84 – 132   There is a partial entry of the theme in E minor, on the upbeat to b.85. Then from the upbeat to b.90 phrase the RH sixths and LH thirds sonorously and smoothly as Haydn evidently intended (see the *legato* slur in b.90). It is effective to play the ornamented solo treble fragments from the upbeat to bb.97, 99, etc. (the three crotchets B, A sharp, B, etc.) in a clear *mezzo-forte*, and to 'answer' with the rejoinders in both hands (from the upbeat to bb.98, 100, etc.) in a quieter, semi-echo effect, *or* vice versa! From the upbeat to b.105 listen acutely to the movement of the three lines, and particularly to the resonances created by the sustained notes in the two RH lines, and also in the inner LH line from the upbeat to b.108, over a resonant held lower pedal point B, again showing the implied emphases on all tied notes. A short partial entry of the theme in the inner LH line on the upbeat to b.114 leads into a 'development' in the treble and inner LH lines, in sixths from the 2nd beat of b.118, and in tenths from the 2nd beat of b.121. Pursue these figures confidently with a feeling of purposeful 'ongoingness', supported by a resonantly sustained lower LH line. 'Retake' the long held lower LH B firmly on the 2nd beat of b.121 (and similarly the E on the 2nd beat of b.124). The theme enters again in the tonic in the inner LH line on the upbeat to b.133. Co-ordinate this entry carefully with your emphasized tied treble upbeat A.

bb.133 – 89   From bb.148 – 51 support the descending RH triplet scale figures with warmly sustained LH lines, showing the implied emphasis on the tied inner minims on the 2nd beat of these bars. Then from bb.152 – 6 similarly support your LH scales with the sustained RH lines. Show the 'concealed' entry of the theme in B minor in the lower RH line on the upbeat to b.157. Phrase the RH thirds smoothly from the upbeat to b.162 as you lead towards the improvisatory passage from b.165. Then listen acutely to the marvellous shifting modulatory resonances of the sustained LH chords and to the inflections of the complementary RH quavers, articulating the RH throughout the passage as indicated in bb.165 and 166. Shape the dynamics as the mood takes you – they will, and should, vary at every performance of such an improvisatory passage. There is, however, an inevitable build-up of sonority and rhythmic tension to around b.181, with perhaps a slight easing out through bb.187 – 8 as you 'resolve' towards the dominant of C major. And *too much* 'fiddling about' with the dynamics will weaken the inexorable onward thrust of this passage, which is dependent above all upon the maintenance of an iron-steady pulse. Always feel that the LH chords are 'leading', and propelling the RH, and *not* the other way about.

bb.189 – 231   Let the RH 'go to' a clear minim third on the 1st beat of b.189 as you poise yourself on the dominant of C major for the RH entry of the theme on the upbeat to b.190. Swing easily into even triplets in the LH here, being careful not to alter your crotchet pulse. Start this passage *piano* in a very simple style, and then from b.203, as Haydn expands into a long melodic passage, let the dynamics undulate freely as the melody sings buoyantly over continuingly evenly pulsating LH triplets, building up in a gradual *crescendo* from b.220 towards b.232. In bb.213 and 217 let the RH semiquavers coincide with the third triplet of the LH group in accordance with the old convention. Give the trills in bb.197, 215, etc. six notes, starting on the upper note (as in the LH in bb.55, 57, etc.), treating the preceding semiquaver again as a triplet, and feeling it as an 'upbeat' prefix to the trill.

bb.232 – 64   Poise yourself on the 1st beat of b.232 as you take over the triplets steadily in the RH, ready for the LH to enter emphatically with the theme on the upbeat to b.233. Keep the RH triplets perfectly even and relatively quiet, or they will 'take over' and swamp the LH 'lead' when they are in cross-rhythm to the LH, bringing about a swift general collapse! The LH, as will be seen, 'leads' from here right through to b.264. Strike off vigorously in the LH with firm bass octaves and vigorously 'plucked' LH crotchets through bb.247 – 8 and 249 – 50. Practise the LH carefully alone from b.251. It is essential that you learn to 'go down' confidently to a strong bass octave on the 1st beat of each bar from *rock-steady* quaver figures. Practise the downward leaps at first from the *3rd* beat of each bar (leaving out the first two quavers of each four-quaver figure), imagining that the two quavers on these 3rd beats (e.g. the B flat and G in b.251 etc.) are slurred, so that the B flat is relatively firm, and the G relatively light. Then practise the whole quaver figure and the downward leap, feeling the quaver figures as *upbeats* to the crotchet octaves. The slurred effect suggested above is for practising purposes only. To achieve the best ultimate effect the quavers need to be detached – however, if when the hands are put together this proves to be too tall an order (like patting the head and circling the stomach!) play them in a strong *legato* curve. The essential is that the beat remains rock-steady, propelled and at the same time controlled by the powerful bass octaves. Balance the LH with 'keenly' articulated RH triplets and help the overall rhythmic and resonant effect with a *short* pedal on each bass octave. It will help to promote steadiness if you at first play the RH in chords when you put 'hands together'. Do not be afraid to exploit the splendid resonances of this passage (though without becoming too heavy and Beethovenian, nor letting the RH triplets swamp your LH).

bb.264 – 340   Poise yourself in b.264, ready to define the 'concealed' RH entry of the theme on the upbeat to b.265. At b.274 Haydn switches into G minor, and then from the upbeat to b.279 embarks on a development of the 'churning' motif (see bb.6 – 9) in broken octaves. Be careful once more to keep a steady crotchet pulse here, treating the broken octaves as if they are slurred, and supporting the RH with very steady and even LH quavers. Practise the RH at first in plain octaves, alone, and then with the LH. Be sure to let the inner RH crotchet line 'lead' up through b.284 (rather than being swamped by the syncopated treble B flats) towards a singing, inner tied minim E flat on the 1st beat of b.285. Then let the descending upper crotchet line 'go to' a singing A on the 1st beat of b.286, and so on. Support these sustained upper lines with steady LH broken octaves, again played as if slurred. Place the grace note figures *on* the 1st beat of bb.311 and 314. From b.323 support the RH triplets with firmly placed octaves on the 1st and 3rd beats, and then from the upbeat to b.327 keep the LH crotchets rock-steady beneath your cleanly articulated RH triplet scale figures. (Feel as if the LH is moving in 'arcs' up from the octaves to the single crotchets and down again, rather than in isolated 'plonks'.) Similarly from the upbeat to b.332, balance the LH triplets with steady and resonant RH thirds and seconds.

bb.340 – 68   After this long triplet passage, poise yourself again in b.340 to show the 'concealed' entry of the theme in the RH on the upbeat to b.341. Then move on purposefully towards the interrupted cadence with the powerful diminished 7th chord with pause at b.349, and the brilliant dominant 7th flourish in b.350. Imagine a pause on the low D at the end of the flourish, and then from the upbeat to b.352 drive on to the end with a final burst of energy, buoying along the resonant RH lines with brilliantly 'whirring' LH semiquavers. Practise the LH slowly and rhythmically, with light, sharp accents with the fifth finger, aiming for immaculate clarity (it is all too easy for the modern piano to sound muddy in this low register). Practising in dotted rhythms will help:

     ♩. ♩ ♩. ♩   and   ♪♫♫ ♪♫♫   etc, particularly   ♪♫♫   in the case of the extremely awkward downward leaps in b.367. It is essential here that you concentrate on leaping down on to *firm* bass notes, letting the relatively light upper notes, taken with the thumb and second finger, 'look after themselves'. End with vigorous clear chords.

Fantasia (or Capriccio) in C major

(Hob. XVII/4) (8 +)

This wild caper must be carried off with joyous humour and panache. Musically it is less demanding than the Capriccio in G major, but to stay the course and arrive at the end in one piece is a considerable test of technical and rhythmic stamina. The pace is unrelenting, save for the momentary respite of the occasional pause (bb.28, 87, 114, etc.) in which to gather yourself for the next onslaught.

Haydn starts plainly enough, as if setting off into an everyday sonata finale.

bb.1 – 28   Set a secure **3/8** pulse, nice and brisk, but not too fast, bearing in mind the extensive semiquaver passage-work to come. If you race, you will steamroller the detailing, and spoil all the fun. Lead off from a clear slurred quaver upbeat and articulate the RH with all brightness through bb.1 – 4 over rock-steady, busily persistent but not heavy, detached LH chords. Place the written out turn clearly *on* the 1st beat of b.2. Then 'lean' on the LH slurred crotchet thirds on the 1st beat of bb.5 and 6, as you neatly articulate the detailing of the RH, also lightly emphasizing the slurred dotted semiquavers on the 2nd beat of these bars. Detach the quavers neatly in both hands in b.7, and finish off the phrase with a clear quaver chord on the 1st beat of b.8; then *feel* the quaver rest as you poise yourself to lead off in the high register in a more 'clattery' tone, with another clear and perfectly timed slurred upbeat to b.9. Support your RH with steady, yet keenly 'ongoing' LH semiquavers through bb.9 – 12, executing the RH turn on the 1st beat of b.10 as in b.2. Be careful to feel the quaver rest precisely again on the 2nd beat of b.16 so that you enter with perfectly co-ordinated, rumbustuous unison semiquavers on the upbeat to b.17. From b.17 Haydn jerks back and forth between a 'normal' rhythm in bb.17, 19 and 21, and a cross-rhythm effect in bb.18, 20 and 22 – 8. Let yourself 'go with' this alternating rhythmic effect, keeping your athletic RH semiquavers steady with the help of a firmly placed LH crotchet on the 1st beat of b.18, and firm and steady LH chords on the 1st beat of bb.19 – 22. Then let yourself *really* 'go with' the cross-rhythm effect through the C major flourish (though without losing the *sense* of your 'normal' pulse) from b.22. 'Join in' confidently with the LH on the second cross-rhythm 'triplet' of b.25, and plunge down recklessly towards resonant unison crotchet G's at b.28.

Collect yourself on the pause, ready to lead off clearly with the LH into the

bb.28 – 69   passage of 'serious' contrapuntal business that follows. Practise carefully 'hands separately' here, and be sure to 'lean' well on the alternating LH-RH slurred upbeats to bb.29 – 34. Take care also to sustain the alternating RH inner and upper dotted crotchets resonantly through bb.35 – 8. Feel that the RH treble semiquavers in b.35 'go to' the dotted crotchet D on the 1st beat of b.36, and that the inner semiquavers in b.36 'go to' the dotted crotchet G on the 1st beat of b.37, and so on. Be sure to sustain the lower LH tied D through bb.39 – 40, beneath your steady ascending inner quaver line. Support your RH semiquavers with resonant LH chords as you *crescendo* through bb.41 – 5. Then drop to *piano* as indicated on the upbeat to b.46, and glide up smoothly to b.47, where Haydn launches into a brief 'development' of the opening theme. Listen to the descending inner LH chromatic line from b.45 as it 'goes on' downwards while the theme enters in b.47, and support the activities of the treble through to b.59 with a clear and steady LH inner line over your sustained lower LH tied D's. (Note that this pedal point (D) continues right through from b.39 to b.58.) Give the illusion (but *only* the illusion!) of running out of control as you veer breathlessly up from b.62 (*piano*) in *crescendo* towards the wild six-four demisemiquaver flourish at b.67. Be sure to arrive on a vigorous detached quaver D precisely on the 3rd beat of this bar, and then 'drop' the hand on to an energetic trill in b.38 over a strong supporting LH dominant 7th chord.

Use the quaver rest at the end of b.69 to poise yourself to enter, *piano*, with

bb.70 – 124   the 'horn-call' motif on the 1st beat of b.70. Follow the detailing precisely, 'leaning' slightly on the slurred semiquaver on the 2nd beat of bb.70 and 71 etc, and on the slurred quaver sixths or fifths on the 2nd beat of bb.76 and 78; and then feel that you are 'going to', and 'lean' well on the appoggiatura third on the 1st beat of b.73, and similarly on the appoggiatura effect quaver third on the 1st beat of b.77.

'Join in' neatly and lightly with the high LH treble fragments in b.74, articulating them just like the corresponding slur- *staccato* figure in the RH, bringing the hand *off* the quaver on each 3rd beat. Take care that the LH does not tend to get heavier as you go along, or it will 'take over', sabotage the RH 'lead', and cause a general collapse. 'Lean' well also on the RH slurred crotchet chords on the 1st beat of bb.80 – 6, making a progressive *diminuendo* towards a *pianissimo* chord and pause at b.87. At b.88 Haydn launches wildly off into B flat major. Support your energetic cross-rhythm effect RH broken chords with resonantly sustained tied LH chords through bb.88 – 99, and with steady octaves through bb.100 – 5, going *piano* as indicated at b.103, to *crescendo* again towards b.106. Carry your *crescendo* right on to b.112 with stentorian *sforzato* LH chords, and increasingly athletic RH semiquavers, and again plunge down towards the tied unison E's on the 1st beat of b.114. Then *listen* to the fading sound (the sound would have faded much more satisfactorily on the early pianos, of course) through the 'written out' pause, and then creep up very smoothly (starting *pianissimo* but in perfect tempo) through the unison chromatic scale ready to burst into the opening theme again at b.124.

bb.124 – 213   Place the offbeat LH fragment neatly at bb.132 – 3, listening accutely to the intervals beneath the RH theme-fragment. 'Take over' clearly with the LH on the upbeat to b.134, and dovetail the offbeat descending treble semiquaver fragment lightly and smoothly. Then pursue the LH and RH lines with spanking clarity through to b.144, giving equal importance to either hand. More 'serious' business follows from b.146. Shape and articulate the curving LH scale figures cleanly beneath *steady* RH quaver chords. *Listen* to the changing intervals rather than just thumping out the RH here. 'Go to' a firm quaver chord on the 1st beat of b.156, and then be sure to let the RH 'lead', placing the quaver sixths neatly on the upbeats to, and on the 1st beats of, bb.157 – 62 over neatly dovetailed (rather than swamping) LH fragments. Haydn then 'develops' the opening motif in a modulating passage of continual RH hand-crossing. Be sure to 'finish off' the previous passage with a clear RH sixth on the 1st beat of b.162, and then to 'enter' clearly with the LH broken thirds on the 2nd beat of the bar. Then be careful to keep a perfectly steady pulse as you cross back and forth scrupulously clearly in the RH, over even pulsating LH semiquavers. Following the *piano* at b.180 – 3, burst into *forte* at b.184, and plunge down energetically as before towards the pause on the unison octave, supported by firm crotchet chords on the 1st beat of bb.188 – 91. '*Tenuto intanto, finché non si sente più il suono*', meaning 'hold till the sound can no longer be heard', is not, of course, a practical possibility, especially on the modern piano. Allow an exaggerated pause though, before you sidle on to the *piano* octave F, 'pointing' this astonishing shift to the dominant of B flat major. Then *count* the two bars before entering precisely on the 1st beat of b.195 with the *piano* horn-call motif. *Diminuendo* as before to *pianissimo* at b.212.

bb.214 – 54   Burst in with the strident shock of the RH augmented fourth on the 1st beat of b.214, and listen to the shifting resonances of the low RH *sforzato* chords through to b.221, as the sharply defined LH fragments flit back and forth in immaculate time. From b.222 Haydn again takes up the 'development' figure from b.164. Be sure here that you mark the first LH semiquaver of bb.224, 226, 228 and 230 – 3 with a neat, sharp accent to 'balance' yourself where the RH has a quaver rest. 'Take over' confidently with the RH semiquavers on the 1st beat of b.234, similarly accenting the 1st beat of bb.234 – 45. Play the offbeat LH quavers with a persistent, niggling 'tick tick', but again keep them relatively light so that they do not swamp the RH and bring about another general collapse! *Crescendo* resolutely from b.242 towards a strong RH sixth on the 1st beat of b.246. Be careful to keep steady here as you slur the upbeats firmly up to the 1st beat of bb.247 and 248, supported by evenly placed LH quaver octaves. Do not give up the ghost at the sight of the double thirds in bb.249 – 50. If you really carry out the cross-rhythm effect indicated by the slurs, and play these thirds as vigorously accented triplets, they are quite easy to manage (although the effect to the listener is calculatedly hectic!). Steady yourself with precisely placed and vigorous 'normal' detached quaver thirds in b.251, and 'go to' a firm crotchet third on the 1st beat of b.252 as you carry out the same effect in the LH. Carry on forcefully with the detached LH thirds ascending through b.254 as you prepare to enter exultantly with the opening theme on the RH upbeat to b.255.

bb.255 – 305   Play the inner LH broken sixths through bb.259 – 61 as if they are slurred, over sturdy lower quavers, and 'go to' a firm crotchet chord on the 1st beat of b.262. From the upbeat to b.263 Haydn 'develops' his idea from b.132 in reversed hands. Be sure that the LH maintains its 'lead' here, and is not overbalanced by your neatly placed RH figures. Then transfer the 'lead' to the RH on the 1st beat of b.268, 'leaning' warmly on the chords on the 1st beat of bb.268 – 72 over a neatly articulated LH. Listen to the treble melodic fragment descending from the upbeat to b.272 to the 1st beat of b.274. Be careful to balance your leap up to the hilarious high F on the 3rd beat of b.279, with a neat LH accent on the 1st beat of b.280, or your rhythm will topple. Go *pianissimo* at b.282, and then keep up the suspense of the protracted joke through to b.294 (keeping a taut pulse, and not forgetting the sudden *forte* bump at b.289). You could either *crescendo* steeply from the *piano* at b.291, or burst in with a sudden *forte* at b.294. Then hurtle down (but in perfect time) to the low F sharps at b.302, with the same effect as at b.192, ready to enter with the horn-call motif at b.305.

bb.305 – 405   From b.324 Haydn develops his cross-rhythm outburst in even more dramatic fashion than at bb.88 – 113. *Crescendo* through bb.346 – 7 up to the 1st beat of b.348, and skip exuberantly down towards strong slurred dotted crotchet thirds on the 1st beat of b.352. Then *diminuendo* towards b.355 with neatly placed detached quaver chords on the 1st beat of bb.354 – 5, ready to lead in boldly with the LH on the upbeat to b.356. Haydn appears to be launching into a restatement of the material from b.29, but nothing is left alone for long, and in b.367 he veers off in a new direction. Lead off enthusiastically in the RH here, supported by even LH semiquavers, and from b.372 drive on towards the 1st beat of b.379 with vigorously articulated semiquavers in both hands, giving clear sharp accents with the fifth fingers on the 1st beat of these bars. Go immediately *piano* on the 2nd beat of b.379, and then burst in with the *fortissimo* dominant 7th chords on the 2nd beat of b.383. Alternatively you could *diminuendo* towards b.379, and then make a steep *crescendo* from b.381. In either case 'go to' an emphatic E flat chord on the 1st beat of b.385, and then articulate the downward run with all possible brilliance, 'joining in' confidently with the LH on the second semiquaver of b.389. 'Lead' clearly with the low LH fragments through bb.393 – 4 etc, starting in each case with a strong *sforzato* quaver, and taking care not to sound muddy (particularly in the RH) in this low register. Drive on forcefully towards firm unison quaver C's on the 1st beat of b.405, supporting your offbeat RH semiquaver fragments with resonant LH thirds on the 1st beat of bb.399 – 402.

bb.406 – 67   Collect yourself on the quaver rest in b.405, ready to lead in with the slurred quaver upbeat for the final onslaught. 'Lean' dashingly in both hands on the slurred upbeats to bb.410 – 12, and 'point' the jokey high quavers on the 2nd beat of bb.406, 409 – 11 and 413. Then pursue the piece of contrapuntal byplay clearly from bb.417 – 21. Support, but do not swamp, the RH with a clear inner LH line from b.423, over a resonant dominant pedal point. Veer hectically upwards from b.438 as from b.62. Then plummet to a firm (and slightly 'held') bass quaver G 'going to' a resonant A flat on the 1st beat of b.445 in a resolute interrupted cadence. Work upwards in a vigorous *forte* through bb.446 – 9, showing the alternating RH-LH *sforzato* upbeats. Then feel that you are 'opening out' from b.449 towards b.453. The octave *glissando* effect intended by Haydn in bb.454, 456 and 458 is unthinkable for most of us on the modern piano. Rip down in both hands therefore to vigorous *staccato* quavers on the 3rd beat of these bars. Give resonant LH chords on the 1st beat of bb.457 and 458, 'going to' an even stronger chord on the 1st beat of b.459. Then place the detached quaver thirds quietly and with immaculate precision on the 3rd and 1st beats of bb.459 – 62. *Wait* through the rests, *feeling* the silent beats, then slur the *pianissimo* LH thirds and RH sixths neatly from the upbeats to bb.465 and 466, and end with ringing final chords, all in perfect time.

20 Variations in G major
(Hob. XVII/2) (2-6)

Arietta in A major with 12 Variations
(Hob. XVII/2) (2-6)

The original version of this set of variations is the one in G major, written *c.*1765. The shortened version in A major was published, along with the Arietta and 12 Variations in E flat, in 1788/9.

20 Variations in G major

Although no one is likely to want to perform (nor to listen to) all twenty Variations, there are several attractive numbers. Variations, by their nature, make excellent teaching material, and various selections could be made for players from Grade 6 downwards. The Theme, with a selection from Variations 1, 2, 4, 11 (omitting the octaves for small hands), and perhaps ending with No. 5, would be good at Grade 3. At Grade 4, a set could be made up to include one or two of the above, with the addition of Nos. 8 and 14, and at Grade 5, perhaps Nos. 6, 7, 12 and 13.

Theme (2 – 3)

The Theme, and by inference the whole work (since the Variations adhere closely to the framework and harmony of the Theme), can be approached either in an easy *Andante* style, or alternatively in a more rumbustious *Allegro*. In either event the musical points remain substantially the same, but where possible differences of style seem particularly marked, I refer below to the *Andante* approach as a), and the more 'virtuosic' *Allegro* style as b). And while my own preference is for style b), style a) is, of course, more appropriate for very young or inexperienced players.

a) Play the Theme with absolute simplicity in an easy *Andante* motion at which the melody line will sing flowingly over unhurried LH triplets. Practise the LH alone until your triplets are perfectly even and secure. Lead in, in the RH, with a clear crotchet upbeat. Here, and through all the Variations, there is the sense of 'lean' on the upbeat leading into bb.1 and 9. Be sure to give these upbeats their full value while at the same time feeling this sense in which they give an onward 'lean'. Then phrase the melody line in gracious curves, supported by your evenly flowing LH triplets, feeling the impulse towards a warm-toned minim on the 1st beat of b.2, and then on towards a warmly slurred crotchet G on the 1st beat of b.4, and so on. Take care to finger this line carefully for a perfect *legato*. This necessitates changing fingers (4 – 5) on the minim A on the first beat of b.6, and also (2 – 3) on the crotchet B on the 2nd beat of b.7, and so on. Be sure to 'finish off' the LH clearly down to the crotchet G on the 2nd beat of b.8 (and similarly at the end of each section throughout the Variations), ready to lead on confidently with the upbeat to b.9. Feel the implied emphasis on the tied crotchet upbeat to bb.10 and 12, giving these notes sufficient tone to sing over the subsequent 1st beats so that the sound 'joins' smoothly with the crotchet on the 2nd beat of bb.10 and 12.

b) Lead off with brightly detached crotchets over 'keen' LH triplets. But as in a), take care to give your detached upbeats their full value and a feeling of onward-leading emphasis; and also as in a), feel the impulse towards the minim in b.2 and the slurred crotchet on the 1st beat of b.4, etc.

In whichever style you play, feel a sense of 'opening out' through the second half of the Theme, and all the Variations, with an overall dynamic curve in every instance towards bb.13 – 14.

Variation 1 (2 – 3)

Lead in from a clear RH upbeat and support your cleanly articulated RH triplets with a firm LH chord on the 1st beat of bb.1 and 5, and with *steady* LH crotchets thereafter. Do observe all LH rests. Take care to keep steady through bb.13 – 14. Feel a clear crotchet pulse through the LH and RH triplets in b.13. Then place the LH crotchet sixth firmly on the 3rd beat (keeping the RH offbeat triplet relatively light) with the feeling of 'going to' a firm LH triplet on the first beat of b.14. Then take care similarly to place the LH crotchet B clearly on the 3rd beat of b.14. You could play the triplets in this Variation a) in gracious and smooth curves, or b) in more rattling triplets underpinned with lively detached LH crotchets.

Variation 2 (2 – 3)

Lead in a) in a rather subdued, very even tone, or b) in a more bucolic 'churning' style, and support your RH with very steady and even LH quavers through bb.1 – 3 and 9 – 12. Feel that your even RH crotchets are 'going to' the 1st beat of b.2, and be sure to place the first of the two demisemiquavers *on* the 1st beat rather than anticipating it. Then feel that your even and steady LH crotchets are 'leading' through bb.5 – 8 and 13 – 16, with the syncopated RH line following smoothly.

Variation 3 (6)

Practise the RH alone until your (memorized) upward and downward leaps are quite secure. Feel that the RH is crossing back and forth in wide 'arcs', not in isolated 'plonks'. Then practise 'hands together', *slowly*, playing at first just one *chord* per bar in the LH (i.e. G major in b.1; D major, 1st inversion in b.2, etc), and then playing three crotchet chords per bar. Then when you practise the Variation as written, ensure that your LH triplets remain perfectly steady, and are not disrupted by the activities of the RH. Play this Variation with the utmost vitality. Lead into bb.1, 5, etc, with vigorous and steady but 'ongoing' upbeat semiquavers, and play the RH crotchet sixths etc, in a lively 'plucked' *staccato*. 'Lean' on the quaver appoggiatura on the 1st beat of bb.10 and 12, making a clear cross-rhythm effect against the LH triplets. If, however, this proves impossibly difficult, abandon the appoggiatura altogether (it is not given in the A major version).

Variation 4 (2 – 3)

Imagine a clear bassoon tone for the low registered RH melody line here. Balance the three lines carefully so that the RH is supported but not swamped by a smoothly sustained bass dotted minim line, and very even (but relatively lighter) inner LH crotchets. Make sure that the second LH crotchet never 'hangs' over the rest on the 1st beat of the subsequent bar.

Variation 5 (2 – 3)

Feel a *crescendo* up through the scale towards a ringing crotchet on the 1st beat of bb.2,

4, etc, always supporting your RH with firm and very steady LH crotchet chords. Then feel a dynamic curve up to and down from the semiquaver C on the 2nd *quaver* pulse of b.6, supported by LH chords which 'go to' a firm chord on the 1st beat of b.6 (but do be sure to come *off* on the 2nd beat). *Crescendo* upwards again towards a ringing crotchet on the 3rd beat of bb.10 and 12. Be sure to give full value to these 3rd beats so that you don't 'fall into' bb.11 and 13.

Variation 6 (5)

Lead in from a clear and accurately timed dotted rhythm upbeat, and then be sure that the RH 'leads' right through the first section, and again from the upbeat to b.13. Feel that the clear and vigorous LH scales are fitting in with your steady but lively detached RH crotchet thirds and *not* the other way about. Then after the double bar support your RH with resonant LH chords on the 1st beat of bb.9 and 11, and with clear and very steady LH fragments from the upbeat to bb.10 and 12. Take care to synchronize the hands immaculately from these upbeats to bb.10 and 12, so that you 'go to' and 'finish off' cleanly with the crotchets on the 2nd beat of bb.10 and 12, ready to lead on with a vigorous RH dotted rhythm upbeat. Take care also to keep the LH steady through b.15 by marking each group of LH semiquavers with a clear accent on the crotchet beat.

Variation 7 (5)

Here take a firm 'lead' with the LH. Go from a firm dominant 7th upbeat chord to a strong crotchet third on the 1st beat of b.1. Enter on the offbeat in the RH without making a bump, and feel you are making a *crescendo* up towards the semiquaver D on the 3rd beat of the bar, supported by your firm LH crotchet third which will in turn 'go to' another firm chord on the 1st beat of b.2 and so on. Then let the RH semiquavers in b.3 'go to' a strong crotchet D on the 1st beat of b.4, with the *LH* this time entering without a bump, and *crescendoing* up to a strong quaver D on the 3rd beat. Then 'place' the LH upbeat dominant 7th quaver chord carefully so that you don't 'fall into' the crotchet third on the 1st beat of b.5. *Crescendo* exuberantly from the double bar through to the end, making a rising 'churning' effect up to a ringing high RH semiquaver on the 3rd beat of each bar, keeping your pulse firmly in control with the help of firm and very steady LH chords.

Variation 8 (4)

Give this Variation a mock 'martial', tin-soldier style. When you practise the little repeated note figure, feel that the relatively light semiquavers are 'going to' a clear detached quaver on each crotchet beat, and that overall you are 'going through' to a firm slurred quaver on the 1st beat of b.2. You can either change fingers 3-2-1 on the repeated notes in the conventional way, or, as many pianists now do, use the same finger, preferably the third. Support your RH with very steady crotchet thirds through bb.1, 5, etc, feeling that the RH is fitting in with these steady LH crotchets and *not* the other way about. Then feel that the LH is continuing to 'lead' through bb.2 – 4, 6 – 8, etc, with the RH detached quavers following evenly and relatively lightly.

Variation 9 (6)

It is by no means easy to balance the rather growly, but at the same time, warm-toned inner LH melody line with the accompanying RH semiquavers. Practise the LH carefully alone until it is perfectly steady and as smooth as possible. Feel in b.1 that you are 'going to' the minim A on the 1st beat of b.2, and similarly in b.3 that you are 'going to' the chord on the 1st beat of b.4, 'leaning' well on the appoggiatura-like crotchet G, while listening at the same time to the resonance of the bass notes. When you put 'hands together' ensure that the RH semiquavers remain even and relatively light so that they balance but do not swamp the LH melody line. You can a) give a quietly contemplative feeling, or b) give the inner LH melody the effect of 'swimming' along in buoyant curves between the upper semiquavers and the lower sustained line. Avoid making a frantic lurch at the wide LH spread in b.2 by playing the lower D on the 1st beat of the bar, with the A more or less coinciding with the *second* RH semiquaver D. Listen to the nice clash of the LH B with the RH C on the 1st beat of b.10, and the LH C sharp with the RH D on the 1st beat of b.12.

Variation 10 (6)

Support your RH with resolute and steady LH crotchet octaves, and listen to the treble *quaver* line, ensuring that the inner semiquavers, particularly the offbeat inner drone (e.g. the D through bb.1 – 4 etc.), remain relatively light. Give these RH quavers and semiquavers an 'onward churning' character, either a) quietly determined, or b) somewhat frenetic (but steady!).

Variation 11 (2 – 3, omitting octaves if necessary)

This makes an excellent little study in the management of repeated and tied notes.

a) Learn to play the repeated LH crotchets (whether single notes or octaves) as smoothly as possible, that is, lifting the notes as little and as late as possible, so that the sound is almost continuous. Likewise with the RH thirds. Always feel that your LH is 'leading' like an evenly beating pulse. Then feel the gentle implied emphasis on the tied RH upbeat thirds, so that they sing over the subsequent 1st beats, but be careful not to let the RH 'hang on' over the rests on the 3rd beat of b.4 or the 1st beat of bb.11 or 13.

b) Alternatively, like John McCabe in his recording of these Variations, you could 'lean' with a slurred effect on the opening upbeat and similarly on the LH upbeat to each bar, then playing the 1st and 2nd LH octaves in each bar, and also all the *untied* RH crotchets, in a quietly detached style.

Variation 12 (5)

Lead in from smooth upbeat quavers and phrase the RH quaver line in expressive curves over very steady LH crotchet chords or single notes. Feel the 'lift' up to and down from the high second quaver in bb.1 and 5, and take care to 'finish off' cleanly in the RH on the 2nd beat of bb.4, 8, etc, ready to give a clear onward lead into bb.5, 9, etc, with the descending upbeat quaver figure. Listen carefully to the wide span of the melody line as it curves down to the low F sharp on the 2nd beat of b.12, and up again to the high D on the 2nd beat of b.14.

Variation 13 (5)

Feel a ländler or waltz-like rhythm here, with a substantial bass octave on the 1st beat of every bar, and rather definite thirds on the 2nd and 3rd beats. Articulate your RH semiquaver upbeat up towards a clear crotchet on the 1st beat of b.1. Then be sure that your downward semiquaver scale enters precisely between your LH crotchet thirds on the 2nd and 3rd beats of b.1, exactly *on* the 4th quaver pulse of the bar, with the feeling of 'going to' a firm slurred crotchet on the 1st beat of b.2, and so on.

Variation 14 (4)

Define your ascending RH dotted rhythm figures very precisely over steady LH crotchet thirds, and with the feeling of 'going to' a strong tied crotchet on the 1st beat of b.2. The Henle edition does not give the turns on the 1st beat of bb.4 – 7, and they are, in practice, almost impossible to 'get in' without completely disrupting your rhythm (certainly so for an inexperienced player). Either resort to short appoggiaturas interpreted as acciaccaturas, as in bb.10 – 12, or leave them out altogether. Increase the tone after the double bar with stronger LH chords, supporting the RH with firm LH chords.

Variation 15 (6)

This Variation with its minuet-like rhythm makes an excellent little rhythmic study. Let your accurately timed semiquaver upbeat 'go to' a firm crotchet on the 1st beat of b.1, and then time the RH dotted rhythm and trill precisely, over evenly placed LH crotchet octaves, feeling that you are 'going to' the slurred crotchet on the 1st beat of b.2. Give

the trill six notes starting on the upper note: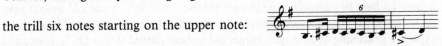

Always feel that you are 'going to' a firm crotchet on the 1st beat of each bar which, in every instance save for b.4, is unaccompanied, and then be sure to place the LH precisely on each 2nd and 3rd beat. Editions vary as to the interpretation of the hemidemisemiquaver upbeats. In practice you will have to play the upbeat to bb.3 and 7 just like four hemidemisemiquavers; then most editions, but not the Vienna Urtext, give the 'upbeats' to the *3rd* beat of b.7 and the *1st* beat of b.8 (and similarly to the 3rd beat of bb.10 and 12) as hemidemisemiquaver *triplets*. To play these as the Vienna Urtext Edition indicates is very difficult, and even if you can manage it, the difference will be almost undetectable! In any event, be sure that you give sufficient value to the rests on the 3rd beat of bb.2 and 6 etc, and to the dotted quavers on the 2nd and 3rd beats of b.7 etc, so that you 'flick' the hemidemisemiquaver 'upbeats' down rapidly and lightly to arrive on a firm slurred crotchet (or dotted quaver) *exactly* on the subsequent crotchet beat. Keep yourself steady throughout with the help of immaculately placed LH crotchet octaves, taking care to place them *equally* on the 1st and 2nd beats of bb.1, 2, etc, and avoiding 'hanging on' over the 1st beat of bb.2, 3, etc.

Variation 16 (6)

Practise the LH thoroughly, alone. Make a sharp light accent with the fifth finger on each bass note, and keep the upper notes relatively light and perfectly articulated. Practising

in dotted rhythms will help:　　♩. ♪♩. ♪　and　♩ ♪♪♪　etc. Ensure that you can

play the LH perfectly rhythmically before you put 'hands together'. Then lead off with resonant RH *legato* thirds, and play the RH throughout in a smooth and sustained style (in contrast to your 'whirling' LH semiquavers), ensuring through slow practice that the hands are perfectly co-ordinated.

Variation 17 (6)

The essential here is to maintain a very steady crotchet pulse so that the semiquaver figures alternate perfectly evenly between the hands. Let your upbeat semiquavers 'go to' a clear *quaver* on the 1st beat of b.1. Then always be quite clear where your crotchet pulse falls, i.e. on the LH then the RH G on the 2nd and 3rd beats of b.1. Then feel that the RH is 'going to' a clear *LH* quaver on the 1st beat of b.2, rather than leaving off in mid-air at the end of b.1, and so on. Be sure that the hands 'take over' cleanly from each other, and never 'hang on' over the rests. Let the LH 'lead' with firm crotchet octaves through b.7, with the RH semiquavers following relatively lightly, but with the RH upbeat 'going to' a firm crotchet third on the 1st beat of b.8. Lead off again in the LH after the double bar with clear and lively 'plucked' quavers, with the RH semiquavers again following relatively lightly. Then let the RH upbeat semiquaver 'go to' a clear quaver on the 1st beat of b.13, with the LH semiquaver in turn 'going to' a clear quaver on the *2nd* beat, and so on.

Variation 18 (6)

Practise carefully 'hands separately'. Give a very sustained quality to the RH lines. Feel the implied emphasis on the tied treble upbeat to b.2, and on the tied inner upbeat to b.3, giving these notes sufficient tone to sing over the subsequent 1st beats. Give the LH

trills six notes, starting on the upper note: 𝄢 When you put

'hands together' make sure that the RH leads, and that you feel a perfectly steady crotchet pulse in both hands. Always feel that you are 'going to' each 1st beat, so that the RH chord on each 1st beat has enough tone to balance the 'hole' left by the LH quaver rest. This effect is not easy to manage, and will require considerable concentration! It is helpful if, when you are practising at first, you forget the upbeat partial ties to bb.2, 3, etc, and play the *whole* of the chord on the 1st beat of bb.2, 3.

Variation 19 (6)

'Lean' well on the dotted quaver upbeat to bb.1, 3, etc, and 'flick' the two demisemiquavers down lightly to a clear quaver on the subsequent 1st beat. Then feel that the LH is 'leading' through bb.1, 3, etc, with perfectly measured detached quavers on the 2nd and 3rd beats, and with the RH detached quavers, also perfectly measured, following relatively lightly, with the feeling that you are 'going to' the subsequent minim chord. Be sure, though, that you do not 'skimp' the 3rd beat of these bars in your anxiety to reach the high RH chord. There is more time than you think, provided that you keep your *LH* perfectly steady through bb.1, 3, etc. (and don't take the easy way out by taking the RH upbeat quaver with the LH − the effect will not be the same; allow a tiny natural break in the RH as you leap upwards, so that you can 'point' the chord with a *sforzato* effect in both hands). Then make sure that your bright, clear chords (bb.6 − 8) are immaculately timed. 'Feel' the silent 2nd beat of b.6 and the 1st beat of b.7, so that you 'come in', precisely in time, with neat, sharp semiquaver 'upbeats' to the 3rd beat of b.6 and to the 2nd beat of b.7. Keep very steady again through bb.13 and 14, always feeling that the LH is 'leading' so that the LH *crotchet* chord on the upbeat to bb.14 and 15 is stronger than the treble *quaver* chord.

Variation 20 (6)(O)

The LH tenths in bb.2, 4, etc. have been the subject of much scholarly discussion. For most of us they are, of course, unplayable, but on the other hand, the 'compressed' alternative given on the lower stave gives a rather thick and growling effect. To play all LH chords in a slightly spread, strumming, 'churning' style gives a splendid hurdy-gurdy effect, but this is a tall order for relatively inexperienced players. Another solution is to play the original version but only on the *1st* beat of bb.2, 4, etc. (with the bass note played first − on the beat − and the upper third played together, rather than spreading the whole

chord) thus: 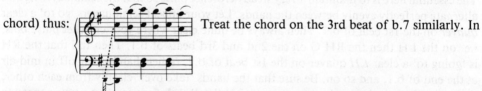 Treat the chord on the 3rd beat of b.7 similarly. In

any event the essential is to keep the LH chords rock-steady, changing the pedal with each chord. Let your RH octave lines curve as smoothly and resonantly as possible (showing the offbeat slurred effect through bb.1, 2, etc.), and be sure to keep the syncopated line in bb.3, 7, and particularly 10 and 12, very steady, feeling that the LH chords are 'leading', and holding the RH crotchets until *after* you have changed the pedal on each LH chord so that the RH line sounds continuous.

Arietta in A major with 12 Variations

In this shortened version of the G major Variations, the Variations are arranged in a different order. If you have only this set, you could again make a little selection for Grade 3 of Variations 1, 4 and 5 (see above – 20 Variations in G major). For comments on the Variations in the Arietta refer to the corresponding Variation in the G major set above, as shown in the following table:

Arietta	G major Variations
1	1
2	5
3	6
4	2
5	7
6	3
7	13
8	14
9	16
10	(see below)
11	17
12	10

Variation 10 (5) is new. Learn to 'snap' the semiquavers neatly *on* the beat (but in a gentle, not too clipped manner) by practising the rhythm in five-finger exercises. Make sure that you give an overall *legato* effect through bb.3, 7, etc, rather than letting the hand come off between each beat, and lean a little on each slurred snapped semiquaver so that each beat is lightly accented. 'Go through' from the crotchet upbeat to a firm semiquaver on the 1st beat of b.1, and be sure that your LH quavers enter precisely (and without a bump) on the 2nd quaver pulse of the bar, that is, immediately after your RH dotted quaver. Then keep the LH quaver line processing in perfectly even and smooth curves to support your quaintly humorous RH 'snaps'. Do take the RH *off* on the 2nd beat of bb.1 and 2, and 'go up' to an emphasized minim on the 2nd beat of bb.5 and 6.

Arietta in E flat major with 12 Variations

(Hob. XVII/3) (7)*

The theme of this entrancing set of Variations is taken from the Minuet from the String Quartet Op. 9 No. 2 (Hob. III/20).

Theme

Set a steadily moving minuet-like **3/4**. Imagine the clear sound of the solo violin, and feel the 'string' quality of the accompanying chords as you play the treble melody with expressive simplicity over very even, just-detached LH crotchet chords. Let the repeated melody notes 'speak' through bb.2 and 3, and feel you are 'going towards' a warmly slurred minim on the 1st beat of b.4 over sustained lower dotted minims. Listen to the contrary motion movement of the inner and lower parts in bb.5 and 6 (with a quiet emphasis on the minim chords on the 2nd beats) as you slur the treble minims up to warmly emphasized (not bumped) crotchets on the 3rd beats. Treat the appoggiatura on the 1st beat of b.7 like a gentle, not too clipped acciaccatura, and curve the melody line eloquently down to the low register in the middle of b.8, and up again towards a warm, gently stressed dotted crotchet on the 2nd beat of b.9. Be sure to 'finish off' the LH neatly down to the 3rd beat of b.10 (and similarly in b.20, and in corresponding instances throughout the Variations), and then continue equally eloquently, perhaps in a rather fuller tone from the double bar. Here, and throughout the Variations, never become so carried away with the beauty of your playing that you forget the quiet 'stepping' pulse of the minuet rhythm!

Variation 1

Support your RH through bb.1 and 2 with very even LH quavers, and then through bb.3 – 4 listen to the sustained LH lines showing the implied emphasis on the inner tied crotchet upbeat to b.4 beneath your evenly slurred RH quavers. Feel the very gentle implied emphasis on the syncopated crotchet B flats in b.2, and on the syncopated crotchets on the 2nd quaver pulse of bb.5 and 6 (and also on the inner and lower minims in bb.5 and 6 and in bb.15 and 16, as in the Theme). Then let your slurred RH quavers curve smoothly through bb.7 – 10 over very even LH crotchets. Shape the treble melodic fragments expressively from the double bar, over continuingly even LH quavers. 'Lean' gently on the tied crotchet on the 1st beat of b.11, and on the slurred quavers on the 1st beat of bb.12 – 14, feeling the rests in these bars like 'breath' points. Then listen acutely to the intervals of the wide-curving treble line from b.15.

Variation 2

As so often, and particularly here, the poise and eloquence of the RH is dependent on the immaculate placing of the LH chords. Support the RH, therefore, with a clearly placed crotchet octave on the 1st beat of b.1, and with precisely placed even-toned crotchet thirds on the 2nd and 3rd beats, and the 1st and 2nd beats of b.1. Take particular care to place the LH crotchet third accurately on the 2nd beat of b.2 beneath the RH tied crotchet to give a neat rhythmic springboard for the ascending RH run. Then ensure that the RH scale, 'entering' exactly on the 4th *quaver* pulse of the bar (without a bump) is perfectly timed to arrive on the top E flat precisely on the 1st beat of b.3. It is essential to the poised execution of this scale run (and similarly to the sextuplet downward runs in bb.5 – 7) that the *LH* crotchets are immaculately placed on the 2nd beats of these bars. Then through bb.8 – 9 feel that the steady LH crotchets are 'leading' with the RH offbeat quaver chords following steadily. From b.12 let your RH semiquaver fragments 'speak' as expressively as possible, feeling the rests again like 'breath' points, supported by quietly but firmly placed LH crotchet chords.

Variation 3

Do be sure to 'feel' the held 2nd beat of b.2, and then listen acutely to the beautiful resonances of the tied treble *and* inner RH notes, held over the LH dotted minim B flat through the 1st and 2nd beats of b.4. Then listen to the subtle chromatic inflections of the syncopated RH line through bb.7 – 10 (and again to the syncopated RH fourths, fifths and sixths, bb.17 – 20) over very even LH crotchets. Listen also to the expressive interplay between the treble and inner lines through bb.11 – 14.

Variation 4

Let your RH semiquavers curl smoothly and expressively over very even LH chords through bb.1 – 4, being careful to show the quaver rest on the 1st beat of b.2. Then be sure to maintain a steady crotchet pulse from b.5 as the semiquaver figuration flows evenly between the hands. Lead off with a clear RH crotchet on the 1st beat of b.5; then feel that the LH semiquaver fragment is 'going to' the crotchet 2nd beat, with the RH semiquavers in turn 'going to' the crotchet on the 1st beat of b.6 and so on. Then support your LH scale figure with steady detached RH crotchets through b.7, and your *RH* semiquavers with firm *LH* crotchets through b.8 and so on.

Variation 5

The eloquence of the ornamented RH line here is once again dependent on the foundation provided by steady and even LH chords. Let the ornamental dotted rhythm figure rise smoothly to a singing tied minim on the 1st beat of b.2 showing the expressive melodic curve onwards up to the high E flat, and down to the G on the 2nd beat of b.3. The turns in b.1 can either be placed *on* the dotted quavers, starting on the upper note, or immediately *after* the dotted quavers. In either case they are tricky to fit in without interfering with the poise of the semiquaver 'upbeat' to the 2nd and 3rd beats of the bar. Place the LH third clearly but *quietly* on the 3rd beat of b.3 so that it supports but does not drown the singing tone of the held dotted crotchet G; then in b.4 be sure to 'feel' and give full value to the held treble A natural on the *2nd* beat of the bar, above the LH minim chord. Slur the RH semiquaver couplets neatly through the 1st beat of bb.5 and 6, and feel that you are 'going to' and 'leaning' upon, the slurred crotchets on the 2nd beat of these bars. 'Lean' also upon the slurred RH quavers on the 1st beat of bb.7 – 10, and let the RH quaver notes and fragments through bb.7 – 10 'speak' expressively over your precisely placed LH fifths and sixths.

Variation 6

Support your swathes of clearly but smoothly articulated semiquavers with firm and perfectly timed LH crotchet octaves on the 1st beat of bb.1 – 3, with clearly placed chords on the 1st and 2nd beats of bb.5 and 6, and with a steady crotchet line from the upbeat to b.8. Hold all the supporting LH crotchets for their exact value and no more. Feel that you are 'going to' a firm slurred minim on the 1st beat of b.4 over perfectly timed LH crotchet B flats.

Variation 7

Do not panic at the sight of the demisemiquaver run on the 1st beat of b.3. This will fit in easily to your crotchet pulse. Start from a rather firm LH semiquaver on the 1st beat of the bar, and run up in an improvisatory manner to arrive on a clear treble G exactly on the 2nd beat of the bar. Feel the slurred quavers on the 1st beat of bb.5 and 6 like little sighs. Nothing in the first six bars prepares us for the startling unison interjections from b.7. Articulate the demisemiquaver turns briskly up to strong *sforzato* quavers on the 2nd beat of bb.7 and 8, then 'pluck' the unison quavers vigorously, and 'finish off' the LH crotchets firmly down to the 3rd beat of b.10. Then resume the serene movement from the double bar, shaping the syncopated RH treble line expressively through bb.12 – 15 over evenly moving lower lines (practise these LH lines carefully alone, listening acutely to the resonances of all tied and held notes).

Variation 8

Start this Variation with a burst of *brio*, and support your vigorously 'plucked' RH triplets with clear LH crotchet chords on the 1st beat of bb.1 – 3. Then phrase the *legato* RH triplets more graciously from b.5 over carefully placed LH chords on the 1st and 2nd beats of bb.5 and 6, and over a smooth LH crotchet line from the 2nd beat of b.7. Let the detached triplets alternate evenly between the hands from b.11, being quite clear (though without too obvious accents) where your crotchet pulse falls, particularly in bb.12 and 14 (i.e. on the B natural, and the A flat and the F in b.12, etc.)

Variation 9

'Lean' lightly with the thumb on the slurred quaver broken octaves in b.2, and treat the semiquaver octaves on the 3rd beat as if they are also slurred, supporting your RH as always with an even and steady LH. Ensure that the treble minims sing clearly through the 1st and 2nd beats of bb.5 and 6 over the inner RH and LH quaver figures, and steady lower LH crotchets. Feel that the LH quavers are 'leading' from the 2nd beat of b.7 and 'going down to' a firm *sforzato* chord on the 2nd beat of b.8. The Vienna Urtext Edition gives the RH in bb.11 and 13 as a tied dotted crotchet with a demisemiquaver 'turn', whereas Henle gives a dotted crotchet and semiquaver triplet. The former version gives a more refined effect. Who, hearing the romantic-sounding broken octave figure in bb.12 and 14 out of context, would attribute these bars to Haydn? Treat the slurred grace notes like expressive and not too clipped acciaccaturas. Feel that you are 'going to' a singing dotted crotchet octave on the 1st beat of b.13, and similarly to the crotchet on the 1st beat of b.15 (and be careful not to hurry the remainder of this bar, taking a fraction of extra time to show the 'lift' up to, and down from the high quaver F at the end of the bar).

Variation 10

Articulate the little offbeat LH interjection in bb.1 and 2 (and the longer semiquaver line through bb.3 and 4) cleanly beneath a resonant RH line. Then in bb.5 and 6 support your ascending treble figure with firm and steady LH crotchet chords on the 1st and 2nd beats. 'Lead' through bb.7 – 8 with clear and steady LH detached crotchets, keeping your neat ornamented RH figures relatively light. Execute the turns thus  and ensure that the last note of each turn does not 'hang over' the subsequent semiquaver rest.

Variation 11

Try to feel the melody line in continuing widely curving arcs from b.3 onwards, rather than in isolated 'plonks', as it rises and dips between the upper and lower register. Show the implied singing emphasis on the high dotted crotchet on the 2nd beat of b.3 and then curve down to 'go to', and to 'lean' warmly on the slurred minim chord on the 1st beat of b.4. Feel also the emphasis on the tied crotchet C flat on the 2nd beat of b.7, on the syncopated crotchet E flat in b.9, and on the tied crotchet on the 2nd beat of bb.12 and 14. Be sure yet again to support all these smooth RH swoops with a perfectly stable LH.

Variation 12

Support your RH with even, yet 'keen' LH semiquavers through bb.1 and 2, and then let the LH quavers 'lead' through b.3 as they rise evenly, over a sustained lower dotted minim, towards a firm 1st beat of b.4. Treat the perky RH grace notes in bb.5 and 6 like acciaccaturas, and steady yourself in these bars with neatly articulated LH semiquaver fragments, 'going to' a rather firm quaver on the 2nd beat. Let the LH quavers 'lead' through b.7 down towards a firm minim on the 1st beat of b.8. Keep your inner LH quavers very steady through bb.11 – 14 over resonant lower dotted minims, as in b.3, as you listen to the diminishing or widening 'broken' intervals of the RH semiquaver figures. Take care to articulate these RH semiquavers cleanly and neatly rather than letting them get 'flappy'. Since this last variation lacks a sense of finality, Franz Eibner, Editor of the Vienna Urtext Edition, makes the excellent suggestion of ending the work by playing the theme again.

6 Easy Variations in C major

(Hob. XVII/5) (6)

Variations in D major

(Hob. XVII/7) (5)

(Not published in the Vienna Urtext Edition, see below.)

Variations on the Anthem 'Gott Erhalte' (7)

We will pass over these three sets of Variations. Although they have a certain tinkling, musical box charm, the patterns of the Variations in C are of too conventional a kind to detain the player, in view of the vast selection of music in the Grade 6 – 7 range. The set of five Variations in D is given by Henle in the Appendix to their volume of miscellaneous pieces. This is a keyboard version of an earlier trio movement. The Variations are built on an unchanging 'ground' with a bass octave 'drone' effect alternating between tonic and dominant, producing an amusing overall 'churning' effect. But this is not really apt material for study or performance, although the Variations might have a use in demonstrating to a student how to let the LH 'take the lead'.

Haydn took immense pains with the commission to compose the melody of 'Gott Erhalte', which was to become the Austrian, then the German National Anthem. This is Haydn's arrangement of the Variation movement from his String Quartet Op. 76 No. 3 *(Emperor)*, which had the anthem as its theme. It feels unseemly, to say the least, to be tinkling around the keyboard with this great string music! But devotees of Haydn will find much of interest in the Variations which, however, are far from easy to bring off. (This arrangement is published for the first time in the Vienna Urtext Edition.)

Andante con Variazione in F minor

(Hob. XVII/6) (8)*

This is the best-known and loved of Haydn's single works for the piano. There are two themes, the first (bb.1 – 29) in F minor, the second (bb.30 – 49) in F major. (Since there are no clear divisions between the variations, the bar numbers run continuously.)

bb.1 – 12   The first theme is wistfully melancholic with the delicately piquant dotted rhythm motif entering as if 'suspended' over the *legato* harmonic movement of the LH. Establish a gently moving **2/4** at which the opening bars 'move' rather than feel sticky, but at which, on the other hand, the demisemiquavers and ornamented figuration from b.14 will not sound rushed. Practise the LH carefully alone, slurring the inner quavers smoothly over the *tenuto* lower crotchet line through bb.1 – 3. Then shape the two sustained LH lines carefully and expressively through bb.4 – 6, listening acutely to the smooth movement of each. Show the implied emphasis on the syncopated inner tied B flat on the 2nd quaver pulse of b.4, giving this note sufficient tone to sing over the 1st beat of b.5, and make sure similarly that the tied crotchet F on the 2nd beat of b.5 sings over the 1st beat of b.6, *listening* to the resonances of these inner notes over the sustained lower notes. Then when you put 'hands together', let this LH give a smooth, quietly moving foundation for your exquisitely poised RH melody line, being sure to listen just as carefully to the LH through bb.4 – 6 as you did when practising it alone. Enter *mezzo-voce* in the treble precisely on the 4th quaver pulse of b.1, with the feeling of 'going to' the slurred quaver on the 1st beat of b.2. Define the dotted rhythms neatly, but in a gently detached 'speaking' manner, and not spikily. *Crescendo* gently to lead into b.4 in a full, rather than loud tone, feeling the peak of your *crescendo* curve on the 2nd beat of b.4 in the RH and on the tied inner B flat in the LH. Incorporate the turn smoothly into your eloquently phrased melody line in b.5, and *decrescendo* downwards to 'lean' quietly but warmly on the treble B natural on the 1st beat of b.6. (Do ensure that the *inner* RH quaver A flat enters quietly on the 2nd quaver pulse of b.6, and in such a manner that it does not sound like a treble melody note.) 'Finish off' the phrase neatly in both hands in b.6 before leading on quietly with the RH from b.7. Practise the *RH* alone here, listening again to the tied and held notes, so that it, in its turn, will give a quiet and smooth foundation for the *LH* melody line. When you put 'hands together', listen acutely to the balance between the hands, taking care that you do not become so carried away by the beautiful resonances of the RH that you allow the LH to be swamped through bb.8 – 9. Then when the dotted rhythm line moves back to the treble in b.10, notice how the inner line moves down to the LH on the emphasized tied quaver upbeat to b.11. Finish off the section with a perfectly timed bass *piano* dotted rhythm broken octave figure.

Lead off with the LH again in b.13 with a rather brighter tone. Phrase the
bb.13 – 29   ornamented treble line smoothly and lightly through bb.14 and 15, over your
continuingly smooth LH, listening particularly to the sustained *lower* line. It is best here if the written out turns *anticipate* the two demisemiquavers, in other words if they follow on almost immediately after the semiquaver on the 2nd beat of these bars (the B flat and A flat respectively). Let the RH skip gently down through b.16 as you 'go to' and lean upon the slurred ornamented crotchet on the 1st beat of b.17, placing the grace notes *on* this 1st beat. (Show also the tied inner LH quaver upbeat to this bar.) 'Finish off' the phrase neatly again before leading on smoothly but purposefully with the semiquaver upbeat thirds to b.18. Let the RH cross deftly and in perfect time back and forth from bass to treble through bb.18 – 19, supported by your continuingly smooth and steady LH. Feel here that the RH is fitting in with this steady LH and *not* the other way about. Then move in an implied *crescendo* towards the 1st beat of b.22, avoiding shrillness as the RH goes higher by giving good support with the LH detached thirds moving in contrary motion. Alternatively you can *diminuendo* expressively towards b.22 (and similarly in corresponding circumstances in the variations). Then, observing the quaver rest, place the quaver chord precisely and quietly on the 2nd beat of b.22, before leading off in a full tone with the RH in b.23. Keep a very steady RH here as the LH in turn crosses from bass to treble as you *crescendo* towards the tremendous *tenuto sforzato* spread G flat major chord at b.25. Most pianists retain this chord, with judicious half-pedalling, through the little cadenza-like descending *piano* figure through b.26 to good effect. Finish the section in immaculate time, right down to the low bass quaver, as in b.12. As will be evident, there is a great deal of detail to attend to. Even an experienced artist coming freshly to this work needs time to understand and fully assimilate the exquisite refinements of this theme. Do not imagine, therefore, that you can dispose of it in a brisk morning's practice.

The second theme is deliciously light and airy. Lead off *piano* with a smoothly
bb.30 – 9   singing RH line supported by even LH quavers as you *crescendo* towards
the 1st beat of b.31. The RH arabesques in bb.31, 35 – 6, etc. lie neatly under the hand, and are not difficult to manage providing that they are immaculately timed. 'Go to' and lean well upon the RH tied quaver on the first beat of b.31. Then having placed the second LH quaver precisely in time beneath your tied RH quaver, articulate

the demisemiquavers lightly in a perfectly clear kind of overall 'flick', showing the curve up to the top note C and down to a clear detached quaver (taken with the second finger) precisely on the 2nd beat of the bar. Then from the upbeat to b.32 articulate the RH figures lightly and neatly over even and steady LH quavers, with the feeling of 'going to' the slurred crotchet third on the 1st beat of b.33. 'Lean' again on the tied quaver on the 1st beat of b.35, and then 'flick' the demisemiquavers down to a firm-toned tied quaver on the 2nd beat of the bar, and so on. Change fingers (2 – 1) on this tied quaver on the 2nd beat of b.35, and similarly on the 1st beat of b.36, to preserve the smoothness of the line. As is so often the case the activities of the RH are entirely dependent on a reliable LH. Support your RH, therefore, with very steady LH quavers, either legato or slightly detached and feel that the RH is fitting in with these LH quavers, rather than the other way about. Keep steady as you *crescendo* through b.37 towards a sustained *sforzato* chord on the 1st beat of b.38. Flick your RH demisemiquavers neatly back to the detached quaver F to coincide precisely with the inner LH quaver D on the 2nd beat of the bar.

bb.40 – 9 Lead off with warm-toned RH thirds in b.40 over lightly articulated LH demisemiquaver figures. Then from the upbeat to b.42, support the RH with even LH quaver chords. Be sure to 'go to' and lean well upon the slurred and tied crotchets on the 1st beat of b.43, being sure to give this crotchet chord its full value, and to 'finish off' the RH cleanly on the 2nd beat, before leading on with the smooth semiquaver upbeat thirds into b.44. Do not panic when you see that the arabesques in bb.46 and 47 have eight *hemi*demisemiquavers instead of seven *demi*semiquavers. Providing that you 'flick' them lightly up to and down from the upmost note as before, the extra note fits in quite comfortably. Be sure as before to keep the supporting LH quavers perfectly steady. Many a player comes to grief in b.48. The secret here, of course, is to keep the *RH* quavers perfectly steady, and this time to let the *LH* fit in with the RH, instead of 'taking over' with the LH and arriving at the top D too soon, causing a general collapse, as usually happens! 'Lean' well on the LH tied quaver B flat and time the upward run so that the D coincides with the RH B flat exactly on the 2nd beat of the bar. This six-note run feels peculiarly leisurely after the eight-note figures in bb.46 and 47, so take special care to keep steady here.

bb.50 – 78 Lead off quietly and steadily in the LH in b.50 in the first variation of the minor theme, letting the offbeat treble semiquavers follow in a lightly detached (not spiky) and 'speaking' style and 'lean' warmly, not harshly, on the syncopated *sforzato* slurred quavers in b.52, observing the rests precisely. From bb.53 – 5 continue to listen to the LH just as carefully as you did in bb.4 – 6 as you let the RH scale 'fall' graciously from the high syncopated quaver, and merge smoothly into the syncopated line moving evenly over your steady LH through bb.54 – 5. Lead off quietly again in the RH in b.56, and be careful to place your LH offbeat semiquavers very quietly and accurately but eloquently (this is not so easy as it was in reverse in bb.50 – 1), particularly when the LH has to cross to the treble and back from the upbeat to b.60. From b.62 phrase the RH syncopated line smoothly and expressively over your even LH. Let the RH descend smoothly to a quiet but definite third on the 1st beat of b.66, so that the LH semiquavers can enter on the offbeat without a bump. Be careful to keep the LH steady through bb.67 – 8 as the RH crosses neatly back and forth. Ensure that each RH fragment 'goes to' the slurred quaver B natural on the 2nd beat of each of these bars, and be very careful not to 'bump' the treble semiquaver third at the end of each bar. Be quite clear that the LH is 'leading' here. Lead on with a firm LH in thirds, in *crescendo* towards the 1st beat of b.71, with the RH offbeat semiquavers, then demisemiquaver fragments following evenly and relatively lightly. Then, conversely, ensure that the RH leads from b.72. 'Draw out' the big RH/LH 'staggered' chords a little in b.74, and then take over the 'lead' with the 'single' LH demisemiquaver on the upbeat to b.75. Let this demisemiquaver flourish descend resonantly, 'pointing' the 'single' LH notes falling on each quaver beat (holding the sound of the big chords within the pedal) towards a strong LH diminished slurred crotchet chord on the 1st beat of b.76. Then 'take over' the lead with the RH again on the 1st beat of b.77, with the LH detached semiquavers following relatively lightly, as you *diminuendo* towards a *piano* ending of this section.

bb.79 – 98   Create a continuous chain of RH trills through b.83. Whether you start the trills on the upper or main note must be a matter of taste or convenience, the important thing is that the trills be continuous, and *that they fit in with steady LH quavers*. In b.84 and on the 1st beat of b.85 (and similarly in b.87), do not try to cram so many notes into the trills that you disrupt the basic dotted rhythm. You can either interpret these trills as suggested in the Vienna Urtext Edition

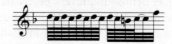

(perhaps with rather fewer notes) or 'stop' the trill fractionally earlier so that the semiquaver is given its precise value (the effect that I prefer). Practise at first without the trills, of course, and when you add the trills *ensure that the LH rules*. Otherwise total derailment is inevitable! (Similarly ensure that your LH trill on the 2nd beat of b.85 fits in with your steady *RH* thirds.) 'Tie over' the upper note of the upbeat third into b.86 so that you start this trill fractionally *after* the 1st beat, and then make another continuous chain of trills through the bar. In b.87 support the RH with firm LH crotchet chords and be sure that you do not skimp the 'plain' semiquavers on the 2nd and 4th quaver pulses of the bar. 'Tie over' the semiquaver G again into the 2nd beat, as with the upbeat to b.86. From b.89 practise the RH thoroughly, alone, and when you add the LH trill, concentrate on the *RH*, keeping the trill running easily and relatively lightly so that it does not (as usually happens) 'take over' and cause another collapse! Allow the inevitable and natural slight break as you leap up in the RH from the end of b.93, instead of lurching hectically upwards. (Few players are likely to take the course, optimistically implied by the fingering in the Vienna Urtext Edition, of playing the trills with the *LH* through b.93.) Fit in the LH trill with the steady RH quavers through the 1st beat of b.95, and vice versa through the 2nd beat. Hold fast to your crotchet pulse through b.96 feeling the quaver pulse running through the crotchet beats, while at the same time feeling that you are 'going towards' each main beat. Again through b.97 fit your ornamented RH in with your *even* LH quavers, defining the dotted rhythms neatly. In the last resort, everyone has to find their own ways of negotiating this alarming passage, which grows increasingly difficult from b.83 onwards. Be comforted by the knowledge that even seasoned performers feel they are walking a tightrope, reaching the most precarious moments at b.96! The vital thing is to keep the basic rhythmic framework steady, and to keep the trills running relatively lightly and easily *within* the framework, rather than allowing the trills to take over and sabotage your rhythmic security.

bb.99 – 127   Do not rush off in relief as you reach calm waters again, but lead off evenly in the LH at b.99, and let your RH demisemiquavers flow easily and fluently, feeling the natural dynamic rise and fall as the curves undulate (and similarly in reverse from b.105). Note the different detailing of the LH lines though bb.102 – 4 (compare with bb.4 – 6). Shape the smooth inner RH line through bb.108 – 10 with a warm tone. Practise the RH hand-crossing carefully through bb.116 – 17: you have to move back and forth very neatly and controlledly to avoid any untoward bumps. Be sure, as before in the corresponding passage in the theme and first variation, that you are leading clearly with the LH from b.116 and conversely with the RH from b.121. Feel the Beethovenian grandeur as you descend from the upbeat to b.124, and 'go to' and give full value to the resonant unison crotchet octaves on the 1st beat of b.125. Articulate the flourishes exuberantly through the 2nd beat of b.125, and the 1st beat of b.126, rising to perfectly placed detached semiquavers on the 4th quaver pulse of b.125 and the 2nd *quaver* pulse of b.126 respectively. Then spread the quaver chords ringingly, and 'finish off' the final flourish cleanly down to the bass quaver on the 2nd beat of b.127.

       In this major variation the essential once more is to keep steady. Lead off *bb.128 – 50* with warm-toned RH thirds, over even inner LH repeated semiquavers and a sustained lower tied F, feeling that you are 'going to' a clear RH semiquaver third and LH quaver on the 1st beat of b.129. Allow a tiny natural break as you leap calmly up to the high A, and as you descend through b.129 (and 131 and 133) keep steady by feeling the quaver pulse moving evenly within your RH triplet demisemiquavers, though without obvious accents. Then from the upbeat to b.130 let your RH *hemi*demisemiquaver figures fit in with your steady LH semiquavers and *not* the other way about. Then be sure that you return smoothly to *demi*semiquavers at the beginning of b.131, and that you do not hurry through this bar as you descend towards a warm crotchet A on the 1st beat of b.132. Note the lightly syncopating effect of the LH slurred offbeat semiquavers from the upbeat to b.134, and let your treble line 'go to' a warmly slurred crotchet sixth on the 1st beat of b.135, as the LH ascends very smoothly to 'meet' the resolving RH semiquaver sixth on the 2nd beat of this bar. Lead off clearly with the RH thirds through b.136 over easy-running LH demisemiquavers, which in turn 'go to' a warm-toned minim sixth to support the RH descending demisemiquavers through b.137. Be careful to time the LH upbeat semiquavers to b.140 accurately, and then to 'lead off' clearly with the LH on the 1st beat of b.140. One you have thoroughly studied this variation, do let the rather complex figuration sound as light and carefree as possible. The Vienna Urtext Edition includes five bars at the end of this variation which will be unknown to most players. See their comments re sources in the 'Critical Notes'. If you have this edition and decide to include these bars, play them in a free, improvisatory style. Support the resonant dominant 7th chords in b.146 with substantial LH demisemiquavers, showing the descending lower line clearly 'going to' a strong crotchet E on the 1st beat of b.147. Be sure that the LH demisemiquavers 'join in' smoothly with the RH on the offbeat in b.147. Spread the quaver chords with a ringing sound in b.149, and finish off the flourish cleanly in b.150 to allow a full quaver rest.

       For those not possessing the Vienna Urtext Edition, bar numberings from *bb.151 – 209* here will of course not tally. Numbers for other editions are given in brackets.

       Start quietly back into b.151 as in the theme. *Crescendo* (or *diminuendo*, see comments re b.22) towards the 1st beat of b.172 (167) as before. Then be sure to *wait* through the rests, *feeling* the silent beats, or you will spoil the magical surprise of the *piano* offbeat entry in b.173 (168) as Haydn leads us towards the final 'free' variation or coda. Time this fragment precisely and wait again, or you will, in turn, spoil the shock of the stentorian *forte* 'answering' chords in b.175 (170). Drop to a hushed *piano* on the 2nd quaver pulse of b.176 (171) and then feel the heightening intensity as you *crescendo* towards b.185 (180). Define the jerking RH dotted rhythms sharply over the ominously swirling LH *legato* thirds, like an approaching storm which will burst out in full fury with the upbeat to b.185 (180). On the other hand, there is a good case for subduing the tension of this passage and winding through bb.176 – 84 (171 – 9) in sinuous sighing curves. In either event, gather your forces on the *sforzato* upbeat chord to b.185 (180) for this searing passage,

referred to by John McCabe as 'one of the most powerful tragic outbursts in piano music',†
and keep the pulse under iron control right through until b.208 (203), where the tension
finally subsides in the approach to the reprise at b.210 (205). Give a ringing tone to the
tied high F on the 2nd beat of b.185 (180), and drive on towards b.191 (186) with a rigorously
rhythmic RH, rising with a lashing fifth finger to the high quavers on the main beats of
bb.186 – 90 (181 – 5), supported by vigorously pulsating LH demisemiquavers. Carry the
LH through to a strong crotchet octave on the 1st beat of b.191 (186), and then let the
RH runs fit in with the trumpeting and again rigorously rhythmic LH chords from bb.191 – 4
(186 – 9). *Crescendo* and *decrescendo* up to and down from the upmost notes of these
runs, timing those of bb.191 (186), 192 (187) and 193 (188) so that the top note falls on
the *2nd* beat of the bar (where the LH has a quaver rest). Above all, ensure that the LH
takes the lead, making the RH fit in with the LH and *not* the other way about. Feel that
the LH upbeat dotted rhythm chords are 'going to' even stronger crotchet chords on the
1st beat of bb.192 – 4 (187 – 9). In b.194 (189) space the run to fit the bar − it is effective
to make a *diminuendo* towards the semiquaver A on the 1st beat of b.195 (190). Allow
the sound to 'billow' from here, up to and down from the upmost notes of each
demisemiquaver sextuplet curve. Because the sextuplets do not divide evenly between the
hands, the rhythm can easily be lost here. Be clear that the 2nd and 4th sextuplet groups
begin on the *2nd* note of each RH group (i.e. the first RH E flat in each RH group, bb.195
and 196 (190 and 191)), though without making obvious accents. Keep steady also by feeling
that each RH group 'goes to' a clear demisemiquaver A natural on the 1st and 2nd crotchet
beats of bb.195 and 196, and so on. Although Haydn seems to imply a continuing *crescendo*
through to the 1st beat of b.199 (194) with a *subito piano* on the 2nd quaver pulse of the
bar, many pianists make a steep *diminuendo* through the second half of b.198 (193) with
good effect. In any event, poise yourself on the 1st beat of b.199 (194) for the return of
the steady LH 'theme' quavers with the RH dotted rhythm figures again crossing neatly
back and forth. Descend to quietest *pianissimo* through bb.201 – 3 (196 – 8) but without
losing the inner rhythmic tension. Then move in a dramatic *crescendo* through bb.204
and 205 (199 and 200) towards the *sforzato tenuto* LH chord held through from bb.206 – 9
(201 – 4) with the jagged RH figure rising towards the end of b.206 (201) and descending
in a gradual *diminuendo,* always in strictest time, save perhaps for the tiniest 'give' at
the very end of b.209 (204).

Lead off again in *pianissimo* and for the last time with your even LH quavers.
bb.210 – 33 Let the groups of five treble demisemiquavers 'curl' easily upwards within
(205 – 28) the LH quaver pulse through b.213 (208). In bb.215 – 16 (210 – 11) let the
LH demi-semiquaver arpeggios ascend cleanly towards the quavers on the 2nd beats, in
precise co-ordination with the steady RH quavers. From this point follow Haydn's detailed
indications scrupulously. Give full value to the powerful *sforzato* syncopated chords from
b.217 (212) and then be sure to hold the long *tenuto* LH chord right through from the
2nd quaver pulse of b.218 (213) as you listen to the beautiful far-away effect of the reiterated
piano treble figure. Show that these treble demisemiquavers are slurred down to the detached
quavers (and similarly in the LH from the upbeat to b.222 (217), beneath quietly placed
treble quaver chords). Give the low RH minim chord, and the tied LH minim E natural
on the 1st beat of b.223 (218) a full singing tone, and gradually 'tail away' the rising broken
dominant 7th, holding the whole within the pedal and *listening* to the sound through a
generous pause. Then allow the momentary silence of the quaver rest before the shock
of the *forte* chords (play these in perfect time) returning to *piano* on the cadential dominant

†*Haydn Piano Sonatas* (BBC Music Guides).

fifth on the 2nd beat of b.226 (221). Then from the b.227 (222) Haydn protracts his return to the final tonic in a tiny, kind of extra coda. Listen to his masterly orchestral colouring in the wide, but gradually decreasing space between the hands from the upbeat to bb.228 (223) and 230 (225), and end in a hushed but clear *pianissimo*, with little, if any, *rallentando* again save perhaps for a little 'give' in the penultimate bar.

Adagio in F major
(Hob. XVII/9) (6)

This short piece of unknown origin is at first sight comparatively unassuming. Yet on closer acquaintance it somehow conveys the expressive weight and import of a symphonic movement. To set a tempo try bb.5 – 6, and settle at a speed at which the RH demisemiquavers will flow easily, expressively, and without a sense of hurry, over even LH quaver thirds. Shape the melody line in 'vocal' curves, as a singer would, feeling the dynamic curve up to and down from the upmost note of each phrase.

bb.1 – 8   Lead off with a singing treble dotted crotchet over a full-toned F major chord. Feel the lift up to and down from the semiquaver F, and phrase the curves of the melody line smoothly through to the 2nd beat of b.2, incorporating the turn unhurriedly. Support the RH with carefully balanced LH chords through bb.1 – 4, and show the 'onward lead' of the three LH rising upbeat quavers through the end of b.2, feeling that you are 'going to' a further strong chord on the 1st beat of b.3. This LH three-quaver figure is important to the sense of continuity between the phrases – see how, in various forms, it again gives an onward lead to bb.5, 9, 15, etc. Play the descending scale in b.3 in a gently detached and 'speaking', not spiky manner. Feel that your RH upbeat semiquavers are 'going to' a singing slurred crotchet on the 1st beat of b.5. Then, observing the demisemiquaver rest like a little breath point, feel similarly that the demisemiquavers in b.5 are 'going to' a singing dotted quaver F on the 1st beat of b.6, supporting your RH through these bars with very even LH quaver thirds. Then show the implied emphasis on the syncopated RH crotchet third on the 2nd *quaver* pulse of b.7, supporting the RH in this bar with steady LH crotchet chords and octave. 'Finish off' cleanly in both hands on the 2nd beat of b.8 ready to lead back to b.1, or on to b.9 with the rising LH quavers.

bb.9 – 30   'Lean' warmly on the RH tied quaver on the 1st beat of b.9 (and 11), and then place the offbeat semiquavers carefully and relatively lightly, again in a 'speaking' manner, over your even LH quaver chords. 'Go up to' a singing high F on the 3rd beat of b.10, and support the RH semiquavers with sustained LH chords in b.12. Then 'go to' and lean well upon the slurred crotchet B natural on the 1st beat of b.13 and again b.14, and be careful not to hurry the 3rd beat of b.14 – in other words, be sure that you differentiate clearly between the semiquavers and the previous demisemiquavers as you shape this wide 'vocal' curve eloquently through the 2nd and 3rd beats of the bar. 'Go to' and again 'lean' well upon the slurred crotchet on the 1st beat of b.15, and allow a little 'give' as you 'finish off' carefully again here, ready to lead into the reprise with the descending LH thirds. Take care to co-ordinate the LH semiquaver seventh neatly with the RH on the upbeat to bb.14 and 15. 'Skip' gently, not spikily, down through b.18 in the slur/*staccato* variant of the scale in b.3. 'Draw out' a little to 'point' the interrupted cadence at bb.22 – 3. You could either approach this in *crescendo* or tail the sound away to *pianissimo*, then be careful to time the recitative-like chords, and rests, accurately from the upbeat to b.24, feeling in each instance that the semiquaver upbeat chord is 'going to' the slurred crotchet chord on the subsequent 1st beat of bb.24 – 6. Then, over warm and steady LH octaves, show the overall melodic curve of the improvisatory RH, up to the top of the arpeggio and down to the quaver upbeat to b.28. Tail away the sound of the ascending F major chords in a *diminuendo* through b.28. Then come in with a warm, not harsh, *forte* LH octave on the 1st beat of b.29, and show another overall curve up to the top of the demisemiquaver scale and down to the final chords.

Adagio in G major
(from Piano Trio in E flat, see Hob. XV/22) (7) (O)*

According to the Vienna Urtext Edition, this remarkable piece is the original version of the second movement of the Piano Trio in E flat. H.C. Robbins Landon writes of the 'violent emotion that wells up through this intensely personal, rhapsodic "Adagio non Troppo", so personal that it sometimes borders on the eccentric'.† The piece is not really suitable for small hands – the numerous long held notes, which create essential resonances, involve wide stretches from time to time.

Find a tempo at which the melody line flows easily over unhurried LH triplets, with an overall two-in-the-bar feeling. If you are too slow, the opening bars will 'stick'. If, on the other hand, you are too fast, the intensely expressive resonances of bb.14 – 15, for example, will merely sound like an exercise in RH fourths and sixths.

bb.1 – 11   Lead off with a warm-toned RH line, supported by sustained lower LH crotchets and even and relatively light inner triplets. Play the repeated D's with a certain intensity, with the feeling of 'going to' a resonantly singing *tenuto* minim D on the 2nd main beat of b.1, and similarly, be sure to give the minim D's in bb.2 and 3 sufficient tone to sing over the 1st beat of the subsequent bars. The editors of the Vienna Urtext Edition consider that the RH semiquavers in bb.1, 2, etc. should be played as written (see their Critical Notes). This will certainly 'point' the melody line with more expressive effect than letting the semiquavers coincide with the LH triplets as in the old tradition. Feel the accented offbeat quavers in the RH, then LH, in b.3, and again in the RH in b.4, as warm melodic 'leans', not bumps. 'Go to' resonantly singing tied minims in the treble and bass on the 1st beat of b.5. Then *listen* to the inner LH line entering clearly on the offbeat, 'joining in' clearly with the RH thirds as you swell a little towards the restatement in b.6. Let the RH 'go' smoothly to a resonant minim D on the 2nd main beat of b.8, allowing this note to sing right through to the 2nd main beat of b.9, while also listening acutely to the movements of the inner RH and LH parts through to b.11, over the warmly sustained bass semibreves. 'Ease' the tempo a little through the second half of b.10 as you return towards the opening motif in b.11.

bb.11 – 17   You could either make a *crescendo* through the second half of b.11, or burst in with a powerfully resonant *subito forte* on the 1st beat of b.12 – either can be equally effective if carried out with conviction. The former suggests the closing of the previous phrase on the 1st beat of b.11, 'overlapping' with the beginning of the next phrase which then 'grows' through b.11 towards the *sforzato* on the 1st beat of b.12. The latter, on the other hand, suggests the ending of the previous phrase in *diminuendo* through b.11, and the bursting forth of the new phrase in b.12. In any event, give the *sforzato* bass A (taken with the RH) and the treble chords a splendid resonance,

†*Haydn: Chronicle and Works*, vol. 3 (Thames & Hudson).

supported by a steady and even LH. Let the LH 'go to' a firm minim chord on the 1st beat of b.13, and then listen carefully to the smooth movement of each of the triplet lines, and to all the warmly sustained tied notes, through to b.16. Let your RH fourths, then sixths, move as resonantly, smoothly and expressively as possible from the middle of b.14 over the sustained lower dominant pedal point. Feel the implied warm 'lean' on the upmost quavers of each descending line of triplets, as in b.3 (i.e. on the 8th triplet pulse of b.14, and the 2nd and 8th in b.15). Then 'ease' a little again as you move towards the 1st beat of b.17.

bb.17 – 23   It is effective to take the descending scale passage (bb.17 – 19) in a *diminuendo* down to a *pianissimo* bass note on the 1st beat of b.19. Then feel a continuous 'arc' of sound as you rise to the high D and 'continue' the downward scale (though allowing the slight and inevitable extra fraction of time, rather than lurching frantically upwards with a bump). The Trio in E flat (see above) is more or less contemporary with the 'London' Sonata in C major, with its controversial pedal effects. Did Haydn, fascinated with the possibilities of the pedal, intend a slightly blurred effect here? (This Trio also anticipates by only a few years the similar effects of the descending *pianissimo* scale passage in Beethoven's Piano Concerto in C major.) Try playing this passage in a gently detached style (as indicated) over a very even LH, 'covered' by judicious half-pedalling in an overall misty effect. Then clear the sound at the beginning of b.21, and follow the upper and lower crotchet melody lines smoothly and resonantly from the 2nd beat of b.21 through to the middle of b.22.

bb.23 – 36   Do not panic at the sight of the ascending scales in bb.23 and 24. It is easier for relatively inexperienced players to divide such runs into definite groups to begin with – then, when confidence has been gained, the groups can be more loosely merged. 'Lean' warmly on the RH dotted quaver C sharp and treat the first three notes of the run as 'upbeat' notes to the main scale starting on the 4th beat as shown; then divide the run into groups of three, four and four notes (or three, three and five) to coincide with each LH triplet note. *Crescendo* sharply towards the *forte* high D, on the 1st beat of b.24 and b.25, and at all costs keep the LH moving perfectly evenly, feeling that the RH scale is fitting in with the steady LH, and *not* the other way about. Then let the LH 'go to' a singing minim third on the 2nd main beat of b.26, with the RH triplets similarly 'going to' a singing minim A on the 1st beat of b.27 and so on. Support your even and expressive RH offbeat octave fragments with resonant LH chords through bb.29 and 30, and take the inner triplet line in the second half of b.31 with the LH as shown, beneath the treble trill, and over a resonant lower third. 'Tail' the sound away as the thirds go down in alternating hands towards a *pianissimo* bass third on the 1st beat of b.35.

bb.36 – 83   Returning to the opening motif again in b.36, sound an immediate warning note with the *sforzato* diminished 7th harmony on the 1st beat of b.37, as you prepare to launch into the turbulent improvisatory passage of 'development' stretching through to b.55. Let the lower LH line 'go to' a firm crotchet E on the 1st beat of b.38 and give full-toned support in the LH as the RH scale descends (resonantly this time) towards a *forte* bass A on the 1st beat of b.40. Give full rein to your own expressive impulses through this long passage (though without losing the sense of your steady two-in-the-bar pulse). Note the *subito piano* on the *2nd* crotchet beat of b.43, and the *subito forte* on the *2nd* crotchet beat of b.44. 'Go to' resonant *sforzatos* in both hands on the 2nd crotchet beat of bb.45 – 7, again noting the subsequent *subito pianos*. Support the upper and inner triplets with a resonantly sustained bass line through bb.48 – 55, and feel the magical hush as the turbulence begins to subside from the end of b.52. Listen also to the inflections of the offbeat inner LH triplets from this point as you prepare to 'ease' back into the reprise at b.56. In his slightly shortened 'recapitulation', Haydn, in typical manner, alters the material of the opening section around in all directions. The scale passages at bb.75 and 76 are much easier to manage since there are only nine notes, giving three to each LH triplet. Tail the sound away towards the end as at bb.34 – 5, giving plenty of time to the final bass third and to the spread upper chord (including the telling F sharp in your even upward spread):

Allegretto in G major
(after a piece for Mechanical
Clock, Hob. XVII/10) (6)*

For this delightful piece, set an easy **6/8** swing at which the opening bar will 'move' but at which, on the other hand, the coming ornamentation and demisemiquaver figuration will not sound rushed. Play the piece with the utmost clarity, delicacy and poise, in a quiet overall dynamic.

bb.1 – 13   Lead off from a quiet, clear quaver upbeat and time the dotted rhythms immaculately in b.1 (placing the grace notes *on* the beat) over gently rhythmic LH quaver chords. 'Stop' the RH trill in b.2 approximately on the 2nd quaver pulse of the bar (and similarly in the RH in bb.14 and 16, and in the LH in b.15) so that the 'single' hemidemisemiquaver is clearly defined. The footnote in the Vienna Urtext Edition, however correct, is excessively difficult to implement! Make a little swell as the three quavers rise through the second half of b.2, and then articulate the slurred semiquaver couplets expressively downwards through the first half of b.3, and shape the curving semiquavers very smoothly through b.4. Support the RH from the upbeat to b.3 through to the middle of b.4 with warm-toned LH chords, listening particularly to the expressive movement of the inner LH line. Then time your RH immaculately and clearly again in b.5, the RH always supported by quiet and very steady LH chords. Practise b.7 slowly and carefully until the LH and RH demisemiquaver figures are perfectly co-ordinated. Swing into easy LH triplets from the 2nd overall beat of b.8 without altering your overall pulse, and shape the treble fragments neatly over your perfectly even LH, making a little *crescendo* towards b.12. Then time the quiet RH 'cuckoo' thirds and the more resolute spread quaver chords with perfect precision.

bb.13 – 35   Find a new and more expressive tone colour as you turn into the minor from the upbeat to b.14. Do not panic and get loud and clumsy when the LH temporarily 'takes over' the trill figure on the 1st beat of b.15. Practise the LH alone through from the previous bar until you can manage the two bars without any bumps, and then when you put 'hands together' listen carefully to make sure that the steadiness of the *RH* is not disrupted through your preoccupation with the LH. The implied lean on the tied inner RH 'upbeat' to the 2nd main beat of b.15 helps steadiness here. Then practise the *RH* alone from bb.17 – 21, preserving your **6/8** swing, keeping the sixths as smooth as possible through b.19 and running up the scale neatly and steadily towards a clear dotted quaver on the 1st beat of b.21. Then when you add the trill, beam your concentration on to the rhythm and shaping of the *RH*, and let the trill run easily and relatively lightly (likewise the demisemiquaver tremolo through b.20) so that it does not get too loud and 'take over', causing a total collapse! Keep your quiet, and evenly pulsating LH semiquavers very steady through bb.29 – 30, as you 'join in' quietly with the RH triplets in cross-rhythm. 'Lean' lightly and melodiously on your RH thumb, imagining that the triplets are slurred, and making sure that your RH thumb and LH fifth finger coincide perfectly on each quaver pulse. Feel that your RH triplets are fitting in with your even and steady LH semiquavers, and *not* the other way about. Treat the demisemiquavers similarly from the upbeat to b.32. End with clear chords in perfect time.

Allegretto in G major
(shortened arrangement of the Finale from the String Quartet in G major, Op. 33 No. 5) (5)

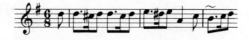

This makes an attractive little piece for a young player. Set a bright but steady **6/8** swing (leaving 'room' for the increase to *Presto* in the final section).

bb.1 – 16 Practise the LH alone, perfectly rhythmically, in an easy, not too spiky *staccato* imagining the sound of *pizzicato* strings. Then when you put 'hands together' do feel that your RH dotted rhythm is fitting in with the secure and ongoing LH rhythmic swing and *not* the other way about. Lead in with the RH from a clear quaver upbeat, and 'lean' slightly on each *dotted* quaver, keeping the semiquavers and quavers relatively light so that you create an easy, lilting two-in-the-bar motion. Place the turns *on* the beat in b.3, and then feel that you are 'going to' a firm slurred and tied chord on the 1st beat of b.4. Then, making a little *crescendo* towards the end of the section, feel that you are 'going to' a further firm slurred chord on the 1st beat of b.8, again playing the ornament *on* the beat.

bb.17 – 32 Keep perfectly steady as you move into the varied version of the first sixteen bars by relying on your continuingly rhythmic LH. Articulate the semiquaver figures neatly (bb.17 – 18) and shape the scale figure smoothly through b.19. Listen to the clash of the RH C sharp and the LH C natural on the 1st and 2nd beats of b.21, and to the inner LH seventh resolving to the A sharp in b.23. Do not panic and lurch blindly downwards at b.31, but 'finish off' the RH quavers neatly up to the high G at the end of b.30, allowing the slight natural break as you 'go down to' a confidently firm low A on the 1st beat of b.31, keeping your LH chords perfectly steady.

bb.33 – 58 Allowing a very tiny break, launch into the *Presto* not only at a faster tempo (still governed by your secure LH rhythm) but with a brighter texture, in contrast to the more 'easy' feel of the *Allegretto*. Be sure that the LH figure in b.40 is clearly articulated, and neatly 'finished off' down to the crotchet on the 2nd beat of the bar, so that you don't 'fall into' the upbeat to b.41. Then listen to the sustained lower LH drone through bb.41 – 4. Carefully practise the 'whirring' LH semiquavers alone at b.46, making a sharp light finger accent with the fifth finger on the bass notes, and keeping the upper notes relatively light. Practice in dotted rhythms will help:

together' feel here that the RH is leading, and make the LH fit in and 'keep up with' your

RH rhythm. Be sure that the unison *forte* figures are perfectly co-ordinated in bb.52 and 54, and 'go to' a firm 1st beat of bb.53 and 55. Then make a *subito piano* with the RH quaver as indicated. Keep steady here by placing the LH crotchet D clearly on the 2nd beat of these bars (53 and 55). Time the *pianissimo* crotchet chords immaculately and end with ringing *forte* chords.

Il Maestro e Lo Scolare
(Hob. XVII/a/1) (4 – 5)

Lo Scolare

Il Maestro

This is an entrancing duet, warmly recommended to teachers, parents and friends of young pupils. The 'teacher' plays each phrase first, followed by the pupil. What better 'lesson' could the pupil have than to listen to, and try to emulate, the perfect phrasing of the teacher! At the same time the pupil has the pleasure of taking the upper part.

A COMPARATIVE TABLE
OF EDITIONS OF HAYDN'S SONATAS

VIENNA URTEXT	KEY	HOBOKEN NUMBER	HENLE URTEXT	PETERS
Volume 1			*Volume 1, Neun Kleine Frühe Sonaten*	*6 Easy Divertimenti*
No. 1	G	XVI/8	No. 3	No. 4
No. 2	C	XVI/7	No. 2	No. 5
No. 3	F	XVI/9	No. 4	No. 6
No. 4	G	XVI/G1	No. 6	–
No. 5	G	XVI/11	1st movement as Finale of above Sonata. 2nd and 3rd movements in Volume 1 Appendix	Appears as No. 11 (*Volume 1*)
			Volume 1, Neun Kleine Frühe Sonaten	
No. 6	C	XVI/10	No. 5	No. 43 (*Volume 4*)
No. 7	D ·	XVII/D1	No. 7	–
			Volume 1, Neun Frühe Sonaten	
No. 8	A	XVI/5	No. 2	No. 23 (*Volume 2*)
			Volume 1, Neun Kleine Frühe Sonaten	*6 Easy Divertimenti*
No. 9	D	XVI/4	No. 9	No. 3
No. 10	C	XVI/1	No. 1	No. 1
			Volume 1, Neun Frühe Sonaten	
No. 11	B flat	XVI/2	No. 7	No. 22 (*Volume 2*)
No. 12	A	XVI/12	No. 3	No. 29 (*Volume 3*)
No. 13	G	XVI/6	No. 6	No. 37 (*Volume 4*)
			Volume 1, Neun Kleine Frühe Sonaten	*6 Easy Divertimenti*
No. 14	C	XVI/3	No. 8	No. 2
			Volume 1, Neun Frühe Sonaten	
No. 15	E	XVI/13	No. 4	No. 18 (*Volume 2*)
No. 16	D	XVI/14	No. 5	No. 15 (*Volume 2*)
No. 17	E flat	–	No. 8	–
No. 18	E flat	–	No. 9	–

VIENNA URTEXT	KEY	HOBOKEN NUMBER	HENLE URTEXT	PETERS
Volume 1B			*Volume 1, Sieben Sonaten 1765-72*	
No. 19	E minor	XVI/47	No. 1	See No. 34 (*Volume 4*), version in F major (see Commentary).
No. 20	B flat	XVI/18	No. 6	No. 19 (*Volume 2*)
			Volume 1 Appendix, Sieben Verschollene Sonaten	
No. 21†	D minor	XVI/2A	No. 1	–
No. 22†	A	XVI/2B	No. 2	–
No. 23†	B	XVI/2C	No. 3	–
No. 24†	B flat	XVI/2D	No. 4	–
No. 25†	E minor	XVI/2E	No. 5	–
No. 26†	C	XVI/2G	No. 6	–
No. 27†	A	XVI/2H	No. 7	–
			Volume 1, Sieben Sonaten 1765-72	
No. 28	D	XVI/5	No. 4	–
No. 29	E flat	XVI/45	No. 2	No. 26 (*Volume 3*)
No. 30	D	XVI/19	No. 3	No. 9 (*Volume 1*)
No. 31	A flat	XVI/46	No. 5	No. 8 (*Volume 1*)
No. 32	G minor	XVI/44	No. 7	No. 4 (*Volume 1*)
			Volume 2, 3rd set of Sechs Sonaten	
No. 33	C minor	XVI/20	No. 6	No. 25 (*Volume 3*)
			Volume 3, Drei Sonaten	
No. 34	D	XVI/33	No. 2	No. 20 (*Volume 2*)
No. 35	A flat	XVI/43	No. 1	No. 41 (*Volume 4*)
Volume 2			*Volume 2, 1st set of Sechs Sonaten (für Fürst Nikolaus Esterházy)*	
No. 36	C	XVI/21	No. 1	No. 16 (*Volume 2*)
No. 37	E	XVI/22	No. 2	No. 40 (*Volume 4*)
No. 38	F	XVI/23	No. 3	No. 21 (*Volume 2*)
No. 39	D	XVI/24	No. 4	No. 31 (*Volume 3*)
No. 40	E flat	XVI/25	No. 5	No. 32 (*Volume 3*)
No. 41	A	XVI/26	No. 6	No. 33 (*Volume 3*)

†Fragments

VIENNA URTEXT	KEY	HOBOKEN NUMBER	HENLE URTEXT	PETERS
			Volume 2, 2nd set of *Sechs Sonaten*	
No. 42	G	XVI/27	No. 1	No. 12 (*Volume 2*)
No. 43	E flat	XVI/28	No. 2	No. 13 (*Volume 2*)
No. 44	F	XVI/29	No. 3	No. 14 (*Volume 2*)
No. 45	A	XVI/30	No. 4	No. 36 (*Volume 4*)
No. 46	E	XVI/31	No. 5	No. 30 (*Volume 3*)
No. 47	B minor	XVI/32	No. 6	No. 39 (*Volume 4*)
			Volume 2, 3rd set of *Sechs Sonaten*	
No. 48	C	XVI/35	No. 1	No. 5 (*Volume 1*)
No. 49	C sharp minor	XVI/36	No. 2	No. 6 (*Volume 1*)
No. 50	D	XVI/37	No. 3	No. 7 (*Volume 1*)
No. 51	E flat	XVI/38	No. 4	No. 35 (*Volume 4*)
No. 52	G	XVI/39	No. 5	No. 17 (*Volume 2*)
Volume 3			*Volume 3, Drei Sonaten*	
No. 53	E minor	XVI/34	No. 3	No. 2 (*Volume 1*)
			Volume 3, Drei Sonaten für Prinzessin Marie Esterházy	
No. 54	G	XVI/40	No. 1	No. 10 (*Volume 1*)
No. 55	B flat	XVI/41	No. 2	No. 27 (*Volume 3*)
No. 56	D	XVI/42	No. 3	No. 28 (*Volume 3*)
No. 57	F	XVI/47	See *Volume 1, Seiben Sonaten um 1765-72*, No. 1.	No. 34 (*Volume 4*)
			Volume 3, Zwei Sonaten 1789/90	
No. 58	C	XVI/48	No. 1	No. 24 (*Volume 3*)
No. 59	E flat	XVI/49	No. 2	No. 3 (*Volume 1*)
			Volume 3, Drei Englische Sonaten	
No. 60	C	XVI/50	No. 2	No. 42 (*Volume 4*)
No. 61	D	XVI/51	No. 3	No. 38 (*Volume 4*)
No. 62	E flat	XVI/52	No. 1	No. 1 (*Volume 1*)